Lecture Notes in Computer Science

Edited by G. Goos and J. Hartmanis

148

Logics of Programs and Their Applications

Proceedings, Poznan, August 23 – 29, 1980

Edited by A. Salwicki

Springer-Verlag
Berlin Heidelberg New York 1983

Editor

Andrzej Salwicki
Institute of Informatics, University of Warsaw
00-901 Warsaw, PKiN PO Box 1210, Poland

ISBN 3-540-11981-7 Springer-Verlag Berlin Heidelberg New York
ISBN 0-387-11981-7 Springer-Verlag New York Heidelberg Berlin

Printed in Germany

Printing and binding: Beltz Offsetdruck, Hemsbach/Bergstr.
2145/3140-543210

F O R E W O R D

The Symposium on Logics of Programs and their Applications was held in Poznań, Poland on August 23 - 29, 1980. It took place in between Zürich meeting on Logics of programs 1979 and Yorktown Heights workshop 1981. The Poznań meeting gathered seventy four participants from nine countries. The contributions were dealing not only with logics of programs but also with their applications to abstract data types, parallel computations and LOGLAN - a programming language designed and implemented at the University of Warsaw. There were also four discussions on logics of programs, abstract data types, models of concurrency and on mutual connections between software and theory of computations.

The presented volume contains 23 selected contributions.

The Symposium has been organized jointly by the Regional Computing Center of the Technical University of Poznań, Institute of informatics of the University of Warsaw and the Mathematical Institute of Polish Academy of Sciences. We wish to thank all authors for their valuable contributions. The main part of the organizational work has been done by dr Jacek Martinek. I sincerely thank him, dr Krystyna Balińska and everyone who helped in the organization of the Symposium.

I hope that the unique atmosphere of that August meeting will remain in the memories of all participants.

Andrzej Salwicki

C O N T E N T S

H. Andréka
Sharpening the characterization of the power
of Floyd method 1

L. Banachowski
On proving program correctness by means of stepwise
refinement method 27

W.M. Bartol, A. Kreczmar, A.I. Litwiniuk, H. Oktaba
Semantics and implementation of prefixing at many levels 45

F. Berman
Nonstandard models in propositional dynamic logic 81

H. Burkhard
On priorities of parallelism :
Petri nets under the maximum firing strategy 86

B. Chlebus
On four logics of programs and complexity of their
satisfiability problems : extended abstract 98

L. Czaja
Are infinite behaviours of parallel system
schemata necessary ? 108

W. Dańko
Algorithmic properties of finitely generated structures 118

P. Enjalbert
Algebraic semantics and program logics:
Algorithmic logic for program trees 132

M. Grabowski
Some model-theoretical properties of logic
for programs with random control 148

H. Kawai
A formal system for parallel programs in discrete time and space 156

G. Mirkowska
On the propositional algorithmic theory of arithmetic 166

I. Németi
Nonstandard runs of Floyd-provable programs 186

E. Orłowska
On some extensions of dynamic logic 205

U. Petermann
On algorithmic logic with partial operations 213

A. Pettorossi
Towards a theory of parallelism and communications for increasing efficiency in applicative languages 224

G. Plotkin
An operational semantics for CSP 250

S.R. Radev
Programming languages and logics of programs 253

A. Skowron
Concurrent programs 258

L. Stapp
Axiomatic approach to the system of files 270

M.E. Szabo
A sequent calculus for Kröger logic 295

M.K. Valiev
On axiomatization of process logic 304

D. Vakarelov
Filtration theorem for dynamic algebras with tests and inverse operator 314

SHARPENING THE CHARACTERIZATION OF THE POWER OF FLOYD METHOD

H. Andréka
Math. Inst. Hungar. Acad. Sci., Budapest
Reáltanoda u. 13-15, H-1053 Hungary

§1. INTRODUCTION

The present paper uses Nonstandard Dynamic Logic (from now on DL) to compare powers of program verification methods and to give explicit characterizations of well known program verification methods, such as e.g. Floyd's method. An exposition of this subject is [23] of which the present paper is a continuation. For more intuitive introductory and motivating material on the lattice of Dynamic Logics and on the lattice of program verification methods the reader is referred to [23].

The present paper is strongly related to [20] (in this volume) in several ways. E.g. both introduce the same Nonstandard DL, but [20] uses the earliest primitive version of Nonstandard DL in the form it was published in 1977 in [1]. The explicit characterization of the information content of Floyd method, which is refined in the present paper, was first published in [1] using the framework of [20]. Section 5 of [20] shows a modest one of the many applications of ultraproducts in the theory of programming. Another one is in the proof of Thm.6 of [23]. A third one is in the proof of Thm.2 of the present paper.

The first part (Section 2) of the present paper recalls the basic notions of Nonstandard DL since it is not as well known as one would like it to be. Hence the first part is rather similar to that of e.g. [23], [3], [4] etc. which may make the misleading impression on the reader that this might be the same paper. No, this isn't. Works belonging to Nonstandard DL are e.g. [4],[3],[27],[28],[1],[11],[9],[13],[20], [5],[14],[26]. A systematic introductory monograph with motivation, examples, overview of the field etc. is [4] which will be sent to anybody on request. A published introduction to Nonstandard DL with at least some of these features is [3]. Intuitive examples, illustrations are in [20],[22],[4]. One of the main ideas of Nonstandard DL is to restrict ourselves to logics with decidable proof concepts (see Def.9) while maintaining a reasonable, intuitively convincing model theory. We are interested in properties of program schemes in axiomatizable classes of models. We cannot understand why some people investigate properties of program schemes either in a single model or in the class of all possible models. Only these two extremes were treated e.g. in the book of Manna.

By Thm.9 of [3], Floyd's method is equivalent with induction over formulas not containing quantifiers of sort time. Recently, E.M.Szabo raised the problem to decide how sharp this characterization is. In the present paper we prove that induction over formulas containing a single universal quantifier of sort time (i.e. Π_1-induction) is already strictly stronger than Floyd's method (see Thm.2 in §4).

NOTATION

In the following we shall recall some standard notations from textbooks on logic (mainly from [19],[8]).

d denotes an arbitrary similarity type of classical one-sorted models. I.e. d correlates arities (natural numbers) to function and relation symbols. See Def.1(i) in this paper.

ω denotes the set of natural nubers such that $0 \in \omega$.

Natural numbers are used in the von Neumann sense, i.e.
$n = \{0,1,\dots,n-1\}$ and in particular

0 is the empty set.

$X = \{x_w : w \in \omega\}$ denotes a set of variables.

F_d is the set of classical first order formulas of type d with variables in X. Cf. e.g. [8]p.22.

τ denotes a term of type d in the usual sense of logic, see [8]p.22 or [19]p.166, Def.10.8(ii).

M_d denotes the class of all classical one-sorted models of type d, see e.g. [8] or [19] Def.11.1, or Defs. 1 and 3 here.

A classical one-sorted model is denoted by an underlined capital like $\underline{T}$ or $\underline{D}$ and its universe is denoted by the same capital without underlining. E.g. T is the universe of $\underline{T}$, and D is that of $\underline{D}$.

By a "valuation of the variables" in a model $\underline{D}$ a function $q : \omega \to D$ is understood, see [19]p.195.

$\tau[q]_{\underline{D}}$ denotes the value of the term τ in the model $\underline{D}$ under the valuation q of the variables, see [8]p.27, Def.13.13 or [19] Def.11.2. If τ contains no variable then we write τ instead of $\tau[q]_{\underline{D}}$, if $\underline{D}$ is understood.

$\underline{D} \models \varphi[q]$ denotes that the valuation q satisfies the formula φ in the model $\underline{D}$.

$L_d = \langle F_d, M_d, \models \rangle$ is the classical first order language of similarity type d, see [27].

^{A}B denotes the set of all functions from A into B, i.e. $^{A}B = \{f : f$ maps A into $B\}$, see [19]p.7.

A function is considered to be a set of pairs.

Dom f denotes the domain of the function f, $\text{Dom } f \overset{d}{=} \{a : (\exists b)\langle a,b\rangle \in f\}$.

Rng f denotes the range of the function f, $\text{Rng } f \overset{d}{=} \{b : (\exists a)\langle a,b\rangle \in f\}$.

A sequence s of length n is a function with $\text{Dom } s = n$.

$\langle U_s : s \in S\rangle$ denotes the function $\{\langle s,U_s\rangle : s \in S\}$. Moreover for an expression $\text{Expr}(x)$ and class S we define

$\langle \text{Expr}(x) : x \in S\rangle$ to be the function $f : S \to \text{Rng } f$ such that $(\forall x \in S)$ $f(x) = \text{Expr}(x)$.

$\text{Sb}(X) \overset{d}{=} \{Y : Y \subseteq X\}$ is the powerset of X.

X^* denotes the set of all finite sequences of elements of X, i.e. $X^* \overset{d}{=} \cup\{^{m}X : m \in \omega\}$. We shall identify X^* with $\{H : H \subseteq X$ and $|H| < \omega\}^*$, and also with $(X^*)^*$. We think of X^* as the set of "words over the alphabet X".

$A \sim B \overset{d}{=} \{a \in A : a \notin B\}$.

§2. THE DEFINITION OF OUR DYNAMIC LOGIC DL_d.

2.1 Syntax of program schemes

Recall d, X, F_d from the list of notations. Now we define the set P_d of program schemes of type d.

The set Lab of "label symbols" is defined to be an arbitrary but fixed subset of the set Tm_d^0 of all constant terms of type d, i.e. d-type terms which do not contain variable symbols. (Lab is chosen this way for technical reasons only. There are many other possible ways for handling labels, see e.g. [28].) Logical symbols: $\{\wedge, \neg, \exists, =\}$. Other symbols: $\{\leftarrow, \text{IF}, \text{GOTO}, \text{HALT}, (,), :\}$.

The set U_d of commands of type d is defined as follows:

$(i : x \leftarrow \tau) \in U_d$ if $i \in \text{Lab}$, $x \in X$, and τ is a term of type d and with all variables in X.

$(i : \text{IF } \chi \text{ GOTO } v) \in U_d$ if $i, v \in \text{Lab}$, $\chi \in F_d$ is a formula without quantifier.

$(i : \text{HALT}) \in U_d$ if $i \in \text{Lab}$.

These are the only elements of U_d.

By a program scheme of type d we understand a finite sequence p of commands (elements of U_d) ending with a "HALT", in which no two members have the same label, and in which the only "HALT-command" is the last one. Further, if (i: IF χ GOTO v) occurs in p then there is u such that the command (v:u) occurs in p. I.e. an element p of P_d is of the form $p = \langle (i_0:u_0),\ldots,(i_{n-1}:u_{n-1}), (i_n:\text{HALT})\rangle$ where $n\in\omega$, $(i_m:u_m)\in U_d$ for $m\le n$ etc.

Convention 1 If a program scheme is denoted by p then its parts are denoted as follows:

$$p = \langle (i_0:u_0),\ldots,(i_{n-1}:u_{n-1}),(i_n:\text{HALT})\rangle .$$

Throughout we shall use the definition:

$$c \overset{d}{=} \min\{w\in\omega : (\forall v\in\omega\sim w)[x_v \text{ does not occur in } p]\}.$$

I.e. $\{x_w : w<c\}$ contains all the variables occurring in the program scheme p, and if $c>0$ then x_{c-1} really occurs in p. We shall use x_c as the control variable of p.

2.2 Semantics of program schemes

By a language with semantics we understand a triple $L = \langle F, M, \models\rangle$ of classes such that $\models \subseteq M\times F\times Sets$ where Sets is the class of all sets. Here F is called the syntax of L, M the class of models or possible interpretations of L, $\models$ the satisfaction relation of L, and $\langle M, \models\rangle$ is called the semantics of L. Instead of $\langle a,b,c\rangle\in\models$ we write $a\models b[c]$, and we say "c satisfies b in a". See [27],[29] p.265.

DEFINITION 1 (one-sorted models)

(i) By a (classical or one-sorted) similarity type d we understand a pair $d = \langle H,d_1\rangle$ such that d_1 is a function $d_1 : \Sigma \to \omega$ for some set Σ, $H\subseteq\Sigma$ and $(\forall r\in\Sigma)d_1(r)>0$.

The elements of Σ are called the symbols of d and the elements of H are called the operation symbols or function symbols of d. Let $r\in\Sigma$. Then we shall write $d(r)$ instead of $d_1(r)$.

(ii) Let $d = \langle H,d_1\rangle$ be a similarity type, let $\Sigma = \text{Dom } d_1$ as above. By a model of type d we understand a pair $\mathfrak{D} = \langle D,R\rangle$ such that R is a function with $\text{Dom } R = \Sigma$ and $(\forall r\in\Sigma)R(r)\subseteq {}^{d(r)}D$ and if $r\in H$ then $R(r) : {}^{(d(r)-1)}D \to D$.

Notation: $\langle D,R_r\rangle_{r\in\Sigma} \overset{d}{=} \langle D,\langle R_r : r\in\Sigma\rangle\rangle \overset{d}{=} \langle D,R\rangle$.

I.e. $\mathfrak{D} = \langle D,R_r\rangle_{r\in\Sigma}$ is a model of type d iff R_r is a d(r)-ary relation over D and if $r\in H$ then R_r is a $(d(r)-1)$ -ary function, for all $r\in\Sigma$.

If $r\in H$ and $d(r)=1$ then there is a unique $b\in D$ such that $R_r = \{\langle b\rangle\}$ and we shall identify R_r with b. If $r\in H$, $d(r)=1$ then r is said to be a <u>constant symbol</u> and $R_r\in D$ is the constant element denoted by r in $\mathfrak{D}$.

The set D is called the <u>universe</u> of $\mathfrak{D}$.

(iii) $M_d \stackrel{d}{=} \{\mathfrak{D} : \mathfrak{D}$ is a model of type $d\}$. <u>End of Definition 1</u>

<u>DEFINITION 2</u> (the similarity type t of arithmetic)

t denotes the similarity type of Peano's arithmetic. In more detail, $t = \langle \{0,sc,+,\cdot\}, t_1\rangle$ where $\mathrm{Dom}\, t_1 = \{\le,0,sc,+,\cdot\}$, $t(\le)=2$, $t(0)=1$, $t(sc)=2$ and $t(+)=t(\cdot)=3$. <u>End of Definition 2</u>

Throughout the paper, t is supposed to be disjoint from any other similarity type, moreover if d is a similarity type then $\mathrm{Dom}(d_1)\cap\mathrm{Dom}(t_1)=0$ is assumed throughout the paper.

<u>DEFINITION 3</u> (many-sorted models, [19])

(i) By a <u>many-sorted similarity type</u> m we understand a triple $m = \langle S,H,m_2\rangle$ such that m_2 is a function $m_2 : \Sigma \to S^*$ for some set Σ, $H\subseteq\Sigma$ and $(\forall r\in\Sigma)m_2(r) \notin {}^0S$.

The elements of S are called the <u>sorts</u> of m. If $r\in\Sigma$ then we shall write $m(r)$ instead of $m_2(r)$.

(ii) Let m be a many-sorted similarity type and let $\Sigma = \mathrm{Dom}\, m_2$ as above. By a (many-sorted) model of type m we understand a pair $\mathfrak{M} = \langle\langle U_s : s\in S\rangle,R\rangle$ such that R is a function with $\mathrm{Dom}\, R = \Sigma$ and if $r\in\Sigma$ and $m(r)=\langle s_1,\dots,s_n\rangle$ then $R(r)\subseteq U_{s_1}\times\dots\times U_{s_n}$ and if in addition $r\in H$ then $R(r)$ is a function $R(r) : U_{s_1}\times\dots\times U_{s_{n-1}} \to U_{s_n}$.

U_s is said to be the <u>universe of sort s</u> of $\mathfrak{M}$.

(iii) $M_m \stackrel{d}{=} \{\mathfrak{M} : \mathfrak{M}$ is a many-sorted model of type $m\}$.

<u>End of Definition 3</u>

<u>DEFINITION 4</u> (the 3-sorted similarity type td)

(i) To any one-sorted similarity type d we associate a 3-sorted similarity type td as follows:

Let $d = \langle H,d_1\rangle$ be any one-sorted similarity type. Recall that t is a fixed similarity type introduced in Def.2 and, by our convention, $\mathrm{Dom}(d_1)\cap\mathrm{Dom}(t_1)=0$.

We shall define the new similarity type td such that the original similarity types t and d will be actual elements of a part of td, namely t and d will be two sorts of td.

Now we define td to be $td \overset{d}{=} \langle S,K,td_2\rangle$ where

a) $S \overset{d}{=} \{t,d,i\}$, $|S|=3$. (S is the set of sorts of td.) Here the elements of S are used as symbols only; we could have chosen $S = \{0,1,2\}$ as well.

b) $K \overset{d}{=} \{ext,0,sc,+,\cdot\}\cup H$. (K is the set of operation symbols of td.)

c) $td_2 : (Dom(t_1)\cup Dom(d_1)\cup\{ext\}) \to S^*$ such that
$td_2(ext) = \langle i,t,d\rangle$,
$td_2(r)\in {}^n\{t\}$ if $t(r)=n$ and
$td_2(r)\in {}^n\{d\}$ if $d(r)=n$.
E.g. $td_2(\leq) = \langle t,t\rangle$, $td_2(+) = \langle t,t,t\rangle$, etc.

By these the 3-sorted similarity type td is defined.

(ii) Let $\mathfrak{M} = \langle\langle U_t,U_d,U_i\rangle,R_r\rangle_{r\in\Sigma}$ be a td-type model. Then (1)-(3) below hold:

(1) $\langle U_t,R_r\rangle_{r\in Dom(t_1)}\in M_t$.

(2) $\langle U_d,R_r\rangle_{r\in Dom(d_1)}\in M_d$.

(3) $R_{ext} : U_i\times U_t \to U_d$.

<u>Notation</u>: $\langle\langle U_t,R_r\rangle_{r\in Dom(t_1)}, \langle U_d,R_r\rangle_{r\in Dom(d_1)}, U_i, R_{ext}\rangle \overset{d}{=}$

$\overset{d}{=} \langle\langle U_t,U_d,U_i\rangle, R_r\rangle_{r\in\Sigma}$.

We define: $\underset{\sim}{T} \overset{d}{=} \langle U_t,R_r\rangle_{r\in Dom(t_1)}$, $T \overset{d}{=} U_t$,

$\underset{\sim}{D} \overset{d}{=} \langle U_d,R_r\rangle_{r\in Dom(d_1)}$, $D \overset{d}{=} U_d$ and $I \overset{d}{=} U_i$.

The sorts t,d, and i are called time, data and intensions respectively. $\underset{\sim}{T}$ is said to be the <u>time-structure of $\mathfrak{M}$.</u>

<u>End of Definition 4</u>

<u>Convention 2</u> Whenever an element of M_{td} is denoted by the letter $\mathfrak{M}$ then the parts of $\mathfrak{M}$ are denoted as follows:

$\langle \underset{\sim}{T}, \underset{\sim}{D}, I, ext\rangle \overset{d}{=} \langle\langle U_t^{\mathfrak{M}}, U_d^{\mathfrak{M}}, U_i^{\mathfrak{M}}\rangle, r^{\mathfrak{M}}\rangle_{r\in\Sigma} \overset{d}{=} \mathfrak{M}$.

Note that $\mathfrak{M}\in M_{td}$ iff $[\underset{\sim}{T}\in M_t, \underset{\sim}{D}\in M_d$, and $ext : I\times T \to D]$.

For more detailed introduction to many-sorted languages, like $L_{td} = \langle F_{td},M_{td},\models\rangle$ defined below, the reader is referred e.g. to the textbook [19].

<u>DEFINITION 5</u> (the first order 3-sorted language $L_{td} = \langle F_{td},M_{td},\models\rangle$ of type td, [19])

Let $d = \langle H, d_1 \rangle$ be any one-sorted similarity type. Recall from Def.s 3 and 4 that t is a fixed similarity type, and td is a 3-sorted similarity type with sorts $\{t,d,i\}$.

(i) We define the set F_{td} of first order 3-sorted formulas of type td.:

Let $X \overset{d}{=} \{x_w : w\in\omega\}$, $Y \overset{d}{=} \{y_w : w\in\omega\}$ and $Z \overset{d}{=} \{z_w : w\in\omega\}$ be three disjoint sets (and $x_w \neq x_j$ if $w\neq j\in\omega$ etc.). We define Z, X, and Y to be the sets of variables of sorts t, d, and i respectively.

F_t^Z denotes the set of all first order formulas of type t with variables in Z, F_d denotes the set of all first order formulas of type d with variables in X, and Tm_t^Z denotes the set of all first order terms of type t with variables in Z.

The set $Tm_{td,d}$ of terms of type td and of sort d is defined to be the smallest set satisfying conditions (1)-(3) below.

(1) $X\subseteq Tm_{td,d}$.

(2) $ext(y_w,\tau)\in Tm_{td,d}$ for any $\tau\in Tm_t^Z$ and $w\in\omega$.

(3) $f(\tau_1,\ldots,\tau_n)\in Tm_{td,d}$ for any $f\in H$ if $d(f)=n+1$ and $\tau_1,\ldots,\tau_n\in$ $\in Tm_{td,d}$.

The set F_{td} of first order formulas of type td is defined to be the smallest set satisfying conditions (4)-(8) below.

(4) $(\tau_1=\tau_2)\in F_{td}$ for any $\tau_1,\tau_2\in Tm_{td,d}$.

(5) $r(\tau_1,\ldots,\tau_n)\in F_{td}$ for any $\tau_1,\ldots,\tau_n\in Tm_{td,d}$ and for any $r\in H$ if $d(r)=n$.

(6) $(y_w=y_j)\in F_{td}$ for any $w,j\in\omega$.

(7) $F_t^Z\subseteq F_{td}$.

(8) $\{\neg\varphi, (\varphi\wedge\psi), (\exists x_w\varphi), (\exists y_w\varphi), (\exists z_w\varphi) : w\in\omega\} \subseteq F_{td}$ for any $\varphi,\psi\in F_{td}$.

By this, the set F_{td} has been defined. Note that $F_d\subseteq F_{td}$.

(ii) Now we define the "meanings" of elements of F_{td}.

By a <u>valuation</u> (of the variables) into $\mathfrak{M}$ we understand a triple $v=\langle g,k,r\rangle$ such that $g \in {}^{\omega}T$, $k \in {}^{\omega}D$ and $r \in {}^{\omega}I$. The statement "<u>the valuation</u> $v=\langle g,k,r\rangle$ <u>satisfies</u> φ <u>in</u> $\mathfrak{M}$" is denoted by $\mathfrak{M} \models \varphi[v]$ or equivalently by $\mathfrak{M} \models \varphi[g,k,r]$.

The truth of $\mathfrak{M} \models \varphi[g,k,r]$ is defined the usual way(see [19]) which is completely analogous with the one-sorted case. E.g.

$\mathfrak{M} \models (y_0=y_1)[g,k,r]$ iff $r_0=r_1$,

$\mathfrak{M} \models (x_1=ext(y_2,z_0))[g,k,r]$ iff $k_1=ext^{\mathfrak{M}}(r_2,g_0)$,

$\mathfrak{M} \models \varphi[g,k,r]$ iff $\underset{\sim}{T} \models \varphi[g]$ for $\varphi\in F_t^Z$,

$\mathfrak{M} \models \varphi[g,k,r]$ iff $\underset{\sim}{D} \models \varphi[k]$ for $\varphi \in F_d$ etc.

The formula $\varphi \in F_{td}$ is valid in $\mathfrak{M}$, in symbols $\mathfrak{M} \models \varphi$, iff

$(\forall g \in {}^{\omega}T)(\forall k \in {}^{\omega}D)(\forall r \in {}^{\omega}I)\ \mathfrak{M} \models \varphi[g,k,r]$.

(iii) The (3-sorted) language L_{td} of type td is defined to be the triple $L_{td} = \langle F_{td}, M_{td}, \models \rangle$ where $\models$ is the satisfaction relation defined in (ii) above. End of Definition 5

Now we define the meanings of program schemes $p \in P_d$ in the 3-sorted models $\mathfrak{M} \in M_{td}$.

Notation: Let $\langle \underset{\sim}{T}, \underset{\sim}{D}, I, ext \rangle \in M_{td}$, see Convention 2. Let $s_0, \ldots, s_m \in I$, $\bar{s} \stackrel{d}{=} \langle s_0, \ldots, s_m \rangle$. Let $b \in T$. Then we define

$ext(\bar{s}, b) \stackrel{d}{=} \langle ext(s_0, b), \ldots, ext(s_m, b) \rangle$.

DEFINITION 6 (traces of programs in time-models)

Let $p \in P_d$ and $\mathfrak{M} \in M_{td}$. We shall use Conventions 1 and 2. Let $s_0, \ldots, s_c \in I$ be arbitrary intensions in $\mathfrak{M}$. Let $\bar{s} = \langle s_0, \ldots, s_{c-1} \rangle$. The sequence $\langle s_0, \ldots, s_c \rangle$ of intensions is defined to be a trace of p in $\mathfrak{M}$ if the following (i) and (ii) are satisfied.

(i) $ext(s_c, 0) = i_0$ and $ext(s_c, b) \in \{i_m : m \le n\}$ for every $b \in T$.

(ii) For every $b \in T$ and for every $j \le c$ if $ext(s_c, b) = i_m$ then statements (1)-(3) below hold.

(1) If $u_m =$ "$x_w \leftarrow \tau$" then

$$ext(s_j, b+1) = \begin{cases} i_{m+1} & \text{if } j \ne w \\ \tau[ext(\bar{s}, b)]_{\underset{\sim}{D}} & \text{if } j = w \\ ext(s_j, b) & \text{otherwise} \end{cases} .$$

(2) If $u_m =$ "IF χ GOTO v" then

$$ext(s_j, b+1) = \begin{cases} v & \text{if } j = c \text{ and } \underset{\sim}{D} \models \chi[ext(\bar{s}, b)] \\ i_{m+1} & \text{if } j = c \text{ and } \underset{\sim}{D} \not\models \chi[ext(\bar{s}, b)]. \\ ext(s_j, b) & \text{otherwise} \end{cases}$$

(3) If $u_m =$ "HALT" then $ext(s_j, b+1) = ext(s_j, b)$.

End of Definition 6

DEFINITION 7 (possible output)

Let $s = \langle s_0, \ldots, s_c \rangle$ be a trace of $p \in P_d$ in $\mathfrak{M} \in M_{td}$.

(i) Let $k \in {}^{\omega}D$. The trace s is said to be of input k iff $(\forall j<c)k(j) = ext(s_j,0)$.

(ii) Recall from Convention 1 that i_n is the label of the HALT-command of p. Let $b \in T$. We say that s terminates p at time b in $\mathfrak{M}$ iff $ext(s_c,b)=i_n$.

(iii) Let $k,q \in {}^{\omega}D$. We define q to be a possible output of p with input k in $\mathfrak{M}$ iff (a)-(d) below hold for some s.

(a) $s = \langle s_0,\ldots,s_c \rangle$ is a trace of p in $\mathfrak{M}$.

(b) s is of input k.

(c) There is $b \in T$ such that s terminates p at time b and $\langle q_0,\ldots,q_{c-1} \rangle = \langle ext(s_0,b),\ldots,ext(s_{c-1},b) \rangle$.

(d) $(\forall j \in \omega)[j \geq c \Rightarrow q_j = k_j]$.

If q is a possible output of p with input k in $\mathfrak{M}$ then we shall also say that $\langle q_0,\ldots,q_{c-1} \rangle$ is a possible output of p with input $\langle k_0,\ldots,k_{c-1} \rangle$. End of Definition 7

By now we have defined a semantics of program schemes.

Remark: A trace $\langle s_0,\ldots,s_c \rangle$ of a program $p \in P_d$ correlates to each variable x_w $(w \leq c)$ occurring in the program p an intension or "history" s_w such that the value $ext(s_w,b)$ can be considered as the "value contained in" or "extension of" x_w at time point $b \in T$. The intension $s_w \in I$ represents a function $ext(s_w,-) : T \to D$ from time points of data values D. This function is the "history" of the variable x_w during an execution of the program p in the model $\mathfrak{M}$. Def.6 ensures that the sequence $\langle ext(s_0,-),\ldots,ext(s_c,-) \rangle$ of functions can be considered as a behaviour or "run" or "trace" of the program p in $\mathfrak{M}$. Here s_c is the intension of the "control variable".

About using Th.: It might look counter-intuitive to execute programs in arbitrary elements of M_{td}. However, we can collect all our postulates about time into a set $Ax \subseteq F_{td}$ of axioms which this way would define the class $Mod(Ax) \subseteq M_{td}$ of all intended interpretations of P_d. Then traces of programs in $Mod(Ax)$ provide an intuitively acceptable semantics of program schemes. Such a set Ax of axioms was proposed in [23] Def.13 and in [3] Part II, Def.14. If one wants to define semantics with unusual time structure e.g. parallelism, nondeterminism, interactions etc. then one can choose an Ax different from the one proposed in [23] or [3].

2.3. The language DL_d for reasoning about programs

We introduce our language DL_d for reasoning about programs or, in other words, the language DL_d of our first order dynamic logic.

DEFINITION 8 (the language DL_d of first order dynamic logic)

Let d be a (one-sorted) similarity type.

(i) DF_d is defined to be the smallest set satisfying conditions (1)-(3) below.

(1) $F_{td} \subseteq DF_d$.

(2) $(\forall p \in P_d)(\forall \psi \in DF_d) \Box(p,\psi) \in DF_d$.

(3) $(\forall \varphi,\psi \in DF_d)(\forall x \in X \cup Y \cup Z)\{\neg\varphi, (\varphi\wedge\psi), (\exists x\varphi)\} \subseteq DF_d$.

By this we have defined the set DF_d of dynamic formulas of type d.

(ii) Now we define the meanings of the dynamic formulas in the 3-sorted models $\mathfrak{M} \in M_{td}$. Let $\mathfrak{M} = \langle \underset{\sim}{T}, \underset{\sim}{D}, I, ext \rangle \in M_{td}$. Let v be a valuation of the variables of F_{td} into $\mathfrak{M}$, i.e. let $v = \langle g,k,r \rangle$ where $g \in {}^{\omega}T$, $k \in {}^{\omega}D$, and $r \in {}^{\omega}I$. We shall define the truth of $\mathfrak{M} \models \varphi[v]$ for all $\varphi \in DF_d$.

(4) If $\varphi \in F_{td}$ then $\mathfrak{M} \models \varphi[v]$ is already defined in Def.5.

(5) Let $p \in P_d$ and $\psi \in DF_d$ be arbitrary. Assume that $\mathfrak{M} \models \psi[v]$ has already been defined for every valuation v of the variables of F_{td} into $\mathfrak{M}$. Let $g \in {}^{\omega}T$, $k \in {}^{\omega}D$, and $r \in {}^{\omega}I$. Then $\mathfrak{M} \models \Box(p,\psi)[g,k,r]$ iff $[\mathfrak{M} \models \psi[g,q,r]$ for every possible output q of p with input k in $\mathfrak{M}]$. For "possible output" see Def.7.

(6) Let $\varphi,\psi \in DF_d$ and let $x \in X \cup Y \cup Z$. Then $\mathfrak{M} \models (\neg\varphi)[g,k,r]$, $\mathfrak{M} \models (\varphi\wedge\psi)[g,k,r]$ and $\mathfrak{M} \models (\exists x\varphi)[g,k,r]$ are defined the usual way.

Let e.g. $w \in \omega$. Then $\mathfrak{M} \models (\exists z_w\varphi)[g,k,r]$ iff (there is $h \in {}^{\omega}T$ such that $(\forall j \in \omega)(j \neq w \Rightarrow h_j = g_j)$ and $\mathfrak{M} \models \varphi[h,k,r]$).

(iii) The language DL_d of first order dynamic logic of type d is defined to be the triple $DL_d \overset{d}{=} \langle DF_d, M_{td}, \models \rangle$ where $\models$ is defined in (ii) above.

End of Definition 8

Notation: Let $p \in P_d$ and $\psi \in DF_d$. Then $\Diamond(p,\psi)$ abbreviates the formula $\neg\Box(p,\neg\psi)$. In our language DF_d we introduced the logical connectives $\neg, \wedge, =, \exists, \Box$ only. However, we shall use the derived logical connectives $\forall, \rightarrow, \leftrightarrow, \vee$, TRUE, FALSE, $\Diamond$,too, in the standard sense.

E.g. $(\varphi\vee\psi)$ stands for the formula $\neg(\neg\varphi\wedge\neg\psi)$.

Remark: Standard concepts of programming theory can be expressed in DL_d. E.g. $\Box(p,\psi)$ expresses that p is partially correct w.r.t. output condition ψ, and $\Diamond(p,\psi)$ expresses that p is totally correct w.r.t. output condition ψ in the weaker sense.

Convention 3 We shall use the model theoretic consequence relation $\models$ in the usual way. I.e. Let $Th\subseteq DF_d$, $\psi\in DF_d$ and $K\subseteq M_{td}$. Then

$\mathfrak{M}\models\varphi$ iff $(\forall g\in{}^{\omega}T)(\forall k\in{}^{\omega}D)(\forall r\in{}^{\omega}I)\ \mathfrak{M}\models\varphi[g,k,r]$,

$\mathfrak{M}\models Th$ iff $(\forall\varphi\in Th)\ \mathfrak{M}\models\varphi$,

$K\models Th$ iff $(\forall\mathfrak{M}\in K)\ \mathfrak{M}\models Th$,

$Mod(Th) \stackrel{d}{=} Mod_{td}(Th) \stackrel{d}{=} \{\mathfrak{M}\in M_{td} : \mathfrak{M}\models Th\}$, and

$Th\models\varphi$ iff $Mod(Th)\models\varphi$.

Note that Mod(Th) is a sloppy abbreviation of $Mod_{td}(Th)$, we shall use it when context helps the reader to guess which similarity type h such that $Th\subseteq F_h$ is used in $Mod(Th) = Mod_h(Th)$.

2.4. Proof concepts

DEFINITION 9 (proof concept [19])

Let $L = \langle F,M,\models\rangle$ be a language. By a proof concept on the set F we understand a relation $\vdash\subseteq Sb(F)\times F$ together with a set $Pr\subseteq F^*$ such that $(\forall Th\subseteq F)(\forall\varphi\in F)[Th\vdash\varphi$ iff $\langle H,w,\varphi\rangle\in Pr$ for some finite $H\subseteq Th$ and for some $w\in F^*)]$. Recall that we identify X^* with $\{H\in Sb(X) : |H|<\omega\}^*$.

The proof concept $(\vdash,Pr)$ is decidable iff the set Pr is a decidable subset of F^* in the usual sense of the theory of algorithms and recursive functions (i.e. if Pr is recursive).

Pr is called the set of proofs, and $\vdash$ is called derivability relation. End of Definition 9

Sometimes we shall sloppily write "$\vdash$ is a decidable proof concept" instead of "$(\vdash,Pr)$ is a decidable proof concept".

Note that the usual proof concept of classical first order logic is a decidable one in the sense of the above definition. As a contrast we note that the so called effective ω-rule is not a decidable proof concept.

THEOREM 1 (strong completeness of DL_d)

There is a decidable proof concept $(\vdash^N, Prn)$ for the language DL_d such that for every $Th \subseteq DF_d$ and $\varphi \in DF_d$ we have $[Th \models \varphi$ iff $Th \vdash^N \varphi]$.

Proof: can be found in [3], as well as in [4] Thm.2 pp.30-38. QED

DEFINITION 10 (the proof concept $(\vdash^N, Prn)$ of DL_d)

By Thm.1 above there exists a decidable set $Prn \subseteq (DF_d)^*$ such that

$(\forall Th \subseteq DF_d)(\forall \varphi \in DF_d)[Th \vdash^N \varphi$ iff $(\exists$ finite $H \subseteq Th)(\exists w)\langle H,w,\varphi\rangle \in Prn]$.

The decision algorithm for Prn is rigorously constructed in [3] Thm.2, and [4]Thm.2, pp.30-38, and in [21].

From now on we shall use Prn as defined in the quoted papers. The only important properties of Prn we shall use are its decidability and its completeness for DL_d. End of Definition 10

DEFINITION 11 (new proof concepts $(Ax \vdash^N)$ from $\vdash^N$)

Let $Ax \subseteq DF_d$ be decidable but otherwise arbitrary.

(i) Let $Th \subseteq DF_d$ and $\varphi \in DF_d$ be arbitrary. We say that φ is $(Ax \vdash^N)$-provable from Th iff $Th \cup Ax \vdash^N \varphi$. That is, φ is provable by the proof concept $(Ax \vdash^N)$ from Th iff $Th \cup Ax \vdash^N \varphi$. Thus $(Ax \vdash^N)$ is a new recursively enumerable "provability" relation.

(ii) $pf(Ax \vdash^N) \stackrel{d}{=} \{\langle H, \langle L,w\rangle, \varphi\rangle \in (DF_d)^* : \langle H \cup L, w, \varphi\rangle \in Prn$ and $L \subseteq Ax\}$. Clearly φ is $(Ax \vdash^N)$-provable from Th iff $(\exists \langle H,w,\varphi\rangle \in Prn) H \subseteq Th \cup Ax$. Clearly $pf(Ax \vdash^N)$ is a decidable subset of $(DF_d)^*$.

(iii) We have defined a new proof concept $\langle (Ax \vdash^N), pf(Ax \vdash^N)\rangle$ where $pf(Ax \vdash^N)$ is the decidable set of all $(Ax \vdash^N)$-proofs. We shall always denote this new proof concept by $(Ax \vdash^N)$. So whenever we write $(Ax \vdash^N)$ we shall mean $\langle (Ax \vdash^N), pf(Ax \vdash^N)\rangle$ but we shall not write it out explicitly. End of Definition 11

§3. THE LATTICE OF PROOF METHODS FOR PARTIAL CORRECTNESS OF PROGRAMS

In [23], it was shown how to use the logic DL_d to compare powers of methods of program verification as well as to generate new methods for program verification. To this end, we had to fix the criteria to be used when we compare program verification methods. We say that one method $\vdash_1$ is stronger than another $\vdash_2$ iff more programs can be proved to be partially correct by $\vdash_1$ than by $\vdash_2$. So we consider the reasoning power to prove partial correctness statements $\varphi \to \Box(p,\psi)$ to be the criterion to compare different methods. This choice has nothing to do with our logic DL_d, namely DL_d is suitable for proving total correctness of programs. It was proved in [3]Thm.7 and in Thm.7 of [4] that the Kfoury-Park [16] negative result on proving total correctness is not true for DL_d.

We shall consider program verification methods only with decidable proof concepts.

On Figure 2 of [23], different proof concepts $(Ax_1 \overset{N}{\vdash})$, $(Ax_2 \overset{N}{\vdash})$ were compared with each other as well as with such classical proof concepts as Floyd's $\overset{F}{\vdash}$, Burstall's $\overset{mod}{\vdash}$ and Pnueli's $\overset{fum}{\vdash}$. Intuitive motivations for investigating Fig.2 can be found in [23] §5.2. Below we recall Fig.2 of [23] (see Fig.1 here) together with the most important definitions.

DEFINITION 12 (ind(φ,z), IA, Ia, Lax)

Let d be a similarity type. Then td, F_{td} and Z were defined in Def.s 4 and 5 in §2.2. Let $z \in Z$ be arbitrary. Let $\varphi \in F_{td}$. We define the induction formula ind(φ,z) as follows:

$$\text{ind}(\varphi,z) \overset{d}{=} ([\varphi(0) \wedge \forall z(\varphi \rightarrow \varphi(sc(z)))] \rightarrow \forall z\varphi),$$

where $\varphi(0)$ and $\varphi(sc(z))$ denote the formulas obtained from φ by replacing every free occurrence of z in φ by 0 and sc(z) resp.

The induction axioms are:

$IA \overset{d}{=} \{\text{ind}(\varphi,z) : \varphi \in F_{td} \text{ and } z \in Z\}$.

$Lax \overset{d}{=} \{(j \neq k) : j \text{ and } k \text{ are two different elements of } Lab\}$.

$Ia \overset{d}{=} IA \cup Lax$.

End of Definition 12

Clearly $IA \subseteq F_{td}$ since if $\varphi \in F_{td}$ and $z \in Z$ then $\varphi(0), \varphi(sc(z)) \in F_{td}$ because 0 and sc(z) are terms of sort t. It is important to stress here that φ may contain other free variables of all sorts. All the free variables of φ are also free in ind(φ,z) except for z. They are the "parameters" of the induction ind(φ,z).

The theory IA says that if a "property" φ changes during time T then it must change "some time", i.e. there is a time point $b \in T$ when φ is just changing.

Our strongest set of induction axioms is Ia. We shall distinguish various subsets of Ia.

DEFINITION 13 (Iq, $I\Sigma_1$, $I\Pi_1$, Il, Ict, If)

$If \overset{d}{=} \{\varphi \in IA : \varphi$ contains no free variable of sort t or d$\} \cup Lax$.

$Il \overset{d}{=} \{\varphi \in IA : (\forall i \in \omega)[i>0 \Rightarrow z_i$ does not occur in φ neither free nor bound}$\cup$Lax.

$\mathrm{Ict} \overset{d}{=} \{ind(\exists x_0 \ldots x_m [(\bigwedge_{j\le m} x_j = ext(y_j, z_0)) \wedge \varphi], z_0) : m\in\omega$ and $\varphi\in F_d\}\cup$Lax.

$(\Sigma_{0,t}F_{td}) \overset{d}{=} \{\varphi\in F_{td} : \varphi$ contains no quantifier of sort t, that is $(\forall i\in\omega)[$"$\exists z_i$" does not occur in $\varphi]\}$.

$\mathrm{Iq} \overset{d}{=} \{ind(\varphi, z_0) : \varphi\in(\Sigma_{0,t}F_{td})\}\cup$Lax.

$\mathrm{I}\Sigma_1 \overset{d}{=} \{ind(\exists z_1 \ldots z_m \varphi, z_0) : \varphi\in(\Sigma_{0,t}F_{td})$ and $m\in\omega\}\cup$Lax.

$\mathrm{I}\Pi_1 \overset{d}{=} \{ind(\forall z_1 \ldots z_m \varphi, z_0) : \varphi\in(\Sigma_{0,t}F_{td})$ and $m\in\omega\}\cup$Lax.

End of Definition 13

DEFINITION 14 (Ts, To, Tpres, Tpa$\subseteq F_t^Z$)

Notation: $sc^0(z_0) \overset{d}{=} z_0$ and $(\forall n\in\omega) sc^{n+1}(z_0) \overset{d}{=} sc(sc^n(z_0))$.

$\mathrm{Ts} \overset{d}{=} \{z_0 \ne 0 \leftrightarrow \exists z_1(z_0 = sc(z_1)),\ sc(z_0)=sc(z_1) \to z_0 = z_1,\ sc^n(z_0)\ne z_0 :$

$: n\in\omega,\ n\ne 0\}$.

$\mathrm{To} \overset{d}{=} \{(z_0\le z_1 \wedge z_1 \le z_2) \to z_0 \le z_2,\ (z_0\le z_1 \wedge z_1\le z_0) \to z_0 = z_1,$

$z_0\le z_1 \vee z_1\le z_0,\ 0\le z_0,\ (z_0\le z_1 \wedge z_0\ne z_1) \leftrightarrow sc(z_0)\le z_1,$

$0=z_0 \vee\ z_1(z_0=sc(z_1))\}$.

Tpres is the deicable set of Presburger's axioms:

$\mathrm{Tpres} \overset{d}{=} \mathrm{To}\cup\{z_0+0=z_0,\ z_0+sc(z_1)=sc(z_0+z_1),\ ind(\varphi, z_0) : \varphi\in F_t^Z$ and "$\cdot$" does not occur in $\varphi\}$.

Tpa is the set of Peano's axioms formulated in the language F_t^Z about the similarity type t, see e.g. Example 1.4.11 in [8]p.42.:

$\mathrm{Tpa} \overset{d}{=} \mathrm{Tpres}\cup\{z_0\cdot 0=0,\ z_0\cdot sc(z_1)=(z_0\cdot z_1)+z_1,\ ind(\varphi, z_0) : \varphi\in F_t^Z\}$.

End of Definition 14

DEFINITION 15 (Floyd-Hoare proof method ($\overset{F}{\vdash}$,Prf))

(i) The set HF_d of Floyd-Hoare statements of type d is an important sublanguage of DF_d.:

$HF_d \overset{d}{=} \{(\varphi \to \Box(p,\psi)) : p\in P_d$ and $\varphi,\psi\in F_d\}$. Clearly $HF_d\subseteq DF_d$.

(ii) Floyd-Hoare language HFL_d is defined to be:

$HFL_d \overset{d}{=} \langle HF_d \cup F_d,\ Mod_{td}(\mathrm{Iq}),\ \models\rangle$.

(iii) The relation $\overset{F}{\vdash} \subseteq \{Th : Th\subseteq F_d\}\times HF_d$ was defined in a rigorous manner in [20]Def.4 (this volume), [3]Def.17, [4]Def.17 p.55, [6],[2]p.118. We shall use this definition of $\overset{F}{\vdash}$ without refor -

-mulating it, but we note that in the quoted papers there is a decidable set $Prf \subseteq (HF_d \cup F_d)^*$ such that $(\forall Th \subseteq F_d)(\forall \varphi \in HF_d)[Th \vdash^F \varphi$ iff $(\exists$ finite $H \subseteq Th)(\exists w)\langle H, w, \varphi\rangle \in Prf]$. Hence Prf is the set of $\vdash^F$-proofs and Prf is decidable. Cf. Def.10. According to Def.10, $(\vdash^F, Prf)$ is a decidable proof concept for the Floyd-Hoare language HFL_d.

End of Definition 15

Here we do not recall the definitions of Dax, Imd, Ifm, Tfm, $\vdash^{\underline{fum}}$, $\vdash^{\underline{mod}}$, they can be found in [23].

Instead of "proof method for program verification" we shall simply say "proof method". By a proof method we understand a proof concept $(X \vdash^Y)$ in the sense of Def.11 or one in the sense of Def.9. Thus e.g. $\vdash^F$ and $(Dax \vdash^N)$ are proof methods. When we call $(X \vdash^N)$ a proof method for program verification then what we intuitively have in mind is the proof concept $(X \vdash^N)$ as a device for proving properties of programs. We shall concentrate on the powers of proof methods $(X \vdash^Y)$ to prove partial correctness of programs.

We define a pre-ordering $\leq$ on the proof methods as follows: $(X \vdash^Y) \leq (Y \vdash^Z)$ is defined to hold iff $[(Th \cup X \vdash^Y \rho) \rightarrow (Th \cup Y \vdash^Z \rho)]$ for every similarity type d, $Th \subseteq F_d$ and $\rho \in HF_d$.

The relation $\leq$ induces an equivalence relation $\equiv$ defined as: $(X \vdash^Y) \equiv (Y \vdash^Z)$ iff $[(X \vdash^Y) \leq (Y \vdash^Z)$ and $(Y \vdash^Z) \leq (X \vdash^Y)]$.

A straight line $X \vdash^Y$ — $Y \vdash^Z$ on Fig.1 indicates the relation $(X \vdash^Y) \leq (Y \vdash^Z)$. A line with $\neq$ added like $X \vdash^Y$ —≠— $Y \vdash^Z$ indicates the strict relation $<$ that is $[(X \vdash^Y) \not\geq (Y \vdash^Z)$ and $(X \vdash^Y) \leq$ $\leq (Y \vdash^Z)]$. A line with $=?$ added like $X \vdash^Y$ —=?— $Y \vdash^Z$ indicates that $(X \vdash^Y) \leq (Y \vdash^Z)$ but we do not know whether $(X \vdash^Y) \geq (Y \vdash^Z)$ holds or not. Broken line $X \vdash^Y$ - -≰- - $Y \vdash^Z$ with $\not\leq$ indicates that $(X \vdash^Y) \not\leq$ $\not\leq (Y \vdash^Z)$ (but we do not know whether $(X \vdash^Y) \geq (Y \vdash^Z)$ holds or not). If $(X \vdash^Y) \not\leq (Y \vdash^Z)$ is not indicated (either by $\neq$ or by $\not\leq$) then we do not know whether or not $(X \vdash^Y) \leq (Y \vdash^Z)$. Hence "=?" is used only to stress that we do not know whether equivalence holds. If two nodes are not connected then we do not know whether they are related in any direction or not that is we do not know whether they are

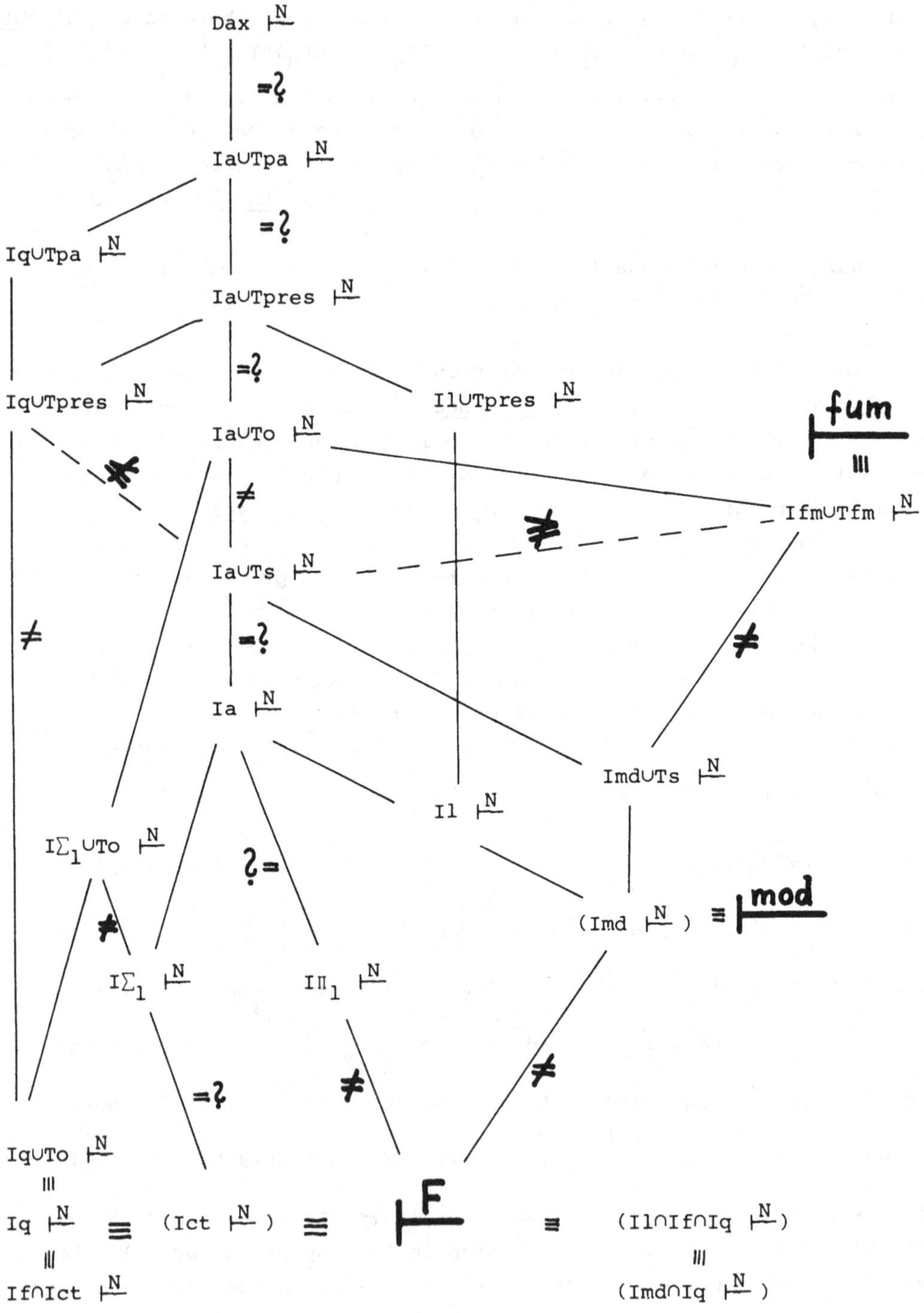
Dax ⊢N
=?
Ia∪Tpa ⊢N
=?
Iq∪Tpa ⊢N
Ia∪Tpres ⊢N
=?
Iq∪Tpres ⊢N
Il∪Tpres ⊢N
⊢fum
≡
Ia∪To ⊢N
≠
≠
Ifm∪Tfm ⊢N
≠
Ia∪Ts ⊢N
≠
=?
≠
Ia ⊢N
Imd∪Ts ⊢N
Il ⊢N
IΣ1∪To ⊢N
?=
(Imd ⊢N) ≡ ⊢mod
≠
IΣ1 ⊢N
IΠ1 ⊢N
=?
≠
≠
Iq∪To ⊢N
≡
Iq ⊢N ≡ (Ict ⊢N) ≡ ⊢F ≡ (Il∩If∩Iq ⊢N)
≡
If∩Ict ⊢N
≡
(Imd∩Iq ⊢N)

FIGURE 1

comparable. For example we do not know whether $(\mathrm{Iq}\cup\mathrm{Tpres} \overset{N}{\vdash}) \leq \leq (\mathrm{Ia}\cup\mathrm{To} \overset{N}{\vdash})$ holds or not. Note that the fact $\mathrm{Iq} \not\equiv \mathrm{Iq}\cup\mathrm{To}$ does <u>not</u> imply $(\mathrm{Iq} \overset{N}{\vdash}) \not\leq (\mathrm{Iq}\cup\mathrm{To} \overset{N}{\vdash})$ since proof methods here are compared only w.r.t. $Th \subseteq F_d$ and $\rho \in HF_d$.

In [23], it is indicated for all statements in Fig.1 where to find proofs for them, e.g. the proof of $\mathrm{Ia}\cup\mathrm{To} \overset{N}{\vdash}) \not\leq (\mathrm{Ia}\cup\mathrm{Ts} \overset{N}{\vdash})$ can be found in [23]. In the present paper we shall prove $(I\Pi_1 \overset{N}{\vdash}) \not\leq \overset{F}{\vdash}$, see Theorem 2. Note the contrast between $(\mathrm{Iq} \overset{N}{\vdash}) \equiv \overset{F}{\vdash}$ and $(I\Pi_1 \overset{N}{\vdash}) \not\leq \not\leq \overset{F}{\vdash}$.

§4. THE MAIN RESULT OF THE PRESENT PAPER

Theorem 2 below says that more programs can be proved to be correct by using induction over universally quantified formulas than by induction over quantifier-free formulas. (Note that $(\mathrm{Iq} \overset{N}{\vdash}) \equiv \overset{F}{\vdash}$.)

<u>THEOREM 2</u> There are a similarity type d, $p \in P_d$, $\psi \in F_d$ and a finite $Th \subseteq F_d$ such that $(Th \cup I\Pi_1) \models \Box(p,\psi)$ but $Th \overset{F}{\not\vdash} \Box(p,\psi)$.

<u>PROOF</u>. Let d consist of the function symbols $0'$, suc with arities $0,1$ respectively. Let p be the program illustrated on Figure 2. Note that in defining p we use fewer labels than required in the formal definition of P_d, but it is easy to see that this change is <u>not essential</u> while it considerably <u>simplifies</u> the traces of p.

Let $Th \subseteq F_d$ be a finite axiomatization of the theory of $\langle \omega, 0, suc \rangle$ where suc is the usual successor function on ω. Let ψ be the formula $x_3 = x_4$.

We shall prove that $Th \cup I\Pi_1 \models \Box(p,\psi)$ but $Th \overset{F}{\not\vdash} \Box(p,\psi)$.

<u>LEMMA 2.1.</u> $Th \cup I\Pi_1 \models \Box(p,\psi)$.

<u>Proof</u>. Let $\mathfrak{M} = \langle \underset{\sim}{T}, \underset{\sim}{D}, I, ext \rangle \in Mod_{td}(Th \cup I\Pi_1)$ be arbitrary and let $s \in {}^6 I$ be a trace of p in $\mathfrak{M}$.

Let $\Sigma_0 F_{td} \overset{d}{=} \{\varphi \in F_{td} : \varphi$ contains no qunatifier$\}$. Then $\Sigma_0 F_{td} \subseteq \subseteq (\Sigma_{0,t} F_{td})$.

<u>Notation</u>: $s_i(z)$ denotes the term $ext(s_i, z)$.

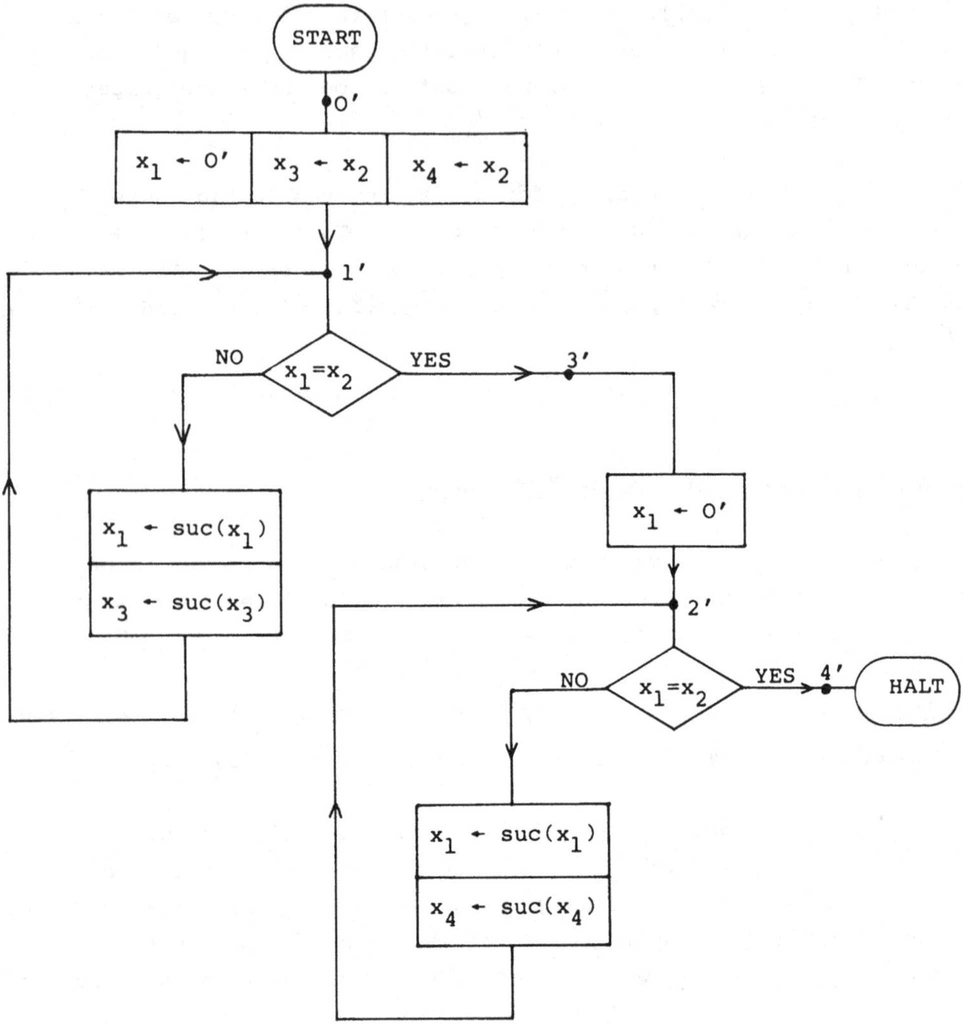

FIGURE 2

We shall extensively use formulas with parameters, e.g. if $\varphi(z_0,y_0)\in F_{td}$ and $s_2\in I$ then we shall sloppily say that $\varphi(z_0,s_2)$ is a formula. Of course, it is not, but the sloppy proof calling $\varphi(z_0, s_2)$ a formula can be translated to a precise one using $\varphi(z_0,y_0)$ and considering the case when y_0 is valuated to denote s_2.

CLAIM 2.1.1. $(\forall z_0)(s_2(z_0)=s_2(0))$.

Proof. Let $\varphi(z_0)$ be the formula $s_2(z_0)=s_2(0)$. Then $\varphi\in\Sigma_0 F_{td}$

hence $ind(\varphi,z_0)\in Iq$. Clearly $\varphi(0)$. Let $b\in T$ and assume $\varphi(b)$. Since s is a trace, $s_2(sc(b))=s_2(b)=s_2(0)$. Thus $\varphi(sc(b))$. Thus $\mathfrak{M}\models\forall z_0(\varphi(z_0)\rightarrow\varphi(sc(z_0)))$. Thus $\mathfrak{M}\models\forall z_0\varphi(z_0)$. QED(2.1.1.)

CLAIM 2.1.2. $\forall z_0[s_5(z_0)\in\{1',3'\}\rightarrow s_4(z_0)=s_2(0)]$.

Proof. Let $\gamma(z_0)$ be the formula $[s_0(z_0)\in\{1',3'\}\rightarrow s_4(z_0)=s_2(0)]$. Clearly $\gamma(0)$, since $s_0(0)=0'\notin\{1',3'\}$ by $\mathfrak{M}\models Th$. Since s is a trace, we have $\forall z_0(\gamma(z_0)\rightarrow\gamma(sc(z_0)))$, since if $s_5(z_0)=1'$ then $s_4(sc(z_0))=s_4(z_0)$ and if $s_5(z_0)\in\{3',2',4'\}$ then $s_5(sc(z_0))\notin\{1',3'\}$ hence $\gamma(sc(z_0))$ is obviously true, and if $s_5(z_0)=0'$ then $s_4(sc(z_0))=s_2(z_0)=s_2(0)$ by 2.1.1. Since $\gamma(z_0)\in\Sigma_0F_{td}$, we have $ind(\gamma,z_0)\in Iq$ and hence by the above, $\mathfrak{M}\models\forall z_0\gamma(z_0)$. QED(2.1.2.)

Let $\chi(z_0,z_1)$ be the formula $[s_5(z_0)=2'\wedge s_5(z_1)=1'\wedge s_1(z_0)=s_1(z_1)]$.

CLAIM 2.1.3. $\forall z_0z_1[\chi(z_0,z_1)\rightarrow s_4(z_0)=s_3(z_1)]$.

Proof. Let $\varkappa(z_0,z_1)$ be the formula $[\chi(z_0,z_1)\rightarrow s_4(z_0)=s_3(z_1)]$. Let $\varphi(z_0)$ be the formula $\forall z_1\varkappa(z_0,z_1)$. Then we have

(1*) $ind(\varphi(z_0),z_0)\in I\Pi_1$

since $\varkappa\in\Sigma_0F_{td}$. Clearly,

(2*) $\varphi(0)$ holds,

since $s_5(0)\neq 2'$ hence $\neg\chi(0,z_1)$. Next we shall prove $\forall z_0(\varphi(z_0)\rightarrow\varphi(sc(z_0)))$. To this end, let $b\in T$ and assume that

(3*) $\varphi(b)$.

We want to prove $\varphi(sc(b))$, which amounts to proving $\forall z_1\varkappa(sc(b),z_1)$. Therefore let $\rho(z_1)$ be the formula $\varkappa(sc(b),z_1)$. Then $\rho(z_1)$ is $[\chi(sc(b),z_1)\rightarrow s_4(sc(b))=s_3(z_1)]$. Clearly

(4*) $\rho(0)$

since $\neg\chi(z_0,0)$ for all z_0. To prove $\forall z_1[\rho(z_1)\rightarrow\rho(sc(z_1))]$ let $k\in T$ and assume that

(5*) $\rho(k)$ holds.

We want to prove $\rho(sc(k))$. If $\neg\chi(sc(b), sc(k))$ then $\rho(sc(k))$ obviously holds, assume therefore

(6*) $\chi(sc(b), sc(k))$.

Therefore we have

(7*) $s_5(sc(b))=2'$ and $s_1(sc(b))=s_1(sc(k))$ and $s_5(sc(k))=1'$

by the definition of χ. Since s is a trace of p, these imply

(8*) $s_5(b)\in\{2',3'\}$ and $s_5(k)\in\{0',1'\}$.

CASE 1 $s_5(b)=3'$.
Since s is a trace, then $s_1(sc(b))=0'$. By (7*), $s_1(sc(k))= =s_1(sc(b))=0'$. Then $s_5(k)=0'$, since otherwise $s_1(sc(k))= =suc(s_1(k))\neq 0'$ would be the case by Th and by s being a trace. (Namely, Th $\models \forall x\, suc(x)\neq 0'$.) Then $s_3(sc(k))=s_2(k)=s_2(0)=s_4(b)= =s_4(sc(b))$, by 2.1.1, 2.1.2. Thus $\rho(sc(k))$ is proved for CASE 1.

CASE 2 $s_5(b)=2'$.
Then by (7*), $s_1(sc(b))=suc(s_1(b))$. Thus if $s_5(k)=0'$ were the case then $s_1(sc(k))=0'\neq suc(s_1(b))=s_1(sc(b))$ would follow (by Th and by s being a trace) contradicting (7*). This proves

(9*) $s_5(k)=1'$.

Thence by (7*) we have $s_1(sc(k))=suc(s_1(k))$ since s is a trace. By (7*) then $suc(s_1(k))=s_1(sc(k))=s_1(sc(b))=suc(s_1(b))$. Since Th $\models$ $\models (suc(x_1)=suc(x_2) \rightarrow x_1=x_2)$ and since $\underset{\sim}{D} \models$ Th (i.e. $\mathfrak{M} \models$ Th), this implies $s_1(k)=s_1(b)$. This together with (9*) and with $s_5(b)=2'$ implies $\chi(b,k)$. By (3*) we have $\varphi(b)$ which implies $\varkappa(b,k)$. Therefore $s_4(b)=s_3(k)$. By $\chi(b,k)$ and $\chi(sc(b), sc(k))$, see (6*), and by s being a trace of p, this implies $s_4(sc(b))=suc(s_4(b))= =suc(s_3(k))=s_3(sc(k))$. This proves $\rho(sc(k))$, for CASE 2.

By Cases 1-2 above we proved $\rho(sc(k))$ from the assumption $\rho(k)$, see (5*). By the choice of k we proved $\mathfrak{M} \models \forall z_1[\rho(z_1) \rightarrow \rho(sc(z_1))]$. This together with (4*) implies $\forall z_1\rho(z_1)$, because by $\rho(z_1)\in\Sigma_0 F_{td}$ we have $ind(\rho(z_1),z_1)\in Iq$. By definition, $\forall z_1\rho(z_1)$ is identical with the formula $\varphi(sc(b))$, hence we proved $\varphi(sc(b))$ from the assumption $\varphi(b)$, see (3*). Thus we proved

(10*) $\forall z_0[\varphi(z_0) \rightarrow \varphi(sc(z_0))]$.

By (1*) we have $ind(\varphi(z_0),z_0)\in I\Pi_1$. By (2*) and (10*) and by $\mathfrak{M} \models I\Pi_1$ we have $\mathfrak{M} \models \forall z_0\varphi(z_0)$. QED(2.1.3.)

Notation: Let $b\in T$. Then $\bar{s}(b) \overset{d}{=} \langle s_i(b) : i\in 6\rangle$ and $\bar{\bar{s}}(b) \overset{d}{=} \langle s_i(b) : i\in 5\rangle$.

Let $e\in T$ be such that $s_5(e)=4'$. (Note that $4'$ is the label of the HALT-command in p.) We want to prove $s_3(e)=s_4(e)$.

Let $\gamma(z_0)$ be the formula $(\bar{s}(z_0)\neq\bar{s}(e))$. Then $ind(\gamma(z_0),z_0)\in Iq$. Clearly $\gamma(0)$ holds. Assume $\forall z_0(\gamma(z_0) \rightarrow \gamma(sc(z_0))$. Then by $\mathfrak{M} \models$ $\models Iq$ we have $\forall z_0\gamma(z_0)$, a contradiction, since $\neg\gamma(e)$ is true. Thus we proved $(\exists c\in T)\neg[\gamma(c) \rightarrow \gamma(sc(c))]$. This means $\gamma(c)$ and $\neg\gamma(sc(c))$. Let this c be fixed. We proved $\bar{s}(c)\neq\bar{s}(e)$ and $\bar{s}(sc(c))=\bar{s}(e)$. Since s is a trace and $s_5(sc(c))=s_5(e)=4'$ we have $s_5(c)\neq 4'$ and hence $s_5(c)=2'$. By $s_5(sc(c))=4'$ and since s is a trace then $s_1(c)=s_2(c)=s_2(0)$ by 2.1.1 and $\bar{\bar{s}}(c)=\bar{\bar{s}}(sc(c))=\bar{\bar{s}}(e)$. We have

(11*) $s_5(c)=2'$ and $s_1(c)=s_2(0)$ and $\bar{\bar{s}}(c)=\bar{\bar{s}}(e)$.

Let $\gamma(z_0)$ be the formula $[s_5(z_0)\in\{2',4'\}\wedge s_3(z_0)=s_3(e)]$. Then $ind(\neg\gamma(z_0),z_0)\in Iq$ and $\neg\gamma(0)$ and $\gamma(c)$ imply that $(\exists b\in T)(\neg\gamma(b)\wedge$ $\wedge\gamma(sc(b)))$. Since s is a trace, we have

(12*) $\forall z_0(s_5(z_0)\in\{2',4'\} \rightarrow [s_5(sc(z_0))\in\{2',4'\}\wedge s_3(z_0)=s_3(sc(z_0))])$.

By (12*) we have $\forall z_0(s_5(z_0)\in\{2',4'\} \rightarrow [\gamma(z_0) \rightarrow \gamma(sc(z_0))])$. This proves $s_5(b)\notin\{2',4'\}$. Then since s is a trace and $s_5(sc(b))\in$ $\in\{2',4'\}$ we have $s_5(b)=3$. Since s is a trace, this implies

(13*) $s_5(b)=3$ and $s_3(b)=s_3(sc(b))=s_3(e)$, by $\gamma(sc(b))$.

Let $\gamma(z_0)$ be the formula $[s_5(z_0)=3' \wedge s_3(z_0)=s_3(e)]$. By (13*) we have $\gamma(b)$. Since $ind(\neg\gamma(z_0),z_0)\in Iq$ and $\neg\gamma(0)$, by $\gamma(b)$ we infer that $(\exists a\in T)[\neg\gamma(a)\wedge\gamma(sc(a))]$. Thus $s_5(sc(a))=3'$ and $s_3(sc(a))=s_3(e)$. Since s is a trace this implies the following

(14*) $s_5(a)=1'$ and $s_3(a)=s_3(sc(a))=s_3(e)$ and $s_1(a)=s_2(a)=s_2(0)$,

by 2.1.1. By (11*) and by (14*), $\chi(c,a)$ holds since $s_1(c)=s_2(0)=$ $=s_1(a)$. Then 2.1.3 implies $s_4(c)=s_3(a)$. By (11*) we have $s_4(e)=$ $=s_4(c)$ and by (14*) we have $s_3(e)=s_3(a)$. We proved $s_4(e)=s_3(e)$.

By the choice of e and s then $\mathfrak{M}\models\Box(p,x_3=x_4)$. By the choice of $\mathfrak{M}$ we proved $Th\cup I\Pi_1 \models\Box(p,x_3=x_4)$. QED(2.1)

Next we prove $Th \not\vdash^F \Box(p,\psi)$. We shall prove more, see Lemma 2.2. Let do be the similarity type d with one binary relation symbol ≤' added. Let $Tho \subseteq F_{do}$ be the complete theory of $\underset{\sim}{\omega} \overset{d}{=} \langle \omega, 0, suc, \leq \rangle$, where ≤ is the usual ordering in ω. Let $\varphi \in F_{do}$ be any formula such that the variable x_2 does not occur in φ and such that $Tho \models \models \exists x_1 \exists x_3 \exists x_4 \varphi$.

<u>LEMMA 2.2.</u> $Tho \not\vdash^F (\varphi \to \Box(p,\psi))$.

<u>Proof</u>. Let $\bar{x} = \langle x_1, x_2, x_3, x_4 \rangle$. Suppose $Tho \vdash^F (\varphi \to \Box(p,\psi))$. Then there is a Floyd-Hoare proof $w \in Prf$ of $(\varphi \to \Box(p,\psi))$ such that w contains inductive assertions attached to the labels 1' and 2' of the program p (see Def.15). Let $\Phi_1(\bar{x}), \Phi_2(\bar{x}) \in F_{do}$ be these inductive assertions attached to the labels 1' and 2' of p. We define

$$
\begin{aligned}
Fl(\bar{x}) \overset{d}{=} \{ & \varphi \to \Phi_1(0', x_2, x_2, x_2), \\
& (\Phi_1(\bar{x}) \wedge x_1 \neq x_2) \to \Phi_1(suc(x_1), x_2, suc(x_3), x_4)), \\
& (\Phi_1(\bar{x}) \wedge x_1 = x_2) \to \Phi_2(0', x_2, x_3, suc(x_4)), \\
& (\Phi_2(\bar{x}) \wedge x_1 \neq x_2) \to \Phi_2\ suc(x_1), x_2, x_3, suc(x_4)), \\
& (\Phi_2(\bar{x}) \wedge x_1 = x_2) \to x_3 = x_4 \}.
\end{aligned}
$$

Then our hypothesis $Tho \vdash^F (\varphi \to \Box(p, x_3 = x_4))$ implies $Tho \vdash Fl(\bar{x})$. Then $\underset{\sim}{\omega} \models Fl(\bar{x})$.

Let $R \overset{d}{=} \{\langle a_1, a_2, a_3, a_4 \rangle \in {}^4\omega : a_1 \leq a_2,\ a_3 = 2a_2,\ a_4 = a_2 + a_1\}$. Here + is the usual addition of natural numbers and $2a_1 = a_2 + a_2$.

<u>CLAIM 2.2.1.</u> $(\forall \langle a_1, a_2, a_3, a_4 \rangle \in R)\ \underset{\sim}{\omega} \models \Phi_2[a_1, a_2, a_3, a_4]$.

<u>Proof.</u> Let $\langle a_1, a_2, a_3, a_4 \rangle \in R$ be arbitrary. Since $Tho \models \exists x_1 \exists x_3 \exists x_4 \varphi$, there are $e_1, e_3, e_4 \in \omega$ such that $\underset{\sim}{\omega} \models \varphi[e_1, e_3, e_4]$. Let $\mathfrak{M} \overset{d}{=} \langle \underset{\sim}{\omega}, \underset{\sim}{\omega}, {}^{\omega}\omega, ext \rangle \in M_{td}$ where $(\forall s \in {}^{\omega}\omega)(\forall b \in \omega) ext(s,b) = s(b)$. Consider the execution of the program p in $\mathfrak{M}$ with input $\langle e_1, a_2, e_3, e_4 \rangle$. We denote the trace of p of input $\langle e_1, a_2, e_3, e_4 \rangle$ by s. By the definition of a trace (Def.6), it is easy to see that there is a time point $b \in \omega$ such that the value of the control variable x_5 at time point b is the label of Φ_2, that is $ext(s_5, b) = s_5(b) = 2$, and the values of the program variables at time point b are: $\langle s_1(b), s_2(b), s_3(b), s_4(b) \rangle = \langle a_1, a_2, a_3, a_4 \rangle$. Then, by $\underset{\sim}{\omega} \models Fl(\bar{x})$ and

$\underset{\sim}{\omega} \models \varphi[s_1(0), s_3(0), s_4(0)]$ and by the definition of a trace we have $\underset{\sim}{\omega} \models \Phi_2[s_1(b), s_2(b), s_3(b), s_4(b)]$. (QED 2.2.1)

By the definition of R we have that $\langle j, 2j, 4j, 3j\rangle \in R$ for every $j \in \omega$. Then by 2.2.1 we have $\underset{\sim}{\omega} \models \Phi_2[j, 2j, 4j, 3j]$ for every $j \in \omega$.

Let U be a nonprincipal ultrafilter over ω. Let $k \overset{d}{=} \langle j : j \in \omega\rangle/U$. For every $n \in \omega$ let $nk \overset{d}{=} \langle nj : j \in \omega\rangle/U$. Let $\underset{\sim}{D}$ be the ultrapower $\underset{\sim}{D} = {}^{\omega}\underset{\sim}{\omega}/U$ of $\underset{\sim}{\omega}$. Then by Los lemma we have $\underset{\sim}{D} \models \Phi_2[k, 2k, 4k, 3k]$. See Figure 3!

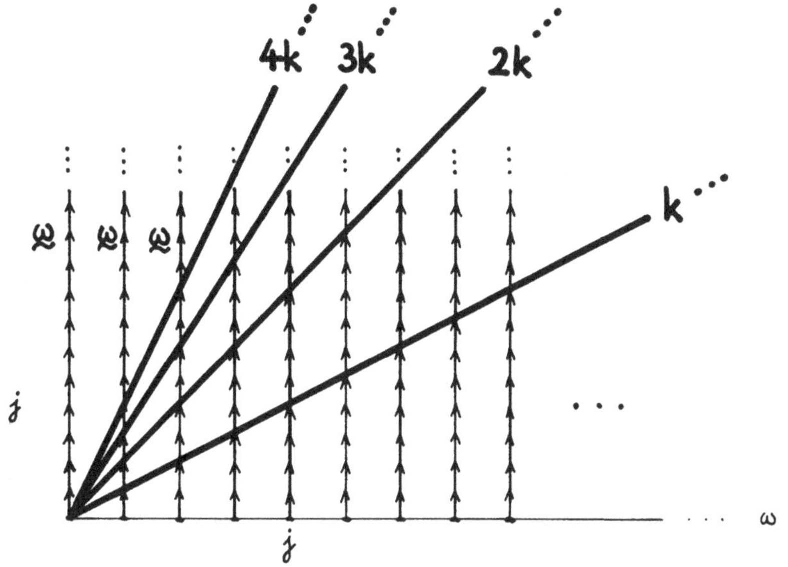

FIGURE 3

We define $suc^n : D \to D$ for every $n \in \omega$ as follows: $(\forall e \in D)[suc^0(e) \overset{d}{=} e$ and $suc^{n+1}(e) \overset{d}{=} suc(suc^n(e))]$.
It is known that $\underset{\sim}{D} = {}^{\omega}\underset{\sim}{\omega}/U$ looks like as it is illustrated on Fig.4 and it is easy to see that the "distance" between any two of k, $2k$, $3k$, $4k$ is <u>infinite</u>, i.e. $(\forall n \in \omega)[suc^n(k) \neq 2k$ and $suc^n(2k) \neq 3k$ etc.$]$.

Now we define $f : D \to D$ as follows. Let $e \in D$ be arbitrary. If there is an $n \in \omega$ such that $suc^n(e) = 4k$ or $suc^n(4k) = e$ then $f(e) \overset{d}{=} suc(e)$, otherwise $f(e) \overset{d}{=} e$. Clearly, f is an automorphism of $\underset{\sim}{D}$. Therefore $\underset{\sim}{D} \models \Phi_2[k, 2k, suc(4k), 3k]$ by $\underset{\sim}{D} \models \Phi_2[k, 2k, 4k, 3k]$. By Los lemma we have that $H \overset{d}{=} \{j \in \omega : \underset{\sim}{\omega} \models \Phi_2[j, 2j, suc(4j), 3j]\} \in U$. Since U is an ultrafilter, there is a $j \in H$. Let this j be fixed.

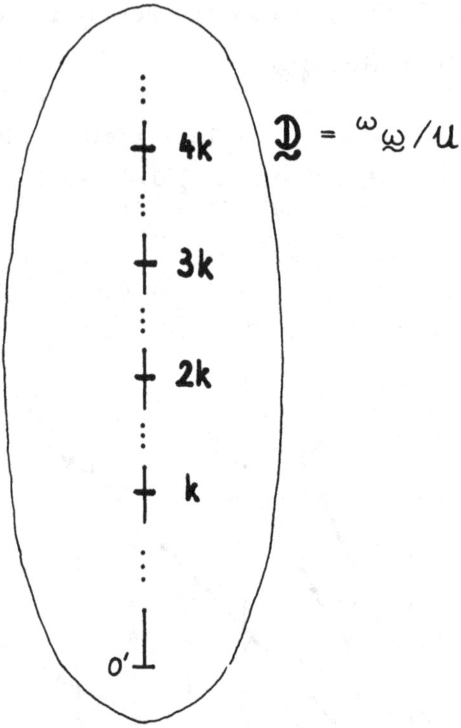

FIGURE 4

Then $\underset{\sim}{\omega} \models \Phi_2[j,2j,suc(4j),3j]$. Since by our hypothesis $\underset{\sim}{\omega} \models Fl(\bar{x})$, we have $\underset{\sim}{\omega} \models ((\Phi_2(\bar{x}) \wedge x_1 \neq x_2) \rightarrow \Phi_2(suc(x_1),x_2,x_3,suc(x_4))$. Thus, from $\underset{\sim}{\omega} \models \Phi_2[j,2j,suc(4j),suc(3j)]$ we can derive $\underset{\sim}{\omega} \models \Phi_2[suc(j),2j,suc(4j),suc(3j)]$ if $j<2j$. If $suc(suc(j))<2j$ then we can repeat this step. Actually, we can repeat this step exactly j times. By induction we can conclude $\underset{\sim}{\omega} \models \Phi_2[2j,2j,suc(4j),4j]$. Then using $\underset{\sim}{\omega} \models ((\Phi_2(\bar{x}) \wedge x_1=x_2) \rightarrow x_3=x_4)$ and $\underset{\sim}{\omega} \models Fl(\bar{x})$ we get from $\underset{\sim}{\omega} \models \Phi_2[2j,2j,suc(4j),4j]$ that $\underset{\sim}{\omega} \models (suc(4j)=4j)$, which is a contradiction. Therefore our hypothesis Tho $\overset{F}{\vdash} (\varphi \rightarrow \Box(p,\psi))$ is false.

<u>QED(Theorem 2)</u>

<u>PROBLEM 3</u> Is $(I\Sigma_1 \overset{N}{\vdash}) \equiv \overset{F}{\vdash}$? I.e. is it true that $(\forall d)(\forall \rho \in HF_d)[I\Sigma_1 \models \rho \Rightarrow \overset{F}{\vdash} \rho]$?

Algebraization of dynamic logic in the spirit of [15] can be found e.g. in [24].

R E F E R E N C E S

[1] Andréka,H. Németi,I., Completeness of Floyd's program verification method w.r.t. nonstandard time models, Seminar Notes Math. Inst. Hungar. Acad. Sci.-SZKI 1977 (in Hungarian). This was abstracted in [2].

[2] Andréka,H. Németi I., Completeness of Floyd Logic, Bull.Section of Logic Wroclaw (1978), Vol 7, No 3, pp.115-121.

[3] Andréka,H. Németi,I. Sain,I., A complete logic for reasoning about programs via nonstandard model theory, Theoret. Comput.Sci., Vol 17(1982) Part I in No 2, pp.193-212, Part II in No 3.

[4] Andréka,H. Németi,I. Sain,I., A complete first order dynamic logic, Preprint, Math.Inst.H.A.S., Budapest, 1980. No.810930.120p.

[5] Andréka,H. Németi,I. Sain,I., Henkin-type semantics for program schemes to turn negative results to positive, Fundamentals of Computation Theory'79 (Proc.Conf.Berlin 1979), Ed. L.Budach, Akademie Verlag, Berlin, 1979. Band 2. pp.18-24.

[6] Andréka,H. Németi,I. Sain,I., A characterization of Floyd-provable programs, In: Mathematical Foundations of Computer Science '81 (Strbské Pleso, Czechoslovakia, 1981), Lecture Notes in Computer Science 118, Springer, Berlin, 1981. pp.162-171.

[7] Burstall,R.M., Program proving as hand simulation with a little induction. IFIP Congress, Stockholm, August 3-10, 1974.

[8] Chang,C.C., Keisler,H.J., Model theory, North-Holland, 1973.

[9] Csirmaz,L., A survey of semantics of Floyd-Hoare derivability, CL&CL - Comput.Linguist, Comput.Lang, 14(1980), pp.21-42.

[10] Csirmaz,L., On the completeness of proving partial correctness, Acta Cybernet., Tom 5, Fasc 2, Szeged, 1981. pp.181-190.

[11] Csirmaz,L. Paris,J.B., A property of 2-sorted Peano models and program verification, Preprint, Budapest, 1981.

[12] Gabbay,D. Pnueli,A. Shelah,S. Stavi,J., On the temporal analysis of fairness, Preprint, Weizmann Inst. of Sci., Dept. of Applied Math., Israel, May 1981.

[13] Gergely,T. Ury,L., Time models for programming logics, In: Mathematical Logic in Computer Science(Proc.Coll. Salgótartján 1978), Colloq.Math.Soc.J.Bolyai Vol 26, North-Holland 1981, pp.359-427.

[14] Hájek,P., Making dynamic logic first-order, In: Mathematical Foundations of Computer Science '81 (Strbské Pleso, Czechoslovakia, 1981) Lecture Notes in Computer Science 118, Springer, Berlin, 1981.

[15] Henkin,L. Monk,J.D. Tarski,A. Andréka,H. Németi I., Cylindric Set Algebras, Lecture Notes in Mathematics 883, Springer-Verlag, Berlin, 1981. v+323p.

[16] Kfoury,D.J. Park,D.M.R., On the termination of program schemes, Information and Control 29(1975), pp.243-251.

[17] Manna,Z. Waldinger,R., Is "Sometime" sometimes better than "Always"? Intermittent assertions in proving program correctness, Preprint, Stanford Research Inst., Menlo Park, June 1976, No. Z173.

[18] Mirkowska,G., PAL - Propositional Algorithmic Logic, In: Logics of Programs, Lecture Notes in Computer Science 125, Springer-Verlag, Berlin, 1981. pp.23-101.

[19] Monk,J.D., Mathematical Logic, Springer Verlag, 1976.

[20] Németi,I., Nonstandard runs of Floyd-provable programs, this volume.

[21] Németi,I., Hilbert style axiomatization of nonstandard dynamic logic, Preprint, Budapest, 1980.

[22] Németi,I., Results on the lattice of dynamic logics, Preprint, Math. Inst. H.A.S., Budapest, 1981.

[23] Németi,I., Nonstandard dynamic logic, In: Proc. Workshop on Logics of Programs (May 1981, New York) Ed.: D.Kozen, Lecture Notes in Computer Science, Springer-Verlag, to appear.

[24] Németi,I., Dynamic algebras of programs, In: Fundamentals of Computation Theory'81 Proc.(Szeged 1981) Lecture Notes in Computer Science 117, Springer-Verlag, Berlin, 1981. pp.281-290.

[25] Parikh,R., Propositional dynamic logics of programs: A survey, In: Logics of Programs, Lecture Notes in Computer Science 125, Springer-Verlag, Berlin, 1981. pp.102-141.

[26] Richter,M.M. Szabo,M.E., Towards a nonstandard analysis of programs, In: Proc. of the Second Victoria Symp. on nonstandard analysis, Victoria, Britisch Columbia, June 1980. Ed. A.Hurd, Lecture Notes in Math., Springer Verlag, 1981.

[27] Sain,I., There are general rules for specifying semantics: Observations on Abstract Model Theory, CL&CL - Comput.Linguist. Comput.Lang., 13(1979), pp.251-282.

[28] Sain,I., First order dynamic logic with decidable proofs and workeable model theory, In: Fundamentals of Computation Theory '81 (Szeged, Hungary 1981), Lecture Notes in Computer Science 117, Springer, Berlin, 1981. pp.334-340.

[29] Stavi,J., Compactness properties of infinitary and abstract languages, In: Logic Colloquium'77, Ed.s A.Macintyre, L.Pacholski, J.Paris,. North-Holland 1978, pp.263-275.

ON PROVING PROGRAM CORRECTNESS BY MEANS OF STEPWISE REFINEMENT METHOD

Lech Banachowski
Institute of Informatics
Warsaw University

The stepwise refinement method [4] and the notion of an implementation of one data structure type by another are formulated on the basis of algorithmic logic [2]. It is shown that the properties of partial and total correctness of an implementation are expressible by means of nondeterministic algorithmic formulas.

1. INTRODUCTION

In the programming practice the following situation occurs frequently. We wish to develop a program correct with respect to some conditions α and β(1). This program is supposed to operate on objects drawn from a certain fixed many sorted algebra $\mathfrak{A}=\langle\{U_s\}_{s\in S},\Theta\rangle$, where $\{U_s\}_{s\in S}$ is a family of basic data types (such as for example integers,

---

(1) We consider two notions of program correctness: partial and total correctness [2]. We assume the following definitions. Suppose we are given program P and two formulas α and β (α describing intended input data, β describing results), all of them written in the algorithmic language [2] of a certain relational system $\mathfrak{A}$. P is said to be partially correct with respect to α and β iff for every input data satisfying α if the computation of P terminates then the resulting output data satisfy β. P is said to be totally correct with respect to α and β iff for every input data satisfying α the computation of P terminates and the resulting output data satisfy β. Thus the partial correctness is expressed by the formula $(\alpha \wedge P\text{true} \Rightarrow P\beta)$ and the total correctness by $(\alpha \Rightarrow P\beta)$.

reals, Boolean values, vectors of integers etc.) and Θ is a set of functions of the form

$$\varphi : U_{s_1} \times \ldots \times U_{s_k} \to U_{s_{k+1}} \qquad (s_1,\ldots,s_k,s_{k+1} \in S).$$

(In this paper for notational convenience we treat relations as functions assuming one of the sets U_s to be the set of Boolean values $\{0,1\}$.) However the problem in question may involve some other objects from a certain larger many-sorted algebra $\mathfrak{B}=\langle\{U_s\}_{s\in S_1}, \Theta_1\rangle$ where we assume that $S \subseteq S_1$ and $\Theta \subseteq \Theta_1$. It is often much easier to write a program over $\mathfrak{B}$ than over $\mathfrak{A}$. Suppose that we have written a program P over $\mathfrak{B}$ correct with respect to conditions α and β. To get a corresponding program P' over $\mathfrak{A}$ correct with respect to α and β, we must replace in some way objects not in $\mathfrak{A}$ by objects in $\mathfrak{A}$ and moreover we must program over $\mathfrak{A}$ all the operations $\varphi \in \Theta_1 - \Theta$ that are used in P i.e. we must provide an implementation for P. For example the standard system of programming (defined by a programming language) is frequently adjoined by the objects like graphs, sets, families of sets etc.

Example 1. Let us consider the following problem. Given a positive integer k and integers e,f,c[1],...,c[l],d[1],...,d[l] drawn from the set $\{1,2,\ldots,k\}$ determine whether the pair (e,f) belongs to the leas equivalence relation containing all the pairs (c[i],d[i]) for $1 \leq i \leq l$. We are to solve this problem over the algebra consisting of Boolean values, integers and vectors of integers. However it is more natural for this problem to think about it in terms of sets of integers and sets of equivalence classes of equivalence relations over the set $\{1,2,\ldots,k\}$. So let R be a variable assuming as its values partitions of the set $\{1,2,\ldots,k\}$ and let A and B be variables assuming as thei values subsets of the set $\{1,2,\ldots,k\}$. Consider the following operations:

(1) init(k) whose value is the partition $\{\{1\},\{2\},\ldots,\{k\}\}$;

(2) find(h,R) whose value is the set of the partition R that contains integer h;

(3) eq(A,B) whose value is either Boolean value 1 if A=B or Boolean value 0 if $A \neq B$;

(4) union(A,B,R) whose value is either the partition $(R-\{A,B\}) \cup \{A \cup B\}$ if sets A and B are in R, or R otherwise.

Now consider the program which uses these operations:

begin

$\{\alpha : k \geq 1 \wedge l \geq 0 \wedge \bigwedge_{u=1}^{l} 1 \leq c[u], d[u] \leq k \wedge 1 \leq e,f \leq k\}$

1: R:=init(k);

for i:=1 to l do

```
        begin{invariant:R is the set of equivalence classes of the least
               equivalence relation containing the pairs (c[u],d[u])
               for 1≤u<i }
2:           A:=find(c[i],R);
3:           B:=find(d[i],R);
4:           R:=union(A,B,R)
        end;
5:      A:=find(e,R);
6:      B:=find(f,R);
7:      q:=eq(A,B)
        {β :q=1⟺(e,f) belongs to the least equivalence relation over
          {1,2,...,k} containing all the pairs (c[u],d[u]) for 1≤u≤l }
   end
```

where q is a Boolean variable and i is an integer variable. Abstract instructions which should be replaced by concrete instructions are preceded by labels in the text. □

After Hoare [4] we shall call the source program P an abstract program and the target program P′ a concrete program. We shall admit the following notational conventions:

(1) a vector of variables of types in S common to both P and P′ will be denoted by x (these variables will be called common variables);

(2) a vector of variables of types in S_1-S appearing only in P will be denoted by y (these variables will be called abstract data structure variables);

(3) a vector of variables of types in S appearing only in P′ will be denoted by z (these variables will be called concrete data structure variables).

Note that in order to represent one abstract data structure variable we must sometimes use several concrete data structure variables. For example if we represent a set A, card(A)=n, by an ordered table T[1:m] such that n≤m and $A=\{T[i] : 1\leq i\leq n\}$ then two concrete data structure variables T and n correspond to one abstract data structure variable S. Hence it follows that the transformation from P to P′ should be accomplished by replacing whole instructions by instructions. Returning to Example 1 the parts of the program that should be replaced are the whole assignment statements: R:=init(k), A:=find(c[i],R), B:=find(d[i],R), R:=union(A,B,R), A:=find(e,R), B:=find(f,R), q:=eq(A,B).

In the opinion of the author input and output specifications should be the same for both P and P′ and should depend only on common variables x. We shall adopt here this point of view assuming "data structures" of P and P′ as local means being initialized at the beginning of computations.

To simplify further considerations relations between values of corresponding data structure variables in the vectors y and z, respectively, will be extended to vectors of values of y and z. The notation I(z)=y will denote the fact that the vector of values of concrete data structure variables z corresponds to the vector of values of abstract data structure variables y. The two main properties which should hold between corresponding computations of P and P′ are: the invariance of the relation I(z)=y and the invariance of the fact that the corresponding vectors of values of variables x are the same. Now it should not be surprising that these two properties allow to infer from partial or total correctness of P with respect to $\alpha(x)$ and $\beta(x)$, partial or total correctness of P′ with respect to the same formulas.

In section 2 we introduce an appropriate notion of a data structure type. In section 3 we define a notion of an implementation of one data structure type by another. In section 4 we introduce notions of partial and total correctness of an implementation and we prove two sufficient conditions for these two kinds of correctness which have the form of validity of some deterministic algorithmic formulas. In section 5 we present the rules which from partial (total) correctness of a source, abstract program P and partial (total) correctness of an implementation allow to infer partial (total) correctness of a target, concrete program P′. In section 6 we prove that both the properties partial and total correctness of an implementation are expressible by means of formulas of certain extended nondeterministic algorithmic logic.

2. Σ(K)-PROGRAMS AND THEIR COMPUTATIONS

Suppose we are given a many sorted universe of objects $\bigcup_{s\in S} U_s$ with operations forming many-sorted algebra $\mathfrak{A}=\langle\{U_s\}_{s\in S}, \Theta\rangle$ where S is a set of sorts and Θ is a set of operations such that for each $\varphi\in\Theta$ there exists $k\geq 0$ and $s_1,\dots,s_{k+1}\in S$ such that

$$\varphi : U_{s_1}\times\dots\times U_{s_k} \longrightarrow U_{s_{k+1}} .$$

We assume that one of the sets U_s is two-element Boolean algebra. Moreover we assume that for this algebra an algorithmic language $L(\mathfrak{A})$ is defined which includes the following sets:

(1) the set of deterministic instructions (programs) FS;

(2) the set of algorithmic terms FST;

(3) the set of algorithmic formulas FSF.

(For the definitions consult [2].)

For notational convenience we shall denote operations and corresponding functors by the same symbols.

Since we wish to abstract from specific programs which contain certain objects and instructions to be implemented, we need to introduce the notion of a computation of a sequence of instructions (drawn from arbitrary programs which use these instructions).

So let $\mathfrak{K}=\{K_0,K_1,\dots,K_n\}$ be a finite set of instructions in FS. We assume that three kinds of variables are distinguished:

(1) common variables x (common to abstract and concrete programs);

(2) data structure variables y (specific for only one program either abstract or concrete);

(3) auxiliary variables (local to a single instruction).

Abstract and concrete programs usually carry out some initializations of values of data structure variables at the beginning. We assume that this is accomplished by the first instruction K_0 which should deliver initial values to all data structure variables in y. In addition we assume that K_0 has the stop property in $\mathfrak{A}$.

By $\Sigma(\mathfrak{K})$ we shall denote the set of all finite sequences

$\sigma=\sigma_0,\sigma_1,\dots,\sigma_m$

where $m\geq 0$, $\sigma_0=K_0$ and $\sigma_i\in\mathfrak{K}-\{K_0\}$ for $1\leq i\leq m$.

The elements of the set $\Sigma(\mathfrak{K})$ will be called $\mathfrak{K}$-programs.

The intuitive meaning of $\mathfrak{K}$-programs is as follows. Let us suppose that the instructions of the set $\mathfrak{K}=\{K_0,K_1,\dots,K_n\}$ are used in a program P. P may be called the main program. Consider a finite computation of P for some initial valuation of variables. During this computation executions of some instructions from $\mathfrak{K}$ take place. Suppose that $\sigma_0,\sigma_1,\dots,\sigma_m$ is the sequence of instructions used consecutively by the main program P. First the execution of $\sigma_0=K_0$ initializes the values of data structure variables. Afterwards some computations take place in P, which however do not change the values of data structure variables. The main program P prepares values of common variables for the instruction σ_1 and then σ_1 is called. The execution of σ_1 can change values of data structure variables and upon the completion σ_1 communicates the values of common variables to the main program P. This process is repeated for the next instructions $\sigma_2,\dots,\sigma_m$, consecutively. At any time values of data structure variables can be changed only by one of the instructions in $\mathfrak{K}$. In this way the values of data structure variables form a certain kind of data type to be distinguished from other data. The main program P may use the values of data structure variables only by calling instructions in $\mathfrak{K}$.

In this paper such a set $\mathfrak{K}$ of instructions will be called a data structure type over α. With the presented above intuitions in mind, we adopt the following definition of a $\mathcal{K}$-program. Namely a computation of a $\mathcal{K}$-program $\sigma=\sigma_0,\sigma_1,\dots,\sigma_m$ consists o three sequences of vectors of values:

(1) $x_0,x_1,\dots,x_m$

(2) $y_1,y_2,\dots,y_{m+1}$

(3) $t_0,t_1,\dots,t_m$

such that the following conditions hold:

(i) for each i, $0\leqslant i\leqslant m$, x_i and t_i are vectors of values of the common variables x;

(ii) for each i, $1\leqslant i\leqslant m$, y_i is a vector of values of the data structu variables y;

(iii) y_1 is the vector of values of data structure variables upon the completion of the execution of $\sigma_0=K_0$;

(iv) for each i, $1\leqslant i\leqslant m$, the computation of σ_i for $x=x_i$ and $y=y_i$ terminates and upon the completion $y=y_{i+1}$ and $x=t_i$. It is convenient to present a computation of a $\mathcal{K}$-program $\sigma=\sigma_0,\sigma_1,\dots,\sigma_m$ by means of the following diagram (assuming the above denotations).

vectors of values of the common variables x before execution of an instruction

vectors of values of the data structure variables y

vectors of values of the common variables x after execution of an instruction

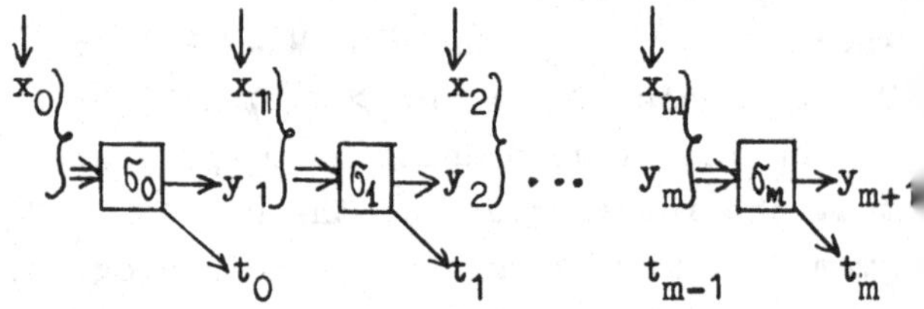

Example 2. Let N be a positive integer. Consider the system whose universe includes the set $\{1,2,\dots,N\}$, the set of Boolean values $\{0,1\}$ and the set P(N) of all subsets of the set $\{1,2,\dots,N\}$. Assume that the following set operations and relations are in the system under consideration:

(1) constant $\emptyset$ (empty set);

(2) two-argument operations $\cup$ and $-$ of union and subtraction of sets, respectively;

(3) two-argument relation $\in$ of being an element of a set;

(4) the operation $\{\ \}$ of composing one-element set.

Let i be a variable assuming its values from the set $\{1,2,\dots,N\}$, let S be a variable assuming its values from the set P(N) and let q be a Boolean variable. Let us consider the following data structure type DICTIONARY=$\{$init, insert, delete, member$\}$ where

init=$[S:=\emptyset]$,

insert= [S:=S∪{i}] ,
delete= [S:=S−{i}] ,
member= [q:=i∈S] .

We assume that i and q are common variables and S is a data structure variable. (N is treated as a constant.) These instructions do not contain any auxiliary variables. For example σ=init, insert, insert, member, delete is a DICTIONARY-program. If we provide the inputs 1,2,2,2 for the common variable i of the consecutive instructions in σ we receive the following computation (only relevant values are indicated).

$$\boxed{\text{init}} \to \left.\begin{matrix} \downarrow \\ i=1 \\ S=\emptyset \end{matrix}\right\} \Rightarrow \boxed{\text{insert}} \to \left.\begin{matrix} \downarrow \\ i=2 \\ S=\{1\} \end{matrix}\right\} \Rightarrow \boxed{\text{insert}} \to \left.\begin{matrix} \downarrow \\ i=2 \\ S=\{1,2\} \end{matrix}\right\} \Rightarrow \boxed{\text{member}} \to \left.\begin{matrix} \downarrow \\ i=2 \\ S=\{1,2\} \\ q=1 \end{matrix}\right\} \Rightarrow \boxed{\text{delete}} \to S=\{1\}$$

□

3. A NOTION OF AN IMPLEMENTATION

Let $\mathfrak{B}=\langle\{U_s\}_{s\in S_1},\Theta_1\rangle$ be an algebra which is an extension of $\mathfrak{A}=\langle\{U_s\}_{s\in S},\Theta\rangle$ (i.e. $S\subseteq S_1$ and $\Theta\subseteq\Theta_1$). We shall assume that $L(\mathfrak{A})$ is a sublanguage of $L(\mathfrak{B})$. Suppose that we are interested in a data structure type $\mathcal{K}=\{K_0,K_1,\ldots,K_n\}$ over $\mathfrak{B}$ and we wish to implement it by another data structure type $\mathcal{M}=\{M_0,M_1,\ldots,M_n\}$ over $\mathfrak{A}$. Assume that x is a vector of common variables of $\mathcal{K}$ and $\mathcal{M}$, y is a vector of data structure variables of $\mathcal{K}$ and z is a vector of data structure variables of $\mathcal{M}$. For example, suppose that we have an abstract program P such that it uses a data structure type $\mathcal{K}$ and all its instructions which cannot be directly carried out by a computer are included in $\mathcal{K}$. We could look for a data structure type $\mathcal{M}$ such that its instructions can be directly carried out by a computer and each instruction in $\mathcal{M}$ simulates the corresponding instruction in $\mathcal{K}$. By replacing the instructions of $\mathcal{K}$ by corresponding instructions of $\mathcal{M}$ in P, we would get a program P′ such that it solves the problem in question and it can run on a computer. Given common inputs for P and P′ the program P calls consecutively some instructions $K_{i_0},K_{i_1},\ldots,K_{i_m}$ of $\mathcal{K}$, while at the same time P′ calls consecutively the corresponding instructions $M_{i_0},M_{i_1},\ldots,M_{i_m}$ of $\mathcal{M}$.

We shall call $\mathcal{K}$ an abstract data structure type and $\mathcal{M}$ a concrete data structure type. We shall use the following notational convention. If

$\sigma= K_{i_0},K_{i_1},\ldots,K_{i_m}$

is a $\mathcal{K}$-program then by σ we denote the corresponding $\mathcal{M}$-program

$\bar{\sigma}=M_{i_0},M_{i_1},\dots,M_{i_m}$

(which is to simulate σ).

To wholly define an implementation of $\mathcal{K}$ by $\mathcal{M}$ we need to establish the connection between values of concrete and abstract data structure variables. We shall use the notion of an interpretation instruction, which is similar to Hoare's [4] concept of "abstract function". Namely to define an implementation we shall provide an instruction I in the language L($\mathcal{Y}$) which is intended to determine the vector of values of abstract data structure variables y which corresponds to a given vector of values of concrete data structure variables z.

Any pair J=($\mathcal{M}$,I) satisfying all the conditions stated above will b called an implementation over $\mathfrak{A}$ of the data structure type $\mathcal{K}$.

Example 3. Let us consider again the data structure type DICTIONARY= {init, insert, delete, member} defined in Example 2. Its implementation can be defined as J=($\mathcal{M}$,I) where

$\mathcal{M}$={ INIT, INSERT, DELETE, MEMBER },

INIT=(for j:=1 to N do T[j]:=false)),

INSERT=[T[i]:=true] ,

DELETE=[T[i]:=false],

MEMBER=[q:=T[i]] ,

i and q are common variables, T is a concrete data structure variable of type Boolean vector of length N, j is an auxiliary variable of type integer and

I=[S:={ j:T[j] =true }] . □

4. PARTIAL AND TOTAL CORRECTNESS OF IMPLEMENTATIONS

The question arises under what conditions $\mathcal{M}$-programs can be regarded as correct simulations of $\mathcal{K}$-programs. We shall adopt the following definitions.

An implementation J=($\mathcal{M}$,I) over $\mathfrak{A}$ of the data structure type $\mathcal{K}$ is said to be partially correct if for every $\mathcal{K}$-program $\sigma=\sigma_0,\sigma_1,\dots,\sigma_m$ and for every computation of the corresponding $\mathcal{M}$-program $\bar{\sigma}=\mu_0,\mu_1,\dots,\mu_m$ given in Figure 1 there exists a computation of σ of the form given in Figure 2 such that for each i, $1\leq i\leq m+1$ the vector of values $I_{\mathfrak{A}}(z=z_i)(y)$ is defined and equal to y_i ((where by $I_{\mathfrak{A}}(z=z_i)(y)$) we denote the vector of resulting values of variables y on the completion of I for $z=z_i$)).

In virtue of the definition partial correctness of an implementation means that if we have a terminating computation of a sequence $\bar{\sigma}$ simulating $\sigma\in\Sigma(\mathcal{K})$, then we can obtain the results of the original sequen-

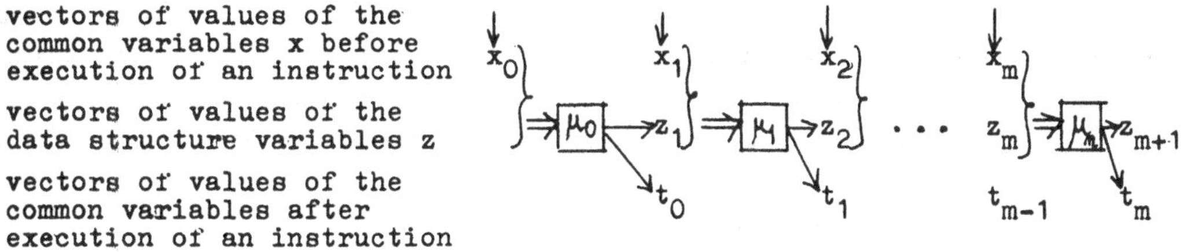

Figure 1. A computation of $\mathfrak{M}$-program $\bar{\sigma}$.

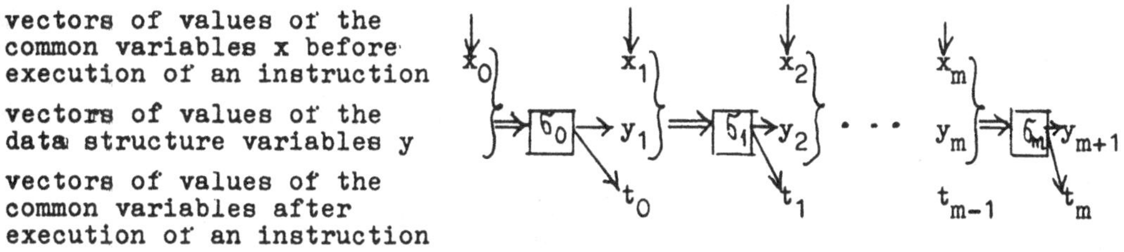

Figure 2. A computation of $\mathfrak{K}$ -program σ .

ce σ directly from this computation. This corresponds (as we shall see in the next section) to the notion of partial correctness of programs. If we get results we know they are correct. Of course sometimes we wish to know something more. Namely if a sequence $\bar{\sigma}$ simulates σ and the computation of σ terminates then the computation of $\bar{\sigma}$ terminates as well.

An implementation $J=(\mathfrak{M},I)$ over $\mathfrak{A}$ of the data structure type $\mathfrak{K}$ is said to be totally correct if for every $\mathfrak{K}$-program $\sigma=\sigma_0,\sigma_1,\ldots,\sigma_m$ and for every its computation of the form given in Figure 2 there exists a computation of $\bar{\sigma}$ of the form given in Figure 1 such that for each i, $1\leqslant i\leqslant m+1$ the vector of values $I_{\mathfrak{A}}(z=z_i)(y)$ is defined and equal to y_i.

Observe that if all the instructions of an abstract data structure type $\mathfrak{K}$ (in practice the instructions in $\mathfrak{K}$ are simply assignment statements or at most sequences of assignment statements) have the stop property in $\mathfrak{D}$ then the total correctness of J implies partial correctness of J. The converse may be not true.

It seems that the definitions of partial and total correctness of implementations cannot be written by means of ordinary deterministic algorithmic formulas. Nevertheless in practical situations we need not go away from algorithmic formulas. Our reasonings about sequences of instructions consists in considering each instruction separately.

Below there are two criteria of partial and total correctness of

an implementation, respectively. They use the notion of validity of al
gorithmic formulas. Let $\Delta(z)$ be an arbitrary algorithmic formula which
plays the role of an invariant of the data structure type $\mathcal{M}$.

Theorem 1. If the following formulas are valid in $\mathcal{J}$

(1) $M_0\Delta(z)$,

(2) $\bigwedge_{1\leqslant i\leqslant n} (\Delta(z)\wedge M_i\,\text{true}\Rightarrow M_i\Delta(z))$,

(3) $K_0 y=M_0 Iy \wedge K_0 x=M_0 x$,

(4) $\bigwedge_{1\leqslant i\leqslant n} (\Delta(z)\wedge M_i\,\text{true}\Rightarrow (M_i Iy=IK_i y \wedge M_i x=IK_i x))$

then $J=(\mathcal{M},I)$ is a partially correct implementation over α of the dat
structure type $\mathcal{K}$.

The validity of the consecutive formulas in Theorem 1 can be expres
sed as follows:

(1) $\Delta(z)$ holds after performing M_0;

(2) $\Delta(z)$ is preserved under each instruction M_i, $1\leqslant i\leqslant n$;

(3) the computations of all the instructions in the diagram below terminate and the diagram is commutative;

$$
\begin{array}{ccc}
x & \xrightarrow{\ K_0\ } & y,t \\
\big\uparrow & & \big\uparrow I \\
x & \xrightarrow[\ M_0\ ]{} & z,t
\end{array}
$$

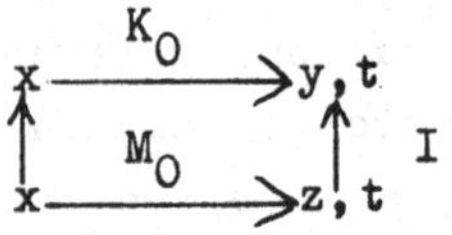

(4) for each i, $1\leqslant i\leqslant n$, if a vector of values of data structure varia
bles z satisfies $\Delta(z)$ and the computation of M_i terminates then the co
mputations of all the instructions in the diagram below terminate and
the diagram is commutative.

$$
\begin{array}{ccc}
y,x & \xrightarrow{\ K_i\ } & y',t \\
I\big\uparrow & & \big\uparrow I \\
z,x & \xrightarrow[\ M_i\ ]{} & z',t
\end{array}
$$

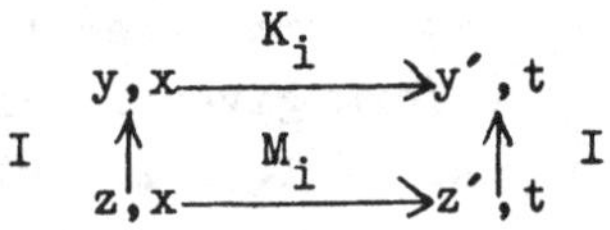

Proof of Theorem 1. Let us consider an arbitrary computation of the
$\mathcal{M}$-program $\overline{\delta}$ given in Figure 1. It follows that during the realizatio
of $\overline{\delta}$ the computation of each instruction μ_i terminates, $0\leqslant i\leqslant m$.
Now carry out δ providing the vector of values x_i for the i-th instruction, $0\leqslant i\leqslant m$.

To prove the thesis of Theorem 1 it is sufficient to show that for
each j, $1\leqslant j\leqslant m+1$, there exists a computation of the $\mathcal{K}$-program $\delta^j=$
$\delta_0,\delta_1,\ldots,\delta_{j-1}$ of the form given in Figure 3 such that for each i,
$1\leqslant i\leqslant j$, the vector of values $I_\alpha(z=z_i)(y)$ is defined and equal to y_i.
The proof proceeds by induction on j. The validity of the formula (3)
implies the initial induction step for j=1. Since by (1) and (2) $\Delta(z)$

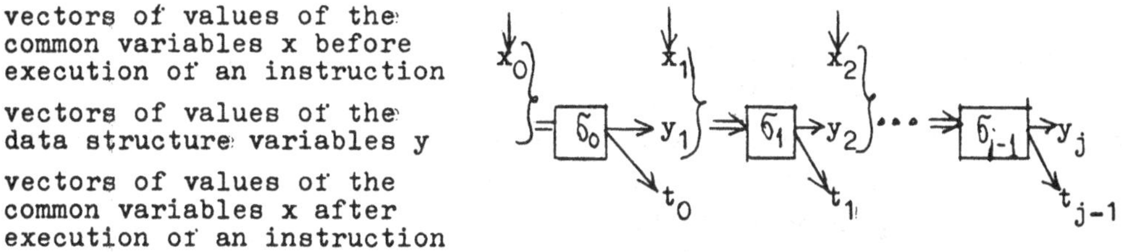

Figure 3. A computation of σ^j.

is an invariant during the computation of $\bar{\sigma}$ the validity of the formula (4) allows to carry out the induction step from j to j+1. □

Theorem 2. If the formulas (1)-(4) of Theorem 1 and the formula

(5) $\bigwedge_{1\leqslant i\leqslant n} (\Delta(z)\wedge IK_i\,\text{true} \Rightarrow M_i\,\text{true})$

are valid in $\mathfrak{B}$ then $J=(\mathcal{M},I)$ is a totally correct implementation over $\mathfrak{A}$ of the data structure type $\mathcal{K}$.

Proof. It is sufficient to observe that the validity of (5) together with the validity of the remaining formulas allows to infer from the termination of the computation of a $\mathcal{K}$-program σ the termination of the corresponding $\mathcal{M}$-program $\bar{\sigma}$. □

In some situations when all the instructions of $\mathcal{K}$ and $\mathcal{M}$ have the stop property and no restrictions on values of concrete data structure variables z are needed, the formulas in Theorems 1 and 2 simplify their form very much.

Corollary. If the following formulas are valid in $\mathfrak{B}$

(1) $M_0Iy=K_0y \wedge M_0x=K_0x$,

(2) $\bigwedge_{1\leqslant i\leqslant n} (M_iIy=IK_iy \wedge M_ix=IK_ix)$

then $J=(\mathcal{M}, I)$ is a totally correct implementation over $\mathfrak{A}$ of the data structure type $\mathcal{K}$.

Proof. It is sufficient to apply Theorem 2 for Δ = true and observe that the validity of (2) ensures the validity of all the formulas $M_i$true and IK_itrue for $1\leqslant i\leqslant n$. □

Example 4. Let us consider again the data structure type DICTIONARY={ init, insert, delete, member} defined in Example 2 and its implementation $J=(\mathcal{M},I)$ defined in Example 3. By Corollary in order to prove the total correctness of this implementation it is sufficient to show the validity of the following formulas (the equalities concerning variables whose values do not change in the corresponding instructions are omitted):

$[S:=\emptyset]S$ = (for j:=1 to N do T[j]:=false; S:={j:T[j]})S,

$(T[i]:=true;\ S:=\{j:T[j]\})S = (S:=\{j:T[j]\};\ S:=S\cup\{i\})S$,
$(T[i]:=false;\ S:=\{j:T[j]\})S = (S:=\{j:T[j]\};\ S:=S-\{i\})S$,
$[q:=T[i]]\ q = (S:=\{j:T[j]\};\ q:=i\in S)q$.

The above formulas can be reduced equivalently by means of simple rule for algorithmic formulas to the following ones:

$\emptyset = (\underline{for}\ j:=1\ \underline{to}\ N\ \underline{do}\ T[j]:=false)\{j:T[j]\}$,
$[T[i]:=true]\{j:T[j]\} = \{j:T[j]\}\cup\{i\}$,
$[T[i]:=false]\{j:T[j]\} = \{j:T[j]\}-\{i\}$,
$T[i] = (i\in\{j:T[j]\})$

which are obviously valid. □

5. PARTIAL AND TOTAL CORRECTNESS OF PROGRAMS WITH DATA STRUCTURES

Let $\mathfrak{A}$ and its extension $\mathfrak{B}$ will be defined as previously. Let $J=(\mathcal{M},I)$ be an implementation of a data structure type $\mathcal{K}$, where $\mathcal{K}=\{K_0,K_1,\ldots,K_n\}$ is an abstract data structure type over $\mathfrak{B}$ and $\mathcal{M}=\{M_0,M_1,\ldots,M_n\}$ is a concrete data structure type over $\mathfrak{A}$. As previously assume that x is a vector of common variables, y is a vector of abstract data structure variables (i.e. of $\mathcal{K}$) and z is a vector of concrete data structure variables (i.e. of $\mathcal{M}$). Now we want to apply the implementation J to transform "abstract" programs over $\mathfrak{B}$ into "concrete" programs over $\mathfrak{A}$. Let P be a program over $\mathfrak{B}$ in which we distinguish instructions of the data structure type $\mathcal{K}$. Let P' be a program resulting from P by textual replacement of each occurrence of the instruction K_i by the instruction M_i for $0\leqslant i\leqslant n$. Let $\alpha(x)$ and $\beta(x)$ be two formulas in the language $L(\mathfrak{A})$.

Theorem 3. If the following conditions hold:

(1) P' is a program in the language $L(\mathfrak{A})$;

(2) P is partially correct (totally correct) with respect to $\alpha(x)$ and $\beta(x)$;

(3) J is a partially correct (totally correct) implementation over $\mathfrak{A}$ of the data structure type $\mathcal{K}$

then P' is partially correct (totally correct) with respect to $\alpha(x)$ and $\beta(x)$.

Proof. Let us consider computations of P and P' for some input data $x=\bar{x}$ satisfying α. Assume that the computation of P' terminates. From this computation of P' we can extract a certain $\mathcal{M}$-program $\mu=\mu_0,\mu_1,\ldots,\mu_m$ and its computation of the form presented in Figure 1. By the assumption (3) it follows that there exists a computation of the corresponding $\mathcal{K}$-program σ, $\bar{\sigma}=\mu$, of the form presented in Figure 2 such that for each i, $1\leqslant i\leqslant n+1$, the vector of values $I_{\mathfrak{A}}(z=z_i)(y)$ is defined and equal to y_i. Consider now the computation of P for input data $x=\bar{x}$. Using the assumption (1) it can be easily proved by induction on the length of computations that excluding steps inside instructions of $\mathcal{K}$ and $\mathcal{M}$ the following three conditions are preserved in the corresponding steps of the computations of P and P′ :

(4) the vector of values of Iy is defined in P′ and equal to the vector of values of y in P;

(5) the vector of values of x in P is equal to the vector of values of x in P′ ;

(6) the statements which are currently carried out in P and P′ are either the same or one is K_i and the other one is M_i for some $0 \leqslant i \leqslant n$.

It follows that the computation of P comes to the end point and the variables x have the same values as the variables x at the end point in P′. By the assumption (2) the values of the variables x satisfy β. We have thus proved Theorem 3 for the case of partial correctness.

The proof for the case of total correctness is similar (the invariance of the same conditions (4),(5) and (6) should also be proved). Therefore we omit it here. □

Example 5. Let us come back to the program in Example 1. We shall treat this program as an abstract one. It uses the following common variables x=(k,l,e,f,c,d,q) and abstract data structure variables y=(A,B,R). To be able to apply the methods presented in this paper we must add to this program two assignment statements which initialize the values of A and B. Thus we shall deal with the following program:

```
P:  begin
      {α: k ≥ 1 ∧ l ≥ 0 ∧ 1 ≤ c[u], d[u] ≤ k for 1 ≤ u ≤ l ∧ 1 ≤ e,f ≤ k }
      begin R:=init(k); A:=∅; B:=∅ end;
      for i:=1 to l do
      begin
        {invariant R is the set of equivalence classes of the least
         equivalence relation containing (c[u],d[u]) for 1 ≤ u < i }
        A:=find(c[i],R);
        B:=find(d[i],R);
        R:=union(A,B,R)
      end;
      A:=find(e,R);
      B:=find(f,R);
      q:=eq(A,B)
     {β: q=1 ⟺ the pair (e,f) belongs to the least equivalence rela-
      tion on the set {1,2,...,k} containing the pairs (c[u],d[u])
      for 1 ≤ u ≤ l}
    end
```

It is easy to prove the total correctness of P with respect to α and β by using the enclosed loop invariant. In P we distinguish seven abstract instructions:

K_0: <u>begin</u> R:=init(k); A:=∅; B:=∅ <u>end</u>,
K_1: A:=find(c[i],R),
K_2: B:=find(d[i],R),
K_3: R:=union(A,B,R),
K_4: A:=find(e,R),
K_5: B:=find(f,R),
K_6: q:=eq(A,B)

forming together a data structure type, call it find-union.

Now we shall present a certain implementation of this data structure type called a tree implementation [1] . An underlying algebra $\mathfrak{A}$ will consist of three basic types: Boolean values, integers and vectors of integers. The set of operations of $\mathfrak{A}$ will consist of all operations used in the concrete data structure type to be defined.

Each subset of the set {1,2,...,k} will be represented as a tree. The whole partition of the set {1,2,...,k} will be represented as a forest of trees, each tree representing one set of the partition. The vertices of this forest are integers 1,2,...,k. The edges of this forest are given by the contents of an integer array T[1:k]. Namely for each i, $1 \leq i \leq k$ the value T[i] is an integer such that $0 \leq T[i] \leq k$ and if for some $1 \leq i,j \leq k$, T[i]=j then the pair (i,j) forms an edge of the forest under consideration. If T[i]=0 then this means that the vertex i is the root of a tree. For example the contents of the array T:

1	2	3	4	5	6	7	8
0	1	1	3	0	5	1	0

determines the following forest

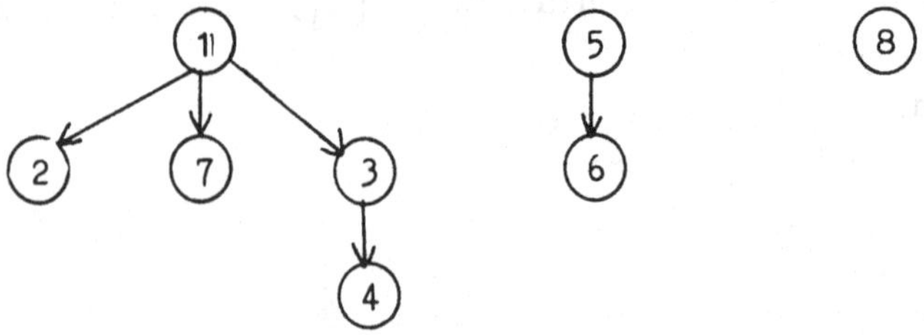

(arrows go from sons to fathers of vertices). The forest above reprents the partition {{1,2,3,4,7},{5,6},{8}}. Each root of a tree represents all vertices composing this tree. For example the root 1 represents the set {1,2,3,4,7} .

Now we shall proceed to the definition of the concrete data structure type FU-tree={INIT, FIND(c[i],a), FIND(d[i],b), UNION, FIND(e,a), FIND(f,b), EQ} with z=(a,b,T) as a vector of concrete data structure variables. (Note that there are four distinct instructions whose names begin with FIND. However they can be considered as distinct calls of the same procedure having two integer parameters u and v called by name.) Let u and v be auxiliary integer variables. We define

```
INIT= begin
        u:=1;
        while u≤k do (u,T[u]):=(u+1,0);
        (a,b):=(0,0)
      end
```

(INIT builds the forest composed of k one-element trees);

```
FIND(v,u)= begin
             (u,v):=(v,T[v]);
             while v≠0 do (u,v):=(v,T[v])
           end
```

(FIND begins at a given vertex v and follows the path to the root of the tree. Upon the completion u is the root of the tree);

```
UNION= if 1≤ a,b≤ l ∧ a≠b then
          if T[a]=0 ∧ T[b]=0 then T[a]:=b
```

(if a and b represent roots of distinct trees then UNION combines these trees into one tree);

EQ=[q:=(a=b)] .

Now we shall proceed to the definition of the interpretation instruction I. Let for a nonnegative integer h and an integer p, $0\leq p\leq k$, the notation $T^h[p]$ means p if $(h=0 \vee p=0)$ or $T^{h-1}[T[p]]$ otherwise. Recall that the contents of the array T and integer i, $1\leq i\leq k$, determine a subset of the set $\{1,2,\ldots,k\}$ consisting of all vertices j, $1\leq j\leq k$, from which the vertex i is reachable in the forest. Denote this set by set(i,T) i.e. $set(i,T)=\{j:\exists\, h, 0\leq h\leq k \wedge T^h[j]=i\}$. It should be evident that this set can be built by a program over the abstract system. The interpretation instruction I can be defined as follows

$I=[\,A:=set(a,T);\ B:=set(b,T);\ R:=\{\, set(u,T): 1\leq u\leq k \wedge T[u]=0\,\}\,]$.

Thus we have completed the definition of the tree implementation of the data structure type find-union, J=(FU-tree,I).

Now using Theorems 1 and 2 we shall show that J is a partially and totally correct implementation. To do this we shall consider consecutive formulas, whose validity is sufficient for partial and total correctness. As an invariant $\Delta(z)$ we take an algorithmic formula stating that the contents of the vector T represents a partition of the set $\{1,2,\ldots,k\}$. It should be clear that such a formula can be constructed if we are provided with classical quantifiers.

(1) Formula (1), namely INIT $\Delta(z)$ states that after initialization T represents a partition of the set $\{1,2,\ldots,k\}$.

(2) Formula (2) states that this property is preserved under any instruction. The instructions EQ and those prefixed with FIND do not change the current forest. The instruction UNION adds new edge only if thi edge links two roots of distinct trees. Hence UNION preserves $\Delta(z)$.

(3) Formula (3) states that the initializations have the following properties:

(i) they possess terminating computations;

(ii) on the completion the values of the common variables k,l,e,f,c,d, i are the same in K_0 and INIT, respectively;

(iii) on the completion the values of abstract data structure variable A,B,R and of concrete data structure variables a,b,T corresponds mutually according to the interpretation instruction I.

The conditions (i) and (ii) are obviously fulfiled. The condition (iii) holds since after initializations $R=\{\{1\},\{2\},\ldots,\{k\}\} = \{set(u,T): 1\leq u\leq k \wedge T[u]=0\}$, $A=\emptyset=set(0,T)$ and $B=\emptyset=set(0,T)$.

(4) Formula (4) states that for each pair of corresponding instruction for every values of common and concrete data structure variables, if T represents a partition of the set $\{1,2,\ldots,k\}$ and the concrete instruction possesses a terminating computation then the following conditions hold:

(i) the interpretation instruction I possesses a terminating computation transforming given values of concrete data structure variables T, a,b into corresponding values of abstract data structure variables R, A,B, respectively;

(ii) the abstract instruction possesses a terminating computation;

(iii) on the completion of both the instructions the values of common variables are the same;

(iv) on the completion of both the instructions the values of abstract data structure variables R,A,B and of concrete data structure variable T,a,b correspond mutually according to the interpretation instruction I

The conditions (i) and (ii) are easy to check. Consider now (iii) and (iv) for each pair of instructions.

Each particular call of FIND(v,u) computes the root u of the tree that contains v. Thus set(u,T)=find(v,R) which equals either A or B. FIND(v,u) computes nothing more, so the conditions (iii) and (iv) hold

Observe that the values a and b are roots of distinct trees iff A=set(a,T) and B=set(b,T) are distinct nonempty sets of the partition R Hence if a and b are roots of distinct trees then the new value of T represents the partition:

$\{set(u,T):T[u]=0 \wedge u \neq a,b\} \cup \{set(a,T) \cup set(b,T)\} = (R-\{A,B\}) \cup \{A \cup B\}$ = union(A,B,R) which is the new value of R. It follows that UNION satisfies (iii) and (iv).

Since A=set(a,T) and B=set(b,T) and the equality set(a,T)=set(b,T) is equivalent to a=b, EQ satisfies (iii) and (iv).

(5) Formula (5) states that if T represents a partition of $\{1,2,\ldots,k\}$ and an abstract instruction has a terminating computation for given values of common variables and for values of abstract data structure variables resulting from given values of concrete data structure variables by applying of the interpretation instruction I, then the corresponding concrete instruction possesses also a terminating computation. Since the values e,f,c[i] and d[i] belong to the set $\{1,2,\ldots,k\}$, all FIND-instructions possess always terminating computations. EQ and UNION evidently possess terminating computations.

By Theorem 1 J is partially correct and by Theorem 2 J is totally correct. Hence by Theorem 3 the program resulting from P by textual replacement of abstract instructions by corresponding concrete instructions is totally correct with respect to the submitted formulas α and β. $\square$

6. EXPRESSIBILITY OF PARTIAL AND TOTAL CORRECTNESS OF AN IMPLEMENTATION BY MEANS OF FORMULAS OF NONDETERMINISTIC ALGORITHMIC LOGIC

Let an algebra $\mathfrak{A}$ and its extension $\mathfrak{B}$ be defined as previously. Let us extend the language of ordinary algorithmic logic by the following three nondeterministic constructs:

(1) for a vector of variables x, [?x] means the nondeterministic assignment to x of values drawn from the appropriate basic types of $\mathfrak{B}$;

(2) for a sequence of statements $P_1,P_2,\ldots,P_s$, <u>choice</u>[$P_1,P_2,\ldots,P_s$] means the nondeterministic choice of one of the instructions $P_1,P_2,\ldots,P_s$ and the execution of it;

(3) for a formula α, $\Box\alpha$ has value 1 if α yields 1 for all possible nondeterministic assignments and choices in α, otherwise $\Box\alpha$ has value 0.

Let J=($\mathcal{M}$,I) be an implementation over $\mathfrak{A}$ of a data structure type $\mathcal{K}$ where $\mathcal{K}=\{K_0,K_1,\ldots,K_n\}$ is an abstract data structure type over $\mathfrak{B}$ and $\mathcal{M}=\{M_0,M_1,\ldots,M_n\}$ is a concrete data structure type over $\mathfrak{A}$. As previously, assume that x is a vector of common variables, y is a vector of abstract data structure variables and z is a vector of concrete data structure variables. Let q be a Boolean variable which appear neither in $\mathcal{K}$ nor in $\mathcal{M}$.

<u>Theorem 4.</u> J is partially correct iff the following formula is valid in $\mathfrak{B}$:

PC: $K_0x=M_0x \wedge K_0y=M_0Iy \wedge \Box(\neg P(\neg\alpha))$ where

P= <u>begin</u>

  [?x]; M_0; [?q];

  <u>while</u> q <u>do</u>

  <u>begin</u>

    [?x]; [?q];

    <u>choice</u>[$M_1, M_2, \ldots, M_n$]

  <u>end</u>; [?x]

<u>end</u> and

$$\alpha = \bigwedge_{1\leq i\leq n} (M_i\,true \Rightarrow (IK_ix=M_ix \wedge IK_iy=M_iIy)) .$$

J is totally correct iff the following formula is valid in $\mathfrak{B}$

TC: $K_0x=M_0x \wedge K_0y=M_0Iy \wedge \Box(\neg P(\neg\beta))$ where P is defined above and

$$\beta : \bigwedge_{1\leq i\leq n} (IK_i\,true \Rightarrow (IK_ix=M_ix \wedge IK_iy=M_iIy)) .$$

<u>Proof.</u> First observe that (Qtrue $\Rightarrow$ Qα) is equivalent to $\neg$ ($\neg\alpha$) fo[r] any deterministic program Q. The next observations concern equivalent formulations of the statements defining the notions of partial and tot[al] correctness of implementations. It follows that:

(1) J is partially correct iff the formula $K_0x=M_0x \wedge K_0y=M_0Iy$ is valid in $\mathfrak{B}$ and for any $\mathcal{M}$-program $\mu = \mu_0, \mu_1, \ldots, \mu_m$, for any terminating computation of it which results in $z=\bar{z}$, for each i, $1\leq i\leq n$, for any values $x=\bar{x}$ such that M_i terminates for $x=\bar{x}$ and $z=\bar{z}$, the formula $IK_ix=M_ix \wedge IK_iy=M_iIy$ is satisfied by $x=\bar{x}$ and $z=\bar{z}$.

(2) J is totally correct iff the formula $K_0x=M_0x \wedge K_0y=M_0Iy$ is valid in $\mathfrak{B}$ and for any $\mathcal{M}$-program $\mu=\mu_0, \mu_1, \ldots, \mu_m$, for any terminating computation of it which results in $z=\bar{z}$, for each i, $1\leq i\leq n$, for any values $x=\bar{x}$ such that K_i terminates for $x=\bar{x}$ and $y=I_{\mathfrak{B}}(z=\bar{z})(y)$, the formula $IK_ix=M_ix \wedge IK_iy=M_iIy$ is satisfied by $x=\bar{x}$ and $z=\bar{z}$.

(1) and (2) imply that PC and TC express the desired properties. $\Box$

REFERENCES

[1] AHO A.V.,HOPCROFT J.E.,ULLMAN J.D., <u>The design and analysis of computer algorithms</u>, Addison-Wesley, Reading, Mass. 1974

[2] SALWICKI A., <u>An introduction to algorithmic logic</u>, Banach Center Publications, vol.2, PWN, Warsaw, 1977

[3] BANACHOWSKI L., <u>On implementations of abstract data types</u>, 26. Mathematical Logic in Computer Science, Salgotarjan 1978, Coll. Math.Soc.Janos Bolyai, 1981, 143-166

[4] HOARE C.A.R., <u>Proof of correctness of data representation</u>, Acta Inf. 1(1972), 271-281

1. Introduction

The prefixing of classes is one of the most attractive and powerful mechanisms incorporated into the programming language Simula 67 (cf [4]). This tool allows a programmer to design a program in a structural, abstract way. To present briefly the main ideas of prefixing we start with the notion of a class.

Let us consider the following scheme of class declaration:

```
class A;
   attributes a1,...,an;
   I1;...;Ip; inner; Ip+1;...;Ir
end A;
```

where $a_1,\dots,a_n$ are attributes (variables or, perhaps, other syntactic units like classes, procedures, functions etc.) and $I_1,\dots,I_p$, $I_{p+1},\dots,I_r$ are instructions of the class A. With the help of an object generator ("new A") one can create an object of the class A, i.e. create a frame (activation record) in the memory for attributes $a_1,\dots,a_n$ and execute the instruction list $I_1,\dots,I_p,I_{p+1},\dots,I_r$. When control returns to the object where the expression "new A" has been executed, the frame is not deallocated and a reference to that frame is transmitted as the value of the expression "new A". Hence, a reference to the object may be retained in a reference variable (e.g.X:-new A, where X is a reference variable qualified by the class A).

The attributes of objects are accessible from outside as well as from inside the object. Remote accessing (e.g.X.a_i) allows one to use the attributes $a_1,\dots,a_n$ from outside. Internal access occurs while executing the instructions of the object of A and any unit nested within it or during calls of the class's procedure attributes.

Consider now declaration scheme of a class B:

```
A class B;
     attributes b1,...,bm;
     J1;...;Js; inner; Js+1;...;Jt
end B;
```

SEMANTICS AND IMPLEMENTATION OF PREFIXING AT MANY LEVELS+

W.M. Bartol
A. Kreczmar
A.I. Litwiniuk
H. Oktaba

Institute of Informatics
University of Warsaw
00-901 Warsaw, P.K.i N. Poland

Abstract

A generalization of Simula's prefixing of classes is presented. The notion of one-level prefixing is first introduced by means of the example of Simula 67; the semantics of a programming language with prefixing at many levels is then discussed and analyzed. The principles for efficiently implementing programming languages with prefixing of classes at many levels are described. A generalized display mechanism is introduced and the correctness of a display update algorithm is proved. A new data structure for efficient identification of dynamic objects is also presented.

Keywords: block structured programming languages, classes, prefixing, methods of implementation, Simula 67.

+This research was supported in part by "Zjednoczenie MERA" of Poland.

Class B is prefixed by A, i.e. B has attributes $a_1,\dots,a_n,b_1,\dots,b_m$ and the instruction list $I_1,\dots,I_p,J_1,\dots,J_s,J_{s+1},\dots,J_t,I_{p+1},\dots,I_r$ and B is called a subclass of A. One can create an object of class B in a similar way as was done for A, i.e. by Y:-<u>new</u> B. Here Y may be a reference variable qualified by class B as well as by class A (for the general rules of this kind of assignment statement see [4]) .

The following class C is a subclass of the classes B and A:

```
B class C;
    attributes c1,...,ck;
    K1;...;Ku; inner; Ku+1;...;Kv
end C;
```

and it has the attributes $a_1,\dots,a_n,b_1,\dots,b_m,c_1,\dots,c_k$ and the instruction list $I_1,\dots,I_p,J_1,\dots,J_s,K_1,\dots,K_u,K_{u+1},\dots,K_v,J_{s+1},\dots,J_t,I_{p+1},\dots,I_r$. The sequence of classes A,B,C is called the prefix sequence of the class C. Class C may in turn be used as a prefix of some other class, and so forth, but no class can occur in its own prefix sequence. Hence prefixing has a tree structure.

Blocks may also be prefixed. For instance, a block:

```
A begin
    attributes c1,...,ck;
    K1;...;Ku
  end
```

is prefixed by the class A, i.e. it has the attributes $a_1,\dots,a_n,c_1,\dots,c_k$ and the instruction list $I_1,\dots,I_p,K_1,\dots,K_u,I_{p+1},\dots,I_r$.

In Simula 67, perhaps because of the method chosen for the original implementation, there is an important restriction on prefixing; namely, a class may be used as a prefix only at the block level at which it has been declared. Before we explain the reasons for this restriction and possible ways of abolishing it, let us look at some examples which illustrate the difficulties arising from this restriction.

Suppose we have a declaration of a class PQ which provides the data structure of a priority queue of integers with maximal capacity defined by an input parametr n:

```
class PQ(n); integer n;
begin
```

```
   integer procedure deletemin;
   ...
   end deletemin;
   procedure insert(x); integer x;
   ...
   end insert;
   ...
end PQ;
```

In the following program:

```
begin
   class PQ(n); integer n;
   ...
   end PQ;
   ...
   begin integer n;
   read(n);
   PQ(n) begin
         ...
         end
   end
end
```

the declaration of PQ is not at the same level as the prefixed block, hence this construction is incorrect in Simula 67.

If the class PQ were translated separately and treated as being declared in the block at level 0, it would never be possible to use this data structure as a prefix in other block except the outermost one.

In Simula 67 this problem has been partially solved, because system classes like SIMSET and SIMULATION may be used at any level. But the user is not able to extend the library of system classes, which still forces him to rewrite the declarations at relevant block levels.

This situation becomes even more cumbersome if we want to make use of two data structures simultaneously and both of them are subclasses of one class. Consider for instance, the data structures A and B using lists as an auxiliary data system. Hence they ought to be subclasses of a class LIST. We have the following declarations:

```
class LIST;
...
```

```
end LIST;
LIST class A;
     ...
     end A;
LIST class B;
     ...
     end B;
```

and now we would like to open two prefixed blocks:

```
A begin
  ...
  B begin
    ...
    end
  end
```

Because of the restriction one must redeclare classes B and LIST at the level where B is used as prefix. Thus, redundancy is unavoidable.

Observe that with the possibility of separate translation and allowing prefixing at many levels we can develop software in a structural way. Any system or user class may be easily extended by the user and attached to the catalog of system classes without the necessity of recompiling already compiled units and without the redundancy of the program text. Moreover, as we showed before, the user is able to make use of arbitrary data structures simultaneously by means of a prefixing mechanism instead of remote accessing (what speeds-up run-time of a program and clarifies its source code).

To conclude, we emphasize that prefixing at many levels is not merely a sophisticated technical problem in programming languages, but an essential step forward in developing an effective software methodology.

The structure of the paper is the following. In section 2 we give an informal insight, illustrated by examples, into some important semantic questions concerning many-level prefixing. Section 3 contains definitions and facts concerning the block structured programming languages, which are well known but necessary. Section 4 contains the formal definition of access to attributes in one-level prefixing (Simula 67). In section 5 we prove that the proposed semantics of the rules for many-level prefixing is correct. Section 6 gives a description of addressing algorithms for many-level prefixing. In particular, a generalized display mechanism is introduced, a mechanism which realizes an efficient access to attributes. In section 7 we discuss the various strategies of storage management and their impact on the semantics of the proposed construct.

2. Many-level prefixing (informal presentation)

The prefixing in Simula-67 is subject to an important restriction: a class may be used as a prefix only at the syntactic level of its declaration. Hereafter we shall call this prefixing "at one level".

In this paper we consider a Simula-like language, in which there is no such restriction and "many-level" prefixing is possible i.e. a class may be used as a prefix whenever its declaration is visible. To speak about such a language we must be able first to determine its semantics. One might think that prefixing "at many levels" is a trivial generalization of prefixing "at one level", but this is not the case.

The semantics of such a language is not obvious: in particular the rules defining access to object attributes cannot be deduced from the analogous Simula rules.

Consider the following program scheme (we follow Simula syntax):

```
L1: begin
    class A; begin real x;
              .
              .
              .
              end A;
    L2: A begin real y;
        class B; begin
                 .
                 .
                 x:=y;
                 .
                 .
                 end B;
        .
        .
        .
        new B;
```

```
        .
        .
        L3: A begin real y;
            B class C; begin
                       .
                       .
                       .
                       y:=x;
                       .
                       .
                       .
                       end C;
            .
            .
            .
            new C;
            .
            .
            .
            end
      end
end;
```

This program has the following block structure: the class A is declared in the outermost block of the program. It prefixes two blocks (one contained in the other) labelled L2 and L3, respectively. Note that the use of the same prefix for two blocks - one nested in the other - is not allowed in Simula-67.

The first prefixed block contains the declaration of a class B, while the second contains the declaration of a class C prefixed by B.

Let us consider the structure of objects created during the execution of the program. Every object of a prefixed class or block contains all attributes belonging to classes from their prefix sequences. In the above program the first object is created upon entry to the block labelled L1. Denote this object by p1. The second, denoted by p2, is created upon entry to the block labelled L2. This object contains two local real variables: x and y. The execution of the statement new B yields a third object (denoted by p3) corresponding to the class B. As indicated in the program scheme, variables x and y occur in the statements of B. Both variables denote attributes of the object p2.

Upon entry to the block L3 a new object p4 containing two variables x and y is created. The execution of the statement <u>new</u> C yields a new object p5 (see Fig.1) of the class C.

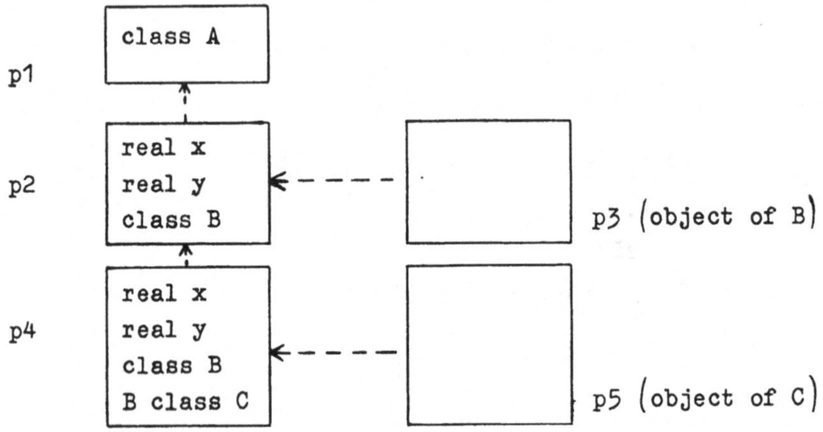

Fig.1.

According to the definition of prefixing the instruction list of C contains the instruction list of B. Therefore we must determine for each occurrence of the variables x and y in the instruction list of C the object from which the appropriate attribute is taken.

Consider first the statement y:=x in the body of C of the object p5. Note that none of the occurrences of the variables x,y is local in C. The object p5 belongs to class C and the nearest block containing the attributes x,y and the declaration of C is the block L3. Hence, both variables denote attributes of the object p4, which represents the block L3.

There are, however, different ways of defining the semantics of the statement x:=y from the class B of the object p5. The semantics of the statement can be based on a purely textual concatenation of the bodies of classes, as in Simula-67. We treat the declaration of class C as if it vere concatenated with class B and declared in the block L3. Therefore both variables denote attributes of the object p4.

The semantics of the statement can be also defined in the following way: the syntactic unit to which the variable x is related is the class A, since A is the class in which x is declared; the syntactic unit to which the variable y is related is block L2. During the execution of statements in the object p5 the sequence of objects statically enclosing p5 is the following: p4,p3,p2,p1. In this sequence p4 is the first object having attributes of the class A. Hence the variable x denotes an attribute of p4. The first object representing block L2 is the object p2, therefore the variable y denotes an attribute of p2.

From the above example it follows that there are some alternative ways of defining the semantics of assignment statement x:=y executed in p5.

In this paper we chose the one described above as the second, and we present its precise and formal definition in Section 5.

Why is this way of defining the semantics preferable?
There are several reasons for this choice. The most important is that we are able to define it in a precise and formal way and we are able to implement it efficiently (cf Section 6).
In the semantics based on a purely textual concatenation we see no way of addressing attributes which would depend only on the place of variable declaration. In particular we are not able to assign a relative displacement (offset) to an identifier occurring in a class statement. Note that an identifier may relate to attributes with different relative displacements depending on the place where a class is used. Compare with the example: in the statement x:=y of B the variable y relates to an attribute of p2 or p4 and these attributes may have different relative displacements. To illustrate the chosen semantics let us consider the program scheme structurally analogous to the example of Section 1.

```
begin
   class LIST;
     begin
     ref (...)head;
     procedure into(...);... head:=...; end;
     .
     .
     .
     end LIST;
    LIST class QUEUE;
     begin
     procedure intoqueue; ... into(...) ...; ... end;
     .
     .
     .
     end QUEUE;
```

```
   LIST class DECK;
     begin
     procedure intodeck; ... into(...) ...; ... end;
     .
     .
     .
     end DECK;
L1:  QUEUE begin
     L2: DECK begin
              .
              .
              .
              S1: intoqueue;
              S2: intodeck;
              end;
           end;
end
```

The above program contains declarations of classes: LIST, QUEUE, DECK. The class LIST describes the general structure of lists and contains the declaration of the variable "head" and the procedure "into", where that variable is used.

The classes QUEUE and DECK use the structure of LIST to describe the structures of queues and decks. In particular, they call the procedure "into" declared in LIST, and they use the variable "head" as its local attribute.

If we want to use both classes: QUEUE and DECK in a program, we may need two blocks prefixed by QUEUE and DECK, respectively. Moreover we wish the procedure "into" called in the body of "intoqueue" to be taken from the object representing the block prefixed by QUEUE; similarly, this procedure when called in the body of "intodeck" is to be taken from the object representing the block prefixed by DECK. Otherwise they should use the same attribute "head", which might destroy completely the proper execution of the program.

Denote the object created upon entry to the outermost block by p1. Objects created upon entries to blocks L1 and L2 will be denoted by p2 and p3, respectively.

The call of the procedure "intoqueue" (statement S1) yields a new object denoted by p4. The procedure "intoqueue" is an attribute of p2, so that the sequence of objects which statically enclose p4 is as follows: p4, p2, p1. The procedure "intoqueue" calls in turn the procedure "into", which is declared in the class LIST: The first object in the sequence p4, p2, p1 which contains attributes of LIST is p2, thus in our semantics "into" is an attribute of p2 and "head" will be taken from p2. Analogous reasoning shows that the procedure "into" when called in the body of "intodeck" is an attribute of p3.

Thus the discussion shows that such informally presented semantics suits our purposes. In the subsequent sections the precise definition of this semantics and its implementation will be given.

3. Syntactic environment in programming languages without prefixing Static containers

Consider first the case of a programming language with block structure and without prefixing. By a syntactic unit in such a language we shall mean a block or a procedure. Arbitrary syntactic units will be denoted by U, V, W with indices or dashes, if necessary.

From the point of view of its block structure, any program may be treated as a tree T. The root of this tree R(T) is the outermost block and for $U,V \in T$, U is the father of V iff V is declared in U (in definition blocks are treated as declarations in units where they appear). For the sake of simplicity of notation we shall write V decl U when V is declared in U (or alternatively, when U is the father of V in T).

Let decl^+ denote the transitive closure of the relation decl and let decl^* denote the transitive and reflexive closure of decl. So we have, in particular, U decl^* U and U decl^* R(T) for any U.

The level of a node in a tree T is introduced as usual, i.e. $\text{level}(R(T))=1$ and $\text{level}(U) = \text{level}(V)+1$ if V decl U.

Any variable and any syntactic unit except a block has a name, called an identifier, introduced at the moment of its declaration. The identifier is then used to represent the variable or the unit in a program. The question of distinction between identifiers and syntactic entities (variables and syntactic units) is essential, because the same identifier may be introduced by different declarations in the program text.

Let id denote an arbitrary identifier. We consider now an occurrence of an identifier id in a statement of a program. Since a declaration associates an identifier with a syntactic entity, for the occurrence of id one must determine a unit U such that a syntactic entity named id is declared in U. For the semantics of a program to be unambiguous, the correspondence between occurrences of identifiers and syntactic entities should be unique, i.e. only one syntactic entity may be associated with the given occurrence of an identifier id. Let us assume that id occurs in a unit V, i.e. V is the innermost unit containing the considered occurrence of id. In the following definition we make precise what is meant by scope of declarations or visibility rules.

Definition 3.1.

By a static container of the occurrence of an identifier id in a unit V, denoted by SC(id,V), we mean a syntactic unit U such that

(a) id is declared in U,

(b) V $decl^*$ U,

(c) there is no unit U' such that V $decl^*$ U' and U' $decl^+$ U and id is declared in U' (i.e. U is the innermost unit enclosing V such that id is declared in U).

If SC(id,V) does not exist, i.e. if there is no U such that (a) and (b) hold then of course the program is incorrect. Otherwise we say that the occurrence of id is local in V if V=SC(id,V), and non--local in V if V≠SC(id,V).

Dynamic containers

During a program's execution we can deal at the same time with many objects of the same syntactic unit, hence a computation of any instruction in an object requires identification and access to all the syntactic entities that it uses. In Algol-60 instances of blocks and procedures may be treated as the examples of objects, (in Simula-67 this is augmented with the objects of classes). The collection of objects of a syntactic unit U will be denoted by $|U|$. The objects themselves will be denoted by small latin letters p,q,r with indices, if necessary.

Consider an object $p \in |U|$. If the occurrence of an identifier id is local in a unit U, then the syntactic entity identified by id is situated within the object p. Hence there is no problem either with identification or with access to this syntactic entity. In general, however, for any id such that SC(id,U) exists, we must determine a unique object q such that $q \in |SC(id,U)|$. Then during the execution of the instruction list of U in the object p, the syntactic entity identified by id will be taken from q. Such an object q will be called a dynamic container of id with respect to p, and will be denoted by DC(id,p). Dynamic containers are unequivocally determined by means of static links.

Upon a unit U is entered an object of this unit is allocated and initialized. It contains some system pointers in addition to declared attributes, for example the dynamic link (DL) which points to the calling object and the static link (SL) pointing to the object which is its syntactic father. We shall write p.SL=q when SL link of the object p points to the object q. (If p.SL is not defined, then we shall write p.SL=none.)

An object q is called the syntactic father of an object p, since q must be the object of a unit V where U is declared, i.e. if p.SL=q, $p \in |U|$, $q \in |V|$, then U decl V.

A sequence $p_k,\ldots,p_1$ of objects is called the SL chain of the object p_k, if p_1. SL=none and p_i. SL=p_{i-1} for i=k,...,2. The SL chain of an object p will be denoted by SL(p).

The SL chains define completely and uniquely syntactic environment of objects. This follows from the well-known results quoted below:

Lemma 3.1.

(a) If $SL(p_k') = p_k,\ldots,p_1$ and $p_i \in |U_i|$ for i=k,...,1, then the sequence $U_k,\ldots,U_1$ is a path from U_k to R(T) in the tree T,

(b) Let $SL(p_k) = p_k,\ldots,p_1$ and $p_k \in |V|$. If SC(id,V) exists, then there is a unique i, $1 \leqslant i \leqslant k$, such that $p_i \in |SC(id,V)|$. □

Lemma 3.1 (b) shows that the SL chain of an object defines completely and uniquely its syntactic environment. All syntactic entities which can be used in V are uniquely situated in $SL(p_k)$. Consequently the dynamic container $DC(id,p_k)$ of the occurrence of id with respect to the object p_k is defined as a unique object p_i belonging to $SL(p_k)$ such that $p_i \in |SC(id,V)|$.

The way SL links are defined during a program's execution induces the semantics of identifiers. The following algorithm determines exactly what should be done with SL links in order to obtain the most natural semantics (cf [7]).

Algorithm 3.1.

We can assume the only one object of the outermost block R(T) may be entered and, of course, for that object SL= none. Consider now the call of a unit U in an object $r_k \in |V|$. If id identifies U, then according to the definition 3.1 U is declared in SC(id,V). The syntactic father of $p \in |U|$ must be the object of the unit SC(id,V), i.e. the unit where U is declared. Let $SL(r_k) = r_k,\ldots,r_1$. By Lemma 3.1 (b) there is a unique i, $1 \leq i \leq k$, such that $r_i \in |SC(id,V)|$. Then define $p.SL=r_i$, i.e. r_i becomes the syntactic father of p. (cf Fig.2).

□

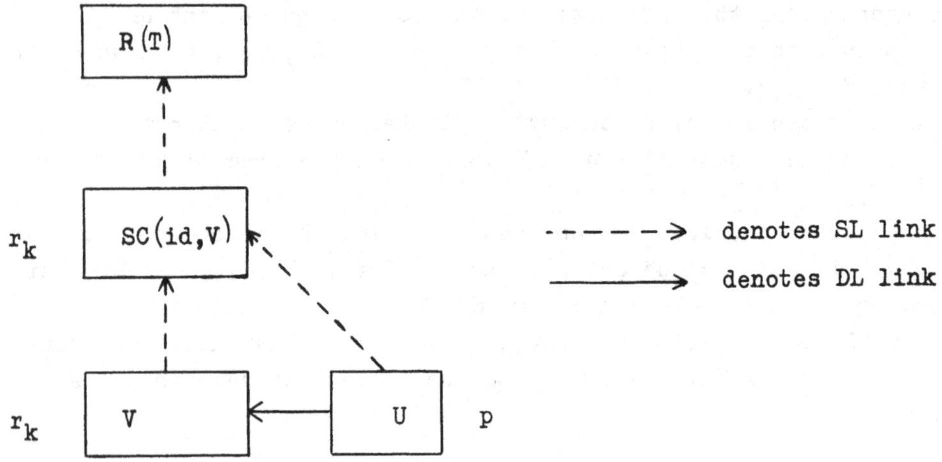

Fig.2.

4. Prefixing at one level

Prefix structure of a program

In this section we shall consider a programming language with block structure and one-level prefixing,i.e. exactly the case of Simula 67.

From the point of view of its prefix structure, any program may be treated as a forest of prefix trees $\{P_i\}$. Each prefix structure of a program is a tree P_i where for $U,V \in P_i$, U is the father of V iff U is the prefix of V and the root of P_i is a unique element of P_i without any prefix. Similarly to the relation decl we introduce the relation pref,i.e. U pref V iff U is the prefix of V.

By a prefix sequence of a unit U (denoted by prefseq(U)) we mean a sequence $V_1,\ldots,V_k$ of units such that $V_k = U$, V_1 has no prefix and V_i pref V_{i+1} for $i = 1,\ldots,k-1$. The example of the block and the prefix structures of a program are illustrated in Figure 3.

```
A: begin ref D Z;
   class B; begin ref(C)X1,X2;
     class C; begin
       class I; begin
                 ...
                 end I;
             end C;
          end B;
   B class D; begin
     C class E; begin ref(I)Y1;
                 ...
                 Y1:- new I;
                 ...
                 end E;
     C class F; begin ref(I)Y2;
                 ...
                 Y2:- new I;
                 ...
                 end F;
               ...
               X1:- new E;  X2:- new F;
               ...
               end D;
  Z:- new D;
  end A;
```

scheme of a block structure

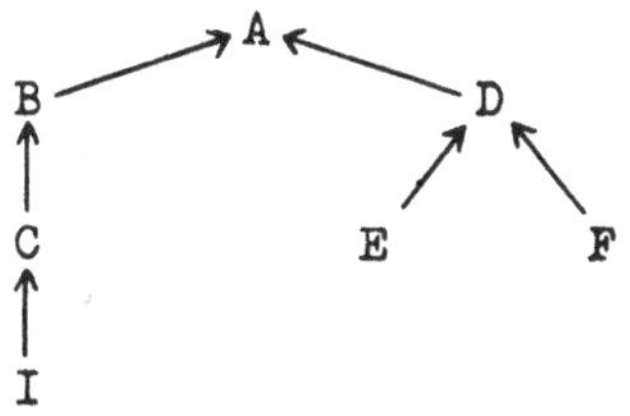

tree T

Tree P_1 Tree P_2 Tree P_3 Tree P_4

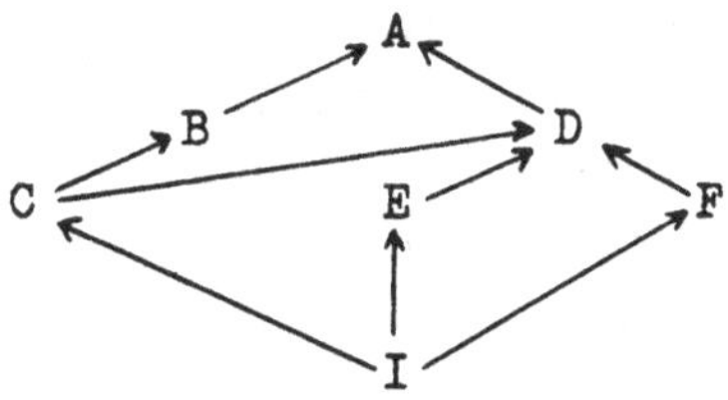

Graph G

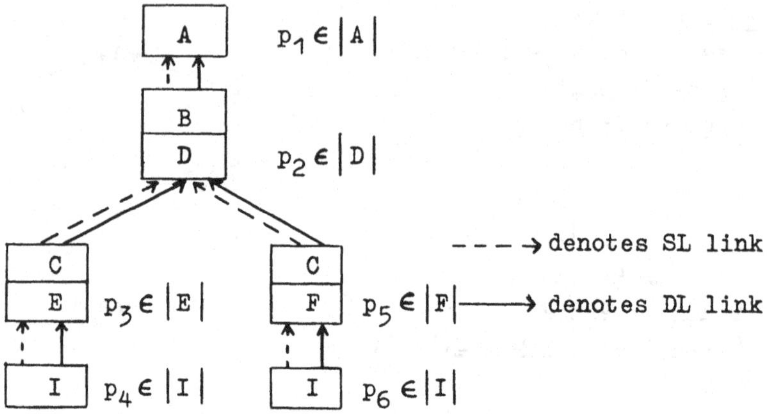

Graphs of SL' and DL's

Fig. 3.

Let $pref^+$ denote the transitive closure of pref and let $pref^*$ denote the transitive and reflexive closure of pref. Then, in particular, U $pref^*$ U for any U, U $pref^*$ V for any U $\in$ prefseq(V) etc.

Note now that if U $pref^*$ V, then an attribute of U is an attribute of V as well. In particular, a syntactic unit W may be an attribute of U and, hence, it will be an attribute of V. Let us denote this extension of the relation decl by attr,i.e. W attr V iff there is a unit U such that W decl U and U $pref^*$ V. While the relation decl always defines a tree, the relation attr need not define a tree. Denote by G the graph determined by the relation attr. Since the relation attr is the extension of decl, the tree T is a subgraph of the graph G.

In Figure 3 the syntactic unit C is the attribute of the syntactic unit D, because C decl B and B pref D. Thus C being the attribute of D may be used as a prefix of the syntactic units E and F. Finally, I decl C and C pref E implies I attr E, similarly I decl C and C pref F implies I attr F.

One-level prefixing is characterized by the following restriction:
(4.1) If U pref V, then level(U) = level(V).
(In words, U may prefix V only if both have the same level in the tree T.) This restriction has many interesting consequences which make the implementation problem almost trivial. First, as an immediate consequence of (4.1) we obtain the following lemma.

Lemma 4.1.

(a) If U attr V, then level(U) = level(V) + 1,

(b) G is a directed acyclic graph with one sink R(T),

(c) Every path in G from U to R(T) has length level(U). □

The definition of a static container for the occurrence of an identifier in a unit is generalized in the following way:

Definition 4.1.

By a static container of the occurrence of an identifier id in a unit V denoted SC(id,V) we mean a syntactic unit U such that id is declared in U and there is a syntactic unit W such that

(a) U $pref^*$ W,

(b) V $decl^*$ W,

(c) there is no unit W' such that V $decl^*$ W' and W' $decl^+$ W and id is the attribute of W',

(d) there is no unit W' such that U $pref^+$ W' and W' $pref^*$ W and id is declared in W'.

In block structured languages without prefixing we search for the innermost unit W such that id is declared in W and W contains a unit V with the occurrence of id. However, according to the definition of prefixing, the attributes of a prefixing unit are contained in the set of attributes of prefixed unit. This implies that the relation pref is stronger than the relation decl in the following sense: in the process of searching for a static container, we search for it first in the prefix sequence and then in the lower levels of the block structure of a program. Conditions (a)-(c) of definition 4.1 require that we search for the innermost unit W such that id is the attribute of W (U is a unit where the searched syntactic entily is declared). Condition (d) says that U is the nearest prefix of W satisfying the conditions (a)-(c).

We now present an algorithm determining the static container SC(id,V).

Algorithm 4.1.

Start from V. If there is no declaration of id, look for it in pref-seq(V) reading from right to left. If id is not an attribute of V, then take V' such that V decl V' and repeat the above process for V'. If id is not an attribute of V', then take V'' such that V' decl V'' and so on. When the algorithm terminates on the outermost block without finding the required declaration, the static container SC(id,V) does not exist and a program is incorrect. □

Look at Figure 3. We have SC(I,E) = C = SC(I,F), SC(Y1,E) = E, SC(Y2,F) = F, SC(X1,D) = SC(X2,D) = B and SC(D,A) = SC(Z,A) = A.

According to the definition of prefixing, the attributes coming from a prefix sequence are the attributes of a prefixed unit, hence, all of them are local in that unit. Thus we say that the occurrence of an identifier id is local in U if SC(id,U) $pref^*$ U, otherwise the occurrence of id is non-local in U.

In the example on Figure 3 all occurrences of identifiers are local.

<u>Dynamic containers</u>

Let prefseq(U_k) = $U_1,\ldots,U_k$ and let us consider an object $p \in |U_k|$. This object consists of layers corresponding to the syntactic units $U_1,\ldots,U_k$. (In Figure 3 p_1 has a layer A, p_2 has layers B,D, p_3 has layers C,E, p_5 has layers C,F, and p_4,p_6 have a layer I.)

Now consider the execution of the instruction lists of units $U_1,\ldots,U_k$. If an identifier id occurs in a unit $U_i, 1 \leq i \leq k$, then for any object $p \in |U_k|$ we must determine a unique object q such that $q \in |V|$ and SC(id,U_i) $pref^*$V. It means that the object q has a layer which corresponds to the static container for the occurrence of id in a unit U_i. The object q will be called a dynamic container of the occurrence of id in a unit U_i with respect to the object p, and will be denoted by DC(id,U_i,p). Dynamic containers will be uniquely determined by means of static links, as before. However, the definition of a syntactic father is more general. In fact, if p.SL = q, $p \in |U|$, $q \in |V|$, then U need not be declared in V.

Look at Figure 3. The object p_2 is created by the instruction Z:-<u>new</u> D, its syntactic father is, of course, the object p_1. In this case D decl A. The object p_3 is created by the instruction X1:- <u>new</u> E and its syntactic father is p_2. In this case E decl D. The object p_4 is created by the instruction Y1:- <u>new</u> I and its syntactic father is evidently p_3. In this case I is not declared in E but in C. Hence the simple rule of Algol 60 does not work. The syntactic father of p_4 is the object p_3 such that I is the attribute of E (not necessarily declared in E). Similarly, the syntactic father of p_5 is p_2, and F decl D, finally the syntactic father of p_6 is p_5, and I attr F.

The example shows the necessity for a more general definition of syntactic father of an object: if $p \in |U|$ and p.SL = q, then q should be an object of a unit V such that U attr V (previously U decl V). The definition of SL chain remains the same as in Section 3. Before we present an algorithm of setting SL links, we prove a lemma analogous to Lemma 3.1 which is of basic importance for the whole construction.

Lemma 4.2.

(a) If $SL(p_k) = p_k,\dots,p_1$ and $p_i \in |U_i|$ for $i=k,\dots,1$, then the sequence $U_k,\dots,U_1$ is a path from U_k to $R(T)$ in the graph G,

(b) Let $SL(p_k) = p_k,\dots,p_1$ and $p_i \in |U_i|$ for $i=k,\dots,1$. If SC(id,V) exists and V pref* U_k, then there is a unique i, $1 \leq i \leq k$, such that SC(id,V)pref* U_i.

Proof

By the definition of the syntactic fathera, if $p_{i+1} \in |U_{i+1}|$ and $p_i \in |U_i|$, then U_{i+1} attr U_i, for $i = k-1,\dots,1$. Hence $U_k,\dots,U_1$ is a path from U_k to R(T) in the graph G. Thus (a) is proved.

Now by Lemma 4.1 level(U_i)=i for $i=k,\dots,1$. Assume that there are two such integers, i, j, $1 \leq i < j \leq k$, that SC(id,V)pref* U_i and SC(id,V)pref* U_j. By the restriction 4.1 level(SC(id,V)) = level(U_i) and level(SC(id,V)) = level(U_j). Hence level(SC(id,V)) = i = j, which is impossible.

The proof that such an i exists is given in Section 5 (Lemma 5.3), where the more general case is considered; namely the case of prefixing at many levels. For this reason we do not repeat this proof in a much simpler case and leave it to the next section.

□

Now we are able to present an algorithm which is an immediate generalization of the algorithm 3.1.

Algorithm 4.2.

We assume the only one object of the outermost block R(T) may be entered, and for that object SL = <u>none</u>.

Consider now an object $p \in |U|$ created in an object $r_m \in |V_k|$. Let prefseq$(V_k) = V_1,\dots,V_k$, and let the instruction which creates p occur in a unit V_i, $1 \leq i \leq k$. If id identifies U, then according to the definition 4.1 U is declared in SC(id,V_i). The syntactic father of p should be an object containing SC(id,V_i) as a layer.

Let $SL(r_m) = r_m,\dots,r_1$. By Lemma 4.2(b) there is a unique j, $1 \leq j \leq m$, such that SC(id,V_i) is the layer of r_j. Then define p.SL = r_j.

□

Figure 4 shows this general situation. When the statement of a unit V_i with the occurrence of id is being executed, in the SL chain of r_m there is a unique object r_j which may be the syntactic father of p.

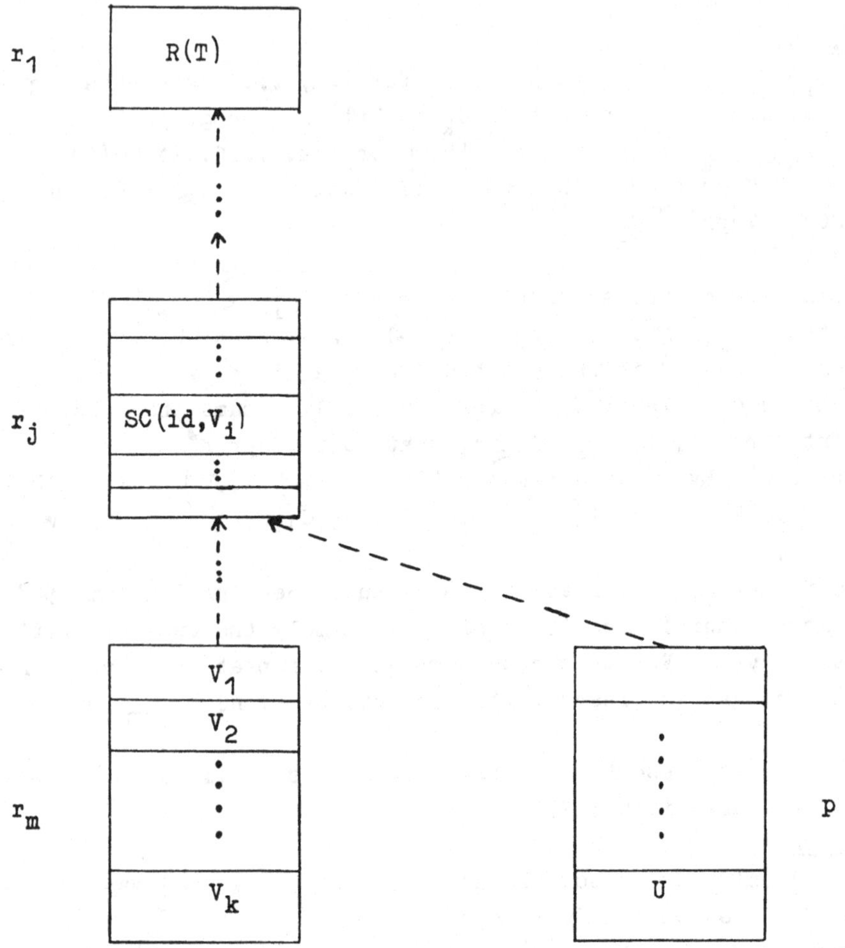

Figure 4

5. Syntactic environment in a programming language with prefixing at many levels.

Existence of a syntactic environment

In this section we shall analyze the situation when Simula's restriction (4.1) is left out. A programming language with block structure and prefixing at many levels, i.e. when (4.1) is not binding, possesses some amazing properties. First we are not able to prove a lemma analogous to Lemma 4.2, where the existence and the uniquness of the syntactic environment for prefixing at one-level is proved. In particular, the analogon of Lemma 4.2(b) does not hold. However, we can show that for a static container SC(id,V) and V $pref^*$ U_k there is at least one i, $1 \leq i \leq k$ such that SC(id,V)$pref^*$ U_i, where SL(p_k)=$p_k,\dots,p_1$, U_i . Lemma 4.2(b) shows the uniquness of such an i, and thus there is no problem with definition of Simula's semantics. Here the situation is not so clear.

The proof of the existence of such an i, $1 \leq i \leq k$, is given in the following three lemmas. Lemma 5.1 is auxiliary and justifies the implication which is used later in the proof of Lemma 5.2. Lemma 5.2 is crucial for the whole proof. It shows that graph G satisfies the desired property. The proof of this lemma is carried out by double induction, with respect to the length of a path $U_k,\dots,U_1$ in G, and with respect to the length of the prefix sequence of U_k. At last Lemma 5.3 is a simple corollary of the Lemma 5.2.

<u>Lemma 5.1.</u>

Let the sequence $U_k,\dots,U_1$ be a path in the graph G from U_k to R(T).

<u>Assumption</u> If V $pref^*$ U_k and V decl W, then there exists j, $1 \leq j < k$, such that W $pref^*$ U_j.

<u>Conclusion</u> If V $pref^*$ U_k and V $decl^*$ W, then there exists t, $1 \leq t \leq k$, such that W $pref^*$ U_t.

<u>Proof</u>.

First note that the above implication has the following meaning. Assumption says that for any V from prefseq(U_k) and declared in W there is U_j on the path $U_{k-1},\dots,U_1$ such that W $pref^*U_j$ (cf Fig.5.). Conclusion generalizes this property. Namely, for any V from prefseq(U_k) and for any W such that V $decl^*$ W there is U_t on the path $U_k,\dots,U_1$ such that W $pref^*$ U_t, (cf Fig.5).

We shall prove the conclusion by induction on the length of path from V to W in the tree T. If V=W and V $pref^*$ U_k, then W $pref^*$ U_k. Hence t=k in this case.

Now consider units V and W such that V $decl^+$ W. Hence there exists a unit W' such that V decl W' and W' $decl^*$ W. If V $pref^*$ U_k and V decl W', then it follows from the assumption that there is $1 \leq j < k$ such that W' $pref^*$ U_j. Now W' $pref^*$ U_j and W' $decl^*$ W, where the length of the path from W' to W is less than the length of the path from V to W. Hence by inductive assumption there exists $1 \leq t \leq j$ such that W $pref^*$ U_t.

□

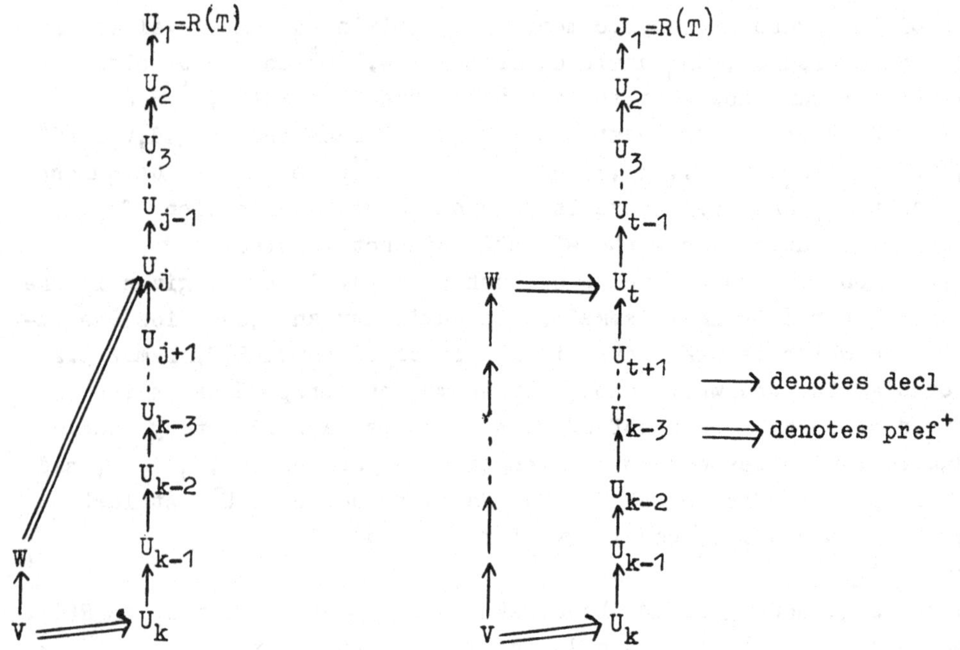

Figure 5

<u>Lemma 5.2.</u>

Let the sequence $U_k,\ldots,U_1$ be a path in the graph G from U_k to R(T). If V pref* U_k and V decl* W, then there exists i, $1 \leqslant i \leqslant k$ such that W pref* U_i.

<u>Proof.</u>

First note that the lemma is simply the conclusion of the previous one. However, it should be proved without the assumption. Since Lemma 5.1 has just been proved, it is sufficient to prove its assumption, i.e.

(5.1) if V decl W and V pref* U_k, then there is j, $1 \leqslant j < k$ such that W pref* U_j.

The proof is carried out by induction on the length of the sequence $U_k,\ldots,U_1$. For k=1, U_k=R(T). Thus V pref* R(T) iff V=R(T) and V decl W for no W.

Assume now that (5.1) holds for all sequences of length less than k, $k \geqslant 2$. For a sequence $U_k,\ldots,U_1$ let V pref* U_k and V decl W. We shall now use induction on the length of the prefix sequence of the unit U_k to prove that W pref* U_j for some $j < k$.

The beginning is simple since for $V=U_k$ we have U_k decl W and consequently W pref* U_{k-1} (by the definition of the relation attr). Assume that (5.1) holds for all prefix sequences of the length less than h. Let V pref* U_k and suppose that the length of the prefix sequence from V to U_k is $h \geq 2$. For some units V', W' we have V pref V' pref* U_k and V' decl W'. The length of the prefix sequence from V' to U_k is h-1. We infer from the inductive assumption that W' pref* U_j for some $j<k$. Now, since V pref V' and V' decl W', the syntactic container SC(id,W') exists, where id identifies V (V occurs in W').
By Definition 4.1 and because V decl W, there is a unit W'' such that W pref* W'' and W' decl* W''. The length of the sequence $U_j,\ldots,U_1$ is less than k and W' pref* U_j so, from the inductive assumption on k, we infer that for a unit $\overline{W}$ such that W' decl $\overline{W}$ there is $m<j$ and $\overline{W}$ pref* U_m.

By Lemma 5.1 if W' decl* $\overline{W}$ and W' pref* U_j there is $1 \leq m \leq j$ such that $\overline{W}$ pref* U_m. Since W' decl* W'' and W' pref* U_j, taking $\overline{W}$ as W'', we obtain W'' pref* U_m. Finally, W pref* W'' and W'' pref* U_m, hence W pref* U_m where $1 \leq m<k$. Thus we have proved (5.1) and the lemma. □

Lemma 5.3.

Let $SL(p_k)=p_k,\ldots,p_1$ and $p_i \in |U_i|$ for $i=1,\ldots,k$. If SC(id,V) exists and V pref* U_k, then there is i, $1 \leq i \leq k$ such that SC(id,V) pref* U_i.

Proof.

From the definition of the SL chain, $U_k,\ldots,U_1$ is a path in the graph G. Since SC(id,V) exists, there is a unit W such that V decl*W and SC(id,V) pref* W. We have V pref* U_k and V decl* W, and by Lemma 5.2 there is i, $1 \leq i \leq k$ such that W pref* U_i. But SC(id,V) pref* W and W pref* U_i implies SC(id,V) pref* U_i. □

Dynamic containers

During the execution of the instruction list of an object $p \in |U|$, we must be able to indicate the dynamic container DC(id,V,p) for any identifier id occurring in any unit V belonging to prefseq(U).
To achieve this goal we wish to use the SL chain of the object p, as in Simula 67. Unfortunately, in the case of many-level prefixing the SL shain does not uniquely define the syntactic environment of p, since the same unit may occur more than once as a layer in SL(p). (Lemma 5.3 quarantees a dynamic container belongs to SL chain but not exactly once).

This new complication is well illustrated on Figure 1. The SL chain of the object $p_5 \in |C|$ contains the layer A twice, in the object p_2 and p_4.

Hence it is necessary to introduce a uniform rule for determining dynamic containers. It seems that there are only two concurrent choices. We may take the nearest or the farthest from the given object on its SL chain. However, the second choice is impossible because it contradicts the standart understanding of locality. Consider an occurrence of id local in V and an object $p \in |U|$ containing a layer corresponding to a syntactic unit V. Assume the chain SL(p) contains another object q with a layer corresponding to V. Then, of course, a dynamic container DC(id,V,p) should be the object p, not the object q (for a concrete example see Section 2, where the program with two data structures QUEUE and DECK is considered).

From the above discussion we can infer a new definition of a dynamic container as well as an algorithm which computes SL links.

Definition 5.1.

Let $SL(r)=r_m,\dots,r_1$ be the SL chain of an object $r \in |V_k|$ and let $prefseq(V_k)=V_1,\dots,V_k$. Consider an occurrence of an identifier id in a unit V_i. We shall say that r_j is the dynamic container for the occurrence of id in a unit V_i with respect to the object r if r_j is the nearest object to r in SL(r) such that $SC(id,V_i)$ is a layer of r_j.

Algorithm 5.1.

The start is the same as usual. Consider an object $p \in |U|$ created in an object $r \in |V_k|$. Let $prefseq(V_k)=V_1,\dots,V_k$ and let the instruction which creates p occur in a unit V_i, $1 \leq i \leq k$. If id identifies U, then according to the definition 4.1., U is declared in $SC(id,V_i)$. Let $SL(r)=r_m,\dots,r_1$ be the SL chain of r. By lemma 5.3. there is j,$1 \leq j \leq m$, such that $SC(id,V_i)$ is the layer of r_j. Let j' be the largest j satisfying this condition i.e. $r_{j'}$ is the dynamic container of the occurrence of id in the unit V_i with respect to r. Then define $p.SL=r_{j'}$.

□

6. The addressing algorithm and its correctness.

In this section we shall describe an addressing algorithm for a language with many-level prefixing. The correctness of this algorithm will be proved.

Addressing in Algol and Simula

Let us start with some remarks on an addressing algorithm for the Algol-like language invented by E.Dijkstra ([6], [7]). Let id be a name of a variable v occurring in U and let SC(id,U)=V. Then the variable v is identified by a pair:

$$(\text{level}(V),\ \text{offset}(v))$$

where offset(v) is a relative displacement of v in a memory frame. Note that both quantities level(V) and offset(v) may be computed at compile time. The run-time address of v is evaluated by a simple formula:

$$\text{DISPLAY}[\text{level}(V)] + \text{offset}(v)$$

where DISPLAY is a running system array updated during run-time. When an object $p \in |U|$ is being executed, DISPLAY[i] for i=level(U),...,1 must point to the members of the SL chain of p.

When an object $p \in |U|$ is being generated, it is sufficient to set

```
DISPLAY[level(U)] :-p;
```

since for m<level(U), DISPLAY[m] must be well defined. But when p is reentered the next time (i.e. through DL or <u>goto</u> statement), the following DISPLAY update algorithm is used:

```
X:-p;
for k:-level(U) step -1 until 1 do
begin
  DISPLAY[k]:- X; X:-X.SL;
end
```

For a language with many-level prefixing we postulate that the addressing algorithm is efficient as in the case described above. However, from the discussion given below, it follows that the same method of attributes identification as in Algol-60 (and Simula-67) is not possible.

Let U be an arbitrary unit with prefix sequence $U_1,\dots,U_n$. It is easv to observe that the prefix sequence has the following property: for every i, $1 \leqslant i \leqslant n$, $\text{level}(U_i) \leqslant \text{level}(U_{i+1})$, where $\text{level}(U_i)$ is determined from the tree T. Due to this property it is not possible to assign one level to all attributes of a given object p since they may be declared in units of different syntactic levels. Hence the local attributes of the object p should be addressed relative to many elements of DISPLAY. (Note that in Simula 67 the equality $\text{level}(U_i)=$ $=\text{level}(U_{i+1})$ holds for all U_i belonbing to the prefix sequence of U. Thus, the addressing algorithm is exactly the same as in Algol 60). Consider the following example:

```
B1:begin
   class A;... end A;
   B2:begin
      A class B;... end B;
      ...
      new B;
      ...
      end;
  ...
  end
```

When the object r of class B (generated by new B) is executed, the SL chain of r is described at Fig.6.

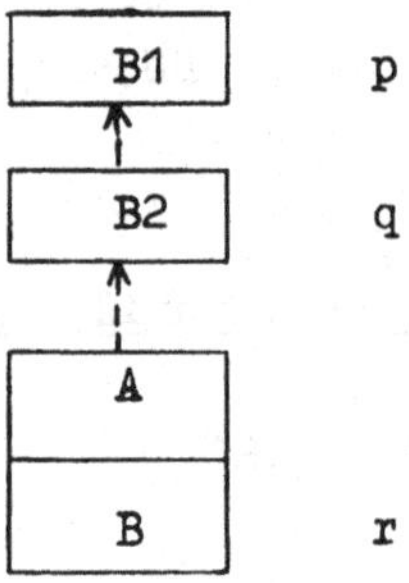

Fig.6.

The Algol-like rule, that DISPLAY[3]=r and DISPLAY[2]=q, is not valid because the attributes of the object r declared in the unit A ought to be addressed with respect to level(A)=2.

In order to avoid these difficulties the assignment of numbers to syntactic units is modified so that levels determined by the program tree T must not be used.

<u>Generalized DISPLAY</u>

To every unit U of a given program we assign a unique number, called a unit number nr(U), determined by any enumeration of tree T. To every id occurring in a unit U we assign a pair of numbers nr(SC(id,U)) and an offset, where the offset is evaluated taking into account all attributes of prefseq(SC(id,U)).

A prefix number sequence pns(U) of a unit U is a sequence

$nr(U_1),\ldots,nr(U_n)$, where $U_1,\ldots,U_n$=prefseq(U).

The vector DISPLAY is replaced by the vector GDISPLAY, the length of which is equal to the number of vertices of T.

Now we present an algorithm which computes relevant items of GDISPLAY every time an object $p \in |U|$ is entered. Let $SL(p)=p_m,\ldots,p_1$; then the GDISPLAY update algorithm has the form:

<u>Algorithm 6.1.</u>

<u>for</u> k:=1 <u>step</u> 1 <u>until</u> m <u>do</u>
update $GD(p_k)$;

The instruction update $GD(p_k)$ consists of the assignment:

$$\text{GDISPLAY}[n_1] :- \text{GDISPLAY}[n_2] :- \ldots :- \text{GDISPLAY}[n_{d_k}] :- p_k,$$

where $p_k \in |U_k|$ and the prefix number sequence of U_k is $pns(U_k)= =n_1,\ldots,n_{d_k}$. □

Observe that for every object $p \in |U|$ the cost of update GD(p) is constant, depending only on the unit U prefix sequence length. The correctness of the GDISPLAY update algorithm can be proved with the help of the following lemma.

<u>Lemma 6.1.</u>
Let $SL(p)=p_m,\ldots,p_1$, where $p_i \in |U_i|$ for i=m,...,1. If id is non-local in V, V pref* U_m and p_j is a dynamic container for id (p_j=DC(id,V,p)), then id is non-local in any U_k for k=j+1,...,m.

<u>Proof</u> follows immediately from the definition 5.1 of a dynamic container. □

<u>Theorem 6.1</u> (correctness of the GDISPLAY update algorithm)
Let $SL(p)=p_m,\ldots,p_1$, where $p_i \in |U_i|$ for i=m,...,1, and assume that the GDISPLAY update algorithm has been executed for an object p. If the occurrence of id is represented by a pair (n,offset) and id occurs in V such that V pref* U_m, then GDISPLAY[n] =p_j ($m \geq j \geq 1$), where p_j=DC(id,V,p).

<u>Proof:</u>

When id is local in U_m, then the dynamic container of id is equal to p and n belongs to $pns(U_m)$. It follows from the algorithm that GDISPLAY [n] =p_m=p.

When id is non-local in V, V pref* U_m and p_j=DC(id,V,p), then by Lemma 6.1 for every k=j+1,...,m id is non-local in U_k, hence nr(SC(id,V)) =n does not belong to $pns(U_k)$. Since p_j is a dynamic container of id, it follows that SC(id,V)pref* U_j; thus n belongs to pns(U_j). Therefore, after executing the update algorithm loop "for k:=j"we have GDISPLAY [n] =p_j and bv the Lemma 6.1 this value will not be changed for k=j+1,...,m. □

This theorem implies the correctness of the run-time addressing algorithm given by a formula:

$$\text{GDISPLAY}\,[n] \;+\; \text{offset}$$

where the pair (n,offset) represents an attribute in a program.

The following example illustrates the use of the GDISPLAY mechanism. Let us consider the extended scheme of the program given in the previous example.

```
B1[1]: begin
          class A[2]; begin real x[2,m];... end A;
       B2[3]: begin real y[3,n];
                 A class B[4]; begin real z[4,k]; ... end B;
                 ...
                 new B;
                 ...
              end;
       ...
       end
```

In this program every unit has a unit number given in brackets and every variable is identified by a pair of numbers: the first is a unit number of the static container of this variable and the second is a displacement in a memory frame. Consider the execution of the statement new B. A new object r of class B is created, the SL chain of r (see Fig.6) consists of the objects r,q (the block B2) and p (the block B1). Before control passes to the object r we must execute the GDISPLAY update algorithm. Fig.7 shows the contents of the vector GDISPLAY after its execution.

1	p
2	r
3	q
4	r

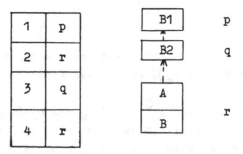

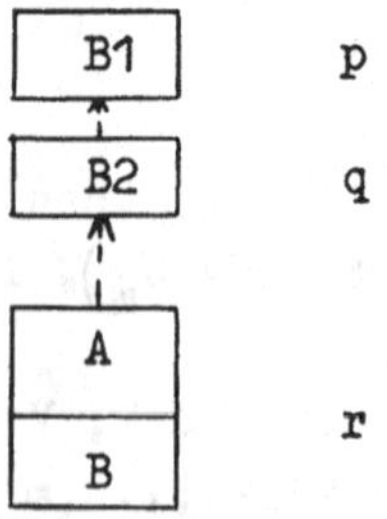

Fig.7.

Note that the attributes x and z of the object r are identified by two different unit numbers. However, due to the GDISPLAY update algorithm, all the elements of the vector GDISPLAY corresponding to the prefix number sequence of the unit B refer to the object r. Thus, the addressing formulas:

$$\text{GDISPLAY}\,[2] + m$$
$$\text{and}\quad \text{GDISPLAY}\,[4] + k$$

compute the addresses of x and z respectively in the frame of the object r.

7. Storage management

In this section we discuss briefly possible strategies of storage management and their influence on the semantics of the language with many-level prefixing. We propose a new approach to the problem and some principles of implementation.

Terminated objects accessibility

Consider first the problem of the accessibility of terminated objects. By a terminated object we mean an object in which control has passed through the final **end**.

Two different cases occur in Simula 67. A block (or a procedure) object is not accessible after its termination while the termination of a class object does not affect its accessibility. The property that a block object becomes inaccessible after its termination results only from the static properties of the correct program and may be statically checked.

Note another important property of Simula 67. The SL chain of the object being executed contains no terminated objects. It follows from the above properties that the activation record for a block or a procedure may be deleted from a memory as soon as this object is terminated.

The situation is quite different when many-level prefixing is allowed. Consider the following example:

```
L1: begin ref(A)X;
      class A;
        ...
    end A;
```

```
L2: begin integer j;
      A class B;
      begin
        procedure P;
        ...
        j:=j+1;
        ...
      end P;
    end B;
    X:-new B;
  end L2;
  XquaB.P; comment XquaB.P denotes instantaneous qualification which
           changes the qualification of X;
end L1;
```

After the execution of the assignment X:-new B there exist three objects: p of block L1, q of block L2 and r of class B, the latter pointed by X. Recall that this assignment is valid because X is qualified by class A and A prefixes B.

Observe now the instruction XquaB.P after the termination of objects r and q. This instruction denotes a call of the procedure P. The created object of the procedure would have in its SL chain two terminated objects: q and r. Note that P may use the attribute j from the terminated block object q. As we see, Simula's access rules are violated. Therefore the semantics of such a call must be determined. (Is the call of procedure P legal or would it cause a runtime error?) Is the access to j of object q legal or would it cause a run-time error? Two solutions are admissible, each implying a possible storage management strategy (cf [2]).

Retention semantics

The first semantics is called "retention". The object remains accessible as long as at least one user's or system pointer (e.g. SL or DL link) refers to that object. The retention strategy of storage allocation corresponds to the above semantics. This strategy may be accomplished either by the use of reference counters or by garbage collection.

Observe however, that within the retention semantics the concepts of block and procedure become trivial. A procedure would be a kind of a crippled class without a remote access mechanism. A block would only be an abbreviation of an anonymous class declaration and a generation at the same time. In this semantics the call of procedure P from the example is legal because the objects q and r are accessible.

Deletion semantics

Following the Simula principles we choose the other semantics, which may be called "deletion". It consists in the principle that a non--class object becomes inaccessible after its termination while a class object remains accessible as long as at least one user's or system pointer refers to that object. We regard this semantics proper for two reasons. First, it keeps the distinction between classes and blocks or procedure. Second, it admits the deletion of terminated non-class objects from a memory (but whether terminated non-class objects are actually deallocated immediately after their termination still depends on the implementation).

Since we are aiming at the possibility of deallocating non-class objects, we must provide the following property:

(7.1) The object being executed has no terminated non-class objects in its SL chain.

The implementation we propose makes use of SL links defining the SL chains for objects. These links are additional attributes of objects. We intend to treat system reference variables and user's reference variables uniformly. Hence, an SL link should become inaccessible after non-class object termination. (Observe also that when an object contains in its SL chain a terminated non-class object, it can not become an active object, because the display update algorithm (Algorithm 6.1) would fail in searching through the SL chain. In such a case a syntactic environment of the object would not be recovered even if the object requiring the display updating does not refer to inaccessible attributes).

Recall the statement X<u>qua</u>B.P from the example. The new created instance of P has a terminated non-class object q in its SL chain. The property (7.1) fails in this case.

Referencing mechanism

The new method of referencing must carry the information about the termination of non-class objects. Thus that method should realize the dictionary operations:insert, delete and member on the collection of all accessible objects.

In this paper we are not concerned with the strategy of allocating new frames for objects. Therefore we may omit some details and assume the existence of the function newframe (appetite) yielding an address of a new allocated frame of length appetite. Similarly we assume the existence of a procedure free(X) which releases the frame indicated by an address X.

The operation insert corresponds to the creation of a new object and should be understood as making the new object accessible. Insert does not deal with memory allocation itself.

Operation delete corresponds to the termination of a non-class object, and member yields information whether a reference points to an accessible object.

We will use an auxiliary data structure, an array H, containing references to objects. Roughly speaking, objects will be addressed indirectly through array H. It is obvious that the operation member should be as efficient as possible, for it is the most frequently used. (In our implementation the cost of member is really low: only two machine instructions).

Array H occupies low addresses of core, from 0 to the position pointed by a variable LASTITEM. (Objects may be allocated in high addresses of core). Each item in H is represented by two words, the physical address of an object and an integer called an object number. The algorithms presented below also use a procedure "intolist", a function "deletefrom" and a boolean function "empty", operating on the auxiliary list of released items of H. Because of their obvious meanings, details are omitted. Let the variable LIST be the head of this list.

Now objects are referenced by the so-called virtual addresses defined as pairs (addres in H, object number). The object number will be used for checking whether the object is accessible, while address in H will be the indirect address of the object (if accessible).

For a reference X denote the first and the second component of the virtual address of X by Xadd and Xob. The method of referencing will satisfy the following properties:

(7.2) If X refers to an accessible object, the H[Xadd] contains the physical address of the object,

(7.3) X refers to an accessible object iff Xob=H[Xadd+1] (i.e. iff object numbers are the same in the virtual address of X and the corresponding item of H).

Hence, the algorithm for the member operation is as follows:

```
boolean procedure member (Xadd,Xob,physical address);
name physical address; integer Xadd,Xob,physical address;
begin
  if Xob=H[Xadd+1] then
  begin physical address:=H[Xadd] ; member:=true
```

```
  end else member:=false
end member;
```

Consider now delete operation. Following property (7.3) it is sufficient to change the object number in an item of H to guarantee that the subsequent executions of a member concerning this item return value false. All items in H which previously pointed to some objects, subsequently being made inaccessible, are linked together into a list (started by the variable LIST)and may be reused for addressing some new objects.

The algorithm of delete operation is as follows:

```
procedure delete (Xadd,Xob);
integer Xadd,Xob;
begin integer addr;
  if member (Xadd,Xob,addr )then
  begin free (addr); comment a frame in memory may be released;
    H[Xadd+1] :=H[Xadd+1]  +1;
    intolist (Xadd,LIST )
  end
end delete;
```

When a new activation record is allocated, a new element must be inserted into H. If the list of released items of H is not empty, one of the previously used elements of H may be reused. Otherwise array H is extended (LASTITEM:=LASTITEM+2).

```
procedure insert (appetite,Xadd,Xob);
name Xadd,Xob; integer appetite,Xadd,Xob;
begin
  if empty(LIST ) then
  begin Xadd:=LASTITEM+1; H[Xadd+1]:=0; LASTITEM:=LASTITEM+2
  end else Xadd:=deletefrom(LIST); comment one element has been
  taken from the list of released elements;
      Xob:=H [Xadd+1];
      H[Xadd]:=newframe(appetite)
end insert;
```

Moreover we intend to treat uniformly references to terminated objects of non-classes and the reference to the empty object none. This is easily accomplished by the following initialization:

```
   none:= (0,0); H[0]:=H[1]:=1;
```

Hence none does not refer to any accessible object because its object number equals 0 and H[1] equals 1.

Finally, we recall now that the SL chain may be cut off. Therefore the display update algorithm must be modified.

Algorithm 7.1.
Let $SL(p)=p_m,\ldots,p_1$, then the GDISPLAY update algorithm has the form:

```
X:-p;
while X.SL =/= none do X:-X.SL;
if X ∉|R(T)| then error else
for k:=1 step 1 until m do updateGD(p_k);
```

□

Let us now discuss the cost of the proposed referencing method. Each accessible object needs two extra words for an item in the array H. Each reference variable needs two words for a virtual address. Thus, with respect to a standard method we lose two words for each accessible object and one word for each reference variable. (However, the pair of integers forming a virtual address may sometimes be packed into one machine word; the same may be done for an item of two words in the array H.)

On the other hand, we profit in an essential increase of the total number of different objects which may be used through the program lifetime without garbage collection. This number exceeds by far the capacity of H, though the number of objects accessible at the same time is limited by H. The new strategy has the advantage of the standard one when a program uses many procedures (what is natural and very common). Then the terminated objects of these procedures are deallocated on line and the corresponding space may be immediately reused by the other objects (as in the case of stack-implementable language). Observe that the lack of on-line deallocation of terminated non-class objects was the main snag to efficient implementations of Simula-67. Mereover, by virtue of this indirect addressing (in case of memory segmentation), the memory compactification may be done without traversing a graph of objects and without updating the reference variables. It may be accomplished by removing inaccessible objects and changing the corresponding addresses stored in the array H.

Finally the time-cost of these three operations (delete, insert, member)is as follows. The cost of the operation member is constant and very low. It may be compared with the cost of testing on none in standard implementation. The cost of insert and delete depends on the cost of other operations like newframe, free, intolist, deletefrom, which maintain the frames of inaccessible objects. Apart from the cost resulting from these operations, the cost of delete and insert is constant. These operations may be implemented in many different methods. However, with the use of good algorithms and data structures (i.e. linear lists, heaps etc.) one can obtain the same time complexity as in the case of standard solutions. Moreover, observe that due to the property (7.1) display may contain physical addresses instead of virtual ones, so an access to the visible attributes is not charged by the cost of member operation.

Programmed deallocation

To end this section, as a consequence of the reference mechanism introduced above, we can propose the new operation to be introduced to the programming language. This new operation is called usually programmed deallocation and may be denoted by kill(X), where X is a reference. The semantics of kill(X) is as follows. If X is a reference to an accessible object, then kill(X) makes this object inaccessible (and in consequence this object may be deallocated). Otherwise kill(X) is equivalent to the empty statement.

We got kill operation as a benefit from the referencing method introduced because of the other reasons. Roughly speaking, kill is realized by the delete operation described previously. Thus, after the execution of kill(X) the object pointed (if any) by X becomes inaccessible. Moreover, any remote access to such a being made inaccessible object will cause a run-time error. The realization of this is possible as a result of the operation member already existing in the set of storage management operations. Here the simple test on none is extended to the test on being accessible (member operation). We showed that the cost of member operation is constant and very low, and may be compared with the cost of the test on none. Thus, with some lost of space and a minimal loss of time we can solve the problem of "dangling reference".

We are confident that a programmer when allowing the use of programmed secure deallocation will be able to perform an efficient storage management by conscious deletions of useless objects. Therefore in most cases the time consuming garbage collection may be omitted.

Acknowledgement

The authors are very grateful to Tomasz Muldner for many useful comments and for careful reading of the manuscript.

References

[1] Bartol W.M. "The definition of the semantics of some instructions of a block structured language with type prefixing.", manuscript, 1980.

[2] Berry D.M., Chirica L., Johnston J.B., Martin D.F. and Sorkin A. "Time required for reference count management in retention block-structured languages." Part 1, Int. J. Comp. and Inf. Sciences, Vol.7, No.1 (March 1978), pp.11-64.

[3] Bobrow D.G., Wegbreit B. "A model and stack implementation of multiple environments", Comm.A.C.M., Vol.16, No.10 (Oct.1973), pp.591-603.

[4] Dahl O-J., Myrhaug B., Nygaard K., "Simula 67 Common Base Language", Norwegian Computing Center 1970.

[5] Dahl O-J., Wang A., "Coroutine sequencing in a block structured environment", B.I.T. Vol.11 (1971), pp.425-449.

[6] Dijkstra E.W., "Recursive programming", Numerische Mathematik 2, Vol.2 (1960), pp.312-318.

[7] Gries D., "Compiler construction for digital computers." New York, Wiley 1971.

NONSTANDARD MODELS

IN

PROPOSITIONAL DYNAMIC LOGIC

Francine Berman
Purdue University
W. Lafayette, Indiana 47907

Propositional Dynamic Logic (PDL) is a formal language for reasoning about flow-hart programs. Although simple in structure, PDL can be used to represent both se-uential and iterative programs and to assert program correctness, termination and ailure.

This paper is based on a lecture given at the 1981 Symposium on Algorithmic Logic nd outlines results from [Be]. We describe three classes of models which differ in heir interpretation of the iterative program operator * (the Kleene star) and show hat these interpretations cannot be distinguished by any PDL assertion, we also discuss hy the continuity of the Kleene star cannot be precisely characterized within a prop-ositional system. We maintain however that continuity is primarily an aid to our ntuition and that nonstandard models of PDL are perfectly adequate for interpreting roperties of flowchart programs.

We briefly introduce PDL. For a more detailed discussion, see [F&L] or [Be].

yntax

PDL assertions and programs are built from primitive sets Φ_0 (basic assertions) nd Σ_0 (basic programs) respectively as follows:

1) Basic assertions are assertions.

2) If P and Q are assertions then so are -P and PvQ.

3) Basic programs are programs. If a and b are programs and P is an assertion then a;b, aUb, a* and P? are programs.

4) If a is a program and P is an assertion then <a>P and [a]P are assertions.

Intuitively, we interpret

a;b as "execute a then execute b,"

aUb as "execute a or execute b,"

a* as "execute a a nondeterministically chosen number of times,"

<a>P as "there is an execution of program a which terminates with P true,"

[a]P as "whenever program a terminates, assertion P is true."

(Note that <> and [] behave as dual operators, i.e. <a>P ≡ -[a]-P).

With the intended interpretation, we can describe a surprising number of properties of programs by PDL assertions. A few examples:

Partial Correctness (P{a}Q) can be represented in PDL by the assertion P→[a]Q interpreted as the statement "Whenever P is true then whenever a halts, Q is true

Nontermination, can be represented in PDL by the assertion [a]false interpreted a the statement "Program a never halts."

A Loop Invariant for a program a can be represented by the PDL assertion [a*]P interpreted as the statement "P is true after any number of iterations of program a."

Semantics

There are several different ways of constructing models faithful to the usual interpretation of the propositional constructs.

A model of PDL is a triple $M = (W,\Pi,\rho)$ where

W is a set of states,
$\Pi:\Phi_0 \to 2^W$ evaluates all basic assertions,
$\rho:\{\text{all programs}\} \to 2^{W\times W}$ evaluates all programs.

We extend Π to evaluate all PDL assertions as follows:

$\Pi(P\vee Q) = \Pi(P) \cup \Pi(Q)$
$\Pi(-P) = W - \Pi(P)$
$\Pi(\langle a\rangle P) = \{w \mid \exists v((w,v)\in\rho(a) \text{ and } v\in\Pi(P))\}$
$\Pi([a]P) = \{w \mid \exists v((w,v)\in\rho(a) \text{ implies } v\in\Pi(P))\}$.

This definition of model ensures that the boolean and modal operators (-, v, <>, []) are interpreted in the usual way but does not constrain the interpretation of the program operators ;, U, *, ?. For example, the generality of this definition permits us to have a model M and a state w in M in which the program aUb ("select a or b") is executable but neither program a nor program b is executable. Therefore, we want to consider models of PDL in which the program operator

; behaves like sequential execution,
U behaves like nondeterministic branching,
* behaves like iteration and
? behaves like test.

A D-sound model is a model of PDL in which the following schemas (D) are valid:

$\langle a;b\rangle P \equiv \langle a\rangle\langle b\rangle P$

$\langle a \cup b\rangle P \equiv \langle a\rangle P \vee \langle b\rangle P$

$\langle P?\rangle Q \equiv P \wedge Q$

$(P \vee \langle a\rangle P \vee \langle a^*\rangle\langle a^*\rangle P) \rightarrow \langle a^*\rangle P$

I: $\langle a^*\rangle P \rightarrow (P \vee \langle a^*\rangle(-P \wedge \langle a\rangle P))$

A Loop Invariant (LI) model is a model in which the valuation function ρ obeys the following rules:

$\rho(a;b) = \rho(a) \circ \rho(b)$

$\rho(a \cup b) = \rho(a) \cup \rho(b)$

$\rho(P?) = \{(w,w) \mid w \text{ is in } \Pi(P)\}$

$\cup\rho(a^n) \subseteq \rho(a^*)$

$\rho(a^*) \circ \rho(a^*) \subseteq \rho(a^*)$

$\Pi(I) = W$.

A Standard model of PDL is a Loop Invariant model in which $\rho(a^*) = \cup\rho(a^n)$.

(Note that this continuity property subsumes the other properties of * in the definition of Loop Invariant model).

How do these classes of models really differ? The following figures illustrate the representation of the program operators ;, U, ?, * as defined within each class of models.

Sequential Execution (;)

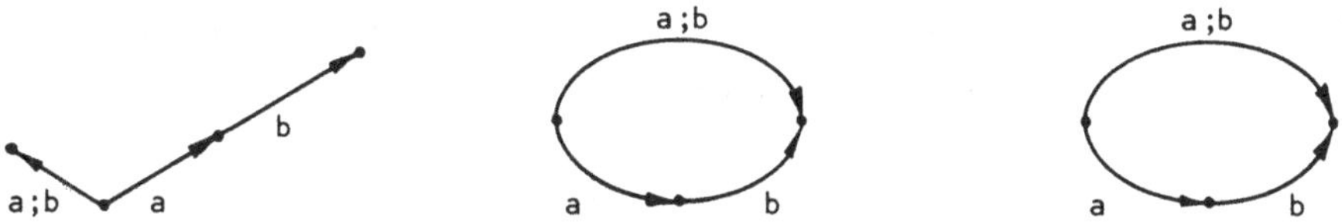

D-Sound Loop Invariant Standard

Nondeterministic Branching (U)

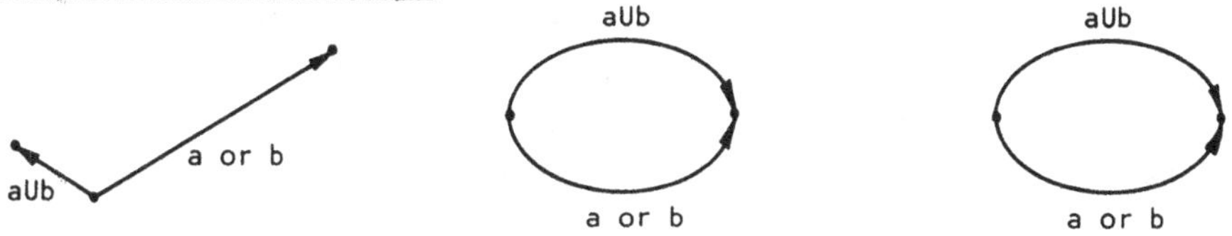

D-Sound Loop Invariant Standard

Tests (?)

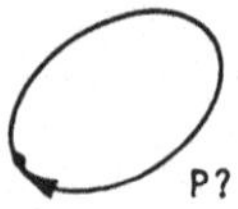

D-Sound

Loop Invariant

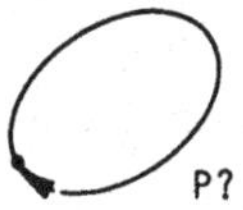

Standard

Iteration (*)

D-Sound

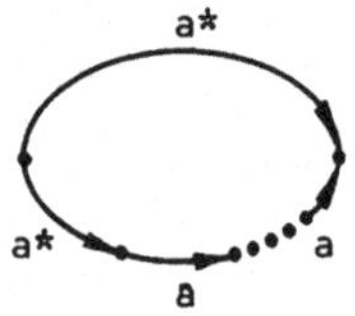

Loop Invariant

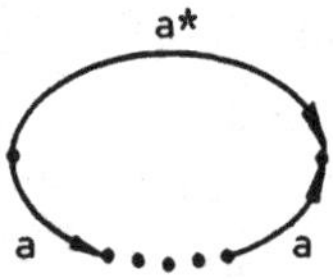

Standard

In particular, Loop Invariant and Standard models differ in their interpretation of iteration. These interpretations are indistinguishable by PDL assertions ([Pa]), i.e., Theory(LI models) = Theory(Standard models).

From these figures, D-Sound models seem much weaker than LI or Standard models. How non-uniform can these models get? Surprisingly enough, the answer is 'not very'. In fact, Theory(D-Sound models) = Theory(LI models). Moreover, every D-Sound model ca be extended to a Loop Invariant model such that if P is an assertion satisfiable at state w in a D-Sound model, P remains satisfiable at w in the extended Loop Invariant model. This is shown in [Be]. The idea of the proof is as follows:

Let M be a D-Sound model. Extend M to a Loop Invariant model M' in stages. At each stage, add new edges (and possibly new states) which "complete" the graph with respect to one of the program operators ;, U, or *. We show that the addition of thes new edges does not change the set of satisfiable assertions at each of the original states. We then show that the resulting model M' is a Loop Invariant model.

The significance of this theorem is that it shows that although the three classes of models interpret the program operators ;, U, ?, * differently, we cannot detect these differences by PDL assertions. In particular,

Theory(D-Sound models) = Theory(LI models) = Theory(Standard models).

Are these classes of models the same? By the definitions, it is easy to show tha

{Standard models} ⊆ {Loop Invariant models} ⊆ {D-Sound models}. In [Be], we showed that each of these inclusions is in fact proper.

What all this means is that by suppressing explicit references to states, PDL is unable to distinguish between models which interpret the regular program operators (;, U, *, ?) in an intuitive way and models in which these operators are much more loosely defined. It is perhaps useful to step back and consider the original aims in defining a propositional programming logic. What properties of programs was it important to represent?

It made sense to express assertions which became true at various points of structured flowchart schemes. It made sense to be able to mention portions of the program itself explicitly so that we could talk about correctness, termination and optimality. It made sense to include iterative programs... but how? Given a flowchart, there are essentially two kinds of assertions we would want to make about a loop. One is that if a loop terminates after we iterate it some fixed number of times (say 17), some particular property P will hold. In fact, we can express this property within PDL by the assertion $[a^{17}]P$. The other is that whenever a loop terminates, no matter how many times it has been executed, a property P will hold. This is expressed within PDL by the assertion [a*]P. What's missing and in fact inexpressible within a propositional programming logic is the continuity property of *. We argue however, that continuity is an aid to our intuition but is not needed to express the necessary properties of loops in flowchart schemes.

These results on nonstandard models of PDL underscore this argument. We have shown that to preserve the correct behavior of the program operators ;, U, ?, *, essentially any class of models in which the schemas D (from the definition of D-Sound) are valid will do. Continuity is helpful to our understanding but not necessary for the correct representation of flowchart properties.

Bibliography

[Be] Berman, F., "Syntactic and Semantic Structure in Propositional Dynamic Logic," Ph.D. Dissertation, University of Washington, August, 1979.

[F&L] Fischer, M.J. and Ladner, R.E., "Propositional Dynamic Logic of Regular Programs," JCSS 18:2, April 1979.

[Pa] Parikh, R., "A Completeness Result for Propositional Dynamic Logic," Symposium on the Mathematical Foundations of Computer Science, Zakopane, Poland, 1978.

ON PRIORITIES OF PARALLELISM: PETRI NETS UNDER THE MAXIMUM FIRING STRATEGY

Hans-Dieter Burkhard

Sektion Mathematik
Humboldt-Universität
DDR-1086 Berlin, PSF 1297

Abstract: The computational power of Petri nets is extended up to the power of counter machines by realizing certain priorities of parallelism. Hence certain concurrent computations can not exactly be reflected by the sets of all sequentialized computations in related systems. Moreover, the reachability, boundedness and liveness problems are undecidable under the modified firing rule.

0. Introduction

The states and the processed sequences in concurrent systems may be heavily affected by the assumptions about the occurences of parallelism. To show this we consider concurrent computations using the Petri net model where we claim that maximal sets of simultaneously firable transitions have to fire in parallel ("Maximum Firing Strategy" 2.1). Petri nets under this firing rule are of more computational power than the nets under the common firing rule (3.2).

While the common firing rule (1.2) for Petri nets corresponds to all possible sequentialized computations (executable by one processor) (1.3), the Maximum Firing Strategy allows only those concurrent computations which make use of the maximally possible parallelism (with a related number of processors). This concept is related to the strategy MAX for concurrent computations, which was introduced by Salwicki and Müldner /SM/ . The extended computational power under the Maximum Firing Strategy implies that there are concurrent computations which can not be faithfully represented by the set of sequentialized runs.

Furthermore, the Petri nets working under the Maximum Firing Strategy are able to simulate counter machines (3.2). As a consequence the boundedness, reachability and liveness problems are undecidable (4.1). This result may be unpleasant with respect to practical use.

But, as it can be seen by the used constructions, these results already hold for parallelism of two processors: If at least two transitions have to fire simultaneously whenever this is possible, then the computational power is again extended up to the power of counter machines (4.4). In this sense it can be stated that the use of parallelism must be paid by undecidability results.

1. Preliminaries. The common firing rule.

1.1 $\mathbb{N}$ is the set of all non-negative integers. For a finite alphabet A, A^* is the free monoid with the empty word e . Operations and relations on vectors are understood componentwise.

A (generalized initial) Petri net is given by $\mathcal{N} = (P, T, F, m_o)$, where P and T are the finite sets of places and transitions, respectively. $F: (P \times T) \cup (T \times P) \longrightarrow \mathbb{N}$ is the flow function, $m_o \in \mathbb{N}^P$ is the initial marking. For a transition $t \in T$ we define the vectors $t^-, t^+ \in \mathbb{N}^P$ by $t^-(p) := F(p,t)$, $t^+(p) := F(t,p)$ $(p \in P)$.

1.2 The transition $t \in T$ is firable under the common firing rule at a marking $m \in \mathbb{N}^P$ iff $t^- \leqq m$. After its firing the new marking is $m + \Delta t$, where $\Delta t := t^+ - t^-$.

A sequence $u = t_1 \ldots t_n \in T^*$ is a firing sequence under the common firing rule iff each transition t_i $(i=1,\ldots,n)$ is firable at the marking $m_o + \Delta t_1 + \ldots + \Delta t_{i-1}$ under the common firing rule, it leads to the new marking $m_o + \Delta u$, where $\Delta u := m_o + \Delta t_1 + \ldots + \Delta t_n$. If only one processor is working, then the firing sequences may be considered as the computational sequences which can be processed by this processor.

1.3 The set of all firing sequences under the common firing rule of a Petri net $\mathcal{N}$ is denoted by $L_{\mathcal{N}}$. The following pumping lemma /B2/ holds:

> There are numbers k, l for each language $L_{\mathcal{N}}$ such that the following holds:
> If the length of a sequence $u \in L_{\mathcal{N}}$ is greater than k ,
> then there is a decomposition $u = u_1 u_2 u_3$ such that
> $1 \leqq$ length of $u_2 \leqq l$ and $u_1 u_2^{n+1} u_3 \in L_{\mathcal{N}}$ for all $n \in \mathbb{N}$.

By the modified firing rule, which we shall define later on (2.1), we get sets of firing sequences which are subsets of $L_{\mathcal{N}}$. In general, such a pumping lemma is not valid for these sets.

1.4 The set of all reachable markings under the common firing rule is defined by $R_{\mathcal{N}} := \{ m_o + \Delta u \; / \; u \in L_{\mathcal{N}} \}$. For a given subset $X \subseteq P$

of places the (non-terminal) Petri net predicate $M_{\mathcal{N},X}$ is defined as the projection of $R_{\mathcal{N}}$ on the places of X :

$M_{\mathcal{N},X} := \{ x \in \mathbb{N}^X \ / \ \exists m \in R_{\mathcal{N}} : m(p) = x(p) \text{ for all } p \in X \}$.

There is again a pumping lemma /B2/:

> There are vectors $y', y'' \in \mathbb{N}^X$ for each set $M_{\mathcal{N},X}$ such that the following holds:
> If $x \in M_{\mathcal{N},X}$ covers y' (i.e. $x \geqq y'$),
> then there exists a vector $z \in (\mathbb{N} \setminus \{0\})^X$ such that
> $z \leqq y''$ and $x + n \cdot z \in M_{\mathcal{N},X}$ for all $n \in \mathbb{N}$.

In general, the Petri net predicates computable by the modified firing rule do not satisfy such a pumping lemma.

2. Firing under the Maximum Strategy.

2.1 The strategy "MAX" for concurrent computations was introduced by Salwicki and Müldner /SM/ : As many processes as possible (limitations may arise by conflicts) have to work concurrently. Thus we want to make use of maximal parallelism. This can be represented in Petri nets by the following firing rule called the Maximum Firing Strategy:

> In a marking m we choose a maximal set T' of simultaneously firable transitions, i.e. $\sum_{t \in T'} t^- \leqq m$ and $\sum_{t \in T''} t^- \nleqq m$ for all $T'' \supsetneqq T'$.
> Then the transitions of T' are fired simultaneously. After this firing the new marking is $m + \sum_{t \in T'} \Delta t$. For that marking a new set T' is chosen ...

2.2 The number of simultaneously firable transitions is bounded by the number of transitions in the net. Additionally it can be bounded by the structure of the net. By adding a "run place" it is possible to change the net (thereby preserving the internal structure) such the not more than a given number n of transitions may fire simultaneously:

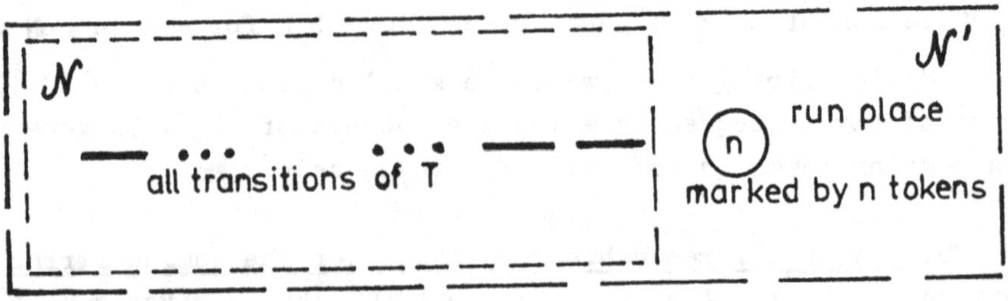

2.3 The set $R^{MAX}_{\mathcal{N}}$ of all reachable markings under the Maximum Firing Strategy contains all those markings which can be reached from m_0 by firing the maximal sets T' of simultaneously firable transitions, i.e., only those markings are valid which are reached when all transitions of a set T' have fired. However, the results presented in this paper remains true if we consider the sets additionally containing the intermediate markings (where some transitions of T' have fired — this would be related to the languages as in 3.4).

The Petri net predicate $M^{MAX}_{\mathcal{N},X}$ under the Maximum Firing Strategy is the projection of $R^{MAX}_{\mathcal{N}}$ on the places of the set $X \subseteq P$. For each net $\mathcal{N}$ we have: $R^{MAX}_{\mathcal{N}} \subseteq R_{\mathcal{N}}$ and $M^{MAX}_{\mathcal{N},X} \subseteq M_{\mathcal{N},X}$.

2.4 As an example we consider the following net (a modified version of Hack's example for the weak computation of 2^i):

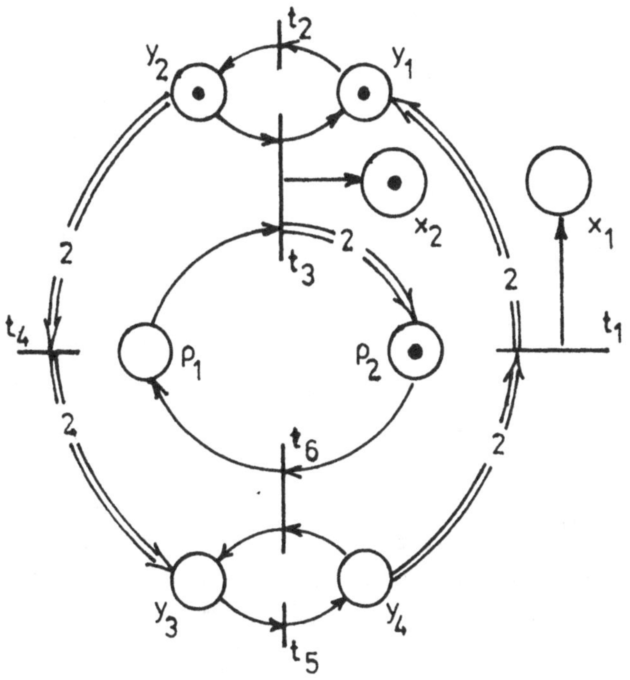

We have $M_{\mathcal{N},X} = \{ (i,j) \ / \ i \in \mathbb{N} \ \wedge \ 1 \leq j \leq 2^i \}$ under the common firing rule for $X = \{ x_1, x_2 \}$.

The computations under the Maximum Firing Strategy lead to the following reachability graph, whereby

$m = (m(x_1), m(x_2), m(p_1), m(p_2), m(y_1), \ldots, m(y_4))$:

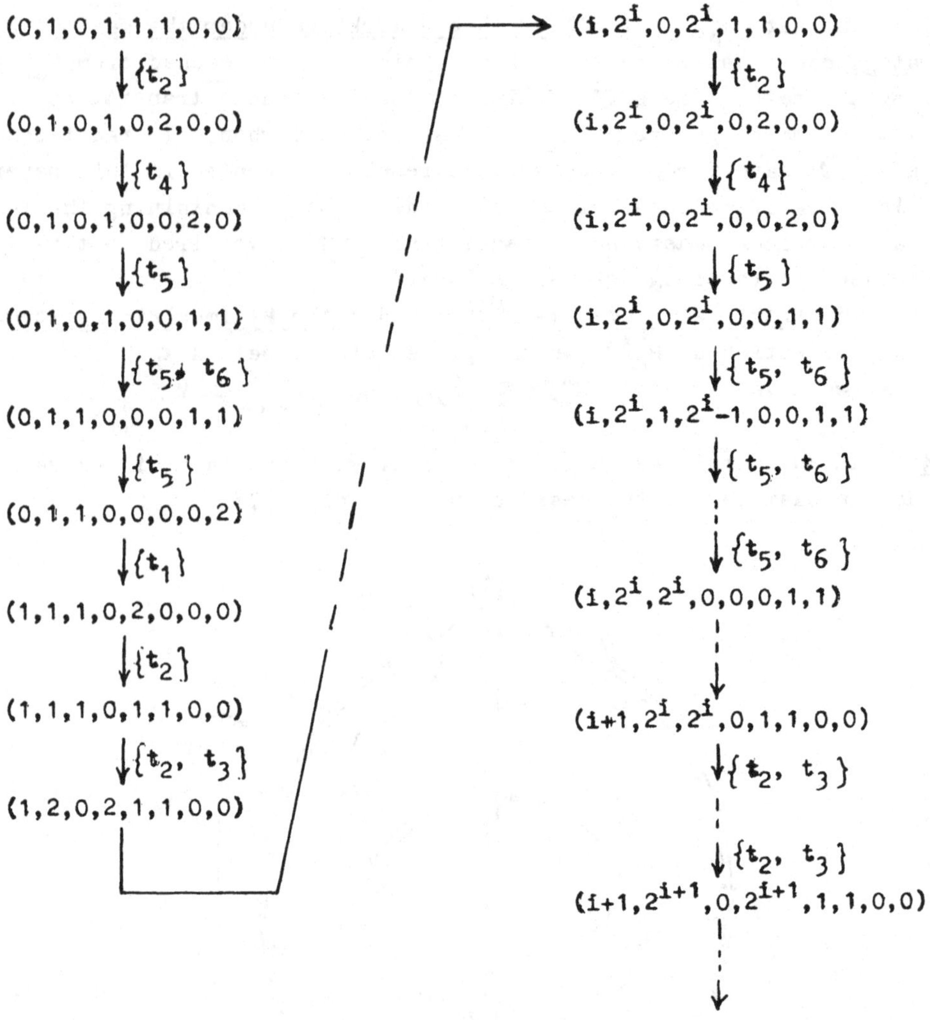

Here we have $M^{MAX}_{\mathcal{N},X} = \left\{ (i,j) \;/\; i \in \mathbb{N} \wedge 2^{i-1} \leq j \leq 2^i \right\}$. Since this set contains no infinite linear subset, it does not satisfy the conditions of the pumping lemma in 1.4 . Hence it can not be computed in any Petri net under the common firing rule.

<u>2.5</u> In the example a <u>while-loop</u> is realized: If the places y_1 and y_2 are each marked by one token, then the transitions t_2 and t_3 have to fire simultaneously as long as there are tokens in place p_1. Thus we have under the Maximum Firing Strategy:

<u>while</u> $m(p_1) > 0$ <u>do</u> <u>begin</u> $m(p_1) := m(p_1) - 1$;
$m(p_2) := m(p_2) + 2$;
$m(x_2) := m(x_2) + 1$ <u>end</u> .

Another while-loop is realized by the transitions t_5 and t_6. Under the common firing rule it can not be possible to realize while-loops in Petri nets. Otherwise the set $M^{MAX}_{\mathcal{N},X}$ of our example would also be computable under the common firing rule.

<u>2.6</u> The reachability graphs under the Maximum Firing Strategy (as well as under the common firing rule) may be infinite as in our example. In general they may also have branchings (if there are two or more maximal sets of simultaneously firable transitions). The reachability graph is finite iff the net is bounded (iff all reachable markings are bounded).

<u>2.7</u> Certain properties of Petri nets - especially boundedness - under the common firing rule can be examined with help of the well-known construction of the coverability tree /KM/, /K1/, /H1/. An important fact used for this construction is the following one (which is also related to the pumping lemma 1.4):

> If a marking m is reachable from m' by firing of a sequence u, then $m + a$ is reachable from $m' + a$ by firing of u under the common firing rule for each $a \in \mathbb{N}^P$.

This is not true for the Maximum Firing Strategy as it can be seen by the example. Hence a coverability tree with respect to the Maximum Firing Strategy can not be constructed. Furthermore, boundedness is not decidable in Petri nets working under this firing rule (4.1) .

3. The computational power of Petri nets under the Maximum Firing Strategy.

<u>3.1</u> The Maximum Firing Strategy is more "selective" than the common firing rule, thus we have $M^{MAX}_{\mathcal{N},X} \subsetneqq M_{\mathcal{N},X}$. By this selecting, the Maximum Firing Strategy is more powerful with respect to computations:

> Let $\mathfrak{M}$ and $\mathfrak{M}^{MAX}$ be the classes of all Petri net predicates $M_{\mathcal{N},X}$ and $M^{MAX}_{\mathcal{N},X}$, respectively. Then we have
>
> $$\mathfrak{M} \subsetneqq \mathfrak{M}^{MAX} .$$

For the proof we refer to 2.2 and 2.4 : If $n = 1$, then we are able to fire in the net $\mathcal{N}'$ constructed in 2.2 exactly all sequences of $L_{\mathcal{N}}$ even under the Maximum Firing Strategy, and hence $M^{MAX}_{\mathcal{N}',X} = M_{\mathcal{N},X}$. For the example 2.4 we have $M^{MAX}_{\mathcal{N},X} \in \mathfrak{M}^{MAX} \setminus \mathfrak{M}$.

3.2 Petri nets under the Maximum Firing Strategy are able to simulate deterministic counter machines. Other possibilities to simulate counter machines by modified Petri nets were given by several authors (cf. 3.5) . The crucial point is the simulation of zero-testing, which is not possible in Petri nets working under the common firing rule /K2 The consequence of the ability to simulate counter machines are the undecidability results given in 4.1 . The instructions of a deterministic counter machine can be simulated by Petri nets working under the Maximum Firing Strategy in the following way (for more details the reader is referred to the literature):

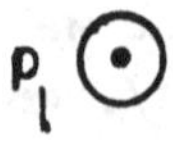

simulates "start in state l"

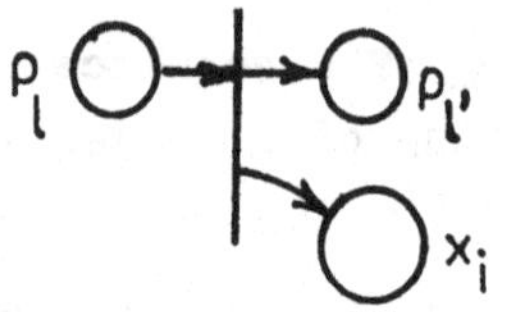

simulates "l: $x_i := x_i + 1$; goto l' ;"

(counters are simulated by the places x_i)

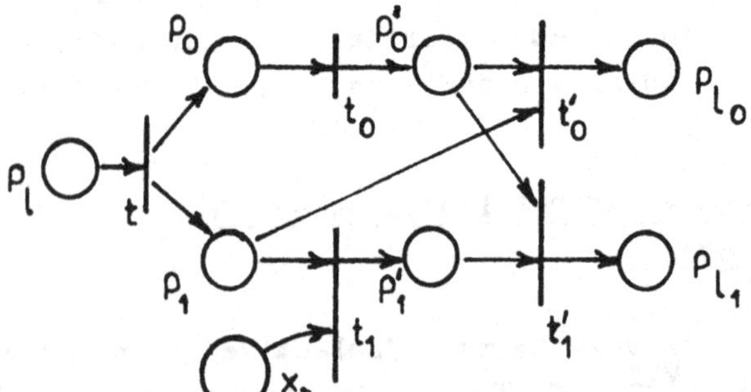

simulates zero-testing :

"l: if $x_i = 0$ then goto l_0 else $x_i := x_i - 1$; goto l_1;"

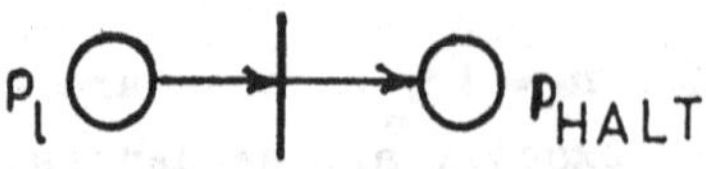

simulates "l: halt"

Non-deterministic counter machines may also be simulated if we make use of the additional choice-construction:

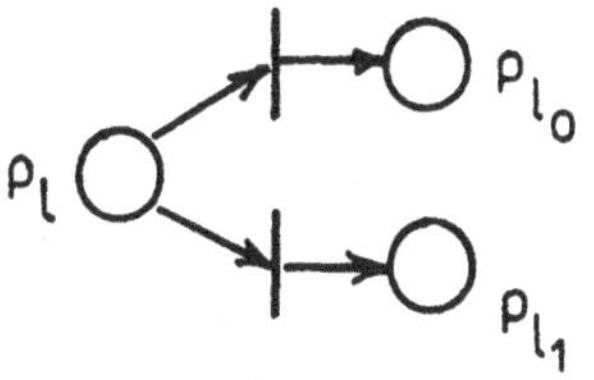

simulates "l: goto l_0 or l_1 ;"

3.3 As it was shown in /B1/, the set $\{(i,2^i) / i \in \mathbb{N}\}$ is not in the class $\mathfrak{M}^{MAX}$, and hence it is not possible to compute all recursively enumerable predicates in the sense of $\mathfrak{M}^{MAX}$. To do this, termination is needed: Only those computations (markings) are valid for which a given submarking $y \in \mathbb{N}^{P \setminus X}$ is reached on the places of the set $P \setminus X$ (where X denotes the places on which the predicate is computed as before). By such predicates

$$M^{MAX}_{\mathcal{N},X,y} := \{x \in \mathbb{N}^X / \exists m \in R^{MAX}_{\mathcal{N}} \; \forall p \in X \; \forall p' \in P \setminus X : \; m(p)=x(p) \wedge m(p')=y(p')\}$$

all recursively enumerable predicates can be represented /B1/.

Remark: It is an open problem which predicates can be represented using termination in Petri nets under the common firing rule. But it is conjectured that not all recursively enumerable predicates can be generated in this way.

3.4 The order of transitions in a firing sequence of $L_{\mathcal{N}}$ may be artificial in the case of concurrently firable transitions. For reasons of comparing results we can also introduce such an artificial order for the firings under the Maximum Firing Strategy: For each maximal set T' of simultaneously firable transitions the transitions of T' may fire in an arbitrary order (each transition exactly once before the next set T' is chosen). Then we obtain that the Maximum Firing Strategy is more powerful also with respect to the representation of languages by Petri nets. Using termination and a transition labelling function (homomorphism) $h: T \rightarrow \Sigma \cup \{e\}$ we can generate all recursively enumerable languages over the alphabet Σ /B1/.

3.5 The power of counter machines is also met by the modified Petri net versions given by several authors. In /H2/ inhibitor arcs and priorities for transitions, respectively, are used. In the nets defined in /JLL/ and /MATTK/ the transitions have to fire during fixed (individual) time intervals after their enabling. Concepts of firing in the order of enabling (realized by certain queue regimes) have thos effects, too /B1/. In /V/ the numbers of transported tokens are modifie by the markings on certain places. The concept in /MPS/ is the closest one to our Maximum Firing Strategy: There the firings of transitions are synchronized by external events such that all enabled transitions connected to the actual event have to fire. The construction for the simulation of inhibitor arcs given in /MPS/ would also work under the Maximum Firing Strategy. But, on the other hand, the construction give there is quite opposite to parallelism since all concurrent firings of the essential transitions are suppressed by a run loop (similar to the construction in 2.2).

4. "The price of parallelism"

4.1 It is well established in the literature that the ability of Petri nets to simulate deterministic counter machines (whereby the Petri nets are modified in some sense) results in the undecidability of the boundedness (are all reachable markings bounded with respect to certain places), the reachability (is a given marking/submarking reachable) and the liveness (can certain transitions always become firable sometime later) problems. Since the halting problem is not decidable for deterministic counter machines, it is not decidable if a token can arrive at the place p_{HALT} (cf.3.2) and hence the reachability problem for submarkings is undecidable. By connecting certain simple subnets to the place p_{HALT} the undecidability of the reachability, boundedness and liveness problems can be proved (cf. for instance /H1/, /JLL/, /B1/).

4.2 In the constructions for the simulation of the counter machines all places excluding the counter-place x_i may only be marked by 0 or 1 It is known from the theory that the halting problem is undecidable even for counter machines with two counters. Hence the undecidability results hold for Petri nets under the Maximum Firing Strategy where the nets have only two unbounded places. By a construction given in /B1/ the number of bounded places can also be limited by two. Hence the total number of places need not be greater than four. On the other hand, the reachability sets $R_{\mathcal{N}}$ of Petri nets with 4 places under the common firing rule are always semilinear /HP/. This illustrates the difference between the firing rules once more.

4.3 Since we always have $M^{MAX}_{\mathcal{N},X} \subseteq M_{\mathcal{N},X}$, a place which is bounded under the common firing rule must also be bounded under the Maximum Firing Strategy. Hence it is possible that a place which was formerly unbounded becomes bounded under the Maximum Firing Strategy. But it is not decidable in general if this happens. Still more important could be the fact that a transition which was live under the common firing rule may become not live with respect to the Maximum Firing Strategy and vice versa /B1/. Here the undecidability results are very strongly affecting the practical use.

4.4 In the Maximum Firing Strategy we make use of maximal parallelism. But for simulating the counter machines the parallelism which is used may also be restricted: Only the parallelism of two transitions is needed for the zero-testing device (3.2): If the transition t_1 is firable (if there are tokens on the place x_i), then the transition t_o' must not become firable (the places p_1 and p_o' must not be marked at the same time). That can be ensured if the transition t_1 must start working (with taking the token from p_1) before the transition t_o has ended its actions (has given the token to p_o'). This condition can be satisfied if we claim that in a net simulating a deterministic counter machine (3.2) at least two transitions have to fire simultaneously whenever this is possible. Moreover, both transitions t_o and t_1 become firable at the same time. Hence it should be reasonably accepted that under the assumptions of a parallel system both transitions are simultaneously acting in reality. Thus deterministic counter machines can be simulated. In this sense we can state that the use of parallelism (the priority of parallelism) must be paid by the undecidability of the reachability, boundedness and liveness problems.

4.5 Of course, the constraints of firings by parallelism of at least two transitions (as far as it is possible) lead also to more computational power (in comparison to the common firing rule as in 3.1). The consequence of those extensions is the impossibility of faithful simulations by all one-processor-computations: There are concurrent computations by nets working under constraints by parallelism such that no net working under the common firing rule can exactly simulate them.

4.6 As it was pointed out in 3.5, all known related extensions of Petri nets (together with termination, cf. 3.3, 3.4) give the nets the power of Turing machines. What we can say now is that already the use of parallelism can give the nets this computational power. The restrictions of this power under the common firing rule result from this point of view from irresolution with respect to parallelism. On the other hand, firing by fair scheduling (sequentializing instead of parallelism) results in the power of Turing machines, too /B1/ (consider the zero-testing device in 3.2 under the assumption that a firable transition has to fire which was enabled the longest time).

Thus the restricted computational power (and the decidability of the boundedness problem, for instance) of Petri nets under the common firing rule can be understood as the consequence of allowing "too much": If there is made a decision concerning parallelism (or fair scheduling or one of the modifications mentioned in 3.5), then these restrictions may be overcome.

5. Conclusions.

The restrictions of firability by the use of parallelism extend the computational power of Petri nets. It is not possible to simulate all these computations by nets working under the common firing rule: The nets under the common firing rule are in general computing "too much". Hence there are concurrent computations executed by several processors using the possibilities of parallel working which cannot be exactly reflected by all computations which one processor could execute in the same system or even in any other system of the same kind.

Under the aspects of practical use the power of Turing machines (or at least of deterministic counter machines) may not be welcome. The decidability of liveness, for instance, is desirable. On the other hand, the use of parallelism as far as it is possible is desirable with respect to efficiency, too. Now the question arises for which classes of nets the mentioned problems (or at least some of them) are decidable with respect to the modified firing rules. A positive answer can trivially be given for the class of bounded nets.

Acknowledgement

The inspiration for the study of the Maximum Firing Strategy was given by Prof. A. Salwicki. I would like to thank him for his suggestions.

References

/B1/ Burkhard, H.D., Ordered Firing in Petri Nets, Elektron.Informationsverarb.Kybernetik 17(1981)2/3,71-86.

/B2/ Burkhard, H.D., Two Pumping Lemmata for Petri Nets. To appear in Elektron.Informationsverarb.Kybernetik.

/H1/ Hack, M., Decision Problems for Petri Nets and Vector Addition Systems, MAC-TM 59, Proj.MAC, M.I.T. 1975.

/H2/ Hack, M., Petri net languages, CSG Memo 124, .Proj.MAC, M.I.T. 1975.

/HP/ Hopcroft, J., Pansiot, J.J., On the reachability problem for 5-dimensional vector addition systems, Theor.Comp.Science 8(1979), 135-159.

/JLL/ Jones, N., Landweber, L., Lien, E., Complexity of some problems in Petri nets, Theor.Comp.Science 4(1977),277-299.

/KM/ Karp, R.M., Miller, R.E., Parallel Program Schemata, Journ. Comp. and System Sciences 3(1969), 147-195.

/K1/ Keller, R.M., Vector replacement systems: a formalism for modelling asynchronous systems, Tech.Rep.117, Comp.Science Lab., Princeton Univ., 1972/74.

/K2/ Keller, R.M., Generalized Petri nets as models for system verification, Tech.Rep.202, Dept.Electrical Eng., Princeton Univ., 1975.

/MATTK/ Mori, M., Araki, T., Taniguchi, K., Tokura, N., Kasami, T., Some decision problems for time Petri nets and applications to the verification of communication protocols, Trans.IECE'77/10 Vol.J60-D, No.10, 822-829.

/MPS/ Moalla, M., Pulou, J., Sifakis, J., Synchronized Petri nets: A model for the description of non-autonomous systems, Lecture Notes in Computer Science 64(1978), 374-384.

/SM/ Salwicki, A., Müldner, T., On algorithmic properties of concurrent programs, Manuscript, Warsaw 1979.

/V/ Valk, R., Self-modifying nets, a natural extension of Petri nets, Lecture Notes in Computer Science 62(1978), 464-476.

ON FOUR LOGICS OF PROGRAMS AND COMPLEXITY OF THEIR SATISFIABILITY PROBLEMS : EXTENDED ABSTRACT

Bogdan S. Chlebus

Institute of Informatics, Warsaw University
00-901, PKiN, Warsaw, Poland.

1. Introduction.

We investigate the problem of space requirements for algorithms recognizing the satisfiable formulas in certain logics of programs. We consider four variants of two basic logical calculi: propositional algorithmic logic /PAL/ and propositional dynamic logic /PDL/. PAL is a deterministic counterpart of PDL (modulo syntactical differences).

PAL was described by Chlebus [2] , [4] . There were proved the decidability of PAL, and given the finitary and infinitary axiomatizations of PAL, with completeness proofs. Other results concerning semantics, axiomatizability and effectivity problems of algorithmic logic may be found in the papers written by Kreczmar [9] , Mirkowska [11] , Salwicki [14] and others.

The semantics of dynamic logic, together with the definability and decidability results, were described by Fischer and Ladner [5], Harel, Meyer and Pratt [6], Pratt [12] , [13] , Valiev[17] and others. Fischer and Ladner [5] discussed thoroughly the semantics of PDL, and proved the small model theorem for PDL. They showed that deciding satisfiability on lenght n formulas requires time $d^{n/\log n}$ for some $d > 1$, and that satisfiability can be decided in nondeterministic time c^n for some c. Pratt [13] showed that satisfiability for PDL can be decided deterministically in exponential time, and Valiev [17] proved this for PDL with program variables interpreted deterministically.

In this paper the space complexity of satisfiability is explored and this leads us to translating the analogies and differences between the semantics of nondeterministic and deterministic logics of programs into the language of computational complexity theory.

We consider logical calculi PAL_0 and PDL_0 which are weakened variants of PAL and PDL. For them there are proved the upper and lower bounds on the space complexity, with relatively small gaps between them. Further we investigate the complexity of decidability for PAL_1 and PDL_1. They are obtained from PAL_0 and PDL_0 by adding a certain program connective. It is called a double-star while. It is a generalized "while" or "repeat" construction in which the logical values of a vector of formulas are checked in a loop, instead of only one formula in the standard while program operator. There are proved exponential lower bounds on the space complexity /nondeterministic and alternating resp./ of the satisfiability in these two logics of programs. It turns out that formulas with the double-star while connective are "abbreviations" of certain /exponentially/ longer formulas with the standard symbols. Hence, these complexity results are in a sense analogous to the results of Meyer and Stockmeyer [10] concerning the lower bounds on the complexity of the problem of equivalence of regular expressions with added symbol for squaring. All the results announced in this report will be treated in detail in [3].

2. Models of computation.

Deterministic, nondeterministic and alternating Turing machines will serve as our models of computing devices. /We will use abbreviation TM for Turing machine/. Alternating TM's were introduced by Chandra, Kozen and Stockmeyer /cf.[1]/ in connection with certain game strategy problems. Nondeterministic TM's are like alternating TM's, except that existential states occur only in their sets of states. Similarly, in a deterministic TM there is at most one next configuration for any given one. Expositions of alternating TM's can be found in [1] and [5]. There were Fischer and Ladner [5] who first noticed the importance of the alternating TM's for investigations concerning the computational complexity of PDL.

Let $S : N \to N$ be a function. Classes $ASPACE(S(n))$, $NSPACE(S(n))$, $DSPACE(S(n))$ denote the sets of languages accepted in space $S(n)$ by the alternating, nondeterministic and deterministic TM's respectively. The following sets are of basic importance for the further considerations:

$PSPACE = \bigcup_{k \in N} DSPACE(n^k)$, $\qquad$ $APSPACE = \bigcup_{k \in N} ASPACE(n^k)$,

$\mathrm{EXPSPACE} = \bigcup_{c>1} \mathrm{DSPACE}(c^n)$, $\mathrm{AEXPSPACE} = \bigcup_{c>1} \mathrm{ASPACE}(c^n)$.

Let Σ_1^*, Σ_2^* be the sets of words over alphabets Σ_1, and Σ_2, and let $A \subseteq \Sigma_1^*$, $B \subseteq \Sigma_2^*$. A is said to be log-space reducible to B iff there is a function $f : \Sigma_1^* \to \Sigma_2^*$ computable in space log(n) and such that $x \in A$ iff $f(x) \in B$, for each $x \in \Sigma_1^*$. /We say $A \leq_{\log} B$ via f/. If C is a class of languages and $L \in C$, then L is said to be log-space complete in C iff $M \leq_{\log} L$ for each $M \in C$.

Let DTIME(S(n)) denote the set of languages accepted deterministically in time S(n). The following fact /Chandra, Kozen and Stockmeyer [1]/ will be helpful later:

Fact1 : Let $S(n) \geq \log n$ for each $n \in N$. Then

$$\mathrm{ASPACE}(S(n)) = \bigcup_{c>0} \mathrm{DTIME}(c^{S(n)}).$$

The following notation is useful when comparing the growth rates of functions. For function $f,g : N \to R$, we write $f(n) = o(g(n))$ iff $\liminf_{n\to\infty} (f(n)/g(n)) = 0$.

3. PAL restricted to one program variable.

Let PAL_0 denote PAL restricted to one program variable and with no program connectives. More precisely, let $V_s = \{p_0, p_1, \ldots\}$ be the infinite set of propositional variables, and K be the unique program variable. The formulas of PAL_0 are defined inductively as follows:

a/ any propositional variable is a formula;

b/ if φ, ψ are formulas, then $(\neg\varphi)$, $(\varphi \wedge \psi)$, $(K\varphi)$, $(\cap K \varphi)$, $(\cup K \varphi)$ are formulas;

c/ the set of formulas is the smallest one satisfying a/ and b/ above.

Let 2^{V_s} be the set of all valuations, i.e. functions from V_s to set $\{0,1\}$. Let X denote any sequence of valuations, $X = (x_0, x_1, \ldots)$, where X may be finite or infinite. For such X, we let X_i denote sequence $(x_i, x_{i+1}, \ldots)$, or the empty sequence Λ if X has less than (i+1) elements. For any formulas φ and ψ, sequence of valuations X, and natural number i, relation $X_i \models \varphi$ /called the satisfaction relation/ is defined inductively as follows:

0. Not $\Lambda \models \varphi$;,
1. $X_i \models p$ iff $x_i(p) = 1$, for $p \in V_s$;,
2. $X_i \models (\neg\varphi)$ iff not $X_i \models \varphi$;
3. $X_i \models (\varphi \wedge \psi)$ iff $X_i \models \varphi$ and $X_i \models \psi$;

4. $X_i \models (K\varphi)$ iff $X_{i+1} \models \varphi$;
5. $X_i \models (\bigcap K\varphi)$ iff $X_n \models \varphi$ for each $n \geq i$;
6. $X_i \models (\bigcup K\varphi)$ iff $X_n \models \varphi$ for some $n \geq i$.

We write $X \models \varphi$ to denote $X_0 \models \varphi$, and say that X is a model of φ . This logical caculus is denoted by PAL_0. It is a subsystem of PAL described in [2] and [4].

If a formula has a model, it is called satisfiable; the set of all satisfiable formulas of PAL_0 is denoted by SAT_0. The space requirements on the algorithms recognizing SAT_0 are summed up in the next theorem:

Theorem.

i/ SAT_0 is log-complete in PSPACE;
ii/ SAT_0 is a member of NSPACE(n);
iii/ SAT_0 is not a member of NSPACE(r(n)), provided function $r : N \rightarrow R$ satisfies condition $r(n) = o(n/\log n)$.

In [3] there is a nondeterministic algorithm described which recoguizes the satisfiable formulas of the whole PAL in space n^2.

4. PAL_0 with the added while-like programs.

The aim this section is to describe a certain extension of PAL_0 with the property that deciding satisfiability in it needs exponential space. Let us extend the syntax and semantics of PAL_0 by adding the following inductive clauses:

i/ if φ, ψ are formulas, $q_1,\ldots,q_n$ are propositional variables, then $([*\varphi K]\psi)$ and $([**q_1,\ldots,q_n K]\psi)$ are formulas;

ii/ $X_i \models ([*\varphi K]\psi)$ iff $X_n \models \neg\varphi$ for some $n \geq i$, and $X_n \models \psi$ for the smallest such number n;

/Let i, j be natural numbers. X_i and X_j are said to be equivalent with respect to variables $q_1,\ldots,q_n$ iff equivalence

$$X_i \models q_k \text{ iff } X_j \models q_k$$

is true for each $1 \leq k \leq n$/

iii/ $X_i \models ([**q_1,\ldots,q_n K]\varphi)$ iff there exists $j > i$ such that X_i and X_j are equivalent with respect to variables $q_1,\ldots,q_n$ and $X_j \models \varphi$ for the smallest such number j.

We denote this logic by PAL_1, and its set of satisfiable formulas by SAT_1. The program connectives defined above are called one-star while and double-star while schemes. The double-star while construct can be "eliminated" from formulas of PAL_1, i.e. for any formula φ there exists formula φ' equivalent to φ, and such that it has the one-star while programs only. The following example illustrates the idea:

$([**q_1,q_2K]\varphi)$ is equivalent to formula

$(q_1 \wedge q_2 \rightarrow K([*\neg(q_1 \wedge q_2)K]\varphi)) \wedge (q_1 \wedge \neg q_2 \rightarrow K[*\neg(q_1 \wedge \neg q_2)K]\varphi)) \wedge$
$(\neg q_1 \wedge q_2 \rightarrow K([*\neg(\neg q_1 \wedge q_2)K]\varphi)) \wedge (\neg q_1 \wedge \neg q_2 \rightarrow K[*\neg(\neg q_1 \wedge \neg q_2)K]\varphi))$

It is clear that if this method of translating is employed, the lenghts of the obtained formulas will grow exponentially. But a more general fact is true: there is no function f, computable in a polynomial space and lenght bounded by some polynomial, such that for any formula φ of PAL_1, $f(\varphi)$ is a formula of PAL_1, without the double-star while programs and equivalent to φ. It follows immediately from the next theorem.

<u>Theorem</u>.

i/ SAT_1 is log-complete in EXPSPACE;
ii/ SAT_1 is a member of NSPACE(2^n);
iii/ SAT_1 is not a member of NSPACE$(c^{n/\log n})$ for some $c > 1$.

5. PDL restricted to one program variable.

The results presented in this section do not pretend to novelty, and are included for the completeness sake. They are stated in this very form to emphasize the analogies with PAL_0 (it should be noticed that APSPACE = EXPTIME). The completeness of SAT_2 in EXPTIME follows from results of Chandra, Kozen and Stockmeyer [1] , Fischer and Ladner [5] , and Pratt [13] . The exponential lower bound on the time complexity of SAT_1 was proved by Fischer and Ladner [5] .

Let PDL_0 denote PDL restricted to one program variable and with no program connectives. More precisely, let $V_s = \{p_0, p_1, \ldots\}$ be the infinite set of propositional variables, K the only program variable, and let the formulas of PDL_0 be defined inductively as follows:

a/ any propositional variable is a formula;
b/ if φ, ψ are formulas, then $(\neg\varphi)$, $(\varphi \wedge \psi)$, $(\langle K\rangle\varphi)$, $(\langle K^*\rangle\varphi)$ are formulas;
c/ the set of formulas is the smallest one satisfying conditions

a/ and b/ above.

A structure suitable for PDL_0 is defined as a 4-tuple $\mathfrak{m} = (U,e,H,G)$ where :

U is a set of states,

$e \in U$ is distinguished in U,

$H \subseteq U \times U$ provides the interpretation of K,

$G : U \times V_s \rightarrow \{0,1\}$ provides the interpretation of the propositional variables.

Sequence of states $s_1,\dots,s_n$ is said to be a computation in $\mathfrak{m}$, if either $n = 1$ or $(s_i,s_{i+1}) \in H$ for each $1 \leq i < n$. Let structure $\mathfrak{m}$ be fixed, For any formula φ and state s, the satisfaction relation $s \models \varphi$ is defined inductively as follows:

1. $s \models p$ iff $G(s,p) = 1$, for $p \in V_s$;
2. $s \models (\neg\varphi)$ iff not $s \models \varphi$;
3. $s \models (\varphi \wedge \psi)$ iff $s \models \varphi$ and $s \models \psi$;
4. $s \models (\langle K \rangle \varphi)$ iff $s' \models \varphi$ for some $s' \in U$ such that $(s,s') \in H$;
5. $s \models (\langle K^* \rangle \varphi)$ iff $s' \models \varphi$ for some $s' \in U$ such that there is a computation $s,\dots,s'$ in $\mathfrak{m}$.

$\mathfrak{m}$ is said to be a model of φ, $\mathfrak{m} \models \varphi$, if $e \models \varphi$. Let SAT_2 denote the set of the satisfiable formulas of PDL_0. The importance of PDL_0 rests on the following theorem:

<u>Theorem.</u>

i/ SAT_2 is log-complete in APSPACE ;

ii/ SAT_2 belongs to ASPACE(n) ;

iii/ SAT_2 is not a member of ASPACE$(r(n))$, provided function $r: N \rightarrow R$ satisfies $r(n) = o(n/\log n)$.

We can translate the lower bound on the alternating space into the lower bound on the deterministic time, and obtain the following slight modification of theorem 4.4 proved by Fischer and Ladner [5]:

<u>Corollary</u>. Let $r: N \rightarrow R$ be a function such that $r(n) = o(n/\log n)$. Then, for each constant $c > 1$, SAT_2 does not belong to DTIME$(c^{r(n)})$.

<u>Proof</u>: Let $w(n) = \max(\log n, r(n))$. Since $w(n) = o(n/\log n)$, we obtain from the previous theorem that $SAT_3 \notin$ ASPACE$(w(n))$. This class equals $\bigcup_{c>0}$ DTIME$(c^{w(n)})$ by Fact 1, and hence includes $\bigcup_{c>0}$ DTIME$(c^{r(n)})$. Q.E.D.

6. PDL_0 with the added while-like programs.

Now we will present a certain extension of PDL_0. Let us add the following inductive clauses to the definition of syntax and semantics of PDL_0 :

i/ if φ , ψ are formulas, $q_1,\dots,q_n$ are propositional variables, then $(\langle * \psi K \rangle \varphi)$ and $(\langle * * q_1,\dots,q_n K \rangle \varphi)$ are formulas;

Let $\mathfrak{m}$ be a structure appropriate for PDL_0 and s be a state in $\mathfrak{m}$.

ii/ $s \models (\langle * \varphi K \rangle \psi)$ iff there is a computation $s_1,\dots,s_n$, where $s = s_1$ such that $s_n \models \neg\varphi \wedge \psi$ and, if there is $1 \leqslant i < n$, then $s_i \models \varphi$;

/States s_1 and s_2 are said to be equivalent with respect to $q_1,\dots,q_n$ iff for each $1 \leqslant i \leqslant n$, the equivalence

$$s_1 \models q_i \quad \text{iff} \quad s_2 \models q_i$$

is true/

iii/ $s \models (\langle * * q_1,\dots,q_n K \rangle \varphi)$ iff there is a computation $s, s_1,\dots,s_m$ such that $s_m \models \varphi$ and

a/ $s \neq s_1$,

b/ s and s_m are equivalent with respect to $q_1,\dots,q_n$,

c/ for any $1 \leqslant i < m$, s and s_i are not equivalent with respect to $q_1,\dots,q_n$.

This logical calculus will be denoted by PDL_1, and the set of the satisfiable formulas of PDL_1 will be denoted by SAT_3. The new program connectives may be defined by the standard PDL connectives as follows:

i/ $(\langle * \varphi K \rangle \psi)$ is equivalent to $(\langle\langle \varphi? ; K\rangle^*; \neg\varphi?\rangle \psi)$ /cf. [5] ,

ii/ the double-star while can be defined by the one-star while similarly as in PAL_1, with the exponential growth of the defining formulas.

Set SAT_3 has some properties analogous to the proved properties of SAT_1, but now the alternating TM is the appropriate model of a computing device:

Theorem.

i/ SAT_3 is log-complete in AEXPSPACE ;

ii/ SAT_3 is a member of ASPACE(2^n).

iii/ SAT_3 is not a member of ASPACE$(c^{n/\log n})$ for some $c > 1$.

Once again we can translate the lower bound into the language of deterministic time and obtain the following result:

<u>Corollary</u>. There is a constant $c > 1$ such that SAT_3 is not a member of $DTIME\left(d^{c^{n/\log n}}\right)$ for each $d > 1$.

<u>Proof</u>: Let c be as in the previous theorem. Then

$SAT_3 \notin ASPACE\left(c^{n/\log n}\right) = \bigcup_{d>0} DTIME\left(d^{c^{n/\log n}}\right)$, by Fact 1. Q.E.D.

7. Final remarks.

It should be remarked that there are two forms of nondeterminism in PDL:

1/ The program variables are interpreted nondeterministically, i.e. for given state s and program variable K, there can be many states which are connected with s by an edge being the interpretation of K;

2/ There is a nondeterministic sum of programs, i.e. given programs P and R, their sum $(P \cup R)$ is interpreted as follows: <u>begin</u> choose either P or R and execute the chosen one <u>end</u>.

It can be shown that any one of these two forms of nondeterminism in PDL is sufficient to yield the completeness result concerning EXPTIME, but in the second case, at least two program variables are needed. A similar fact holds for AEXPSPACE and PDL extended by adding the double-star while from the previous section.

Now, since SAT_0 is complete in PSPACE and SAT_1 is complete in EXPSPACE, we can derive the following conclusions:

<u>Conclusion 1</u>.

The presence of nondeterminism in the semantics of PDL_0 is essential as regards the complexity of satisfiability /i.e. set SAT_2 is not a member of PSPACE/

iff

$$PSPACE \neq APSPACE$$

iff

There is a language acceptable deterministically in time c^n for some c, which cannot be accepted deterministically in polynomial space.

Conclusion 2.

The presence of nondeterminism in the semantics of PDL_1 is essential as regards the complexity of satisfiability /i.e. set SAT_3 is not a member of EXPSPACE/

iff

$$\text{EXPSPACE} \neq \text{AEXPSPACE}$$

iff

There is a language acceptable deterministically in time c^{2^n} for some $c > 1$, which cannot be accepted deterministically in space d^n, for any $d > 0$.

All these problems are open.

References

1. A.K. Chandra, D. Kozen, and L.J. Stockmeyer, Alternation, J. Assoc. Comput. Mach. 28 /1981/, 114-133.
2. B.S. Chlebus, Completeness proofs for some logics of programs, Zeitschr. f. math. Logik und Grundlagen d. Math., to appear.
3. B.S. Chlebus, On the computational complexity of satisfiability in propositional logics of programs, Theoretical Computer Science, to appear.
4. B.S. Chlebus, On the decidability of propositional algorithmic logic, Zeitschr. f. math. Logik und Grundlagen d. Math., to appear.
5. M.J. Fischer and R.E. Ladner, Propositional dynamic logic of regular programs, J. Comput. System Sci. 18/1979/, 194-211.
6. D. Harel, A.R. Meyer and V.R. Pratt, Computability and completeness in logics of programs : preliminary report, 9th ACM Symposium on Theory of Computing /1977/, 261-268.
7. J.E. Hopcroft, and J.D. Ullman, Introduction to Automata Theory, Languages and Computation, Addison-Wesley, Reading, 1979.
8. N.D. Jones, Space-bounded reducibility among combinatorial problems, J. Comput. System Sci. 11 /1975/ 68-85.
9. A. Kreczmar, Effectivity problems of algorithmic logic, Lecture Notes in Computer Science 14 /1974/, 584-600.
10. A.R. Meyer and L.J. Stockmeyer, The equivalence problem for regular expressions with squaring requires exponential space, Proc.

13th Annual IEEE Symposium on Switching and Automata Theory /1972/, 125-129.

11. G. Mirkowska, Algorithmic logic and its applications in the theory of programs, Fund. Inform. 1 /1977/, 147-165.
12. V.R. Pratt, Semantical considerations on Floyd-Hoare logic, 17th IEEE Symposium on the Foundations of Computer Science /1976/, 109-121.
13. V.R. Pratt, A near optimal method for reasoning about action, J. Comput. System Sci. 20 /1980/, 231-254.
14. A. Salwicki, Formalized algorithmic languages, Bull. Acad. Pol. Sci., Ser. Math. 18 /1970/, 227-232.
15. W.J. Savitch, Relationships between nondeterministic tape complexities, J. Comput. System Sci. 4 /1970/, 177-192.
16. J.I. Seiferas, M.I. Fischer and A.R. Meyer, Refinements of the nondeterministic time and space hierarchies, Proc. 14th Annual IEEE Symposium on Switching and Automata Theory /1973/, 130-137.
17. M.K. Valiev, Decision complexity of variants of propositional dynamic logic, Lecture Notes in Computer Science 88 /1980/, 656-664.

ARE INFINITE BEHAVIOURS OF PARALLEL SYSTEM SCHEMATA NECESSARY?

Ludwik Czaja
Institute of Informatics, University of Warsaw
PKiN VIIIp, 00-901 Warsaw, Poland

Summary

A behaviour of a parallel system schema is a sequence of suitably choosen events occuring in progress of a computation induced by the schema. There is an evidence that any "resonable" parallel system schema is describable by means of elementary-recursive formulas with finite behaviours as operand values. There are some features usually inexpressible in any recursive way but nonetheless expressible by formulas with finite behaviours as operand values. In their number: deadlock, strong form of fairness and starvation. A weak, more adequate, form of fairness and starvation seem to exemplify features expressible by formulas with operands assuming merely infinite behaviours as their values. It turns out, however, the later formulas have their equivalent counterparts with finite behaviours as operand values. The paper discusses the issues in detail.

1. A model of parallel system schemata

Empirically, a parallel system schema may be looked upon as a collection $p_1,\dots,p_n$ of sequential processors, a collection $a_1,\dots,a_m$ of shared actions (i.e. procedures operating on shared resources) being executed by the processors, and a supervisor: a processor controlled by a collection $\{\alpha_{ij}\}$ $(i=1,\dots,n,\ j=1,\dots m)$ of synchronization rules such that p_i is permitted to start executing a_j provided that α_{ij}, a boolean function of the state of computing assumes value true. States of computing are constructed as follows. Processor p_i when running a program, can issue a signal r_{ij} of request for action a_j. This makes p_i suspend. On completion of executing a_j processor p_i issues a signal t_{ij} of termination. This makes p_i resume the program which called for a_j. Signals s_{ij} of start permission for p_i to execute a_j are being issued by the supervisor in accordance to given synchronization rules. The "timeless" signals r_{ij}, s_{ij}, t_{ij} are events and are assumed to exclude one another in time, so that time-sequences can be considered. Some of event-sequences are legal computation histories which, for the purpose of this paper will also be referred to as states of computing or behaviours. The structure of a parallel system schema is in Fig.1. The formal model is the following. Let E be a finite set of objects of three kinds called events r_{ij}, s_{ij}, t_{ij} $(i=1,\dots,n,\ j=1,\dots,m)$. E^* is the set of all the finite event-

sequences (denoted by lower case letters u,v,w,...) with empty sequence $\mathcal{E}$. E^{ω} is the set of all the infinite event-sequences (denoted by upper case letters U,V,W,...). Events r_{ij}, s_{ij}, t_{ij} are said to be caused by processor p_i. A performance of action a_j by processor p_i, denoted by p_i/a_j, is an event-sequence $r_{ij}us_{ij}wt_{ij}$ such that:
1. u contains no event caused by p_i, 2. w either contains no event caused by p_i or w contains a performance p_i/a_k (for a certain k) as its subsequence.

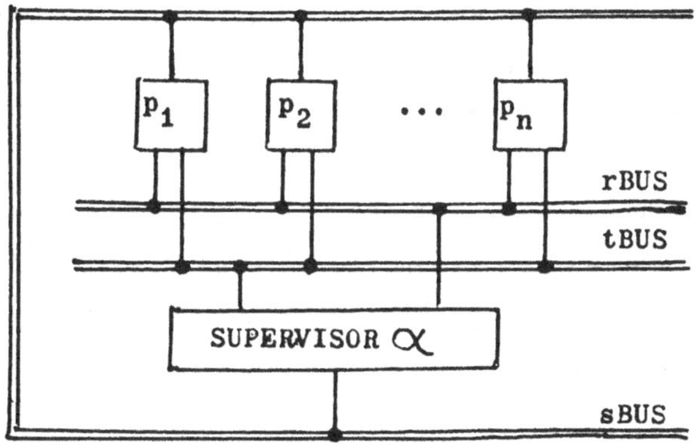

Fig.1. Structure of system schemata. Processors $p_1,\ldots,p_n$ send requests on rBUS and terminations on tBUS. The SUPERVISOR takes them and sends starting signals on sBUS, form which they are taken and performed by the processors.

Definition 1.1 (Set E^*_{corr} - general case)

An event-sequence v is said to be correct provided that either it is $\mathcal{E}$, or else for any i,j,k:

1. any s_{ij} in v must be preceded by an r_{ij} with no event caused by p_i in between,
2. any t_{ij} in v is the final event of a performance p_i/a_j contained in v, as its subsequence,
3. any r_{ij} in v must not be preceded by an r_{ik} unless s_{ik} occurs in between.

The set of all the correct finite event-sequences is denoted by E^*_{corr}. In general case a processor is allowed requesting actions while executing an action. If the processors are forbiden doing this then the structure of E^*_{corr} simplifies:

Definition 1.2 (Set E^*_{corr} - simple case)

Replace in Definition 1.1 point 2 by the text: " any t_{ij} in v must be preceded by an s_{ij} with no event caused by p_i in between" and 3 by the text: "any r_{ij} in v must not be preceded by an r_{ik} unless t_{ik} occurs in between".

Usually, in a particular system, not every correct event-sequence can appear as a time-sequence of events due to some constraints imposed by synchronization rules. They are two-valued partial functions: $\alpha_{ij} : E^* \to \{\underline{true}, \underline{false}\}$, their collection for i=1,..,n, j=1,..,m denoted by α. Their domain is E^*_{corr}. $\alpha_{ij}(v)$ is an authorization condition for s_{ij} in the state v. It is assumed $\alpha_{ij}(v) \supset wait_{ij}(v)$ as an axiom, where $wait_{ij}(v)$, meaning "processor p_i waits for action a_j", is defined below. The axiom ensures that the start signal s_{ij} will not be issued unless processor p_i waits for action a_j, or equivalently, unless $vs_{ij} \in E^*_{corr}$.

Definition 1.3 (Parallel system schema and the set E^*_{PS})

A parallel system schema, PS schema in short, is a pair $PS=(E,\alpha)$. The set E^*_{PS} of all the finite computation histories generated by PS is defined recursively: $\varepsilon \in E^*_{PS}$; if $v \in E^*_{PS}$ then:

(1) $vr_{ij} \in E^*_{PS}$ iff $vr_{ij} \in E^*_{corr}$

(2) $vt_{ij} \in E^*_{PS}$ iff $vt_{ij} \in E^*_{corr}$

(3) $vs_{ij} \in E^*_{PS}$ iff $\alpha_{ij}(v) = \underline{true}$

Definition 1.4 (Set E^ω_{PS})

The set of infinite computation histories generated by PS is:

$$E^\omega_{PS} = \{V \in E^\omega: \forall_{v \in E^*} ((\exists_{W \in E^\omega} V = vW) \supset v \in E^*_{PS})\}$$

In words: E^ω_{PS} is the set of all the infinite event-sequences whose prefixes are in E^*_{PS}.

In the sequel some notational conventions are used:

(1) Auxiliary predicates. Let $e \in E$, $v \in E^*$, $V \in E^\omega$.

$$e \ \underline{in} \ v = \exists_{u,w \in E^*} v = uew \qquad (e \ \underline{in} \ V = \exists_{u \in E^*, W \in E^\omega} V = ueW)$$

In words: event e occurs in the sequence v (V).

$$wait_{ij}(v) = \exists_{u,v \in E^*} (v = ur_{ij}w \wedge \neg\, s_{ij} \ \underline{in} \ w)$$

In words: processor p_i requesting action a_j has not been served up to current, i.e. by the time when the computation history became v; thus, p_i currently is waiting for a_j.

(2) Derivative. Let $S \subseteq E^*$ or $S \subseteq E^\omega$, $v \in E^*$. Then the set: $S/\!/v = \{z: vz \in S\}$ ($z \in E^*$ or $z \in E^\omega$) is said to be a derivative of S with respect to v.

(3) Denotations. $\emptyset$ denotes the empty set, N the set of all nonnegative integers, $|v|$ the length of $v \in E^*$, $\exists_{i,j}$ abbreviates $\exists_{1 \leq i \leq n} \exists_{1 \leq j \leq m}$ (similarly for $\forall$).

<u>Examples</u>

1.1. First Come First Served (FCFS) scheduling

Processors requesting actions are served in FCFS order, which is specified by the following synchronization rules:

$\alpha_{ij}(v) = \text{wait}_{ij}(v) \wedge \text{FCFS}_{ij}(v)$, where $\text{FCFS}_{ij}(v)$ is constructed as follows. Let $w\ \underline{\text{suffix}}\ v = \exists_{u \in E^*}\ v = uw$ and let

$l_{ij}(v) = \min\{|w| : w\ \underline{\text{suffix}}\ v \wedge \text{wait}_{ij}(w)\}$. In words: $l_{ij}(v)$ is the length of the shortest suffix of v, which begins with r_{ij} and contains no event caused by p_i to the right of r_{ij} (if there is no such suffix then $l_{ij}(v) = 0$). Thus $\text{FCFS}_{ij}(v) = \forall_{k,t}\ l_{kt}(v) \leq l_{ij}(v)$

1.2. Readers-Writers with priority to the readers

Let a_1 be WRITE, a_2 - READ actions, thus, a processor executing a_1 is a writer and executing a_2 is a reader. No processor may request an action while it is executing an action, so the set E^*_{corr} is as in Definition 1.2. For a writer p_i to be admitted to execute a_1 no processor may be executing, no processor may be waiting for a_2 and of all the processors waiting for a_1, p_i is waiting longest. For a reader p_i to admitted to execute a_2 no writer may be writing and of all the processors waiting for reading, p_i is waiting longest. Formally, these synchronization rules are expressed as:

$$\alpha_{ij}(v) = \text{wait}_{ij}(v) \wedge \text{mutex}_{ij}(v) \wedge \text{sched}_{ij}(v)$$

where $\text{mutex}_{ij}(v)$, $\text{sched}_{ij}(v)$ are factors responsible for mutual exclusion and scheduling respectively and are defined for the writers and the readers separately as follows. Let

$$\text{exec}_{ij}(v) = \exists_{u,w \in E^*} (v = us_{ij}w \wedge \neg\, t_{ij}\ \underline{\text{in}}\ w)$$

In words: processor p_i is currently executing a_j. Indeed, this is by virtue of simplified E^*_{corr}. For a writer p_i:

$$\mathrm{mutex}_{i1}(v) = \forall_{k,l} \neg\, \mathrm{exec}_{kl}(v)$$

$$\mathrm{sched}_{i1}(v) = (\neg \exists_k \mathrm{wait}_{k2}(v)) \wedge \forall_k l_{k1}(v) \leqslant l_{i1}(v)$$

For a reader p_i:

$$\mathrm{mutex}_{i2}(v) = \forall_k \neg\, \mathrm{exec}_{k1}(v)$$

$$\mathrm{sched}_{i2}(v) = \forall_k l_{k2}(v) \leqslant l_{i2}(v) \qquad (l_{ij}(v) \text{ is as in Example 1.2}).$$

Note that $\alpha_{ij}(v)$ defined above provide deadlock-free system. An example of a deadlock-sensitive system is obtained if the readers were scheduled e.g. by the formula:

$$\mathrm{sched}_{i2}(v) = (\neg \exists_k \mathrm{wait}_{k1}(v)) \wedge \forall_k l_{k2}(v) \leqslant l_{i2}(v)$$

2. Some properties

(1) $E^*_{PS} = E^*_{corr} \cap E^*_{syn}$, where $E^*_{syn} =$

$$\{v \in E^* : \forall_{i,j} \ \forall_{1 \leqslant k \leqslant |v|} \ \forall_{u,w \in E^*} ((|u| = k-1 \wedge v = us_{ij}w) \supset \alpha_{ij}(u))\}$$

(So, the factor E^*_{syn} is responsible for synchronization).
The proof is by noting that

$$ve \in E^*_{PS} \text{ iff } v \in E^*_{PS} \wedge ve \in E^*_{corr} \wedge (e = s_{ij} \supset \alpha_{ij}(v))$$

and applying induction on the length of event-sequences.

(2) Simplified E^*_{corr} (Definition 1.2) is a regular set over the alphabet E. Proof is in [1].

(3) The mutex-Rseq-FCFS class. This is the class of schemas of the following features:

(a) a statically imposed mutual exclusion among some performances (e.g. "in no state, p_i/a_j may overlap with p_k/a_l"). For an example refer to the factor mutex in Readers-Writers.

(b) a limited sort of statically imposed sequencing of mutually exclusive performances - the one expressible in any regular way, e.g. by finite-state machines, regular expressions or left (right) linear grammars (cf. [1]).

(c) FCFS scheduling, possibly with priorities: of all the processors waiting and enabled according to the rules (a) and (b) the one of the highest priority is scheduled to start; if there are a number of such processors, the longest waiting one is scheduled to start.

(d) no processor is allowed requesting actions while executing an action. Thus, E^*_{corr} is simplified, hence regular.

PS schemas from the mutex-Rseq-FCFS class generate regular sets E^*_{PS}. Proof is in [2]. Note that for this class the synchronization rules are of the form:

$$\alpha_{ij}(v) = wait_{ij}(v) \wedge mutex_{ij}(v) \wedge seq_{ij}(v) \wedge sched_{ij}(v)$$

where mutex, seq, sched are responsible for (a), (b), (c) features respectively. They have been constructed in [1,2].

(4) The set E^*_{PS} is a tree structure: ε is the root, the nodes are elements of E^*_{PS}, v is the father of u iff u=ve for a certain $e \in E$. A leaf represents either a total deadlock (see below) or an ultimate termination of PS. The set $E^*_{PS}/\!/v$ is a subtree of E^*_{PS}, with v as the root. The tree structure of E^*_{PS} suggests using in some considerations on PS schemas the following, a slightly modified:

<u>König's Lemma</u> (cf.[4])

Let S be a set and T be a tree of the properties:

(a) there are a finite number of sons of each node,

(b) for any $k \in N$ there exists a finite branch b such that $|b| \geqslant k$ and $b \subseteq S$.

Then, there exists an <u>infinite</u> branch B such that $B \subseteq S$.

The Lemma is applied in the proof of Theorem 3.1.

(5) Mutual exclusion, sequencing and scheduling are expressible in terms of <u>finite</u> behaviours (cf.[1]). Also are deadlocks: a PS = (E,α) is said to be in a common, "stabilized" and "total" deadlock in the state v iff the respective formula:

$$\exists_{i,j}\ wait_{ij}(v) \wedge D_{ij}(v) \qquad \text{(common)}$$

$$\left(\exists_{i,j}\ wait_{ij}(v)\right) \wedge \forall_{i,j}\ \left(wait_{ij}(v) \supset D_{ij}(v)\right) \qquad \text{(stabilized)}$$

$$\forall_{i}\ \exists_{j} \left(wait_{ij}(v) \wedge D_{ij}(v)\right) \qquad \text{(total)}$$

holds, where

$$D_{ij}(v) = \bigvee_{w \in E^*} (vw \in E^*_{PS} \supset \neg\, s_{ij} \ \underline{\text{in}}\ w).$$

Some necessary and suffucient conditions for deadlock are in [3].

3. Two descriptions of fairness and their equivalence

A PS schema is fair in a state v if each waiting in this state processor will start after a finite time - regardless of further progress of computing. PS is fair if it is fair in each state. Intuitively it might seem that there are two different cases possible:

(1) a "strong" fairness, when there always is a deadline in time up to which each waiting processor will start, no matter how the computation of the whole system develops; and more adequate

(2) a "weak" fairness - when such a deadline can grow limitlessly, depending on a progress of computation. Let us construct formulas for these two cases.

Strong fairness: formula SF(v)

A PS schema is strongly fair in the state v, if all the possible computation histories may be jointly ("uniformly") bounded in length, so that start signals of all the waiting (in v) processors occur in the sector of each computation history between v and this boundary. A formula expressing this property is:

$$\exists_{d \in N} \bigvee_{i,j} (\text{wait}_{ij}(v) \supset F_{ij}(v,d)) \qquad \text{where}$$

$$F_{ij}(v,d) = \bigvee_{w \in E^*} ((vw \in E^*_{PS} \wedge |w| \geq d) \supset s_{ij} \ \underline{\text{in}}\ w)$$

Formula $F_{ij}(v,d)$ expresses: any "sufficiently long", i.e. not shorter than d, continuation of the history v comprises s_{ij}. Since $\bigvee_{i,j}$ is the finite conjunction, $d' \leq d''$ implies $F_{ij}(v,d') \supset F_{ij}(v,d'')$ and $\text{wait}_{ij}(v)$ does not depend on d, the formula SF(v) expressing strong fairness is:

$$SF(v) = \bigvee_{i,j} (\text{wait}_{ij}(v) \supset \exists_{d \in N} F_{ij}(v,d))$$

Weak fairness: formula WF(v)

A PS schema is weakly fair in the state v, if start signals of all the waiting (in v) processors occur in each infinite computation history beginning in v. The formula WF(v) expressing it is:

$$WF(v) = \forall_{i,j} \left(wait_{ij}(v) \supset \forall_{W \in E^{\omega}} \left(vW \in E_{PS}^{\omega} \supset s_{ij} \ \underline{in} \ W \right) \right)$$

The main theorem of this paper establishes equivalence of strong and weak fairness:

Theorem 3.1

SF(v) iff WF(v), for any $v \in E_{PS}^{*}$

Proof

It suffices to show that

$$\exists_{d \in N} F_{ij}(v,d) \quad \text{iff} \quad \forall_{W \in E^{\omega}} \left(vW \in E_{PS}^{\omega} \supset s_{ij} \ \underline{in} \ W \right)$$

The "$\Rightarrow$" is obvious, it remains to demonstrate "$\Leftarrow$".

Suppose $\neg \exists_{d \in N} F_{ij}(v,d)$, that is:

$$\forall_{d \in N} \exists_{w \in E^{*}} \left(\left(vw \in E_{PS}^{*} \wedge |w| \geqslant d \right) \wedge \neg s_{ij} \ \underline{in} \ w \right)$$

In words: there exists an arbitrarily long finite branch beginning in v and comprising no s_{ij}. Thus, for $T = E_{PS}^{*}$, $S = E_{PS}^{*}/\!/v - E^{*}s_{ij}E^{*}$ all premisses of the König's Lemma are met, since S is the set of all finite branches of the subtree $E_{PS}^{*}/\!/v$ comprising no s_{ij}. Hence, there exists an infinitely long branch W_0 beginning in v, such that all the nodes of W_0, i.e. prefixes of the event-sequence W_0 belong to S. By Definition 1.4 and defintion of derivative $/\!/$:

$W_0 \in E_{PS}^{\omega}/\!/v - E^{*}s_{ij}E^{\omega}$ - a contradiction with the formula

$\forall_{W \in E^{\omega}} \left(vW \in E_{PS}^{\omega} \supset s_{ij} \ \underline{in} \ W \right)$ equivalent to $E_{PS}^{\omega}/\!/v - E^{*}s_{ij}E^{\omega} = \emptyset$ (cf. [3]).

Q.E.D.

Theorem 3.1 and some results from [3] bring to:

Corollary 3.1

$$WF(v) \quad \text{iff} \quad \forall_{i,j} \, (wait_{ij}(v) \supset E^{*}_{PS}/\!\!/v - E^{*}s_{ij}E^{*} \ \underline{\text{is finite}})$$

thus, weak fairness decision problem for a class $\mathcal{P}$ of PS schemas is equivalent to the finiteness decision problem for the family of sets $\{E^{*}_{PS}/\!\!/v-E^{*}sE^{*}\}(PS \in \mathcal{P},\ v \in E^{*}_{PS},\ s \in \{s_{ij}\}$, $i=1,..,n$, $j=1,..,m)$. For example, weak fairness decision problem for PS schemas generating context-free sets E^{*}_{PS}, is algorithmically solvable.

From the Corollary 3.1 and Section 2, point 3 we obtain:

Corollary 3.2

Weak fairness decision problem for the class mutex-Rseq-FCFS of PS schemas is algorithmically solvable. Moreover, for a fixed PS schema from this class, the family $\{E^{*}_{PS}/\!\!/v - E^{*}s_{ij}E^{*}\}$ $(v \in E^{*}_{PS}$, $i=1,\dots,n$, $j=1,\dots,m)$ is finite, since E^{*}_{PS} is a regular set. Thus, there is a universal procedure, capable of statically (i.e. before the run) detecting all the potentially unfair (i.e. starving) situations in any fixed schema from the class mutex-Rseq-FCFS - if these situations follow from a description of the schema, not from its interpretation.

4. Conclusion

Theorem 3.1 establishes that the two seemingly different concepts of fairness which we named here strong and weak fairness, turn out to be two different descriptions of the same phenomenon: fairness, as commonly understood property of a parallel system in which each waiting processor will continue its work after a finite time. Although, description by the formula WF(v) (second order formula) is perhaps more appealing, the formula SF(v) (first order formula) is simpler logically, as it does not require introducing infinitely long event-sequences. Since neither relatively simple features, like mutual exclusion, scheduling , sequencing, nor more complicated, like deadlocks or starvation (i.e. negation of fairness) require infinitely long event-sequences, the question arises: are there any realistic features which essentialy require infinite event-sequences in order to be expressed?

Acknowledgment

The remark on using König's Lemma in proving Theorem 3.1 is due to Mr. P.Urzyczyn.

References

[1] L.Czaja, A specification of parallel problems, Information Processing Letters, 8(4)(1979) 162-167

[2] L.Czaja, Parallel system schemas and their relation to automata, Information Processing Letters, 10(3) (1980) 153-158

[3] L.Czaja, Deadlock and fairness in parallel schemas: a set-theoretic characterization and decision problems, Information Processing Letters, 10 (4,5) (1980) 234-239

[4] D.König, Über eine Schlussweise aus dem Endlichen ins Umendliche, Acta Litt. Ac. Sci. Hung. Fran. Josep. 3 (1927), 121-130

ALGORITHMIC PROPERTIES OF FINITELY GENERATED STRUCTURES

Wiktor Dańko

Institute of Mathematics
University of Warsaw, Białystok Division
Akademicka 2, 15-267 Białystok, Poland

Abstract

We consider abstract structures and relations definable in those structures by formulas of Algorithmic Logic [1,3,14]. We notice that in the case where a structure is finitely generated every relation defined by an algorithmic formula can be defined by an algorithmic formula without classical quantifiers. Using the above fact we prove analogons of Łoś-Tarski Theorem for Algorithmic Logic and for $L_{\omega_1\omega}$.

1. Introduction

In this paper we shall deal with abstract structures and algorithms over them. We shall consider properties of structures which can be formulated in terms of algorithms. For instance, if the algorithm

<u>begin</u> x:= 1 ; <u>while</u> x $\neq$ 0 <u>do</u> x:= x + 1 <u>end</u>

halts in a field then the characteristic of this field is finite. However, algorithms will be rather tools than objects of our investigations.

We have at our disposal several formal definitions of the notion of algorithm program over a structure [1,3,7,11,20,22]. We choose the definition contained in the system of Algorithmic Logic. We shall use the language of Algorithmic Logic with tables and classical quantifiers [3] which is an extension of the first order language and contains two additional kinds of expressions

- algorithms (programs)
- algorithmic formulas describing properties of programs

Every algorithmic formula may be treated as a formula from $L_{\omega_1\omega}$ (compare [12,22]). We recall basic notions concerning Algorithmic Logic in Section 2.

Used here system of Algorithmic Logic is the system best known to the author. It is equivalent to the logic of effective definitions defined by J.Tiuryn in [22]. The logic of effective definitions LED was constructed in order to express properties of algorithms interpreted as Friedman's schemes [7]. The "computational" powers of programs with tables and Friedman's schemes are the same and many other classes of program schemes are inter-translatable with the Friedman's schemes (compare [22]). These facts motivate our choice of the notion of algorithm.

By an algorithmic theory we shall mean a theory based on a language and the consequence operation of Algorithmic Logic (compare [1,3, 13]). In [3] it was proved the completeness theorem for theories based on Algorithmic Logic with tables and classical quantifiers.

We first consider algorithmic theories of finitely generated structures. It is easy to prove that every relation defined in a finitely generated structure by an algorithmic formula may be defined by an algorithmic formula without classical quantifiers. As a corollary we obtain that for a given finitely generated structure $\mathfrak{A}$ we are able to find a set of algorithmic formulas such that every model of it is isomorphic to $\mathfrak{A}$. Moreover, it is possible to find such a set of formulas consisting of formulas without classical quantifiers.

The following problem arises in a natural way: when is a given algorithmic theory equivalent to an algorithmic theory based on axioms not containing classical quantifiers ?

In the case of first order theories this problem was solved by Łoś and Tarski (cf. for example [21]). We prove an analogon of Łoś-Tarski Theorem for Algorithmic Logic with tables and classical quantifiers. The method of reasoning can be also used in the case of $L_{\omega_1\omega}$.

Algorithmic theories axiomatizable without classical quantifiers have a property similar to the property of open first order theories: Let T be an algorithmic theory based on axioms not containing classical quantifiers. Then every theorem of T not containing classical quantifiers can be proved (in T) by means of axioms and rules of inference which do not contain classical quantifiers.

The next problem considered in this paper is concerned with the number of generators of models of algorithmic theories. It can be formulated in the following way:
Let T be an algorithmic theory such that for every natural number n there is a model of T with at least n generators. Is there a model of T with infinite number of generators? In Section 3 we show that the answer is negative.

2. Algorithmic Logic and its semantics, notation and basic facts.

We first recall some notions concerning the system of Algorithmic Logic with tables and classical quantifiers defined in [3] . The presented here version is a simplification of the version contained in [

Let $\mathfrak{A} = \langle A, f_1,\ldots,f_n, r_1,\ldots,r_m \rangle$ be a structure with universe A, functions $f_1,\ldots,f_n$ and relations $r_1,\ldots,r_m$. We associate with an algorithmic language with tables and classical quantifiers which is a modification of the language described in [3]. The alphabet of this language contains the following sets of symbols

$\Phi = \{ \varphi_1,\ldots,\varphi_n \}$ - the set of functors

$P = \{ \varrho_1,\ldots,\varrho_m \}$ - the set of predicates

$\mathfrak{X} = \{X,Y,Z, \ldots \}$ - the set of names of tables of individual variables

$V_N = \{ i,j,k, \ldots \}$ - the set of index variables which are interpreted as natural numbers

$\{ 0,s,= \}$ where s denotes the successor function in the set of natural numbers, 0 denotes the number zero and = denotes the identity relation

The set I of indices is the set of terms constructed with the use of the constant symbol 0, the index variables from V_N and the symbol s of the successor function.

The set T of terms is the least set of expressions containing all expressions of the form X[t] where $X \in \mathfrak{X}$, $t \in I$ and such that if $\varphi \in \Phi$ is an r-argument functor and $\tau_1,\ldots,\tau_r \in T$ then $\varphi(\tau_1,\ldots,\tau_r) \in T$.

The set V_i of individual variables is the set of all expressions of the form $X[\bar{n}]$ where $X \in \mathfrak{X}$, n is a natural number and $\bar{n}$ denotes the index $\underbrace{s(\ldots s(0)\ldots)}_{n \text{ times}}$.

The set F_o of open formulas is the least set of expressions containing all expressions of the form $\varrho(\tau_1,\ldots,\tau_r)$ where $\varrho \in P$ is an r-argument predicate and $\tau_1,\ldots,\tau_r \in T$ and such that if α, $\beta \in F_o$ then $\neg\alpha$, $(\alpha \wedge \beta)$, $(\alpha \vee \beta)$, $(\alpha \rightarrow \beta)$, $(\alpha \leftrightarrow \beta) \in F_o$.

The set S of assignements is the set of all expressions of the form $z := w$ where z is an index variable and w is an index or z is a term of the form X[t] and w is a term.

The set Pr of programs is the least set of expressions containing all assignements and such that if $K,M \in Pr$ and γ is an open formul then

$\underline{\text{begin}}$ K ; M $\underline{\text{end}}$, $\underline{\text{if}}$ γ $\underline{\text{then}}$ K , $\underline{\text{while}}$ γ $\underline{\text{do}}$ K

are in Pr.

Let K be a program and let v be a valuation of variables. By $K_{\alpha}(v)$ we shall denote the valuation of variables after execution of the program K ($K_{\alpha}(v)$ may be undefined).

In the whole paper we shall use the same notation and terminology as in [3,1,13,16].

Let us consider an example. Let K denote the following program

$\underline{\text{begin}}$ i:= 0 ; $\underline{\text{while}}$ X[i] $\neq$ a $\underline{\text{do}}$ i:= i+1 $\underline{\text{end}}$

This program stops if and only if the sequence of values of variables v(X[0]) , v(X[1]) , v(X[2]) , ... contains the element denoted by a. The realization of the program K depends on values of infinite number of variables.

We now define a set $Pr_o \subset Pr$ of programs such that for every program M from Pr_o we can effectively find a finite set V(M) of individual and index variables such that the realization of the program M depends on the values of variables from V(M) only.

Let K be a program from Pr such that the symbol s of the successor function occurs only in assignements of the form j:= t . We also assume that t contains at most one occurrence of the symbol s. Let $\mathcal{X}_K = \{X_1, \ldots, X_p\}$ be the set of all names of tables of individual variables occurring in K and let $I_K = \{i_1, \ldots, i_r\}$ be the set of all index variables occurring in K. Let i be an index variable not occurring in K. By $K_{(i)}$ we shall denote the program obtained from K after simultaneous replacing all assignements of the form j:= s(k) by the subprogram

```
begin
    j:= s(k)  ;
    if  j > i  then
        begin
            i:= s(i)  ;
            X1[j] := X1[0]  ; . . . ;  Xp[j] := Xp[0]
        end.
end
```

One can prove that the realization of the program

$\underline{\text{begin}}$ i:= 0 ; $K_{(i)}$ $\underline{\text{end}}$

only depends on the values of variables $X_1[0], \ldots, X_p[0], i_1, \ldots, i_r$.

(compare [3]). Thus individual variables with indices greater than zero play a role of auxiliary variables and every program of the above form can be viewed as a program with finite number of input variables and infinite number of auxiliary variables.

The set Pr_0 of programs is the least set of programs containing all programs of the form <u>begin</u> i:= 0 ; $K_{(i)}$ <u>end</u> and such that if $K,M \in Pr_0$ and γ is an open formula without subexpressions of the form X[t] where t contains an index variable then

<u>begin</u> K ; M <u>end</u> , <u>if</u> γ <u>then</u> K , <u>while</u> γ <u>do</u> K

belong to Pr_0.

It is easy to see that for every program M from Pr_0 we can effectively find the set V(M) of variables such that the realization of M only depends on the values of variables from V(M) .

The set of formulas is the least set of expressions containing all open formulas without subexpressions of the form X[t] where t contains an index variable and satisfying the following conditions

- if $\alpha,\beta \in F$ then $\neg\alpha$, $(\alpha \vee \beta)$, $(\alpha \wedge \beta)$, $(\alpha \rightarrow \beta)$, $(\alpha \leftrightarrow \beta) \in F$
- if $\alpha \in F$ and x is an individual variable then $\exists x \alpha$, $\forall x \alpha \in F$
- if $\alpha \in F$ and M is a program from Pr_0 then $M\alpha$, $\bigcup M\alpha$, $\bigcap M\alpha \in F$

The logical value of a formula of the form $M\alpha$ is defined in the following way

$$M\alpha_{\mathfrak{a}}(v) = \begin{cases} 1 & \text{if the valuation } v' = M_{\mathfrak{a}}(v) \text{ is defined} \\ & \quad \text{and } \alpha_{\mathfrak{a}}(v') = 1 \\ 0 & \text{otherwise} \end{cases}$$

The meaning of iteration quantifiers is defined as follows

$$\bigcup M\alpha_{\mathfrak{a}}(v) = \sup_{i \in N} M^i\alpha_{\mathfrak{a}}(v)$$

$$\bigcap M\alpha_{\mathfrak{a}}(v) = \inf_{i \in N} M^i\alpha_{\mathfrak{a}}(v)$$

N denotes the set of natural numbers

where M^i denotes the composition i times of the program M.
For every formula α we can find a finite set of individual and index variables such that the logical value of the formula α only depends on values of the variables from this set. We shall denote this set by $V(\alpha)$. The variables from $V(\alpha)$ we shall call free variables of the formula α .

The language of Algorithmic Logic with tables and classical quantifiers defined above we shall denote by $L_{\exists T}$. We shall also consider some sublanguages of $L_{\exists T}$. All of them are based on the sets of functors predicates and individual variables of the language $L_{\exists T}$:

$L_{\exists}$ - the language of Algorithmic Logic with classical quantifiers defined and investigated in [1] (without tables)

L - the language of Algorithmic Logic (without tables and classical quantifiers) defined and investigated in [13]

L_1 - the language of first order logic

Obviously

$$\left.\begin{matrix} L \subset \\ L_1 \subset \end{matrix}\right\} L_{\exists} \subset L_{\exists T}$$

The sets of programs of the languages L, $L_{\exists}$ are identical and every program from L ($L_{\exists}$) does not contain index variables.

For every language $\mathcal{L} \in \{L, L_1, L_{\exists}, L_{\exists T}\}$ we have a corresponding consequence operation $\mathcal{C} \in \{C, C_1, C_{\exists}, C_{\exists T}\}$ defined in [14], [15], [1], [3] respectively. The consequence operations C, $C_{\exists}$, $C_{\exists T}$ are based on recursive sets of logical axioms and ω-rules of inference.

By a theory T based on the language $\mathcal{L}$ and the consequence operation $\mathcal{C}$ we shall mean a system $T = \langle \mathcal{L}, \mathcal{C}, Ax \rangle$ where Ax is a fixed set of formulas from $\mathcal{L}$ called nonlogical axioms of T. Formulas from $\mathcal{C}(Ax)$ we shall call theorems of the theory T. We shall often write $T \vdash \alpha$ instead of $\alpha \in \mathcal{C}(Ax)$. We shall also use the notation $T \models \alpha$ and $\mathfrak{A} \models \alpha$. We assume that its meaning is known.

For every language $\mathcal{L} \in \{L, L_1, L_{\exists}, L_{\exists T}\}$ and corresponding consequence operation $\mathcal{C} \in \{C, C_1, C_{\exists}, C_{\exists T}\}$ the completeness theorem holds

$$T \vdash \alpha \quad \text{iff} \quad T \models \alpha$$

(compare [14,15,1,3]).

Similarly to the case of the language of the language $L_{\exists}$ we can prove theorems on normal forms of programs and formulas for the language $L_{\exists T}$ (compare [1]).

In the sequel we shall assume that the set of predicates contains the sign = of equality. A structure for $\mathcal{L}$ will be called proper for equality if the sign = is realized as the identity relation.

We shall only consider structures of finite signature.

As we have mentioned above programs with tables with finite number of input variables i.e. programs from Pr_0 and Friedman's schemes are equally powerfull. In the sequel we shall use some properties of Friedman's schemes formulated in terms of programs with tables.

3. Finitely generated structures.

We recall some facts from [2] useful in further considerations. It is also possible to infer these facts from the relationship between programs with tables and Friedman's schemes.

Let $L_{\exists T}$ be a language of Algorithmic Logic with tables and classical quantifiers described in Section 2. Let $\{Y_1,\ldots,Y_k\}$ be a set of names of tables of individual variables. By Nr we shall denote the following enumeration of symbols of the language $L_{\exists T}$:

0	(	)	s	,	[	]	φ_1	...	φ_n	Y_1	...	Y_k
0	1	2	3	4	5	6	7	...	n+6	n+7	...	n+k+6

We extend Nr on the set of terms constructed from the functors $\varphi_1,\ldots,\varphi_n$ and the variables $Y_1[0]$, ..., $Y_k[0]$ (we adopt a standard Godel coding; cf. for example [21]) . We shall often denote the variable $Y_i[0]$ by y_i .

Let $\tau_0, \tau_1, \tau_2, \ldots$ be the sequence of all terms from $L_{\exists T}$ constructed with the use of the functors $\varphi_1,\ldots,\varphi_n$ and the variables $y_1,\ldots,y_k$ ordered with respect to the enumeration Nr. The following lemma is essential for our further investigations of finitely generated structures (compare [2] p.105) .

Lemma 1 ([2])

There is a program K with input variables $i, y_1, \ldots, y_k$ and an output variable x such that

$v(i) = n$ implies $v'(x) = \tau_{n\,\mathfrak{A}}(v)$

where v' denotes the valuation $K_{\mathfrak{A}}(v)$.

We shall denote this program by K_{term} .

Let w be an expression of $L_{\exists T}$, $V(w) = \{y_1,\ldots,y_k, i_1,\ldots,i_r\}$ We shall often write $w(y_1,\ldots,y_k, i_1,\ldots,i_r)$ instead of w .

Let $\mathfrak{A} = \langle A, f_1,\ldots,f_n, r_1,\ldots,r_m,=\rangle$ be a structure and let $a_1,\ldots,a_k \in A$. By $[a_1,\ldots,a_k]_{\mathfrak{A}}$ we shall denote the substructure of $\mathfrak{A}$ generated by the set $\{a_1,\ldots,a_k\}$. We shall often write $[a_1,\ldots,a_k]$ instead of $[a_1,\ldots,a_k]_{\mathfrak{A}}$ if it does not lead to any confusion.

Let us make two simple remarks:

Remark 1

Let $\mathfrak{A} = \langle A, \ldots\rangle$ be a structure and let $\mathfrak{A}_0 = \langle A_0, \ldots\rangle$ be a substructure of $\mathfrak{A}$. Let $L_{\exists T}$ be a language for $\mathfrak{A}$ and let K be a program. If $v(x) \in A_0$ for every individual variable x from V(K) and $v' = K_{\mathfrak{A}}(v)$ is defined then for every individual variable z $v(z) \neq v'(z)$ implies $v'(z) \in A_o$.

Remark 2

Let $\mathfrak{A} = \langle A, \ldots \rangle$ be a structure and let $L_{\exists T}$ be a language for it. Let $\alpha(y_1,\ldots,y_k, i_1,\ldots,i_r) \in L_{\exists T}$ be a formula without classical quantifiers. Then

$$\alpha_{\mathfrak{A}}(v) = \alpha_{\mathfrak{A}_o}(v)$$

where $\mathfrak{A}_o$ denotes the substructure of $\mathfrak{A}$ generated by elements $v(y_1)$, $\ldots, v(y_k)$.

The following lemma is fundamental

Lemma 2

Let $\mathfrak{A} = \langle A, \ldots \rangle$ be a structure and let $L_{\exists T}$ be a language for it. For every formula $\alpha(x_1,\ldots,x_p, i_1,\ldots,i_r)$ there is a formula $\alpha_k^o(x_1,\ldots,x_p, y_1,\ldots,y_k, i_1,\ldots,i_r)$ without classical quantifiers such that for every substructure $[b_1,\ldots,b_k]$ of $\mathfrak{A}$ the following implication holds:

if $v(y_i) = b_i$ for $i = 1,\ldots,k$ and $v(x_i) \in [b_1,\ldots,b_k]$ for $i = 1,\ldots,p$ then

$$\alpha^o_{k\,\mathfrak{A}}(v) = \alpha_{[b_1,\ldots,b_k]}(v)$$

The idea of the proof.

The proof of Lemma 2 proceeds by induction on the length of a formula. It makes essential use of Remarks 1,2 and the idea of the proof is to eliminate the classical quantifiers by iteration ones. The method of elimination can be illustrated informally:

$$y \in [y_1,\ldots,y_k] \leftrightarrow y = \tau_0 \vee y = \tau_1 \vee y = \tau_2 \vee \ldots$$

The countable disjunction of the right side of the above equivalence can be expressed by a formula of $L_{\exists T}$

$$y \in [y_1,\ldots,y_k] \leftrightarrow i:= 0 \bigcup \underline{\text{begin}}\ K_{term}\ ;\ i:= s(i)\ \underline{\text{end}}\ (x = y)$$

where the meaning of K_{term}, τ_n is the same as in Lemma 1.

Thus, we have

$$\exists y\,(y \in [y_1,\ldots,y_k] \wedge \beta(y)) \leftrightarrow i:= 0 \bigcup \underline{\text{begin}}\ K_{term}\ ;\ i:= s(i)\ \underline{\text{end}}\ \beta(x)$$

$$\forall y\,(y \in [y_1,\ldots,y_k] \rightarrow \beta(y)) \leftrightarrow i:= 0 \bigcap \underline{\text{begin}}\ K_{term}\ ;\ i:= s(i)\ \underline{\text{end}}\ \beta(x)$$

The induction step in the definition of the formula α_k^o we only illustrate in the case where α is of the form $\exists\gamma\ \beta(\gamma,x_1,\dots,x_p,i_1,\dots,i_r)$. The formula α_k^o is defined as

$$i:=0 \bigcup \underline{\text{begin}}\ K_{term}\ ;\ i:=s(i)\ \underline{\text{end}}\ \beta_k^o(x,x_1,\dots,x_p,y_1,\dots,y_k,i_1,\dots,i_r)$$

Corollary 1

Let $\mathfrak{A} = \langle A, f_1,\dots,f_n,a_1,\dots,a_k, r_1,\dots,r_m,=\rangle$ be a structure generated by the set $\{a_1,\dots,a_k\}$. Let $L_{\exists T}$ be a language for $\mathfrak{A}$. There is a set Ax of formulas without classical quantifiers such that

if a structure $\mathfrak{A}'$ for $L_{\exists T}$ is a model of Ax proper for equality then it is isomorphic to $\mathfrak{A}$.

Obviously, the theory based on the set of axioms Ax is complete.

The idea of the proof.

The set Ax consists of all open formulas without variables which are valid in $\mathfrak{A}$ and of the following formula which express that is generated by $\{a_1,\dots,a_k\}$:

$$\underline{\text{begin}}\ y_1:=a_1\ ;\ \dots\ ;\ y_k:=a_k\ ;\ i:=0\ \underline{\text{end}} \bigcup \underline{\text{begin}}\ K_{term}\ ;\ i:=s(i)\ \underline{\text{end}}\ (x=y)$$

This Corollary has been also proved by J.Tiuryn (compare [22]). The algorithmic arithmetic of natural numbers (compare [13]) is an example of a theory of a structure generated by one element.

At the end of this section we shall be concerned with a problem similar to the following problem of first order logic contained in the Theorem

If for every natural number n there is a model of T proper for equality with at least n-element universum then there is an infinite model of T.

Problem.

Let T be an algorithmic theory with the property: for every natural number n there is a model of T proper for equality such that every set of generators contains at least n elements. Is there a model of T proper for equality with infinite number of generators i.e. model not finitely generated ?

We can express by a formula of $L_{\omega_1\omega}$ that all models are finitely generated. But this formula cannot be written in $L_{\exists T}$. This suggest tha the answer is positive. However, the answer is negative. The idea of the construction of an example which shows this is similar to the idea of axiomatization of finite dictionaries [17] .

Example 1

The language of the theory T contains the following symbols

a - zero argument functor

p,r - one argument functors

T,D - one argument predicates

The set of nonlogical axioms of the theory T consists of the following formulas

$$(T(x) \vee D(x)) \wedge \neg (T(x) \wedge D(x))$$

$$T(x) \longrightarrow \bigcup x:= p(x) \ (x = a)$$

$$p(a) = a \wedge [(T(x) \wedge T(y) \wedge x \neq a \wedge y \neq a) \longrightarrow (p(x) = p(y) \longrightarrow x = y)]$$

$$D(z) \longrightarrow \exists x \ [T(x) \wedge \bigcup z:= r(z) \ (z = x)]$$

$$\forall x \{ T(x) \longrightarrow \exists t \ [D(t) \wedge \forall z \ (\bigcup z:= r(z) \ (z = x) \longrightarrow y:= t \bigcup y:= r(y) \ (y = z))]\}$$

$$T(x) \longrightarrow r(x) = x \quad , \quad D(z) \longrightarrow p(z) = z$$

$$(D(z) \wedge D(t)) \longrightarrow (r(z) = r(t) \longrightarrow z = t)$$

$$\exists x_o \{ T(x_o) \wedge \forall x \ [T(x) \longrightarrow y:= x_o \bigcup y:= p(y) \ (y = x)]\}$$

Every model of the theory T is of the form:

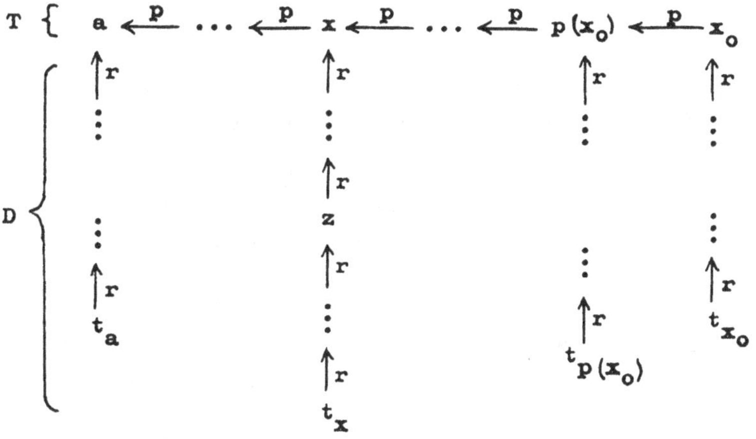

This is an informal description of such a model; $x \xleftarrow{p} y$ means that $p(y) = x$ and letters different from p,r denote elements of universum. A index of t is connected with fifth axiom.

4. Algorithmic theories axiomatizable without classical quantifiers.

We shall say that a theory $T = \langle L_{\exists T}, C_{\exists T}, Ax \rangle$ is axiomatizab without classical quantifiers if there is a set Ax_o of formulas not c taining classical quantifiers such that for every formula $\alpha \in L_{\exists T}$

$\alpha \in C_{\exists T}(Ax)$ if and only if $\alpha \in C_{\exists T}(Ax_o)$.

We start from the theorem on open first order theories [16] . Let C_1^o denote the consequence operation obtained from the consequence operation C_1 (defined in [16]) after removing all logical axioms and rules of inference containing classical quantifiers.

Theorem ([16])

Let $T = \langle L_1, C_1, Ax \rangle$ be an open first order theory and let $\alpha \in L_1$ be an open formula. Then

$\alpha \in C_1(Ax)$ if and only if $\alpha \in C_1^o(Ax)$.

In an analogous way we can prove the following theorems:

Theorem 2

Let $T = \langle L_{\exists}, C_{\exists}, Ax \rangle$ be an algorithmic theory such that every formula from Ax does not contain classical quantifiers. Let α be a formula from $L_{\exists}$ (L) not containing classical quantifiers. Then α is a theorem of the theory T if and only if α is a theorem of the theory $T' = \langle L, C, Ax \rangle$.

Theorem 3

Let $T = \langle L_{\exists T}, C_{\exists T}, Ax \rangle$ be an algorithmic theory such that every formula from Ax does not contain classical quantifiers and let $\alpha \in L_{\exists T}$ be a formula without classical quantifiers. Then

$\alpha \in C_{\exists T}(Ax)$ if and only if $\alpha \in C_{\exists T}^o(Ax)$

where $C_{\exists T}^o$ denotes the consequence operation obtained from $C_{\exists T}$ after removing all axioms and rules of inference containing classical quantifiers.

As we have mentioned above the proofs of Theorems 2,3 are similar to the proof of the preceding theorem and therefore we omit them.

We shall now characterize model theoretical properties of algorithmic theories axiomatizable without classical quantifiers. In the case of first order logic model theoretical properties of theories axiomatizable without classical quantifiers (open theories) are characterized by Łoś-Tarski Theorem.

Łoś-Tarski Theorem ([21])

A first order theory T is equivalent to an open theory iff every substructure of a model of T is a model of T.

This theorem is not valid in the case of Algorithmic Logic with tables and classical quantifiers.

Example 2

Let us consider the algorithmic theory T with one argument functor s and two argument predicate = based on axioms for equality and the following axioms:

$$s(x) = s(y) \rightarrow x = y$$

$$\exists x \forall y \{ \neg s(y) = x \wedge \underline{\text{while}}\ y \neq x\ \underline{\text{do}}\ x := s(x)\ (x = y) \}$$

It is easy to see that every model of T proper for equality is isomorphic to the set of natural numbers with the successor function and the identity relation (compare [18]).

The theory T is not equivalent to an algorithmic theory with axioms not containing classical quantifiers. This fact immediately follows from the following

Lemma 3

Let α be an algorithmic formula of the theory T without classical quantifiers. Let $\mathcal{N}$ denote the structure of natural numbers with the successor function and the identity relation and let $\mathcal{Z}$ denote the structure of integers with the successor function and the identity relation. Then

$$\mathcal{N} \models \alpha \text{ if and only if } \mathcal{Z} \models \alpha .$$

The proof of Lemma 3 is typical of Algorithmic Logic. By induction on the length of the formula α we can prove that for every natural number n

$$\alpha(x_1,\ldots,x_p,i_1,\ldots,i_r)_{\mathcal{Z}}(v) = \alpha(x_1,\ldots,x_p,i_1,\ldots,i_r)_{\mathcal{Z}}(v^n)$$

where v^n denotes the valuation obtained from v by replacing the value $v(x_i)$ of the variable x_i by the number $v(x_i) + n$. The thesis of our lemma is an immediate consequence of the above equality.

We now prove the main theorem of this section.

Theorem 4 (an analogon of Łoś-Tarski Theorem)

Let $T = \langle L_{\exists T}, C_{\exists T}, Ax \rangle$ be an algorithmic theory. The theory T is axiomatizable without classical quantifiers if and only if for every structure $\mathfrak{A}$ for $L_{\exists T}$ the following equivalence holds :

$\mathfrak{A}$ is a model of T iff every finitely generated substructur of $\mathfrak{A}$ is a model of T

The idea of the proof.

The proof of the fact that every algorithmic theory axiomatizabl without classical quantifiers satisfies the equivalence of the theore immediately follows from Remark 2.

Let us assume that T is a theory satisfying the above equivalenc One can assume that all axioms of T are sentences. We define the set Ax_0 (of formulas without classical quantifiers) in the following way

$$Ax_0 = \{ \alpha_k^o(y_1,\dots,y_k) \ : \ \alpha \text{ is an axiom of T } (\alpha \in Ax) \text{ and k is a natural number} \}$$

where the meaning of the formula α_k^o is the same as in Lemma 2. Let us notice that in virtue of Lemma 2 $\mathfrak{A} \models Ax_0$ means that all sentences from Ax are valid in every finitely generated substructure of $\mathfrak{A}$. In virtue of our assumption this implies that $\mathfrak{A} \models Ax_0$ iff $\mathfrak{A} \models Ax$ which ends the proof of Theorem 4.

A similar reasoning can be repeated for $L_{\omega_1\omega}$. We shall say that a sentence of $L_{\omega_1\omega}$ is a simple universal sentence if it is of the for $\forall x_1 \dots \forall x_n \gamma$ where γ does not contain quantifiers.

Theorem 5

Let α be a sentence of $L_{\omega_1\omega}$ with finite number of functors and predicates. There is a set Ax of simple universal sentences equivalen to α (i.e. $\mathfrak{A} \models Ax$ iff $\mathfrak{A} \models \alpha$) if and only if for every stru ture $\mathfrak{A}$ the following equivalence holds :

$\mathfrak{A}$ is a model of α iff every finitely generated substructur of $\mathfrak{A}$ is a model of α.

The method of the proof is the same as in the case of Theorem 4. Remark 2 and Lemma 2 can be easily modified for $L_{\omega_1\omega}$.

References

[1] L.Banachowski, Investigations of properties of programs by mean of the extended algorithmic logic, Fundamenta Informaticae I, 1977

[2] W.Dańko, Programs with tables and procedures on the ground of algorithmic logic, doctoral dissertation, University of Warsaw, 1976

[3] W.Dańko, Algorithmic logic with tables and classical quantifiers Zeszyty naukowe Filii UW w Białymstoku, (in print)

[4] E.Engeler, Algorithmic properties of structures, Math. Sys. Theory I, 1967

[5] M.Grabowski, The set of all tautologies of the zero order algorithmic logic is decidable, Bull.Acad.Polon.Sci. Sèr.Math.Astr.Phys., 20, 1972

[6] H.Friedman, Algorithmic procedures, generalized Turing algorithms and elementary recursion theory, Logic Colloquium'69 Nôrth-Holland Publ. Co., Amsterdam 1971

[7] D.Harel, A.Meyer, V.Pratt, Computability and completeness in logic of programs, MIT Cambridge Mess. May 1977

[8] C.Hoare, An axiomatic basis of computer programming, Com. ACM 12, 1969

[9] A.Kreczmar, Programmability in fields, Fundamenta Informaticae I 1977

[10] D.Luckham, D.Park, M.Paterson, On formalized computer programs, ICSS 4, 1970

[11] E.G.Lopez-Escobar, The interpolation theorem for denumerable long formulas, Fund.Math. 57, 1968

[12] H.J.Keisler, Model theory for infinitary logic, North-Holland Publ. Co., Amsterdam 1972

[13] G. Mirkowska, Algorithmic logic and its applications in program theory, Fund. Inf. I, 1977

[14] G.Mirkowska, On formalized system of algorithmic logic, Bull. Acad.Polon.Sci.Sèr.Math.Astr.Phys. 19, 1971

[15] H.Rasiowa, R.Sikorski, Mathematics of metamathematics, PWN, Warszawa, 1963

[16] H.Rasiowa, On logical structure of programs, Bull.Acad.Polon. Sci.Sèr.Math.Astr.Phys. 20, 1972

[17] A.Salwicki, On algorithmic theory of dictionaries, Fund. Inf. (in print)

[18] A.Salwicki, Programmability and recursiveness, Dissertationes Mathematicae, (in print)

[19] A.Salwicki, Formalized algorithmic languages, Bull.Acad.Polon. Sci.Sèr. Math.Astr.Phys. 18, 1970

[20] J.C.Shepherdson, Computation over abstract structures, Logic Colloquium'73,North-Holland, Amsterdam 1973

[21] J.Shoenfield, Mathematical logic, Addison-Wesley Publ. Co., 1967

[22] J.Tiuryn, Logic of effective definitions, Fundamenta Informatice, (to appear) and R.W.T.H. Aachen Report 55, 1979

ALGEBRAIC SEMANTICS AND PROGRAM LOGICS:

ALGORITHMIC LOGIC FOR PROGRAM TREES

PATRICE ENJALBERT
Laboratoire Central de Recherches - THOMSON-CSF
Domaine de Corbeville - B.P. 10 - 91401 ORSAY, France

ABSTRACT

The aim of this paper is to ground Algorithmic (or Dynamic) Logic on Algebraic semantics in the french acceptation of the term, i.e. theory in which the meaning of a program is a tree resulting from an infinite formal unfolding. We present an algorithmic system in which programs are program-trees and also an example of how it can be applied in order to design systems for programs. Another feature is the use of techniques of $L_{\omega_1\omega}$ (the notion of Consistency Property) for proving completeness and Model Existence theorems.

INTRODUCTION

This paper presents an attempt to bind the concepts of Algorithmic (or Dynamic) Logic, with those of Algebraic semantics.

Let us recall that the term "Algebraic Semantics" in the french acceptation of the term specifies an approach of Semantics in which the meaning of a program is an infinite tree representing all possible formal computations.

This idea of associating formal trees with programs is an ancient one [17], but has been mainly developped first by M. Nivat, B. Courcelle, I. Guessarian and others in the case of so-called Recursive Program Schemes [2] and then by G. Cousineau in the case of imperative programs [3,4]. It is this last theory known as "theory of trees with indexed leaves", which we consider.

In this framework, with every (imperative) program π is associated a program-tree $t(\pi)$ which is the result of a - possibly infinite - complete unfolding of the program.

Example 1 :

π_1 = IF $x < y$ THEN $z := x$ ELSE $z := y$ FI

```
t(π1)  =     x < y
              /   \
          z:=x   z:=y
            |      |
            ω0     ω0
```

where ω_0 can be considered so far as an END instruction.

Example 2 :

π_2 = A:=N;R:=1 ; WHILE A > 0 DO R:=RxA ; A:=A-1 OD (computing R=N!)

$t(\pi_2)$ =

```
                A:=N
                  |
                R:=1
                  |
                 A>0
                / \
           R:=RxA  ω₀
              |
           A:=A-1
              |
             A>0
            / \
       R:=RxA  ω₀
          |
       A:=A-1
          |
         A>0
        / \
   R:=RxA  ω₀
     .
     .
     .
```

In the case of a program with loops (like π_2), the associated tree is infinite.

The interesting point with these trees is that they can be considered either as semantic or syntactic objects. Indeed they are mathematical objects, belonging to a certain free algebra (cf I.1 below), hence can be defined and handled by means of the corresponding algebraic operations and relations. This is the fact which permits to speak of "Algebraic semantics". But on the other hand, they are rather formal objects, very close to original programs as can be seen from the previous examples, and keep a great deal of syntactic aspects.

In other words, Algebraic semantic can be viewed as a "universal" one, in the following sense. Let I be any interpretation, i.e. algebraic structure, of domain $|I|$. With every program π the variables of which are $(x_1,\dots,x_k)$, is traditionnaly associated a partial function $Val^{prog.}(\pi, I): |I|^k \to |I|^k$.

This function can be defined for example by means of fixpoint techniques. The operator Val^{prog} defines the denotational semantics of programs.

As will be shown later, the same operation can be carried out for program-trees, and we have for every p.t. τ a function
$Val^{tree}(\tau, I) : |I|^k \to |I|^k$ (if the variables of τ are again $x_1,\dots x_k$) .

Now, we have the following relation :

$$Val^{prog}(\pi, I) = Val^{tree}(t(\pi), I)$$

for any program π, t (π) being his associated p.t. or, if one likes diagrams, the following one is commutative:

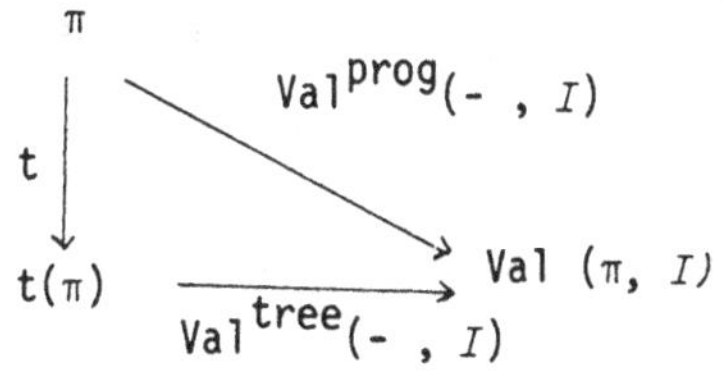

This universal property leads one step further to formulate the following "Postulate of Algebraic Semantics" :

Postulate :

The notion of program-tree is the basic one. The various classes of programs are only different ways of describing p.t.'s by means of finite expressions.

This postulate can be lighted and made more precise by another aspect of Cousineau's theory, namely: its relation with classical language theory.

A language is a set of words. Languages can be defined by means of regular (or rational) expressions, or different classes of grammars. Each of these notions have their counterpart in Cousineau's theory: languages are replaced by trees, grammars by equations (or "actions") systems, and there is also a notion of "rational expression".

Now it happens that all these notions can be interpreted as natural program construct either well known ("actions" - systems are systems of procedures without parameters) or extensions of them (Cousineau's rational expressions are a general "do forever" loop).

Hence we can consider that these programs are nothing but finite expressions defining p.t.'s (our "postulate"), in the same way as grammars or regular expressions define languages; and program constructs do nothing but reflecting the algebraic operations on trees.

Now let us turn to program logic and see what consequences have the above considerations.

One is obvious: if we consider p.t.'s and algebraic operations on them as the basic concepts, we should begin by defining an algorithmic logic in which programs are program-trees.

This was done, first in the restricted case of partial correctness ("Hoare") Logic [8] and then in the general framework of "Algorithmic" logic [9]. It is the main ideas of this last work that we present here.

In the logical system we propose for p.t.'s, among classical connectives (including quantifiers), we introduce the following constructs :

$$\Box\, t\, \alpha \quad \text{and} \quad \Diamond\, t\, \alpha$$

where t is a p.t. and α an algorithmic formula. The meaning of such formulas is respectively: after a terminating computation in t, α is true, and: the computation in t terminates and the result satisfies α.

We define a deductive system for those expressions, which axiomatically defines the algebraic relations and operations on p.t.'s. Especially we have axioms for the order relation on trees and a rule for the least-upper-bound (l.u.b.) operation.

These notions of order and l.u.b. on programs play an important part in other branches of programs semantics. They appear also in the theory of "predicate transformers" [1], which can be considered as close to program logic, but is situated in the framework of set theory. And, to our knowledge, and though obviously present in certain completeness proof using Q-filters [15], the link between formal "algorithmic" systems and order and continuity had never been established. On contrary, our system for p.t.'s makes an explicite and essential use of these notions.

Especially, our system includes an infinitary rule which is a "l.u.b" one :

$$\frac{\{\alpha \to \Box\, t^i\, \beta\}\ i \in I}{\alpha \to \Box\, \underset{i \in I}{\mathrm{l.u.b}}\, (t^i)\, \beta}$$

(where $(t_i)_{i\in I}$ is a directed family of p.t.'s). In fact this rule is a general framework for other known infinitary ones [14, 16], which can all be shown to be "continuity rules" [10].

Let us recall that infinitary rules are necessary in order to have complete axiomatisation of the semantic consequence operation. And our system is complete in that strong acceptation of the word.

Once such a logical system for trees has been designed, we can use the "universal property" of Algebraic Semantics and derive sound systems for various classes of programs in a uniform way. One of them is briefly presented in this paper. The method is essentially the same as for p.t.'s; especially: infinitary rules involve standard sets of approximants.

Proofs can be found in [9] together with further details and aspects among which we mention:

- Propositionnal systems (in the sense of PDL) for p.t.'s and programs, which emphasize the algebraic aspects of the theory.

- A calculus of weakest preconditions in $L_{\omega_1\omega}$, as always first for p.t.'s and then for programs.

Hence links between the logical and algebraic approaches are carried out in various frameworks. Let us also mention some work about "Hoare systems"and program transformations performed in the same framework, with practical applications [6,12]

Notations

Let : μ be a denumerable set of predicate, function, constant symbols defining a 1st order similarity type.

$V = \{x_1, \ldots, x_k\}$ be a finite set of variables among a given set of cardinality $\aleph_1$.

We define the following sets :

$F_o(\mu)$ [resp $F_o(\mu,V)$] : 1st order formulas [resp. with free variables in V] (greek letters : α,β ...)

$U(\mu)$ [resp $U(\mu,V)$] : 1st order terms [resp. with variables in V]. (letters: u, v, w ...)

$As(\mu,V)=\{x \leftarrow u \,/\, x\in V,\ u\in U(\mu,V)\}$: set of assignments (letters : A, B, C ...)

$E = \{e_o, e_1, \ldots, e_n, \ldots\}$:denumerable set of new symbols ("exit" symbols)

If α is a formula, x a variable, u a term, $[\alpha]^u_x$ is the result of the substitution of u to every free occurrence of x (with the usual precaution if variables in u should become bound).

I - LOGICS FOR PROGRAM-TREES

I.1 - Program trees

The definitions and notations are those of [2],[3,4] and [9].

Definitions

Let Ω be a new symbol and :

$$W(\mu,\nu) = F_\circ(\mu,\nu) \cup As(\mu,\nu) \cup (E \cup \{\Omega\})$$

the alphabet whose elements have the arity 2,1, 0 respectively. (W for short if there is no ambiguity). We call ρ this arity function.

We denote by $M_\Omega(W(\mu,\nu))$ the free magma (or "free algebra") on this alphabet, and by $M^\infty_\Omega(W(\mu,\nu)^\Omega)$the complete free magma on W. This last set in the set of program trees on μ and ν. $M_\Omega(W)$ is the set of finite p.t.'s.See [2] for full definitions.

Another definition we shall mainly use is known as Doner formalism [7]. In this formalism, a p.t. is a partial function :

$$t : (N_+)^* \rightarrow W$$

which respects the arity on W, i.e. such that :

$$\forall n \in Dom(t) \; : \; t(m) \text{ has } \rho(t(m)) \text{ sons}$$
$$\Leftrightarrow \forall m \in Dom(t) \quad m1, \ldots, m\rho(t(m)) \in Dom(t)$$
$$\wedge \forall i > \rho(t(m)) \; \neg mi \notin Dom(t)$$

The two definitions can be shown to be equivalent [3].

Operations and order

The elements of $F_\circ$, As , $E \cup \{\Omega\}$ define free algebra operations on $M^\infty_\Omega(W)$, with the corresponding arity. For instance, if $P \in F_\circ$, P defines a binary operation :

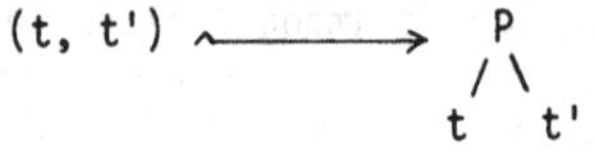

The order on $M^\infty_\Omega(W)$ is the least order relation containing : $\Omega < t$ for all t in $M^\infty_\Omega(W)$ and compatible with the free algebra operations. In other words, a tree t is smaller than t' iff t' is obtained by replacing in t certain occurrences of Ω by new trees.

Example 3 :

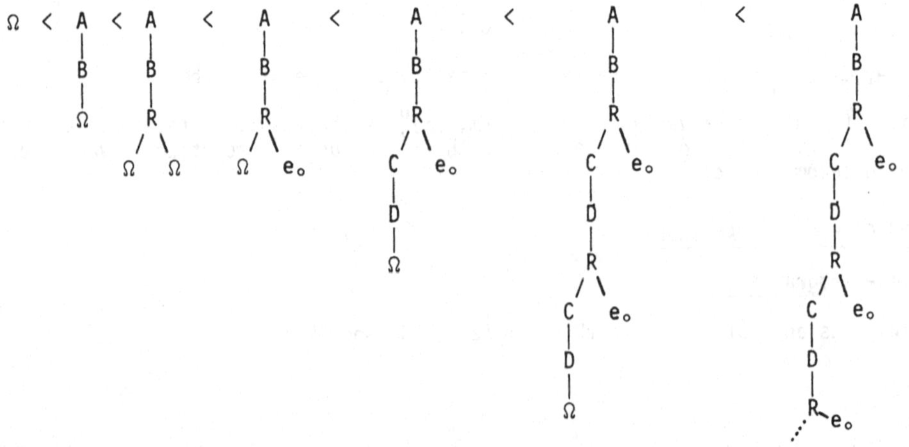

<u>Property</u> : Every directed family of p.t.'s has a l.u.b.

<u>Example 4</u>:

In example 3 we have a chain with its l.u.b., which is exactly the tree of example 2, with obvious correspondance for A, B, C, ...

Another important operation is the <u>substitution</u>. A general substitution operation can be defined. But we shall only need here an informal definition of a special case - Namely :

Let $t, t_1, \ldots, t_n$ be $n + 1$ trees. The <u>parallel substitution</u> of $t_1, \ldots, t_n$ in t <u>to the leaves</u> $e_{i_1}, \ldots, e_{i_n}$ is the result of replacing, for all k $(1 < k < n)$, every occurrence of e_{i_k} by t_k - Notation $t\,[e_{i_k} \searrow t_k : k = 1 \ldots n]$

<u>Example 5:</u>

```
          R
         / \
t =     A   B            t1 =    C             t2 =   D
        |   |                    |                    |
        e0  e1                   e0                   e3


t = [e0 ↘ t1 , e1 ↘ t2]     =       R
                                   / \
                                  A   B
                                  |   |
                                  C   D
                                  |   |
                                  e0  e3
```

<u>Semantics of p.t.'s</u>

Up to now we considered p.t.'s as formal algebraic objects (trees). But we can also consider them as <u>programs</u>.

Let I be an interpretation, i.e. a structure of type μ, $t \in M_\Omega^\infty (W(\mu, v))$, and $\bar{d} \in |I|^k$, where $|I|$ is the domain of I. It is straightforward to define what a <u>computation</u> of t in I with input $\bar{d}$ is : we start from the root with value $\bar{d}$ for the variables, perform any encountered assignment, switch to either branch according to the value of the test when meeting one, and stop when reaching a leaf. If the leaf is an e_i, then the <u>result</u> is the present value of the variables, and if the leaf is Ω , then undefined.

Hence every p.t. t defines a (partial) function :

$$\mathrm{Val}^{\mathrm{tree}}(t, I) \; : \; |I|^k \to |I|^k.$$

There is another way of defining $\mathrm{Val}^{\mathrm{tree}}(t, I)$, which uses two special functions named "Cond" and "Res". For every p.t. t and $m \in \mathrm{Dom}(t)$,

- $\mathrm{Cond}_t(m)$ is a first order (open) formula and $\mathrm{Res}_t(m)$ a string of k terms, defined recursively as follows :

. $Cond_t(\varepsilon) = True \qquad Res_t(\varepsilon) = \langle x_1, \ldots, x_k \rangle$

. If $t = (x \leftarrow u)(t')$, then $m = 1\,m'$ and

$Cond_t(m) = [\,Cond_{t'}(m')\,]^u_x$

$Res_t(m) = [\,Res_{t'}(m')\,]^u_x$

. If $t = R(t', t'')$ $(R \in F_\circ)$

* if $m = 1\,m'$ $\quad Cond_t(m) = R \wedge Cond_{t'}(m')$

$\qquad Res_t(m) = Res_{t'}(m')$

* if $m = 2\,m''$ $\quad Cond_t(m) = \sim R \wedge Cond_{t''}(m'')$

$\qquad Res_t(m) = Res_{t''}(m'')$

The intuitive meaning of $Cond_t(m)$ is to be the relation on the input which forces the computation to reach the node m - $Res_t(m)$ formally represents the function computed along that path (symbolic execution).

Then we have, for any interpretation I, and "data" $\overline{d}$: $\forall\, m \in Dom(t)$

$$Cond_t(m)(\overline{d}) \Rightarrow (Val^{tree}(t, I)(\overline{d}) = Res_t(m)(\overline{d}))$$

I.2 - Logic for program trees

Throughout this section μ will be constant and A will denote a family of p.t.'s about which we only suppose :

- A is denumerable
- $M_\Omega(W(\mu)) \subseteq A \subseteq M^\infty_\Omega(W(\mu))$

Syntax : The language L_A

For any such family, the language L_A is defined as follows :

(i) All atomic formulas are in L_A

(ii) L_A is closed by usual $\wedge$, $\vee$, $\sim$, $\exists x$, $\forall x$ connectives

(iii) If $t \in A$, $\alpha_\circ, \ldots, \alpha_n \in L_A$,

$\Box t \langle \alpha_\circ, \ldots, \alpha_n \rangle$ and $\Diamond t \langle \alpha_\circ, \ldots, \alpha_n \rangle$ are in L_A

we shall denote: $\overline{\alpha} = \langle \alpha_\circ, \ldots, \alpha_n \rangle$ and, accordingly ,

$\Box\, t\, \overline{\alpha}$ and $\Diamond\, t\, \overline{\alpha}$ the above formulas. The length of $\overline{\alpha}$ is $|\overline{\alpha}| = n + 1$.

$\sim \overline{\alpha}$ is : $< \sim \alpha_0 , \ldots , \sim \alpha_n >$ - Similar definitions for $\overline{\alpha} \wedge \overline{\beta}$, $\overline{\alpha} \vee \overline{\beta}$, $\overline{\alpha} \Rightarrow \overline{\beta}$.

A closed formula (every variable is bound) is also called a sentence.

Semantics :

U being an interpretation, α a formula of L_A, we use the notation :

$$U \models \alpha$$

for : U satisfies α (or: U is a model of α)

The definition of this relation is classical for the above clauses (i) and (ii). For (iii) we use the function Cond and Res and set, if $\Box\, t\, \overline{\alpha}$ (and $\Diamond\, t\, \overline{\alpha}$) have variables among $\{ x_1 , \ldots , x_k\}$ and $(u_1 , \ldots , u_k) \in |U|^k$:

* $U \models \Box\, t\, \overline{\alpha}\, [u_1 , \ldots , u_k]$ iff

$\forall\, m \in \mathrm{Dom}\,(t)\ \ \forall i\ \ 0 < i < |\overline{\alpha}|$ s. t. $t(m) = e_i \in E$

$U \models \mathrm{Cond}_t\,(m)\, [u_1 , \ldots , u_k]$

$\Rightarrow U \models \alpha_i\, [\mathrm{Res}_t\,(m)\, [u_1 , \ldots , u_k]]$

* $U \models \Diamond\, t\, \overline{\alpha}\, [u_1 , \ldots , u_k]$ iff :

$\exists\, m \in \mathrm{Dom}\,(t)\ \ \exists i\ \ 0 < i < |\overline{\alpha}|$ s.t. $t\,(m) = e_i$

and $U \models \mathrm{Cond}_t\,(m)\, [u_1 , \ldots , u_k]$

and $U \models \alpha_i\, [\mathrm{Res}_t\,(m)\, [u_1 , \ldots , u_k]]$

Comments :

First notice that in formulas $\Box\, t\, \overline{\alpha}$ and $\Diamond\, t\, \overline{\alpha}$ we have a set of "postconditions" $\alpha_0 , \ldots , \alpha_n$, and not a single one as in other logics (Dynamic or Algorithmic). This is due to the fact that p.t.'shave possibly different types of leaves $e_0, \ldots , e_n, \ldots$, which we interpret as different types of exits. It is indeed practical to distinguish exits, as will be seen in Part II, and it is natural to associate a different formula with each of them.

Hence a formula $\Box\, t\, \overline{\alpha}$, for instance, will be true if whenever the computation reaches a leaf e_i ($U \models \mathrm{Cond}_t\,(m)$), the result ($\mathrm{Res}_t\,(m)$) satisfies the corresponding formula α_i. (And no condition if there is no attached formula α_i, i.e. if $i > |\overline{\alpha}|$.). For $\Diamond\, t\, \overline{\alpha}$, the computation must reach a leaf e_i ($\exists\, m\ U \models \mathrm{Cond}_t\,(m)$) and there must be an attached formula α_i which must be satisfied.

A formula α is true in U iff its universal closure is :

$U \models \alpha\, [x_1 , \ldots , x_k]$ iff $U \models \forall x_1 , \ldots , x_k\ \ \alpha\ \ [x_1, \ldots , x_k]$

A formula α is valid ($\models \alpha$) if, for all structures U , $U \models \alpha$.

Obviously, for all t, $\overline{\alpha}$:

$$\models \Box\ t\ \overline{\alpha} \iff \sim \Diamond\, t \sim \overline{\alpha}$$

Theories - Semantic consequence operation

A theory Γ is a set of sentences. We say that U is model of Γ ($U \models \Gamma$) iff $U \models \alpha$ for every α in Γ.

A sentence α is a semantic consequence of Γ ($\Gamma \models \alpha$) iff every model of Γ is a model of α ($\forall U : U \models \Gamma \Rightarrow U \models \alpha$).

Proposition 1 (Non-Compactness)

The semantic consequence operation is not compact i.e. : There is a set of sentences Γ and a sentence α s.t.

$$\Gamma \models \alpha \quad \text{and} \quad \text{Not } \Gamma_f \models \alpha$$

$$\text{for any finite } \Gamma_f \subseteq \Gamma .$$

Corollary :

There cannot exist any complete finitary axiomatisation of the semantic consequence operation.

Accordingly our axiom system will include an infinitary rule (i.e. with infinitely many premisses).

The deductive system T.

For any formula α, let $\varphi\sim$ be the formula obtained by "moving the negation inside", defined by obvious rules like :

- If α is atomic : $\varphi \sim$ is $\sim \varphi$
- $(\sim \alpha) \sim$ is α
- $(\alpha \wedge \beta) \sim$ is $\sim \alpha \vee \sim \beta$

 .
 .
 .

- $(\Box\, t\, \overline{\alpha}) \sim$ is $\Diamond t\, (\overline{\alpha} \sim)$

We also denote : $\Box\, x \leftarrow u\, \alpha$ for $\Box\, (x \leftarrow u)\, (e_0)\, \alpha$

and : $\Box\, X \leftarrow U\, \alpha$ for $\Box\, (x_1 \leftarrow u_1) \ldots \Box x_n \leftarrow u_n\, \alpha$ for some $n < \omega$.

Definition :

The deductive system T is the following one :

Axioms :

1) All instances of tautologies of Propositionnal Calculus.

2) $(\sim \alpha) \Leftrightarrow (\alpha \sim)$

3) (i) $\square\, e_i\, \overline{\alpha} \Leftrightarrow \alpha_i$ if $i < |\overline{\alpha}|$

$\square\, e_i\, \overline{\alpha} \Leftrightarrow$ True if $i \geq |\overline{\alpha}|$

$\square\, \Omega\, \overline{\alpha} \Leftrightarrow$ True.

(ii) $\square\, (x \leftarrow u)\, (t)\, \overline{\alpha} \Leftrightarrow \square\, (x \leftarrow u)\, \square\, t\, \overline{\alpha}$

(iii) $\square\, R\, (t_1, t_2)\, \overline{\alpha} \Leftrightarrow (R \Rightarrow \square\, t_1\, \overline{\alpha} \wedge \sim R \Rightarrow \square\, t_2\, \overline{\alpha})$ where t, t_1, t_2 are finite.

4) $\square\, t\, \overline{\alpha} \Rightarrow \square\, t'\, \overline{\alpha}$ if $t' < t$

5) (i) $\square\, (x \leftarrow u)\, \alpha \Leftrightarrow [\alpha]^u_x$ if α is atomic

(ii) $(\square\, (x \leftarrow u)\, \alpha \wedge \square\, (x \leftarrow u)\, \beta) \Leftrightarrow \square\, (x \leftarrow u)\, \alpha \wedge \beta$

(iii) $\sim \square\, (x \leftarrow u)\, \alpha \Leftrightarrow \square\, (x \leftarrow u) \sim \alpha$

6) (i) $\forall x\, \alpha \Rightarrow \square\, (x \leftarrow u)\, \alpha$ for all terms u (instanciation)

(ii) $(\forall y\, \square\, (x \leftarrow y)\alpha) \Leftrightarrow (\forall x \alpha)$

7) (i) $x = x$

(ii) $x = y \Rightarrow y = x$

(iii) $\alpha \wedge x = u \Rightarrow \square\, (x \leftarrow u)\, \alpha$ for α atomic and u a term.

<u>Deduction rules</u> :

1. Modus Ponens:

$$\frac{\alpha \quad \alpha \Rightarrow \beta}{\beta}$$

2. Generalisation:

$$\frac{\alpha \Rightarrow \square\, (X \leftarrow U)\, \beta}{\alpha \Rightarrow \square\, (X \leftarrow U)\, \forall\, y\, \beta}$$

If y is not free in α nor occurs in $X \leftarrow U$.

3. Induction :

$$\frac{\{\, \alpha \Rightarrow \square\, t_i\, \overline{\beta}\,\}\ i \in I}{\alpha \Rightarrow \square\, (\underset{i \in I}{\text{l.u.b.}}\, (t_i))\overline{\beta}}$$

if $(t_i)_{i \in I}$ is a directed family.

[α, β are any formulas; $t, t', t_1, t_2 \ldots$ any p.t.'s in A, $x, y, \ldots$ any variables]

Remark :

The notion of free variable in an algorithmic formula of type $\Box\, t\, \bar{\alpha}$ or $\Diamond t\, \bar{\alpha}$ should be defined (Rule 2). Intuitively, a variable x_i occurs free in such a formula if there is a variable x_j which occurs free in some α_k (or in a test R in t) and there is some occurrence in t of e_k (or of R), such that the result (Res_t (m)) in that point depends on x_j.

For instance, $\Box\, x \leftarrow 0\; R(x)$ is closed (in fact equivalent to R (0)).

If t =

```
        x = y
       /     \
     e₀      x←x+1
               |
             x = y
            /     \
          e₀      x←x+1
                    .
                    .
                    .
```

The variables free in $\Box\, t\; S(x,y)$ are x and y.

In $\Box\; (x \leftarrow z)(t)\; S(x,y)$, it is y and z

Completeness theorem

The set of syntactic consequences of a theory Γ is the smallest set of formulas containing Γ, axioms of T and closed by application of the rules of T.

Notation : $\Gamma \vdash_T \alpha$.

Theorem 1 (completeness theorem)

For any theory Γ and sentence α :

$$\Gamma \vdash_T \alpha \quad \Leftrightarrow \quad \Gamma \models \alpha \; .$$

In the "soundness direction" (⇒), the proof uses a translation of formulas of L_A in formulas of $L_{\omega_1,\omega}$. Axioms and rules of T then become more or less axioms and rules of $L_{\omega_1,\omega}$.

For the other direction (<=) we made an adaptation of the notion of consistency Property (C.P.) of [13]. We have a first Model Existence theorem which says that every element of a C.P. has a model. The rest of the proof is moreover less like in [13].

Model Existence Theorem :

The same method gives :

Theorem 2 :

Any consistent theory has a model.

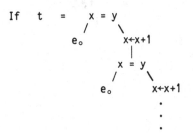

Remark :

In order to compare with $L_{\omega_1\omega}$, remember that since A is countable, so is L_A. Hence we are in fact inside a fragment of $L_{\omega_1\omega}$.

Derived rule and theorem

The following rule can be derived in T :

4. Necessitation
$$\frac{\alpha}{\square\,(x\leftarrow u)\,\alpha}$$

We also have the following useful and general "Theorem for substitution" :

Let $|\overline{\alpha}| = |\overline{\beta}| = n + 1$ and $\forall j \in J \subseteq [n] \quad \alpha_j = \square\, t_j\ \overline{\beta}$.

If the following "coherence condition" is satisfied :

$\forall_i \in [n] \setminus J$, if e_i has an occurrence in t , then $\alpha_i = \beta_i$.

Then : (Theorem for substitution)

$$\vdash_T (\square\, t\, \overline{\alpha} \iff \square\, t\, [e_j \setminus t_j : j \in J]\, \overline{\beta})$$

Let $t' = t\,[e_j \setminus t_j : j \in J]$. Intuitively the theorem means that in order to evaluate $\square\, t'\, \overline{\beta}$, one can "replace" some subtree t_j of t' by the formula $\square\, t_j\, \overline{\beta}$.

II - LOGICS FOR PROGRAMS

Now let us consider some class K of programs whose algebraic semantics is a class A of p.t.'s. From the logic L_A and its axiomatisation we can derive a logic for K. In order to illustrate this statement we shall consider the programming language EXEL [5] (whose constructs exactly fit the algebraic operations on trees), and from this language, the subclass of programs corresponding to regular expressions in the parallel with language Theory.

II.1 - Structured Programs (S.P.'s)

Syntax :

The definition of S.P.'s is :

SP :: = Ω $|\omega_i|$ x $\leftarrow$ U ; SP | IF R THEN SP ELSE SP FI | SP ; SP | DO SP OD

The only thing to explain is the DO ... OD loop and the ω_i's. The intuitive idea is: "Do forever until you find an ω_i; then jump out of i nested loops"; Ω is introduced for technical reasons which will appear in section II.2. The formal semantics will be given in term of p.t.'s. Before, we need to define the corresponding class R of p.t.'s and new operations on it.

The class R of Rationnal Trees

The set of exit symbols E is in this case denoted $\{ \omega_i \mid i \in N \}$. We define the following operations :

- Concatenation : $t \bullet t' = t [\omega_0 \searrow t']$

  and : $t^n = t \bullet t \bullet \ldots \bullet t$ n times.

- $\downarrow$: $\downarrow t = t [\omega_0 \searrow \Omega ; \omega_i \searrow \omega_{i-1} ; i = 1 \ldots n]$.

- $*$: $t^* = \underset{n \in N}{\text{l.u.b.}} (\downarrow t^n)$

Example 6

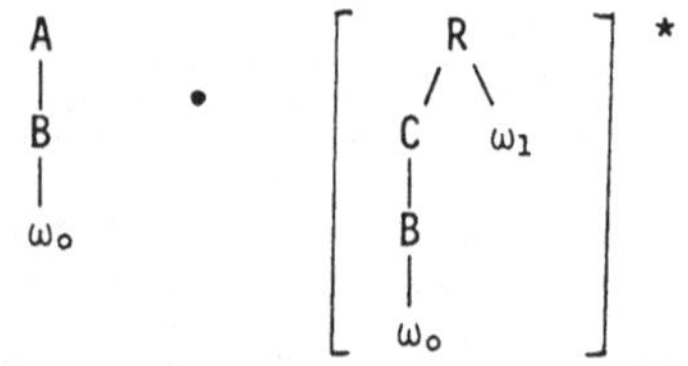

is the tree of Example 4

These operations are the algebraic ones on p.t.'s corresponding to program constructs of S.P.'s.

The class R of rational trees is the smallest one containing Ω, the ω_i's and closed by algebra and star operations. A theorem says that rational trees are exactly those who only have a finite number of subtrees [3,4] (Again, the parallel with language theory).

Remark 7 :

$(\downarrow t^n)_{n\in N}$ is the standard set of approximants of t^*.

Remark that in $\mathcal{L}_R$, $\square \downarrow t^n (\alpha_0 ,\dots, \alpha_k) \iff \square\, t^n (\text{True}, \alpha_0 ,\dots, \alpha_k)$

Semantics of SP's

The application t from SP's to p.t.'s is defined by :

$$\omega_i \mapsto \omega_i$$

$$\Omega \mapsto \Omega$$

$$x\leftarrow U;S \mapsto \begin{array}{c} x\leftarrow U \\ | \\ t(S) \end{array}$$

$$\text{IF } R \text{ THEN } S_1 \text{ ELSE } S_2 \text{ FI} \longmapsto \begin{array}{c} R \\ / \quad \backslash \\ t(S_1) \quad t(S_2) \end{array}$$

$$S_1 \,;\, S_2 \longmapsto t(S_1) \bullet t(S_2)$$

$$\text{DO } S \text{ OD} \longmapsto (t(S))^*$$

Thus we can check that the abstract operations on p.t.'s formalize natural program constructs (which is not the case of the language theory formalism used in DL [11] in order to define programs). t completely defines the meaning of SP's, via the already established semantics of p.t.'s.

II.2 - Logics for SP's

Syntax

The language L_R is defined by the classical conditions and :

If S is a SP and $\overline{\alpha} = (\alpha_0 ,\dots, \alpha_n)$ formulas :

$\square\, S\, \overline{\alpha}$ and $\Diamond\, S\, \overline{\alpha}$ are formulas .

Semantics

Defined via the semantics of $\mathcal{L}_R$. t above can be extended into an application from L_R to $\mathcal{L}_R$, by setting :

$$t(\square\, S\, \overline{\alpha}) = \square\, t(S)\, t(\overline{\alpha}) , \quad t(\Diamond\, S\, \overline{\alpha}) = \Diamond\, t(S)\, t(\overline{\alpha}),$$

$t(\alpha \wedge \beta) = t(\alpha) \wedge t(\beta) \dots$

We say that $\alpha \in L_R$ is satisfied in a structure U if t (α) is . Of course :

Theorem : The semantic consequence operation is not compact.

Deductive system S

It is easy to adapt Axioms 1 - 3, 5 - 7, and rules 1 - 2. Then, we have an axiom which defines composition : An immediate consequence of the Theorem for Substitution).

8) $\square\,(S_1 \bullet S_2)\ \overline{\alpha} \iff \square\, S_1\,(\square\, S_2\ \overline{\alpha})$

The adaptation of axiom (4) for order and rule (3) for l.u.b. involves the standard approximants of DO S OD, and use the above remark 7.

Axiom 4 : $\square$ DO S OD $\overline{\alpha}$ $\Rightarrow$ $\square\, S^n\,(\text{True}, \overline{\alpha})\ \ \forall n \in N$

($S^n = S\ ;\ S;\ldots;\ S$ n times)

Rule 3 : $$\frac{\{\alpha \rightarrow \square\, X \leftarrow U\ \ \square\, S^n\,(\text{True}, \overline{\beta})\}\ n < \omega}{\alpha \leftarrow \square\, X \leftarrow U\ \ \square\,\text{DO}\ \ S\ \ \text{OD}\ \overline{\beta}}$$

This system has the following properties :

Theorem 3 : (completeness)

For any theory Γ and formula α of L_R :

$\Gamma \vdash_{S} \alpha \iff \Gamma \models \alpha$.

Theorem 4 : (Model existence)

Any consistent theory has a model.

II- 3 - Other classes of programs

Similar systems can be given for other classes of programs, namely : EXEL "actions systems", which are set of procedures without parameters, and various combinations of actions systems and SP's. At the present time, some work is being performed in order to give an algebraic semantics to programs with procedures, block instructions etc ... ; the method described here will then be applied to these classes of programs.

REFERENCES

[1] J.W. DE BAKKER : Recursive programs as predicate transformers, in: Formal descriptions of programming concepts, E.J. NEUHOLD ed. North Holland, 1978 p. 165-202.

[2] B. COURCELLE, M. NIVAT : The Algebraic Semantics of Recursive Program Schemes, in Proc. 7th MFCS Symposium, 1978, Lecture Notes in Computer Science, Vol. 62, p. 16-30.

[3] G. COUSINEAU : Les arbres à feuilles indicées: un cadre algébrique de définition des structures de contrôle. Thèse d'Etat, Paris, 1977.

[4] G. COUSINEAU : An algebraic definition of control structures, Theoretical Computer Science 12, 1980, p. 175-192.

[5] G. COUSINEAU : La programmation en EXEL; revue technique THOMSON-CSF, Vol. 10, n° 2, 1978, p. 209-234 et Vol. 11, n° 1, 1979, p. 13-35.

[6] G. COUSINEAU, P. ENJALBERT : Program Equivalence and provability, Lecture notes in Computer Science n° 74, p. 237-245.

[7] DONER : Tree acceptors and some of their applications, J. Comput. System Science, Vol. 4, 1970, p. 406-451.

[8] P. ENJALBERT : Systèmes de déduction pour les arbres et les schémas de programmes, RAIRO Informatique Théorique, Vol. 15, n° 1, 1981, p. 3 - 21 et Vol. 14, n° 4, 1980.

[9] P. ENJALBERT : Contribution à l'étude de la logique Algorithmique...Thèse d'Etat Paris VII, 1981.

[10] P. ENJALBERT : ω -rules and continuity. To appear in: Proceedings of Bialowieza Conference on program logics, 1981.

[11] D. HAREL : First order dynamic logic, springer lecture notes in Computer Science, n° 68, 1979.

[12] C. HENRY : Etude des transformations de programmes EXEL, réalisation d'un transformateur automatique, contrat SESORI n° 218, Rapport final, 1980.

[13] H.J. KEISLER : Model theory for infinitary Logic, Studies in logic and the foundations of Mathematics, Vol. 62, North Holland, 1971.

[14] F. KRÖGER : Infinite proof rules for loops. Acta Informatica, Vol. 14, Fas. 4, 1980.

[15] G. MIRKOWSKA : Propositional algorithmic logic. Internal report, Institut de Mathématiques, Université de Varsovie, 1979.

[16] A. SALWICKI : Formalized algorithmic languages, Bull. Acad. Pol. Sci. Ser. Math. Astr. Phys. 18, 1970, p. 227-232.

[17] D. SCOTT : The lattice of flow diagrams in: Symposium on semantics of algorithmic languages (E. ENGELER ed.), Lecture notes in Math., n° 188, Springer Verlag, Berlin, 1971.

SOME MODEL-THEORETICAL PROPERTIES

OF LOGIC FOR PROGRAMS WITH RANDOM CONTROL

Extended Abstract

Michał Grabowski
Institute of Computer Science
Warsaw University

1. INTRODUCTION

Let K be a nondeterministic program, let α be a formula. In dynamic logic /also in algorithmic logic/ we consider a formula $\Box K\alpha$ which means that every possible computation of K is finite and the valuation obtained as a result satisfies α. Natural question arises: how often α is satisfied by the result of a computation of K? In order to consider this question we treat nondeterministic choice either M or N, where M,N are programs, as probabilistic choice: simply, if control is passing to an instruction either M or N then program tosses a coin; with probability 1/2 control can pass to M and with probability 1/2 control can pass to N.

Let us make two remarks:

1. Conception of program with random control is an analogue of probabilistic Turing machine investigated by Gill [1].

2. The term "probabilistic program" is used, usually, for programs with random data /x:= RANDOM, cf. Rabin [5]/, so let us call the programs with random control-the coin-toss programs.

If K is a coin-toss program and α is a formula then for a given real number $r \in (0,1)$ we consider a formula $\Box_r K\alpha$ which means:

with measure $\geqslant$ r formula α holds after executing program K. The consideration of logic $\mathcal{L}_r$ with such formulas is the subject of this paper.

In the author's opinion, model-theoretical properties of $\mathcal{L}_r$ does not depend on properties of the number r. Though, some model-theoretical properties of $\mathcal{L}_r$ are established under the assumption that r is an arithmetical number /i.e. real number which binary representation is an arithmeticaly defined function/.

The result states that if r is an arithmetical number, then the downward Skolem-Lovenheim theorem holds for $\mathcal{L}_r$ and the Hanf's number of $\mathcal{L}_r$ is the same as the Hanf's number of ordinary algorithmic logic. It is proved by the way that the set of tautologies of $\mathcal{L}_r$ /r is arithmetical/ is Π^1_1 - complete.

The proof of the result is elementary and it is obtained by transferring properties of full weak second-order logic, in abbreviation $\mathcal{L}^f_w$, where by full weak second order logic we mean first-order predicate calculus extended by relational variables and quantifiers: "there exists a finite relation" and "for every finite relation".

Parts 2 and 3 contain exact formulation of syntax and semantics of $\mathcal{L}_r$. Part 4 contains formulation of the result and a sketch of proof.

2. COIN-TOSS PROGRAMS AND FORMULAS OF $\mathcal{L}_r$

We assume that for every $n\in\omega$ a similarity type contains countably many n-ary relational symbols and countably many n-ary function symbols. The sign of equality is one of the relational symbols.

Coin-toss programs are built up from ordinary assignment instructions by means of the following program connectives:

... ; ...	-superposition
if...then...else...	-branching

while...do... -loop

either...or... -probabilistic choice.

Formulas of $\mathcal{L}_r$ are defined as follows:

I ordinary atomic formulas are formulas of $\mathcal{L}_r$,

II if α, β are formulas of $\mathcal{L}_r$ and K is a coin-toss program then $(\alpha \& \beta)$, $\neg\alpha$, $(\alpha \vee \beta)$, $(\alpha \rightarrow \beta)$, $(\forall x)\alpha$, $(\exists x)\alpha$, $\Box_r K\alpha$ are formulas of $\mathcal{L}_r$.

For the sake of simplicity we do not take under consideration iteration quantifiers. The result remains valid for the case of iteration quantifiers.

3. SEMANTICS

The set of oracles - $\{0,1\}^\omega$ - consists of all infinite 0-1-sequences. Treating every oracle as binary representation of a real number from $(0,1)$, we have ordinary Lebesgque measure, Pr, on the set of oracles.

Let v be a valuation of variables in a certain structure, K be a coin-toss program. We can define the tree $T(v)$ of all possible computations of a program K in the same manher as for nondeterministic program cf. Mirkowska [3] or Havel [4].

Let ξ be an oracle. Then $K(v,\xi)$ denotes the valuation obtained as a result of the computation selected in $T(v)$ by oracle ξ. So, if computation is finite, only a finite segment of ξ is used.

Let $\mathfrak{A}$ be a structure, v be a valuation in $\mathfrak{A}$. Now we define the satisfiability of a formula α by a valuation v in the structure $\mathfrak{A}$, $\mathfrak{A} \models \alpha[v]$:

I The ordinary definitions for propositional connectives and classical quantifiers are adopted.

II Let us assume that satisfiability has been defined for a formula α. Then the set

$$X \stackrel{df}{=} \{\xi \mid K(v,\xi) \text{ is defined and } \mathfrak{A} \models \alpha[K(v,\xi)]\}$$

is measurable /it is an event/. We define

$$\mathfrak{A} \models \Box_r K\alpha\,[v] \quad \text{iff} \quad Pr(X) \geqslant r.$$

Validity, $\mathfrak{A} \models \alpha$, is defined in the usualy way.

Let us introduce two auxiliary definitions:

Def. 1 A real number $r \in (0,1)$ is called arithmetical iff there exists a function $f:\omega \rightarrow \{0,1\}$ such that f is definable in standard model of Peano Arithmetic by a first-order arithmetical formula and $r = \sum_{n=0}^{\infty} f(n)\cdot 2^{-n}$.

Def. 2 $\mathcal{L}_r$ - theory of $\mathfrak{A} = \{\alpha \in \mathcal{L}_r \mid \mathfrak{A} \models \alpha\}$
$\mathcal{L}_w^f$ - theory of $\mathfrak{A} = \{\alpha \in \mathcal{L}_w^f \mid \mathfrak{A} \models \alpha\}$

4. THE RESULT AND A SKETCH OF PROOF

Theorem

If $r \in (0,1)$ is an arithmetical number then

1. Downward Skolem-Lovenheim theorem holds for $\mathcal{L}_r$.
2. The set of tautologies of $\mathcal{L}_r$ is Π_1^1 - complete.
3. The Hanf's numbers of $\mathcal{L}_r$ and of ordinary algorithmic logic are equal.
4. The $\mathcal{L}_r$-theory of the field of complex numbers is recursively isomorphic to the set of all true /in standard model/ sentences of Peano Arithmetic.

Outline of proof

The proof makes use of two effective mappings between appropriate sets of formulas:

$$\mathcal{L}_r \underset{I\text{ - interpretation}}{\overset{t\text{ - translation}}{\rightleftarrows}} \mathcal{L}_w^f$$

The mappings t,I possess the following properties:

(I) For every infinite model $\mathfrak{A}$ proper for identity and for every formula $\alpha \in \mathcal{L}_r$

$$\mathfrak{A} \models \alpha[v] \text{ iff } \mathfrak{A} \models t(\alpha)\,[v]$$

(II) For every formula $\beta \in \mathcal{L}_w^f$

$$\models \beta \text{ iff } \models I(\beta)$$

(" $\models \varphi$ " means that φ is a tautology).

Then we conclude that

a/ thesis 1 follows from the property (I) and from the fact that the downward Skolem-Lovenheim theorem holds for $\mathcal{L}_w^f$;

b/ thesis 2 follows from the properties (I) and (II) and from Π_1^1- completness of the set of tautologies of $\mathcal{L}_w^f$;

c/ It is implicitly proved in [2] that $\mathcal{L}_w^f$ -theory of the field of complex numbers is recursively isomorphic to the set of all true /in standard model/ sentences of Peano Arithmetic. We can transfer this property to $\mathcal{L}_r$ by the translation t.

Thesis 3 follows from the property (I) and from certain properties of interpretation I.

We shall explain the idea of I by example.

Let $\mathcal{P}_{fin}(X)$ be the family of all finite subsets of X. We are able /as in [5]/ to construct a finite set

$$Ax(S, E, =, \varepsilon, \ldots)$$

sets elements identity ϵ some other symbols

of formulas of ordinary algorithmic logic - occuring symbols are listed between brackets - such that for every structure $\mathfrak{A}$ proper for identity

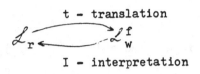

$\mathfrak{A} \models Ax(S,E,=,\varepsilon,\ldots)$ iff $\mathfrak{A}$ is isomorphic to structure

$$\langle \mathcal{P}_{fin}(E_{\mathfrak{A}}) \cup E_{\mathfrak{A}} ; \mathcal{P}_{fin}(E_{\mathfrak{A}}), =, \in, \ldots \rangle$$

of finite subsets of $E_{\mathfrak{A}}$.

Then, for instance, we interpret quantifiers for finite sets in the following way:

let X be a unary relational variable, y be an individual variable;

$X(y) \xrightarrow{I} \varepsilon(y,x) \,\&\, E(y) \,\&\, S(x)$

$(\forall X)\alpha \xrightarrow{I} \bigwedge Ax(S,E,\ldots) \,\&\, (\forall x)(S(x) \rightarrow I(\alpha))$

$(\exists X)\alpha \xrightarrow{I} \bigwedge Ax(S,E,\ldots) \,\&\, (\exists x)(S(x) \,\&\, I(\alpha))$

$(\forall y)\alpha \xrightarrow{I} \bigwedge Ax(S,E,\ldots) \,\&\, (\forall y)(E(y) \,\&\, I(\alpha))$

$(\exists y)\alpha \xrightarrow{I} \bigwedge Ax(S,E,\ldots) \,\&\, (\exists y)(E(y) \,\&\, I(\alpha))$

Let $\mathfrak{A}$ be a structure. We define two-sorted structure

$$fin(\mathfrak{A}) = \langle |\mathfrak{A}| \cup \mathcal{P}_{fin}(|\mathfrak{A}|) \text{ ; primitive operations and relations of } \mathfrak{A}, \mathcal{P}_{fin}(|\mathfrak{A}|), |\mathfrak{A}|, =, \in, \ldots \rangle$$

Thesis 3 in the theorem is derived from the property (I) and the properties of the following type:

(III) For every structure $\mathfrak{A}$ and for every set X of formulas of $\mathcal{L}^f_w$ with relational variables beeing unary

$$\mathfrak{A} \models X \text{ iff } fin(\mathfrak{A}) \models \{ I(\alpha) \mid \alpha \in X \}$$

In the sequel an idea of the translation t is presented. The assumption "r is arithmetical" is used here.

The only case whis is not quite trivial is a formula of the form $\Box_r K\alpha$. Let us represent program K as a set of instructions of the form:

(a) k:do s go to CHOICE(k_1,k_2)

(b) l:if φ then goto CHOICE(l_1,l_2) else goto CHOICE(l_3,l_4)

(c) k: STOP

Let v be a valuation in a certain structure $\mathfrak{A}$.

We define a process P evaluating a sequence S of pairs: $\langle$valuation, instruction$\rangle$. The sing ^ denotes concatenation and for a substitution s, s(v) denotes the valuation obtained from v by s. For a label k, ins(k) denotes the instruction in K labelled by k.

```
P:    S := ⟨v,first instruction of K⟩;
      l := 0; f := 0;
       while f<r do
  begin  l := l+1;  X := empty sequence;
          for each pair ⟨w,i⟩ in S do
       if i is the halting instruction then x:=X ^⟨w,i⟩ ^ ⟨w,i⟩ else
       if i is the of form (a) then X:=X^⟨s(w),ins(k1)⟩^⟨s(w),ins(k2)
  else {i is of the form (b)}
       if φ then x:=X ^⟨w,ins(l1)⟩^⟨w,ins(l2)⟩
            else X:=X ^⟨w,ins(l3)⟩^⟨w,ins(l4)⟩;
       S := X;
       k := the number of elements in S with valuations satysfing α;
       f := k/2↑l
  end
```

It can be proved zhat

$$\mathfrak{A} \models \Box_r K\alpha\,[v] \qquad \text{iff} \qquad \text{process P halts.}$$

If r is an arithmetical number then the relation $f<r$ can be described by an arithmetical formula hence logic $\mathcal{L}^{f}_{w}$ is powerfull enough to express the property : process P halts.

q. e. d.

Let us notice at the end that the same result holds for a first order dynamic logic of probabilistic programming described by Reif in [4].

REFERENCES

[1] Gill, Computational complexity of probabilistic Turing Machines, SIAM Journ. on Comp., vol.6, No 4, 1977 pp.675-695

[2] Grabowski M., Kreczmar A., Dynamic theories of real and complex numbers, Proc. of MFCS 1978 Zakopane, Lect. Notes in Comp. Sc. vol.64, Spr. Ver.

[3] Havel D., First order dynamic logic, Lect. Notes in Comp. Sc. vol.68, 1979, Spr. Ver.

[4] Mirkowska G., Algorithmic logic with nondeterministic programs, Fund. Inf. 3 1979 pp.45-64

[5] Rabin M., Probabilistic algorithms, Proc. of Symp. Algorithms and complexity, Carnegie-Mellon UNIV., April 7-9, 1976, edited by J. Traub

[6] Reif J.H., Logics for probabilistic programming, Proc. of STOC conf., 1980, pp.

[7] Salwicki A., On algorithmic theory of stacks, Proc. of MFCS 1978, Zakopane, Lect. Notes in Comp. Sc. vol.64, Spr. Ver.

A Formal System for Parallel Programs in Discrete Time and Space

Hiroya Kawai, Computation Center of Osaka University,
Mihoga Oka 5-1, Ibaraki City, Osaka 567, Japan

§1 Introduction

The investigation of mathematical theory of parallel programs will be considerablly enhanced in this ten years. However, at the present stage, a reasonable axiomatic system for such programs is not yet enough developped. In this paper, we present a formal system which enables us to prove important properties of parallel programs as well as those of deterministic and nondeterministic programs.

Our main idea is some kind of a reduction of nondeterminism into determinism. To be a little precise, we presume a chóice series of all nondeterminancy at each time point before a "Gedanken-execution". To prove existential properties, it is enough to show that they hold for one of such choice series and to prove universal properties, we verify that they hold for every such choice series. Such a choice series is incorporated in our method as a direction sequence which is an infinite sequence of processes of which statements are executed one after another at each time point.

This paper consists of three sections. In §1, we present a new logic IT_ω (logic of ω-time with intensions). IT_ω is a kind of discrete tense logic in which the always-operator is characterized by a ω-rule. This is a first-order extension of von Wright-Segerberg-Sundholm's tense logic but it is merely a ω-logic and is not so strong as an "infinitary logic". Further, it has a character of intensional logic of Montague type [5]. That is, it includes intensions besides ordinary extensions to deal more naturally and simply with the assignment statement such as x:=x+1. In §2, we define a fragment of a programming language which includes parallel processing and give the translation rules of programs into flow graphs. In this section, we also give the axioms for the execution of programs. In §3, we demonstrate the proofs of existential and universal properties of well known example programs. For this purpose, we enrich the logic with the (extensional) natural number theory.

§2 Logic of ω-Time with Intension: IT_ω

The language of IT_ω contains the set EX of extensional symbols, the set IN of intensional symbols, the set PR^{nm} of (n, m)-ary predicate symbols, the extensional (contigent) identity =, the extensionalizer operator $\vee$ and logical connectors $\supset$, $\neg$, $\forall$, J(next) and G(always). We have the set EXT of extensional terms and the set INT of intensional terms such that EXT:= EX $\cup$ $\{{}^\vee x\colon x \in IN\}$ and INT:= IN. An atomic formula of IT_ω has the form $x = y$, where $x, y \in EXT$, or $Fx_1 \ldots x_n y_1 \ldots y_m$, where $x_1, \ldots, x_n \in EXT$, $y_1, \ldots, y_m \in INT$, and $F \in PR^{nm}$. Well formed formulas are defined as follows: (1) an atomic formula is a wff, (2) if A and B are wff's and $x \in EX \cup IN$, $(\neg A)$, $(A \supset B)$, $(\forall x A)$, (JA), and (GA) are wff's. (We omit the parenthesis if no confusion occurs.) J^nA is an abbreviation for the formula which has n prefixed J's before A. A[x] denotes a wff in which $x \in EXT \cup INT$ occurs freely and A[x/a] is the wff which is constructed from A by the substitution of all x's that occur freely in A for a.

AXIOMS AND RULES OF INFERENCES OF IT_ω

(1) All tautologies of the classical propositional logic.

(2) UI: $\forall x A \supset A[x/a]$. GEN: $A[x/a] \vdash \forall x A$.
($x \in EX$ and $a \in EXT$ or $x \in IN$ and $a \in INT$.)

HUI: $\forall x A[{}^\vee x] \supset A[{}^\vee x/a]$. HGEN: $A[{}^\vee x/a] \vdash \forall x A[{}^\vee x]$.
($x \in IN$ and $a \in EXT$.)

(3) J1: $J(A \supset B) \supset (JA \supset JB)$. J2: $JA \equiv \neg J \neg A$.

G: $GA \supset A$. GJ: $GA \supset JGA$.

BF: $\forall x JA \supset J \forall x A$.

RJ: $A \vdash JA$. RG: $\{A \supset J^nB\}_{n \in \omega} \vdash (A \supset GB)$.

(4) ID1: $x = x$ ($x \in EXT$). ID2: $x \neq y \supset G(x \neq y)$ ($x, y \in EX$).

ID3: $x = y \supset (A[x] \supset A[x/y])$. (If not $x, y \in EX$, then x does not freely occur in the scope of J and G.)

SEMANTICS of IT_ω

The IT_ω-structure S is a kind of non-standard structure such that $S = \langle N, D_e, D_i, \langle D_{nm} \rangle_{n,m \in \omega} \rangle$, where $N = \langle I, ', \leqslant \rangle$ is a Peano structure with successor' and the order relation $\leqslant$, $D_i \subseteq {}^I D_e$, and $D_{nm} \subseteq \wp({}^I({}^nD_e \times {}^mD_i))$. An assignment g over S is a function such that $g(x) \in D_e$ for $x \in EX$, $g(x) \in D_i$ for $x \in IN$, and $g(F) \in D_{nm}$ for $F \in PR^{nm}$.

Let s and t be elements in I. The valuation $\| . \|^g_t$ is defined as follows:

(1) $\| x \|^g_t = g(x)$ for $x \in IN \cup EX$. (2) $\| {}^\vee x \|^g_t = g(x)(t)$ for $x \in IN$.

(3) $\| F \|^g_t = g(F)(t)$ for $F \in PR^{nm}$.

(4) $\| Fx_1 \ldots x_n y_1 \ldots y_m \|^g_t = 1$ iff $\langle \| x_1 \|^g_t, \ldots, \| x_n \|^g_t, \| y_1 \|^g_t, \ldots, \| y_m \|^g_t \rangle \in \| F \|^g_t$.

(5) $\| x = y \|^g_t = 1$ iff $\| x \|^g_t = \| y \|^g_t$.

(6)-(8) the usual clauses for $\supset$, $\neg$, and $\forall$.

(9) $\| JA \|^g_t = 1$ iff $\| A \|^g_{t'} = 1$. (10) $\| GA \|^g_t = 1$ iff for each $s \geqslant t$ $\| A \|^g_s = 1$.

Along the line of thought of Gallin [5], we obtain the completeness theorem for our system IT_ω.

EXTENSION OF IT_ω

To prove properties of programs, we add the set NUM of numerals to EX and the set SEQ to IN. Then, we put

AXSEQ: $\{J^n(\checkmark s = s_n)\}_{n\in\omega}$, where $s \in$ SEQ and $s_n \in$ NUM $(n \in \omega)$

as the axiom for the members of SEQ. As the axioms for the numerals, we assume that of Peano arithmetic, where we extend appropriately the extensional terms. Then, we introduce the set FUN_i^{01} of functions such that $f(x) \in$ INT for $f \in FUN_i^{01}$ and $x \in$ INT and we regard $\checkmark f(x) = y$ as a wff for $y \in$ EXT. The logic extended as above is called IT_ω*.

§2 Parallel Programs and Their Logical Counterparts

First, we introduce a fragment of a programming language which allows parallel processing. Here, we assume the reader has some knowledge of BNF.

A FRAGMENT OF A PROGRAMMING LANGUAGE

Though we don't present the full definition, we believe that the following definition is enough for our purpose. Our fragment contains the data types of integer and boolean. The respective part of our syntax is given as follows:

program ::= <declaration> ;<parallel process> ; <process> ; [<process>].

parallel process ::= cobegin <process name> [// <process name>] coend.

process ::= <process name>: proc <process body>.

process body ::= [<declaration>] <directives> .

directives ::= <label> : <statement> ; [<directives>].

statement ::= x:= a | ?B(<label> , <label>), where x is a variable, a is a term, and B is an Boolean expression.

FLOW GRAPH

We assume the program has n processes $P^1, \ldots, P^n$. The flow graph S^i of the i-th process P^i is a triple $\langle \Sigma^i, T^i, \phi^i \rangle$, where Σ^i is the set of all labels in P^i, $T^i \subseteq \Sigma^i \times \Sigma^i$, and ϕ^i is a mapping from T^i onto the set of assignment statements and (the negation of) Boolean expressions in P^i. The members of T^i and the values of ϕ^i are defined simultaneously as follows:

(1) If k_i: x:= a; h_i:... in P^i, then $\langle k_i, h_i \rangle \in T^i$ and $\phi^i(k_i, h_i)$ = x:=a.

(2) If k_i: ?B(h_i, h_i') in P^i, then $\langle k_i, h_i \rangle, \langle k_i, h_i' \rangle \in T^i$ and $\phi^i(k_i, h_i) = B$ and $\phi^i(k_i, h_i') = \neg B$.

The flow graph S of the program P is a triple $\langle \Sigma, T, \phi \rangle$ such that $\Sigma = \Sigma^1 \times \ldots \times \Sigma^n$, $T \subseteq \Sigma \times \Sigma$, and for each $\langle k_i, h_i \rangle \in T^i$, $((\ldots, k_i, \ldots), (\ldots, h_i, \ldots)) \in T$ and $\phi((\ldots, k_i, \ldots), (\ldots, h_i, \ldots)) = \phi^i(k_i, h_i)$, where the elements of the both tuples are same except for the i-th.

AXIOMS FOR THE EXECUTION OF PROGRAMS

The central idea of dealing with the non-determinism of parallel programs is that of direction sequence $d \in IN$ which denotes the sequence of the successibly executed processes of the program. Program variables $x_1, \ldots, x_m$ are translated into the functions of direction sequence d. $\pi = (\pi^1, \ldots, \pi^n)$ plays the role of program counters. Let $s = (s^1, \ldots, s^n)$ be an element of Σ. We denote $\bigwedge_{i=1}^{n}(\check{\pi}^i(d) = s^i)$ simply by $\check{\pi}(d) = s$. We define $Fair_n(d)$ by

$$Fair_n(d) \equiv G((\bigvee_{i=1}^{n}(\check{d} = i) \wedge \bigwedge_{i=1}^{n} F(\check{d} = i)) \quad (n \geqslant 2).$$

The axioms for the execution of programs are given as follows:

AXPC: $G(\bigvee_{s \in \Sigma}(\check{\pi}(d) = s))$.

Let $u = (u_1, \ldots, u_m)$ for each $u_j \in EX$ $(j = 1, \ldots, m)$ and a be a term.

AXE1: If $\phi(s, t) = \phi^i(s^i, t^i) = x_w := a(x)$, then

$$G((\check{\pi}(d) = s \wedge \bigwedge_{k=1}^{m}(\check{x}_k(d) = u_k) \wedge \check{d} = i) \supset J(\check{\pi}(d) = t \wedge \check{x}_w(d) = a(u) \wedge \bigwedge_{j \neq w}(\check{x}_j(d) = u_j))).$$

AXE2: If $\phi(s, t) = \phi^i(s^i, t^i) = B$ and $\phi(s, t') = \phi^i(s^i, t'^i) = \neg B$, then

$$G((\check{\pi}(d) = s \wedge \bigwedge_{k=1}^{m}(\check{x}_k(d) = u_k) \wedge \check{d} = i) \supset ((B \supset J(\check{\pi}(d) = t \wedge \bigwedge_{k=1}^{m}(\check{x}_k(d) = u_k)) \wedge (\neg B \supset J(\check{\pi}(d) = t' \wedge \bigwedge_{k=1}^{m}(\check{x}_k(d) = u_k))))).$$

IMPORTANT PROPERTIES OF PROGRAMS

Let the initial condition of the program P be denoted by A_{init} and the program be translated into its flow graph P_{ax} with axioms.

(1) A is universally correct with respect to P iff

$$P_{ax} \vdash (A_{init} \supset \forall d\ (Fair_n(d) \supset FGA)).$$

(2) A is existentially correct with respect to P iff

$$P_{ax} \vdash (A_{init} \supset \exists d\ (Fair_n(d) \wedge FGA)).$$

(3) A is invariant with respect to P iff

$$P_{ax} \vdash (A_{init} \supset \forall d\ (Fair_n(d) \supset GA)).$$

§3 Proof of Example Programs

First, we shall prove some kind of existential properties i.e. the existential deadlock. Though it cannot be called "correctness", we can prove it by the same technique as that of the existential correctness.

The following example program is originally due to Dijksta [2].

```
declaration  a, b, c : var of integer;
init  a:= 1; b:= 1; c:= 0;
cobegin  P1 // P2  coend;

P1: proc 1:  a:= 0;                  P2: proc 1:  b:= 0;
         2:  ?(b ≠ 0)(3, 2);                  2:  ?(a ≠ 0)(3, 2);
         3:  c:= 1;                           3:  c:= 2;
         4:  a:= 1;                           4:  b:= 1;
         5:  ?true (1, 5);                    5:  ?true (1, 5)
```

The flow graph of the program is given in Appendix 1. We show that this program falls into a deadlock at (2, 2) with an appropriate direction sequence d.

Let $A_{init} \equiv \forall d\ ({}^{\vee}\pi(d) = (1, 1) \wedge {}^{\vee}a(d) = {}^{\vee}b(d) = 1 \wedge {}^{\vee}c(d) = 0)$.

Theorem 1.1

$P_{ax} \vdash (A_{init} \supset \exists d\ (Fair_2(d) \wedge FG({}^{\vee}\pi(d) = (2, 2) \wedge {}^{\vee}a(d) = {}^{\vee}b(d) = 0)))$.

To prove this theorem, we need the next lemma.

Lemma 1.2 $P_{ax} \vdash \forall d\ (Fair_2(d) \supset (({}^{\vee}\pi(d) = (2, 2) \wedge {}^{\vee}a(d) = {}^{\vee}b(d) = 0)$

$\supset G({}^{\vee}\pi(d) = (2, 2) \wedge {}^{\vee}a(d) = {}^{\vee}b(d) = 0)))$.

In order to prove the theorem, we shall take some fair direction sequence d which begins with 1 and at the next time with 2.

(1) $P_{ax} \vdash A_{init} \supset ({}^{\vee}\pi(d) = (1, 1) \wedge {}^{\vee}a(d) = {}^{\vee}b(d) = 1)$.

(2) $\vdash {}^{\vee}d = 1$ (by AXSEQ).

(3) $P_{ax} \vdash A_{init} \supset J({}^{\vee}\pi(d) = (2, 1) \wedge {}^{\vee}a(d) = 0 \wedge {}^{\vee}b(d) = 1)$

(by (1), (2), and AXE1).

(4) $\vdash J({}^{\vee}d = 2)$ (by AXSEQ).

(5) $P_{ax} \vdash A_{init} \supset J^2({}^{\vee}\pi(d) = (2, 2) \wedge {}^{\vee}a(d) = {}^{\vee}b(d) = 0)$

(by (3), (4), and AXE1).

(6) $P_{ax} \vdash A_{init} \supset J^2G({}^{\vee}\pi(d) = (2, 2) \wedge {}^{\vee}a(d) = {}^{\vee}b(d) = 0)$

(by (5) and Lemma 1.2).

(7) $P_{ax} \vdash A_{init} \supset FG({}^{\vee}\pi(d) = (2, 2) \wedge {}^{\vee}a(d) = {}^{\vee}b(d) = 0)$ (by (6)).

(8) $\vdash Fair_2(d)$ (from our assumption).

(9) $P_{ax} \vdash A_{init} \supset (Fair_2(d) \wedge FG({}^{\vee}\pi(d) = (2, 2) \wedge {}^{\vee}a(d) = {}^{\vee}b(d) = 0))$

(by (7) and (8)).

(10) $P_{ax} \vdash A_{init} \supset \exists d\ (Fair_2(d) \wedge FG({}^{\vee}\pi(d) = (2, 2) \wedge {}^{\vee}a(d) = {}^{\vee}b(d) = 0))$.

Next, we shall prove the universal correctness of the following program due to Kröger [10].

```
declaration  a, b, c : var of integer;
init  a:= n; b:= 2n; c:= 0; comment  n≥1;
cobegin  P^1 // P^2  coend;

P^1: proc 1:  ?(a>0)(2, 6);          P^2: proc 1:  ?(b>n)(2, 6);
          2:  ?(f(a)>c)(3, 4);                 2:  ?(f(b)>c)(3, 4);
          3:  c:= f(a);                        3:  c:= f(b);
          4:  a:= a - 1;                       4:  b:= b - 1;
          5:  ?true(1, 5);                     5:  ?true(1, 5);
          6:  ?true(6, 6);                     6:  ?true(6, 6)
```

The flow graph of this program is given in Appendix II.

Let $A_{init} \equiv \forall d\ ({}^{\checkmark}\pi(d) = (1, 1) \wedge {}^{\checkmark}a(d) = {}^{\checkmark}b(d) = 2n \wedge {}^{\checkmark}c(d) = 0)$. Then, the universal correctness of the program is formulated in the following theorem.

Theorem 2.1 (Strong Correctness)

$$P_{ax} \vdash \forall n\ (A_{init} \supset \forall d\ (Fair_2(d) \supset FG({}^{\checkmark}\pi(d) = (6, 6) \wedge {}^{\checkmark}c(d) = \max_{1 \leq i \leq 2n} f(i)))).$$

To prove this theorem, we begin with the invariance theorem. For the sake of convenience, we put

$I_1 \equiv 0 \leq {}^{\checkmark}a(d) \leq n$, $I_1' \equiv 0 < {}^{\checkmark}a(d) \leq n$, $I_2 \equiv n \leq {}^{\checkmark}b(d) \leq 2n$, $I_2' \equiv n < {}^{\checkmark}b(d) \leq 2n$,

$K \equiv {}^{\checkmark}c(d) = \max_{\substack{{}^{\checkmark}a(d) < i \leq n \\ {}^{\checkmark}b(d) < i \leq 2n}} f(i)$, $K_1^1 \equiv {}^{\checkmark}c(d) = \max_{\substack{{}^{\checkmark}a(d) \leq i \leq n \\ {}^{\checkmark}b(d) < i \leq 2n}} f(i)$, $K_2^1 \equiv {}^{\checkmark}c(d) < \max_{\substack{{}^{\checkmark}a(d) \leq i \leq n \\ {}^{\checkmark}b(d) < i \leq 2n}} f(i)$

$K_1^2 \equiv {}^{\checkmark}c(d) = \max_{\substack{{}^{\checkmark}a(d) < i \leq n \\ {}^{\checkmark}b(d) \leq i \leq 2n}} f(i)$, $K_2^2 \equiv {}^{\checkmark}c(d) \leq \max_{\substack{{}^{\checkmark}a(d) < i \leq n \\ {}^{\checkmark}b(d) \leq i \leq 2n}} f(i)$, $K_1^3 \equiv {}^{\checkmark}c(d) = \max_{\substack{{}^{\checkmark}a(d) \leq i \leq n \\ {}^{\checkmark}b(d) \leq i \leq 2n}} f(i)$,

$K_2^3 \equiv {}^{\checkmark}c(d) < \max_{\substack{{}^{\checkmark}a(d) \leq i \leq n \\ {}^{\checkmark}b(d) \leq i \leq 2n}} f(i)$, and $K_3^3 \equiv {}^{\checkmark}c(d) \leq \max_{\substack{{}^{\checkmark}a(d) \leq i \leq n \\ {}^{\checkmark}b(d) \leq i \leq 2n}} f(i)$.

Let A_{ij} $(i, j = 1, \ldots, 6)$ and A_{inv} be formulas defined in Appendix III.

Theorem 2.2 (Invariance)

$$P_{ax} \vdash \forall n\ (A_{init} \supset \forall d\ (Fair_2(d) \supset G(A_{inv}(d)))).$$

To prove this, we use the next lemma.

Lemma 2.2.1

(1) $A_{init} \supset A_{inv}(d)$ and (2) $({}^{\checkmark}d = 1 \vee {}^{\checkmark}d = 2) \supset (A_{inv}(d) \supset JA_{inv}(d))$.

From the invariance theorem, we have

Theorem 2.3 (Weak Correctness)

$$P_{ax} \vdash \forall n\ (A_{init} \supset \forall d\ (Fair_2(d) \supset G({}^{\checkmark}\pi(d) = (6, 6) \supset {}^{\checkmark}c(d) = \max_{1 \leq i \leq 2n} f(i)))).$$

Next, we shall prove

Theorem 2.4 (Termination)

$$P_{ax} \vdash \forall n\,(A_{init} \supset \forall d\,(Fair_2(d) \supset FG({}^{\vee}\pi(d) = (6, 6)))).$$

We prove this using the following lemmas.

Lemma 2.4.1.1

$$P_{ax} \vdash \forall d\,(Fair_2(d) \supset (({}^{\vee}\pi^1(d) = 1 \wedge {}^{\vee}a(d) = k > 0) \supset F({}^{\vee}\pi^1(d) = 2 \wedge {}^{\vee}a(d) = k))).$$

Proof. Let $A \equiv {}^{\vee}\pi^1(d) = 1 \wedge {}^{\vee}a(d) = k > 0$, $B \equiv {}^{\vee}\pi^1(d) = 2 \wedge {}^{\vee}a(d) = k$, and $C \equiv {}^{\vee}\pi^1(d) = 1 \wedge {}^{\vee}a(d) = k > 0 \wedge ({}^{\vee}\pi^2(d) = 1 \vee \ldots \vee {}^{\vee}\pi^2(d) = 6)$. From AXPC, we have (1) $A \equiv C$. From AXE1 and AXE2, we have (2) ${}^{\vee}d = 2 \wedge C \supset JC$. From (1) and (2), we have (3) ${}^{\vee}d = 2 \wedge A \supset JA$. On the other hand, from AXE2, we have (4) ${}^{\vee}d = 1 \wedge A \supset JB$. Therefore, we have (5) $\forall d\,(Fair_2(d) \supset (A \supset FB))$ from (3), (4), and the definition of $Fair_2(d)$. Q.E.D.

Similarly, we have

Lemma 2.4.1.2

$$P_{ax} \vdash \forall d\,(Fair_2(d) \supset (({}^{\vee}\pi^1(d) = 2 \wedge {}^{\vee}a(d) = k) \supset F(({}^{\vee}\pi^1(d) = 3 \vee {}^{\vee}\pi^1(d) = 4) \wedge {}^{\vee}a(d) = k))).$$

Lemma 2.4.1.3

$$P_{ax} \vdash \forall d\,(Fair_2(d) \supset ((({}^{\vee}\pi^1(d) = 3 \vee {}^{\vee}\pi^1(d) = 4) \wedge {}^{\vee}a(d) = k) \supset F({}^{\vee}\pi^1(d) = 5 \wedge {}^{\vee}a(d) = k - 1))).$$

Lemma 2.4.1.4

$$P_{ax} \vdash \forall d\,(Fair_2(d) \supset (({}^{\vee}\pi^1(d) = 5 \wedge {}^{\vee}a(d) = k - 1) \supset F({}^{\vee}\pi^1(d) = 1 \wedge {}^{\vee}a(d) = k - 1))).$$

From lemmas 2.4.1.1 - 2.4.1.4, we have

Lemma 2.4.1.5

$$P_{ax} \vdash \forall d\,(Fair_2(d) \supset (({}^{\vee}\pi^1(d) = 1 \wedge {}^{\vee}a(d) = k > 0) \supset F({}^{\vee}\pi^1(d) = 1 \wedge {}^{\vee}a(d) = k - 1))).$$

On the other hand, we have

Lemma 2.4.1.6

$$P_{ax} \vdash \forall d\,(Fair_2(d) \supset (({}^{\vee}\pi^1(d) = 1 \wedge {}^{\vee}a(d) = 0) \supset FG({}^{\vee}\pi^1(d) = 6))).$$

Then, from lemmas 2.4.1.5, 2.4.1.6, and the induction axiom of Peano arithmetic, we have

Lemma 2.4.1

$$P_{ax} \vdash \forall n\,\forall d\,(({}^{\vee}\pi^1(d) = 1 \wedge {}^{\vee}a(d) = n) \supset (Fair_2(d) \supset FG({}^{\vee}\pi^1(d) = 6))).$$

Similarly, we have

Lemma 2.4.2

$$P_{ax} \vdash \forall n \forall d \, (({}^{\vee}\pi^2(d) = 1 \wedge {}^{\vee}b(d) = 2n) \supset (Fair_2(d) \supset FG({}^{\vee}\pi^2(d) = 6))).$$

Using lemmas 2.4.1 and 2.4.2, we have Theorem 2.4. Hence, we finally obtain Theorem 2.1 from theorems 2.3 and 2.4.

Reference

[1] Banachowski, L., Kreczmar, A., Mirkowska, G., Rasiowa, H., and Salwicki, A.: An introduction to algorithmic logic: Mathematical investigations in the theory of programs, Math. Found. of Comp. Sci., Vol. 2, 7-99. Banach Center Pub., Warsaw (1977).

[2] Dijkstra, E.W.: Cooperating sequential processes. In: Programming Languages Ed. Genuys, F.. Academic Press, New York (1968).

[3] Dod: Reference manual for the Ada programming language (1980).

[4] Floyd, R.W.: Assigning meaning to programs. In: Proc. Symp. in Appl. Math., Ed. Schwarz, J., 19-32. AMS, Providence, R.I. (1967).

[5] Gallin, D.: Intensional and higher-order modal logic. North-Holland, Amsterdam, Oxford (1975).

[6] Harel, D.: First order dynamic logic. In: Lecture Notes in Comp. Sci., Vol. 68. Springer, Berlin-Heidelberg-New York (1979).

[7] Hoare, C.A.R.: Axiomatic basis for computer programming. Comm. ACM, 10, 565-583 (1969).

[8] Janssen, T.M.V. and van Emde Boas, P.: On the proper treatment or referencing, dereferencing, and assignment. In: 4 th Colloq. of Automata, Languages, and Programming, Lecture Notes in Comp. Sci., Vol. 52. Springer, Berlin-Heidelberg-New York (1977).

[9] Kröger, F.: LAR: A logic of algorithmic reasoning. Acta Informatica, 8, 243-266 (1977).

[10] Kröger, F.: Unendliche Schlussregeln zur Verifikation von Programmen. TUM-I80009, Juli (1980).

[11] Manna, Z.: Logics of programs. In: Proc. of IFIP Congress 80, Ed. Lavinton, S.. North-Holland, Amsterdam-New York-Oxford (1980).

[12] Németi, I.: Nonstandard dynamic logic. Preprint, Math. Inst. of the Hungarian Academy of Sciences (1981).

[13] Pnueli, A.: The temporal semantics of concurrent programs. In: Semantics of Concurrent Computation, Ed. Kahn, G., Lecture Notes in Comp. Sci. Vol. 70, 1-20. Springer, Berlin-Heidelberg-New York (1979).

[14] Pratt, V.R.: Semantical considerations on Floyd-Hoare logic. In: Proc. 17 th Ann. IEEE Symp. on Foundations of Comp. Sci., 109-121. Oct. (1976).

[15] Sundholm, G.: A completeness proof for an infinitary tense logic. Theoria, 43, 47-51 (1977).

Appendix I

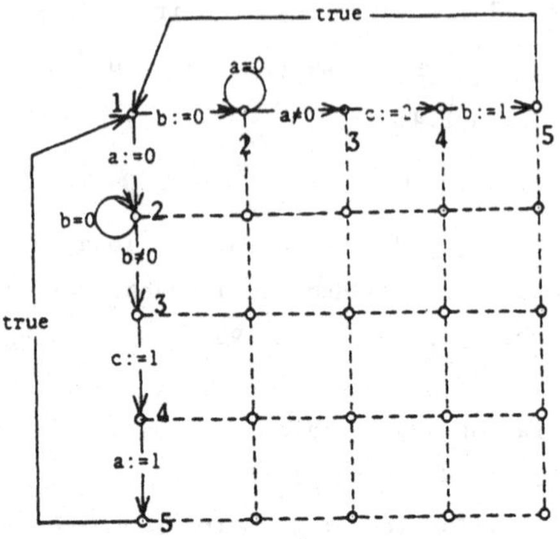

Appendix II

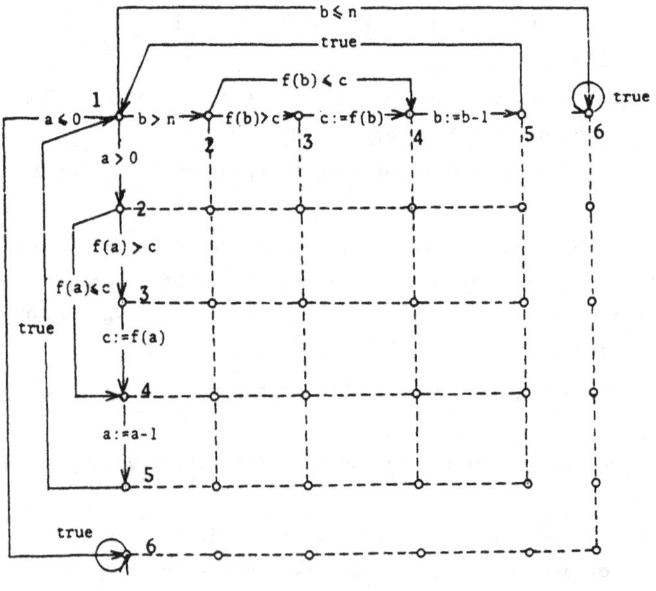

Appendix III

Let A_{ij} denote that $(\check{\pi}^1(d) = i \wedge \check{\pi}^2(d) = j) \supset q_{ij}$. Then, $q_{ij}(i, j = 1, \ldots, 6)$ and A_{inv} are defined as $q_{11} \equiv q_{51} \equiv q_{15} \equiv q_{55} \equiv I_1 \wedge I_2 \wedge K$, $q_{21} \equiv q_{25} \equiv I_1' \wedge I_2 \wedge K$, $q_{31} \equiv q_{35} \equiv I_1' \wedge I_2 \wedge K_2^1$, $q_{41} \equiv q_{45} \equiv I_1' \wedge I_2 \wedge K_1^1$, $q_{61} \equiv q_{65} \equiv \check{a}(d) = 0 \wedge I_2 \wedge K$, $q_{12} \equiv q_{52} \equiv I_1 \wedge I_2' \wedge K$, $q_{22} \equiv I_1' \wedge I_2' \wedge K$, $q_{32} \equiv I_1' \wedge I_2' \wedge K_2^1$, $q_{42} \equiv I_1 \wedge I_2' \wedge K_1^1$, $q_{62} \equiv \check{a}(d) = 0 \wedge I_2' \wedge K$, $q_{13} \equiv q_{53} \equiv I_1 \wedge I_2' \wedge K_2^2$, $q_{23} \equiv I_1' \wedge I_2' \wedge K_2^2$, $q_{33} \equiv I_1' \wedge I_2' \wedge K_2^3$, $q_{43} \equiv I_1' \wedge I_2' \wedge K_3^3$, $q_{63} \equiv \check{a}(d) = 0 \wedge I_2' \wedge K_2^2$, $q_{14} \equiv q_{54} \equiv I_1 \wedge I_2' \wedge K_1^2$, $q_{24} \equiv I_1' \wedge I_2' \wedge K_1^2$, $q_{34} \equiv I_1' \wedge I_2' \wedge K_3^3$, $q_{44} \equiv I_1' \wedge I_2' \wedge K_1^3$, $q_{64} \equiv \check{a}(d) = 0$

$\wedge I_2' \wedge K_1^2$, $q_{16} \equiv q_{56} \equiv I_1 \wedge {}^{\vee}b(d) = n \wedge K$, $q_{26} \equiv I_1' \wedge {}^{\vee}b(d) = n \wedge K$, $q_{36} \equiv I_1' \wedge$ ${}^{\vee}b(d) = n \wedge K_2^1$, $q_{46} \equiv I_1' \wedge {}^{\vee}b(d) = n \wedge K_1^1$, $q_{66} \equiv {}^{\vee}a(d) = 0 \wedge {}^{\vee}b(d) = n \wedge K$, and $A_{inv} \equiv \bigwedge_{1 \leq i, j \leq 6} A_{ij}$.

Appendix IV

We shall sketch the proof of the completeness theorem for IT_ω.

Completeness Theorem For any wff A, $\vdash A$ iff $\models A$.

The proof of the only if part is straightforward. So, we concentrate ourselves on the if part. It is carried out by the Henkin's method of the canonical model construction (cf. Gallin [5]).

A set Σ of wff's is called to be saturated iff (1) Σ is consistent, (2) either $J^nA \in \Sigma$ or $J^n(\neg A) \in \Sigma$, (3) if $J^n(A \supset B) \in \Sigma$ then $J^nA \in \Sigma$ implies $J^nB \in \Sigma$, (4) if $J^nA[x/a]$ for each $a \in EXT \cup INT$ then $J^n(\forall\ x\ A) \in \Sigma$, and (5) if $J^{n+i}A \in \Sigma$ for each $i \in \omega$ then $J^nGA \in \Sigma$.

Lemma 1 Let Σ be a consistent set of wff's.

(1) $\{J^{n+k}A \supset J^nGA\}$ is consistent for some $k \in \omega$.

(2) $\{J^nA[x/a] \supset J^n(\forall\ x\ A)\}$ is consistent for some $a \in EXT \cup INT$.

The proof of (1) is the same as that of Sundholm [15] and (2) is verified by the proof of the first order analogue with a slight modification. From this, we have

Lemma 2 (Saturation) Let Σ' be a consistent set of wff's. Then, it can be extended to some saturated set Σ which contains Σ'.

We shall construct the canonical model. First, we take $I = \omega$, $s' = s + 1$, and $s \leq t$ as the usual order relation, where ω is regarded as the number of prefixed J's in each wff's in some saturated set Σ. Next, we define an equivalence relation on EXT such that $x \simeq y \pmod t$ iff $J^t(x = y) \in \Sigma$. This equivalence relation is independent on $t \in I$ for the members of EX because of $J^t(x = y) \supset J^s(x = y)$ for x, $y \in EX$. So, in this case, we write $x \simeq y$. The assignment g and D's are defined simultaneously as follows.

(1) Let $D_e = EX/\simeq$ and $g(x) = x/\simeq$ for $x \in EX$.

(2) For $x \in IN$, we take some $a \in EX$ such that ${}^{\vee}x \simeq a \pmod t$ and define $g(x)(t) = a/\simeq$. The existence of such a is guaranteed by $\forall\ x\ G\ \exists\ y\ ({}^{\vee}x = y)\ (y \in EX)$. Let $D_i = \{g(x) : x \in IN\} \subseteq {}^{I}D_e$.

(3) For $F \in PR^{nm}$, let $g(F)(t) = \{\langle g(x_1), \ldots, g(x_n), g(y_1)(t), \ldots, g(y_m)(t)\rangle : J^tFx_1 \ldots x_ny_1 \ldots y_m,\ x_1, \ldots, x_n \in EXT$, and $y_1, \ldots, y_m \in INT\}$ and $D_{nm} = \{g(F) : F \in PR^{nm}\} \subseteq \wp({}^{I}({}^{n}D_e \times {}^{m}D_i))$.

The rest of the proof is to check that $\|A\|_t^g = 1$ iff $J^tA \in \Sigma$. This is a well known routine. So, we rest it for the reader.

ON THE PROPOSITIONAL ALGORITHMIC THEORY OF ARITHMETIC

Grażyna Mirkowska
University of Warsaw
Institute of Mathematics
00-901 Warsaw, POLAND

INTRODUCTION

Propositional algorithmic logic [3,4] aims to study properties of program connectives. It appears that this logic enables to axiomatize and study data structures [4] .

Here we present a propositional algorithmic theory of arithmetic of natural numbers. The idea of propositional arithmetic appeared during a discussion with V.Pratt and A.Salwicki on MFCS'79 conference in Olomouc [5] . It was observed that it is possible to express the property " to be a natural number " by means of formulas of propositional algorithmic logic PAL [3] .

The theory developed here use two kinds of atomic program variables for successors and predecessors. Program schemes of the theory represent arbitrary recursive functions [6] . The main result states that every one-argument partial recursive function can be represented by a scheme of program.

This result seems to be interesting since it was already proved by Chlebus [1] that deterministic propositional algorithmic logic is decidable. Our result states that by adding a finite set of formulas to the set of axioms of PAL we can obtained undecidable theory .

. PRELIMINARY DEFINITIONS

We shall consider propositional algorithmic language without non-determinism [3,4] . Let V_o denote the set of all propositional variables and V_p denote the set of all program variables.

The set of all formulas F forms an algebra generated by V_o with the usual logical connectives $\vee, \wedge, \Rightarrow, -$ and such that if $\alpha \in F$ then for every program scheme M , $M\alpha \in F$.

The set of all program schemes Π forms an algebra with program connectives : begin-end ,if-then-else, while-do , generated by the set $V_o \cup \{I\}$, where I is a constant.

By a semantic structure we shall understand a triple $\langle S, \mathfrak{I}, w \rangle$ where S is a nonempty set of states, $\mathfrak{I}$ is a function which to every program variable assigns a partial function from S to S and w is a function which to every state assigns a valuation of propositional variables in the two-element Boolean algebra .

Let $\mathfrak{M}$ be a fixed semantic structure. The meaning of an arbitrary program scheme M in $\mathfrak{M}$ is a partial function M : S $\to$ S such that

$$M_{\mathfrak{M}}(s) = \begin{cases} s' & \text{iff there exists a finite computation [3] of M in the structure } \mathfrak{M} \text{ such that its initial state is } s \text{ and its final state is } s' \\ \text{undefined in the opposite case .} \end{cases}$$

The semantic consequence operation is defined as in propositional algorithmic logic [3,4]. Let us recall only a part of the definition:

$$\mathfrak{M}, s \models M\alpha \quad \text{iff} \quad M_{\mathfrak{M}}(s) \text{ is defined and } \mathfrak{M}, M_{\mathfrak{M}}(s) \models \alpha .$$

In the sequel we shall use the following definition.
The semantic structure $\mathfrak{M} = \langle S, \mathfrak{I}, w \rangle$ is normalized iff for every state s and for every state s′ from the set S the following condition holds

$$s = s' \quad \text{iff} \quad (\forall \alpha \in F)(\mathfrak{M}, s \models \alpha \equiv \mathfrak{M}, s' \models \alpha .).$$

Let " true " denote a formula of the form $(-\alpha \vee \alpha)$ and let (if γ then M fi) be a shortened form of (if γ then M else I), where γ is a formula and M is a program scheme .

2. DETERMINISTIC PROPOSITIONAL ALGORITHMIC LOGIC

In this section we shall describe a deductive system DPAL of deterministic propositional algorithmic logic. This system is an inconsiderable modification of the system defined in [3] .

AXIOMS of DPAL

all axioms of classical propositional calculus and

$M(\alpha \vee \beta) \equiv M\alpha \vee M\beta$

$M(\alpha \wedge \beta) \equiv M\alpha \wedge M\beta$

$M(-\alpha) \equiv -M\alpha \qquad I\alpha \equiv \alpha$

$(\text{begin } M ; M' \text{end})\alpha \equiv M(M'\alpha)$

$(\text{if } \gamma \text{ then } M \text{ else } M' \text{fi})\alpha \equiv (\gamma \wedge M\alpha) \vee (-\gamma \wedge M'\alpha)$

$(\text{while } \gamma \text{ do } M \text{ od})\alpha \equiv (-\gamma \wedge \alpha) \vee (\gamma \wedge M(\text{while } \gamma \text{ do } M \text{ od})\alpha)$

RULES

r1 $\dfrac{\alpha, (\alpha \Rightarrow \beta)}{\beta}$ r2 $\dfrac{(\alpha \Rightarrow \beta)}{M\alpha \Rightarrow M\beta}$

r3 $\dfrac{\{(\text{if } \gamma \text{ then } M \text{ fi})^i(-\gamma \wedge \alpha) \Rightarrow \beta\}_{i \in \omega}}{(\text{while } \gamma \text{ do } M \text{ od})\alpha \Rightarrow \beta}$

In all the above formulas M,M′ are arbitrary program schemes, α , β are formulas and γ is a formula of classical propositional calculus.

The syntactic consequence operation C of DPAL assigns to every set of formulas X a set C(X) which contains all axioms and the set X and is closed with respect to the rules r1, r2, r3.

By a theory we understand a system $T = \langle L, C, A \rangle$ where L is a language of propositional logic described in the section1, C is the syntactical consequence operation and A is a set of formulas called a set of specific axioms of T.

By a model of the theory T we understand a semantic structure $\mathfrak{M}$ such that for every formula $\alpha \in A$ and evety state s in $\mathfrak{M}$,
$\mathfrak{M}, s \models \alpha$.

Below we shall mention two important theorems : the completeness theorem which states that the semantical and syntactical consequence operations coincide , and the theorem on decidability of the set of tautologies of DPAL.

THEOREM 2.1 [3,4]
For every formula α in a consistent theory T the following conditions are equivalent

(i) α is a theorem of the theory T,
(ii) α is valid in every model of the theory T,
(iii) α is valid in every normalized model of the theory T . □

THEOREM 2.2 [1]
The system of deterministic propositional algorithmic logic is decidable . □

3. PROPOSITIONAL THEORY OF ARITHMETIC

Let us consider the language L_n of propositional algorithmic logic, where n is a fixed natural number, such that $V_0 = \{z_1, \dots, z_n\}$ and $P = \{N_1, P_1, \dots, N_n, P_n\}$.

By the propositional algorithmic arithmetic AR_n we shall undertand an algorithmic theory based on the language L_n

$$AR_n = \langle L_n, C , Axar \rangle$$

uch that the set of specific axioms Axar contains all instances of he following schemes

ar1 $N_i(-z_i)$ $(z_i \Rightarrow -P_i \text{true})$

ar2 $(\alpha \Rightarrow N_i P_i \alpha)$ ar3 $(-z_i \Rightarrow (\alpha \Rightarrow P_i N_i \alpha))$

ar4 (while $-z_i$ do P_i od)true

ar5 $(-z_i \Rightarrow P_i \beta_{-i} \equiv \beta_{-i})$ ar6 $(N_i \beta_{-i} \equiv \beta_{-i})$

ar7 $(N_i N_j \alpha \equiv N_j N_i \alpha)$ ar8 $(P_i P_j \alpha \equiv P_j P_i \alpha)$

ar9 $(N_i P_j \alpha \equiv P_j N_i \alpha)$ for $i \neq j$.

In all the above schemes α is an arbitrary formula, β_{-i} is a formula in which z_i does not appear and k.l.i.j are natural numbers not greater than n .

THEOREM 3.1
The following schemas are theorems in AR_n for arbitrary $n,m,k \in \mathcal{N}$

$$N_i^k P_i^m \alpha \equiv \alpha \quad \text{for } k=m$$

$$N_i^k P_i^m \alpha \equiv P_i^{m-k} \alpha \quad \text{for } k<m$$

$$N_i^k P_i^m \alpha \equiv N_i^{k-m} \alpha \quad \text{for } k>m$$

$$-z_i \Rightarrow (P_i(-\alpha) \equiv -P_i \alpha)$$

$$N_i(-\alpha) \equiv -N_i \alpha$$

where $i \leq n$ and α denotes an arbitrary formula . □

EXAMPLE of a MODEL

Let us consider the semantic structure $\mathfrak{M} = \langle S, \mathfrak{I}, w \rangle$ such that $S = N^n$, and for all $i \leq n$.

$\mathfrak{I}(N_i) = \{(f,g) \in S \times S : f(j)=g(j)$ for $j \neq i$ and $g(i)=f(i)+1$

$\mathfrak{I}(P_i) = \{(f,g) \in S \times S : f(i) \neq 0, f(j)=g(j)$ for $j \neq i$ and $g(i)= f(i)-1$

$w(s) = v$ such that $v(z_i)$=true iff $s(i)=0$, for $i \leq n$ and $s \in S$.

By an easy verification we can prove that the structure $\mathfrak{M}$ is a model of the set Axar. We shall call this model standard.

THEOREM 3.2
The propositional algorithmic arithmetic AR is consistent . □

THEOREM 3.3
Every normalized model of Axar is isomorphic to the standard model .

PROOF.
Let $\mathfrak{M}$ be a normalized model of AR_n. The proof of the theorem is devided into three parts

A. We shall prove that there is only one state s_0 in $\mathfrak{M}$ such that for all $i \leq n$, $\mathfrak{M}, s_0 \models z_i$.

B. Cardinality of $\mathfrak{M}$ is at least $\aleph_0$.

C. The structures $\mathfrak{M}$ and $\mathfrak{N}$ are isomorphic.

Part A.

Let $\mathfrak{M} = \langle S', \mathfrak{I}', w' \rangle$ and suppose that there are two states s_o and s_o' in S' such that

$$\mathfrak{M}, s_o' \models z_i \quad \text{and} \quad \mathfrak{M}, s_o \models z_i \quad \text{for all } i \leq n .$$

Since $\mathfrak{M}$ is a normalized structure then there exists a formula α such that

(1) $$\mathfrak{M}, s_o \models \alpha \quad \text{and} \quad \mathfrak{M}, s_o' \models -\alpha .$$

Let us consider the minimal, in the sense of the length, formula α with the property (1). This formula cannot be of the form $(\gamma \vee \beta)$, $(\gamma \wedge \beta)$, $(\gamma \Rightarrow \beta)$, $-\gamma$ since in all these cases the formulas γ and β are shorter than α and at least one of them satisfies (1).

The formula α cannot be of the form (while γ do M od)β since there exists $i \in N$ such that

$$\mathfrak{M}, s_o \models (\text{if } \gamma \text{ then M fi})^i(-\gamma \wedge \beta) \quad \text{and} \quad \mathfrak{M}, s_o' \not\models (\text{if } \gamma \text{ then M fi})^i(-\gamma \wedge \beta).$$

Hence there exists a formula which is submitted to α and which satisfies (1). From the same reason, α cannot be of the form

$$(\text{if } \gamma \text{ then } M_1 \text{ else } M_2 \text{ fi})\beta \quad \text{or} \quad (\text{begin } M_1 ; M_2 \text{ end})\beta .$$

Thus the only possible situation is $\alpha = \text{pref } z_k$ where $k \leq n$ pref $\in V_p^*$. By the theorem 3.1 the last formula is equivalent to

$$N_k^{\,l} z_k \quad \text{or} \quad P_k^{\,m} z_k .$$

The first formula is false in both states s_o and s_o' and the second formula is true in both states.

Hence there is at most one state with the property (1) in the structure $\mathfrak{M}$. Observe that by axiom ar4 there is at least one state s in S' with the propoerty (1) . Thus there exists exactly one state s_o such that for every $i \leq n$ $\mathfrak{M}, s_o \models z_i$.

Part B.

Let us suppose thet there is a normalized model $\mathfrak{M} = \langle S', \mathfrak{I}', w' \rangle$ such that S' is a finite set. Let $S' = \{s_o, \ldots, s_m\}$ and let s_o has the property (1). Suppose $i \leq n$, since s_o is not a value of N_i for any argument, then there are at least two states s_k and s_l such that $k \neq l$ and

$$N_{i\mathfrak{M}}(s_k) = s_j \quad , \quad N_{i\mathfrak{M}}(s_l) = s_j \quad \text{for some } s_j \neq s_o$$

By axioms ar2 and ar3, for all $i \leq n$ and any $s, s' \in S'$

$$N_{i\mathfrak{M}}(s) = s' \quad \text{iff} \quad P_{i\mathfrak{M}}(s') = s \;\&\; s' \neq s_o .$$

Hence

$$P_{i\,\mathfrak{M}}(s_j) = s_k \quad \text{and} \quad P_{i\,\mathfrak{M}}(s_j) = s_1$$

contrary to the fact that $P_{i\mathfrak{M}}$ is a function.

Part C.

Let $\mathfrak{N}$ be a standard model of Axar and $\mathfrak{M}$ be any normalized mode of Axar

$$\mathfrak{N} = \langle S, \mathfrak{I}, w\rangle \quad \text{and} \quad \mathfrak{M} = \langle S', \mathfrak{I}; w'\rangle .$$

We shall define a mapping $h\colon \mathfrak{N} \to \mathfrak{M}$ such that

$$h(g) = \begin{cases} s_0 & \text{for } g = g_0 \\ N_1^{\,i_1}\ldots N_n^{\,i_n}(s_0) & \text{for } g \neq g_0 \text{ and } g(k) = i_k ,\ k \le n \end{cases}$$

where s_0 and g_0 are elements of $\mathfrak{M}$ and $\mathfrak{N}$ respectively that satisfy the property (*).

By axioms ar2 and ar3 $N_{i\,\mathfrak{M}}$ is a one-one mapping, hence for every $g, g' \in S$, if $g \neq g'$ then $h(g) = h(g')$.

Let s' be an element of S' and

$$\mathfrak{M}, s' \models (z_1 \wedge \ldots \wedge z_k) \quad , \quad \mathfrak{M}, s' \not\models (z_{k+1} \vee \ldots \vee z_n) .$$

By axiom ar4 there are naturel numbers $i_{k+1}, \ldots, i_n$ such that

$$\mathfrak{M}, P_{k+1}^{\,i_{k+1}} \ldots P_n^{\,i_n}{}_{\mathfrak{M}}(s') \models (z_1 \wedge \ldots \wedge z_n) .$$

By Part A

$$P_{k+1}^{\,i_{k+1}} \ldots P_n^{\,i_n}{}_{\mathfrak{M}}(s') = s_0 .$$

By the definition of h we have $h(0\ldots 0 i_{k+1} \ldots i_n) = s'$, i.e h is a function on $\mathfrak{M}$.

It remains to show that h is a homomorphism.

$$h(N_{j\,\mathfrak{N}}(i_1 \ldots i_n)) = h(i_1 \ldots, i_j + 1, \ldots i_n) = N_{j\,\mathfrak{M}}(N_{1\,\mathfrak{M}}^{\,i_1} \ldots N_{n\,\mathfrak{M}}^{\,i_n}(s_0)) = N_{j\,\mathfrak{M}}(h(i_1 \ldots i_n$$

$$h\, P_{j\,\mathfrak{M}}(i_1 \ldots i_n) = \begin{cases} h(i_1 \ldots i_j, \ldots i_n) & \text{iff } i_j = 0 \\ h(i_1, \ldots, i_j - 1, \ldots i_n) & \text{iff } i_j \neq 0 \end{cases} = P_{j\,\mathfrak{M}} N_{1\,\mathfrak{M}}^{\,i_1} \ldots N_{j\,\mathfrak{M}}^{\,i_j} \ldots N_{n\,\mathfrak{M}}^{\,i_n}(s$$

$$= P_{j\,\mathfrak{M}}\, h(i_1 \ldots i_j \ldots i_m) .$$

Hence h is an isomorphism.

From A, B, C follows immediately that any normalized model of algorithmic arithmetic is isomorphic to the standard model.

$\square$

4. PROGRAMMABILITY

We shall say that an m-argument partial function $f: \mathcal{N}^m \to \mathcal{N}$ is programmable in the propositional arithmetic AR_n, $n \geq m+1$, iff there exists a program scheme M such that for every model $\mathfrak{M}$ of Axar and for every natural numbers $i_1, \ldots, i_m$, for every state s the following condition holds

$$\text{if} \quad \mathfrak{M}, s \models P_1^{i_1} \ldots P_m^{i_m}(z_1 \wedge \ldots \wedge z_m) \quad \text{then}$$

(1) if $f(i_1, \ldots, i_m)$ is defined then $\mathfrak{M}, s \models M\, P_{m+1}^{f(i_1 \ldots i_m)} z_{m+1}$

or

(2) if $f(i_1 \ldots i_m)$ is not defined then $\mathfrak{M}, s \models -M\, \text{true}$.

If f is a total m-argument function then the above condition is reduced to the following form

$$(3) \quad \mathfrak{M} \models M\text{true} \wedge \left(P_1^{i_1} \ldots P_m^{i_m}(z_1 \wedge \ldots \wedge z_m) \Rightarrow M\, P_{m+1}^{f(i_1 \ldots i_m)} z_{m+1}\right).$$

By the completeness theorem 2.1 it is equivalent to

$$AR_n \vdash M\text{true} \wedge \left(P_1^{i_1} \ldots P_m^{i_m}(z_1 \wedge \ldots \wedge z_m) \Rightarrow M\, P_{m+1}^{f(i_1 \ldots i_m)} z_{m+1}\right).$$

If f is programmable by M then we shall say that M represents the function f .

In all the examples below we shall denote by x the propositional variable storing an information about argument of a programmable function , by y the variable storing an information about result and by u,v,w - auxiliary variables.

EXAMPLE 4.1

The following program $M(x_1, x_2, y)$ represents the function f, $f: \mathcal{N}^2 \to \mathcal{N}$, $f(x_1, x_2) = x_1 + x_2$ for all $x_1, x_2 \in \mathcal{N}$.

```
begin
  while -y do P_y od;
  while -x_1 do P_x1; N_y od;
  while -x_2 do P_x2; N_y od;
end;
```

PROOF.

Observe that by axiom ar4

$$AR \vdash M \text{ true} .$$

For the sake of simplicity let J_1, J_2, J_3 denote the three instructio of the program scheme M and let α denote the formula $(x_1 \wedge x_2 \wedge y)$. Below we shall show that f is programmable in propositional algorithmic theory AR_3 .

$AR \vdash J_1 y$ by axiom ar4

(4) $AR \vdash P_{x_1}^{i} P_{x_2}^{j} (x_1 \wedge x_2) \Rightarrow J_1 \; P_{x_1}^{i} \; P_{x_2}^{j} \; N_y^{i} \; P_y^{i} \; \alpha$ by ar2, ar3

(5) $AR \vdash P_{x_1}^{i} P_{x_2}^{j} (x_1 \wedge x_2) \Rightarrow J_1 J_2 \; P_y^{i} \; P_{x_2}^{j}$ by (4)

(6) $AR \vdash P_y^{i} P_{x_2}^{j} \; \alpha \Rightarrow N_y^{j} \; P_y^{j} \; P_{x_2}^{j} \; P_y^{i} \; \alpha$ by ar2, ar3

(7) $AR \vdash P_y^{i} \; P_{x_2}^{j} \; \alpha \Rightarrow J_3 \; P_y^{j+i} \; \alpha$ by (6)

$AR \vdash P_{x_1}^{i} \; P_{x_2}^{j} (x_1 \wedge x_2) \Rightarrow M \; P_y^{j+i} \; \alpha$ by (5) and (7)

$AR \vdash P_{x_1}^{i} \; P_{x_2}^{j} (x_1 \wedge x_2) \Rightarrow M \; P_y^{j+i} \; y$. □

EXAMPLE 4.2

The following program $M(x_1, x_2, y, v)$ represents function g such that for every $x_1, x_2 \in \mathcal{N}$, $g(x_1, x_2) = x_1 \cdot x_2$.

```
M:          begin
              while -v do P_v od;
              while -y do P_y od;
              while -x_1
                do
                  while -x_2 do P_x2; N_y; N_v od;
                  while -v do N_x2; P_v od;
                  P_x1
                od
            end:
```

PROOF.

Let us denote by $J_1 - J_5$ all instructions of the form "while-do" in the program M and by α the formula $(v \wedge x_2 \wedge y)$.

$$AR \vdash J_1 J_2(v \wedge y) \qquad \text{by ar4}$$

(8) $$AR \vdash P_{x_1}^{\ i} P_{x_2}^{\ j} (x_1 \wedge x_2) \Rightarrow J_1 J_2 P_{x_1}^{\ i} P_{x_2}^{\ j} (x_1 \wedge x_2 \wedge v \wedge y) \qquad \text{by r2}$$

For every natural number k we have

(9) $$AR \vdash P_{x_2}^{\ j} P_y^{j\ k} \alpha \Rightarrow J_4 J_5 P_{x_2}^{\ j} P_y^{j\cdot(k+1)} \alpha \qquad \text{by ar2, ar3, (8)}$$

(10) $$AR \vdash P_{x_2}^{\ j} \alpha \Rightarrow J_4 : J_5^{\ i} P_{x_2}^{\ j} P_y^{j\cdot i} \alpha \qquad \text{by induction and (9)}$$

(11) $$AR \vdash P_{x_1}^{\ i} P_{x_2}^{\ j} (x_1 \wedge \alpha) \Rightarrow J_3 P_{x_2}^{\ j} P_y^{j\cdot i} (x_1 \wedge \alpha) \qquad \text{by (10)}$$

(12) $$AR \vdash P_{x_1}^{\ i} P_{x_2}^{\ j} (x_1 \wedge x_2) \Rightarrow M P_{x_2}^{\ j} P_y^{j\cdot i} (x_1 \wedge \alpha) \qquad \text{by (11), (8)}$$

$$AR \vdash P_{x_1}^{\ i} P_{x_2}^{\ j} (x_1 \wedge x_2) \Rightarrow M P_y^{j\cdot i}\ y \qquad \text{by (12)}$$

□

The natural question arises : which functions can be defined in the propositional algorithmic arithmetic by a program scheme ? The answer is -all partial recursive functions .We shall consider first one-argument functions. The main theorem states that every one-argument partial recursive function can be defined by means of a program scheme in AR_5 . The number 5 is not the smallest possible. For us the most essential was the fact that the number of variables used is bounded.

For that reason we shall introduce two auxiliary functions

$$p(x,u) = 2^x \cdot 3^u \qquad \text{and} \qquad p'(2^x \cdot 3^u) = (x,u)$$

which allow us to interpret a variable as a stack storing informations.

LEMMA 4.1

The following program scheme $M_p(x,u,w,v)$ represents the function $p(x,u)$. More precisely , for every natural numbers i and j

$$AR_5 \vdash P_x^i P_u^j (x \wedge u) \Rightarrow M_p(P_x^{\ i}\ x \wedge P_u^{2^i\ 3^j}\ u)$$

where

M_p : begin

M_1: { while -v do P_v od ;
while -w do P_w od ;

```
    N_w ;
    while -u do
      while -w do P_w; N_v;N_v;N_v od;
      while -v do P_v ;N_w od;
      P_u
    od:
    while -w do P_w; N_u od;
    while -x do P_x; N_w; N_v od;
    while -v do P_v; N_x od
    while -x do
      while -u do P_u;N_v;N_v od;
      while -v do P_v; N_u od;
      P_x
    od;
    while -w do P_w; N_x od
  end M_p ;
```

□

LEMMA 4.2

The following program scheme $M_{p'}(x,u,w,v)$ represents the function p', i.e for every natural numbers i,j

$$AR_5 \vdash P_u^{2^i \cdot 3^j} u \Rightarrow M_{p'}\left(P_x^{\,i}\, x \wedge P_u^j\, u\right) \quad .$$

$M_{p'}$:

```
begin
  while -x do P_x  od;
  while -v do P_v  od;
  while -w do P_w  od;
  while v do
    while -u do
       P_u: if -u then P_u;N_w else N_v fi
    od;
    if v then
       N_x;
       while -w do P_w;N_u od
    else
```

```
          N_u;
          while -w do P_w;N_u;N_u od
        fi
      od;
      while -v do P_v od ;
      while -u do
         P_u;
         if -u then
           N_u;
           while -u do P_u;P_u;P_u N_w od;
           N_v;
           while -w do P_w; N_u  od
         fi
      od:
      while -v do P_v;N_u od
    end M_p. ;
```

□

THEOREM 4.3

Every primitive recursive one-argument function is programmable in the propositional algorithmic arithmetic AR_5 .

PROOF.

Using the result of A.Robinson [2] it is enough to prove that the following functions are programmable

1. $s(x) = x+1$
2. $q(x) = x - [\sqrt{x}]^2$
3. $Jf(x) = f^x(0)$
4. $f \circ g(x) = f(g(x))$
5. $(f + g)(x) = f(x) + g(x)$.

For every case 1.-5. we shall construct a corresponding program M in such a way that for every $i, j \in \mathcal{N}$,

$$AR_5 \vdash (P^i_x\, x \wedge P^j_u u) \Rightarrow M(P^i_x\, x \wedge P^j_u\, u) \quad .$$

ie. the initial values of x and u are not changed by M .

Ad 2. The following program $M_q(x,y,v,w)$ represents the function q, where $q(x) = x - [\max_n (1+3+\ldots+2n-1 \leq x)]^2$.

```
M_q :          begin
               ⎧ while -w do Pw od ;
        M_1:   ⎨ while -y do P_y od ;
               ⎩ while -v do P_v od ;
```

```
        N_v ;
        while -x do
          ⎧ while -v ∧ -x do P_x;N_w;P_v;N_y od ;
          ⎪ if v -x then
     M_3: ⎨    ⎧while -y do P_y;N_v od;
          ⎪ M_2⎩N_v; N_v
          ⎩ fi
        od ;
   M_4: ⎧ if v then while -y do P_y od fi;
        ⎩ while -w do P_w ;N_x od
       end M_q ;
```

Let us denote by α the formula $(x\wedge y\wedge v)$ and let $\mathfrak{N}$ be the standard mode of AR_5 . Below we present the proof that M_q represents q .

(13) $\mathfrak{N} \models M_1 N_v P_v (y\wedge v\wedge w)$ by axiom ar4

For every natural number i and every $m < \max_n (1+3+\ldots+(2n-1) \leq i)$

(14) $\mathfrak{N} \models P_x^{i-(1+3+\ldots+2m-1)} P_v^{2m+1} \alpha \Rightarrow$

$$P_x^{2m+1} P_x^{i-(1+\ldots+2m+1)} N_y^{2m+1} P_y^{2m+1} P_v^{2m+1} \alpha$$

(15) $\mathfrak{N} \models P_y^{2m+1}(-x\wedge v\wedge y) \Rightarrow M_2 P_v^{2m+3} (-x\wedge v\wedge y)$ by ar2 and ar3

(16) $\mathfrak{N} \models P_x^{i-(1+\ldots+2m-1)} P_v^{2m+1} P_w^k (w\wedge\alpha) \Rightarrow$

$$M_3 P_x^{i-(1+\ldots+2m+1)} P_v^{2m+3} P_w^{k+2m+1} (w\wedge\alpha)$$ by (14), (15

If $m = n = \max_j (1+3+\ldots+ 2j-1 \leq i)$ then we have two cases

a. $i = 1+3+\ldots+2n-1$ b. $i > 1+3+\ldots+2n-1$.

(17a) $\mathfrak{N} \models P_x^{i-(1+\ldots+2n-3)} P_v^{2n-1} P_w^k (w\wedge\alpha) \Rightarrow M_3 P_y^{2n-1} P_w^{k+2n-1} (w\wedge\alpha$

(18a) $\mathfrak{N} \models P_x^i P_v (w\wedge\alpha) \Rightarrow M_1 N_v M_3^n P_y^{2n-1} (P_w^i \ w\wedge\alpha)$ by (17a) and induction

(19a) $\mathfrak{N} \models P_x^i (x\wedge w) \Rightarrow M_1 N_v (\text{while } -x \text{ do } M_3 \text{ od}) P_y^{2n-1} (P_w^i \ w\wedge\alpha)$

by (18 a)

(20a) $\mathfrak{N} \models (x\wedge v\wedge P_w^k w) \Rightarrow M_4 (y\wedge w\wedge P_x^k x)$ by ar4 and axioms of logic

(21a) $\mathcal{T} \models P_x^i\, x \Rightarrow M_q\, P_x^i\, x \wedge y$ by (20a), (19a)

(17b) $\mathcal{T} \models P_x^k\, P_v^{2n+1}\, P_w^l (w \wedge \alpha) \Rightarrow M_3\, P_y^k\, P_v^{2n+1-k} (\alpha \wedge P_w^{l+k}\, w)$

where $k = i - 1+3+\ldots+2n-1$

(18b) $\mathcal{T} \models P_x^i\, \alpha \Rightarrow M_1\, N_v\, M_3^n\, P_v^{2n+1-k} (P_w^i\, w \wedge \alpha)$ by (17b) and induction

(19b) $\mathcal{T} \models P_x^i\, x \Rightarrow M_1\, N_v\, (\text{while } -x \text{ do } M_3 \text{ od}) P_y^k\, P_v^{2n+1-k}\, P_w^i (w \wedge \alpha)$

by axioms AX

(20b) $\mathcal{T} \models P_v^{2n+1-k}\, P_y^k\, P_w^i\, (w \wedge \alpha) \Rightarrow M_4 (P_y^k\, y \wedge P_x^i\, x)$ by ar4 and ar2

(21b) $\mathcal{T} \models P_x^i\, x \Rightarrow M_q\, P_y^k\, P_x^i\, (x \wedge y)$ by (20b), (19b)

where $k = i - [\max_n (1+\ldots+2n-1 \leq i)]^2$

$\mathcal{T} \models P_x{}^i\, x \Rightarrow M_q (P_y{}^{q(i)}\, y \wedge P_x{}^i\, x)$ by (21a) and (21b)

Ad 3. Let $M_f(x,y,u,v,w)$ represents the function $f(x)$, then the following program $M_{Jf}(x,y,u,v,w)$ represents the function Jf .

```
M_Jf :
          begin
     M_1: { while -y do P_y od ;
          { M_p(x,u,v,w) ;
     M_2:  while -x do
              M_p(x,u,v,w) ;
     M_3 :    while -x do P_x od ;
M_5: M_4 :    while -y do P_y ; N_x od ;
              M_f(x,y,u,v,w);
              M_p'(x,u,v,w);  P_x
           od:
           M_p'(x,u,v,w )
       end  M_Jf  :
```

(22) $\mathcal{T} \models M_1\, y$ by ar4

(23) $\mathcal{T} \models P_u^j\, P_x^i\, (u \wedge x) \Rightarrow M_p (P_x^i\, x \wedge P_u^{2^i 3^j}\, u)$ by lemma 4.1

(24) $\mathcal{T} \models P_x^i\, x \Rightarrow M_3\, x$ by ar4

$\mathfrak{M} \vdash P_y^k (y \wedge x) \Rightarrow (P_y N_x)^k (y \wedge P_x^k x)$ by ar2 and ar3

(25) $\mathfrak{M} \vdash P_y^k (y \wedge x) \Rightarrow M_4 (y \wedge P_x^k x)$ by axioms AX and induction

(26) $\mathfrak{M} \vdash P_u^j P_x^i P_y^k (u \wedge x \wedge y) \Rightarrow M_p M_3 M_4 (P_u^{2^i 3^j} u \wedge P_x^k x \wedge y)$

by (25) and (24)

(27) $\mathfrak{M} \vdash (x \wedge P_u^j u) \Rightarrow M_f (P_y^{f(0)} y \wedge P_u^j u)$ by assumption

(28) $\mathfrak{M} \vdash (P_u^j u \wedge P_x^i x \wedge y) \Rightarrow M_5 P_u^j u (P_x^{i-1} x \wedge P_y^{f(0)} y)$ by (27) (26) and lemma 4.2

(29) $\mathfrak{M} \vdash (P_u^j u \wedge P_x^i x \wedge y) \Rightarrow M_5^k (P_u^j u \wedge P_x^{i-k} x \wedge P_y^{\underbrace{f(\dots f}_{k\times}(0))} y)$

for $k \leq i$

(30) $\mathfrak{M} \vdash (P_u^j u \wedge P_x^i x \wedge y) \Rightarrow (\text{while } {-x} \text{ do } M_5 \text{ od}) \; (x \wedge P_u^j u \wedge$

$P_y^{\underbrace{f(\dots f}_{i\times}(0))} y)$ by AX and (29)

$\mathfrak{M} \vdash (P_x^i x \wedge P_u^j u) \Rightarrow M_{Jf} (P_x^i x \wedge P_u^j u \wedge P_y^{f^i(0)} y)$

by (22) and (30)

Ad 4. Let $M_f(x.y,u,v,w)$ represents the function $f(x)$ and let $M_g(x,y,u,v,w)$ represents the function $g(x)$, then the following program $M_{fog}(x,y,u,v,w)$ represents the function fog .

```
Mfog :      begin
               Mp (x,u,v,w) ;
               Mf ;
        M1: {  while -x do Px od ;
            {  while -y do Py; Nx  od ;
               Mg ;
               Mp-(x.u,v,w) ;
            end  Mfog ;
```

(31) $\mathfrak{M} \vdash (P_x^i x \wedge P_u^j u) \Rightarrow M_p (P_x^i x \wedge P_u^{2^i 3^j} u)$ by lemma 4.1

(32) $\mathfrak{N} \vdash (P_x^i\, x \wedge P_u^j\, u) \Rightarrow M_g(P_x^i\, x \wedge P_y^{g(i)}\, y \wedge P_u^j\, u)$

by assumption

(33) $\mathfrak{N} \vdash (P_x^i\, x \wedge P_y^k\, y) \Rightarrow M_1(P_x^k\, x \wedge y)$ for every $k \in \mathcal{N}$

by ar4 ,ar2 and axioms AX

(34) $\mathfrak{N} \vdash (P_x^i\, x \wedge P_u^j\, u) \Rightarrow M_p\, M_g\, M_1(P_x^{g(i)}\, x \wedge y \wedge P_u^{2^i 3^j}\, u)$

by (33), (32), (31)

(35) $\mathfrak{N} \vdash (y \wedge P_u^{2^i 3^j}\, u \wedge P_x^{g(i)}\, x) \Rightarrow M_f(P_y^{f(g(i))}\, y \wedge P_x^{g(i)}\, x \wedge P_u^{2^i 3^j}\, u)$

by assumption

$\mathfrak{N} \vdash (P_x^i\, x \wedge P_u^j\, u) \Rightarrow M_{fog}(P_y{}^{f(g(x))}\, y \wedge P_x^i\, x \wedge P_u^j\, u)$

by (35) and (34)

Ad 5. Let $M_f(x,y,u,v,w)$ represents the function $f(x)$ and let $M_g(x,y,u,v,w)$ represents the function $g(x)$. then the following program $M_{f+g}(x,y,u,v,w)$ represents the function $f+g$.

```
Mf+g :     begin
               Mp (x,u,v, w);
               Mf ;
               Mp(y,u,v,w);
               Mg ;
               Mp'(x,u,v,w) ;
               while -x do Px; Ny od ;
               Mp'(x,u,v,w )
           end  Mf+g ;
```

(36) $AR_5 \vdash (P_x^i\, x \wedge P_u^j\, u) \Rightarrow M_p(P_x^i\, x \wedge P_u^{2^i 3^j}\, u)$ by lemma 4.1

(37) $AR_5 \vdash P_x^i\, x \Rightarrow M_f(P_y^{f(i)}\, y \wedge P_x^i\, x)$ by assumption

(38) $AR_5 \vdash (P_x^i\, x \wedge P_y^k\, y \wedge P_u^j\, u) \Rightarrow M_p(y.u.v,w)(P_u^{2^i 3^j}\, u \wedge P_y^k\, y \wedge P_x^i x)$

by lemma 4.1

(39) $AR_5 \vdash (P_x^i\, x \wedge P_u^j\, u) \Rightarrow M_p(x,u,v,w)\ M_f\ M_p(y,u,v,w)\left[P_x^i\, x \wedge P_y^{f(i)}\, y \wedge P_u^{2^{f(i)} \cdot 3^{2^i \cdot 3^j}}\, u \right]$ by (37) and (38)

(40) $AR_5 \vdash (P_x^i\, x \wedge P_y^k\, y \wedge P_u^j\, u) \Rightarrow M_g\ (P_y^{g(i)}\, y \wedge P_x^i\, x \wedge P_u^j\, u)$ by assumption

(41) $AR_5 \vdash (P_x^i\, x \wedge P_y^k\, y \wedge P_u^{2^n \cdot 3^m}\, u) \Rightarrow M_g\ M_{p'}(x,u,v,w)(P_u^m\, u \wedge P_x^n\, x \wedge P_y^k\, y)$ by (40) and lemma 4.2

(42) $AR_5 \vdash (P_x^i\, x \wedge P_y^k\, y \Rightarrow (\text{while } \neg x \text{ do } P_x; N_y \text{ od})(x \wedge P_y^{k+i}\, y)$ by axioms AX

$AR_5 \vdash (P_x^i\, x \wedge P_u^j\, u) \Rightarrow M_{f+g}\ (P_y^{f(i)+g(i)}\, y \wedge P_x^i\, x \wedge P_u^j u)$ by (42),(41) and (40)

This ends the proof of the theorem 4.3 . □

THEOREM 4.4
Every total one-argument recursive function is programmable in the propositional algorithmic arithmetic AR_5 .

PROOF.

To prove the theorem we shall use the result of J.Robinson [2]. By the theorem 4.3 it is enough to prove that the inverse operation is programmable ,i.e. if f is a total programmable function and $\mu_y(f(y) = x)$ is always defined then the function g is also total programmable function

$$g(x) = \mu_y(f(y) = x) .$$

Let $M_f(x,y,u,v,w)$ represents the function f then the following program scheme $M_{\mu f}(x,y,u,v,w)$ represents the function g . The program $M_p(y,u,v,w)$ / $M_{p'}(y,u,v,w)$ / mentioned in the text below , is obtained from the text of the program $M_p(x,u,v,w)$ / $M_{p'}(x,u,v,w)$ / by simultaneous replacement of all occurrences of the variable x by the variable y .

```
M_µf :  begin
            ⎧ while -y do P_y od;
            ⎪ M_p(y,u,v,w);
      M_1 : ⎨ M_p(x,u,v,w);
            ⎪ while -x do P_x od ;
            ⎩ N_y ;
      M_2:    while -(x ∧ y) do
                   M_f(x,y,u,v,w) ;
                   M_p'(x,u,v,w) ;
         M_3 : ⎧   while -v do P_v od ;
               ⎩   while -x ∧ -y do P_x;P_y;N_v od;
         M_4 :     if -(x ∧ y) then
                      ⎧  while -v do P_v ;N_x od ;
                      ⎪  M_p'(y,u,v,w) ;
                M_5:  ⎨  N_y ;
                      ⎪  M_p(y,u,v,w) ;
                      ⎩  M_p(x, u,v,w);
                         while -x do P_x od ;
                         while -y do P_y; N_x od ;
                   fi ;
              od ;
              while -v do P_v; N_x od ;
              M_p'(y,u,v,w)
        end M_µf ;
```

Let us denote by M_6 all the instructions between"od" and " do " in M_2 and let i, j, k, n, m , in all formulas below, denote arbitrary natural numbers .

(43) $$AR_5 \vdash (P_x^i x \wedge P_y^k y \wedge P_u^j u) \Rightarrow M_p(y,u,v,w)(P_x^i x \wedge P_y^j y \wedge P_u^{2^k \cdot 3^j} u)$$

by lemma 4.1

(44) $$AR_5 \vdash (P_x^i x \wedge P_y^k y \wedge P_u^j u) \Rightarrow M_p(x,u,v,w)(P_x^i x \wedge P_y^k y \wedge P_u^{2^i \cdot 3^j} u)$$

(45) $AR_5 \vdash (P_x^i\, x \wedge P_y^k\, y \wedge P_u^j\, u) \Rightarrow M_1\left(P_y y \wedge x \wedge P_u^{2^i \cdot 3^{2^0 \cdot 3^j}} u \right)$

by (43) and (44)

(46) $AR_5 \vdash (P_x^n x \wedge P_u^j u) \Rightarrow M_f\, (P_x^n x \wedge P_u^j u \wedge P_y^{f(n)} y)$ by assumption

(47) $AR_5 \vdash (P_u^{2^i \cdot 3^m} u \wedge P_y^k y) \Rightarrow M_{p'}(x.u.v.w)\left(P_x^i x \wedge P_y^k y \wedge P_u^m u\right)$

by lemma 4.2.

(48) $AR_5 \vdash (P_x^i x \wedge P_y^k y) \Rightarrow M_3\, \left(P_x^{i-l} x \wedge P_v^l v \wedge P_y^{k-l} y\right)$ by axioms Axar

where $l = \min(i,k)$

(49) $AR_5 \vdash (P_x^n x \wedge P_u^{2^i \cdot 3^m} u) \Rightarrow M_f\, M_{p'}\, M_3\left(P_y^{f(n)-l} y \wedge P_x^{i-l} x \wedge P_u^m u \wedge P_v^l v\right)$

where $l = \min(i, f(n))$ by (46), (47), (48)

(50) $AR_5 \vdash (P_u^{2^n \cdot 3^j} u \wedge P_v^l v \wedge P_x^{i-l} x) \Rightarrow M_5\, (P_x^i x \wedge P_y^{n+1} y \wedge P_u^{2^i \cdot 3^{2^{n+1} \cdot 3^j}} u)$

by lemmas 4.1

If $f(n) \neq i$ then

(51) $AR_5 \vdash (P_x^{i-l} x \wedge P_y^{f(n)-l} y \wedge P_u^{2^n 3^j} u) \Rightarrow M_4\, (P_x^{n+1} x \wedge P_u^{2^i \cdot 3^{2^{n+1} \cdot 3^j}} u \wedge y)$

by (50) and Axar

If $f(n) \neq i$ then

(52a) $AR_5 \vdash (P_x^n x \wedge P_u^{2^i \cdot 3^{2^n \cdot 3^j}} u) \Rightarrow M_6\, (P_x^{n+1} x \wedge y \wedge P_u^{2^i \cdot 3^{2^{n+1} \cdot 3^j}} u)$

by (51) and (49)

If $f(n) \neq i$ then

(52b) $AR_5 \vdash (P_x^n x \wedge P_u^{2^i \cdot 3^{2^n \cdot 3^j}} u) \Rightarrow M_6\, \left(x \wedge y \wedge P_u^{2^n \cdot 3^j} u \wedge P_v^i v\right)$ by (49)

By the assumption there exists n such that $f(n) = i$, hence for $n' = \mu_n(f(n) = i)$ we have

(53) $AR_5 \vdash (x \wedge P_y y \wedge P_u^{2^i \cdot 3^{2^0 \cdot 3^j}} u) \Rightarrow M_6^{\,n'}(y \wedge x \wedge P_u^{2^{n'} \cdot 3^j} u \wedge P_v^i v)$

by (52a), (52b)

(54) $AR_5 \vdash (P_x^i x \wedge P_u^j u) \Rightarrow M_1 M_2\, (y \wedge x \wedge P_u^{2^{n'} \cdot 3^j} u \wedge P_v^i v)$

by (45) and (53)

$AR_5 \vdash (P_x^i x \wedge P_u^j u) \Rightarrow M_{\mu f}\, (P_x^i x \wedge P_y^{g(x)} y \wedge P_u^j u)$ by (54). □

Let us observe that if in the last theorem $f(y)$ is not defined for some y or $\mu_y\, f(y)=x$ is not defined then for every model of AR_5 we have

$$\mathfrak{M} \models \neg M_{\mu f} \text{ true}$$

i.e. program $M_{\mu f}$ never stops. As a corollary we have the following theorem .

THEOREM 4.5

Every one-argument partial recursive function is programmable in the propositional theory of arithmetic AR_5 . □

The above result can be strengthened as follows :
Every n-argument partial recursive function is programmable in the propositional theory of arithmetic with $n+5$ variables, AR_{n+5} .

Indeed, for every partial recursive function $f(x_1,\dots,x_n)$ there exists one argument partial recursive function F such that for arbitrary natural numbers $x_1,\dots,x_n$. $f(x_1,\dots,x_n) = F(nb(x_1,\dots,x_n))$, where nb is one-one enumeration of n-tuples of natural numbers . It can be proved that the function nb is programmable in AR_{n+5} and therefore the function f is programmable too .

REFERENCES

[1] Chlebus B., On decidability of propositional algorithmic logic Inst.of Informatics Reports, University of Warsaw, 1979 .

[2] Malcev A.I., Algorithms and recursive functions, Moscow 1965.

[3] Mirkowska G., On the propositional algorithmic logic, Proc.of MFCS'79 . Olomouc, Lecture Notes on Computer Science, Springer Verlag 74 .

[4] Mirkowska G., Complete axiomatization of algorithmic properties of program schemes with bounded nondeterministic interpretations Proc. 12 th Ann. ACM Symp. on theory of Computing, Los Angeles 1980 .

[5] Pratt V.,Salwicki A., personal communication,

[6] Rogers H., The theory of recursive functions and effective compitability ,Mc.Graw-Hill, New York 1967 .

NONSTANDARD RUNS OF FLOYD-PROVABLE PROGRAMS

I. Németi
Mathematical Institute of the Hungarian Academy of Sciences
Budapest, Reáltanoda u. 13-15, H-1053 Hungary

The question is investigated: "exactly which programs are provable by the Floyd-Hoare inductive assertions method?".

Theorem 1 of this paper says that from any theory T containing the Peano axioms exactly those programs are Floyd-Hoare provable which are partially correct in the models of T w.r.t. continuous traces. Intuitively: the provable programs are the ones which are correct in every perhaps nonstandard machine functioning perhaps in a nonstandard time. Of course every nonstandard machine and time has to satisfy our axioms T. This result was first proved in Andréka-Németi [1] in Hungarian. It was announced in English in [2], [3] and was quoted in Salwicki [23], Csirmaz [13], Richter-Szabo [20] etc.

In section 5 concrete examples of simple nonstandard runs of programs are constructively defined and illustrated on figures. The emphasis in section 5 is on simplicity, with the aim to make nonstandard runs and nonstandard models less esoteric, less imaginary, easy to draw, easy to touch. In the proof of Proposition 3 it is demonstrated how ultraproducts can be used to test applicability of Floyd's method in concrete situations.

We are specifically interested in the behaviour of programs (or "program schemes") in first order *axiomatizable classes* of models (or "interpretations").

The central notion of the present paper is that of continuous traces. Properties of continuous traces were investigated in Csirmaz [13]. A simpler and much more natural notion was introduced in [5], [6], [21], [4], [7], [19]. This improved approach was used in Csirmaz-Paris [15], Sain [22], Csirmaz [14]. The quoted works use the general methodology elaborated in Dahn [16] and Sain [21] for investigating new logics.

The most readable introduction is [4] or if that is not available then [7]. Further important works in the present nonstandard direction are Hájek [17], Richter-Szabo [20]. For more uses of ultraproducts (cf. Proposition 3 here) see [19], [4] and a little in [7]. Copies of all the above quoted papers of Andréka, Csirmaz, Németi or Sain *are available* from the present author except [2] and [12].

1. SYNTAX

Let t be a *similarity type* assigning arities to function symbols and relation symbols. ω denotes the set of *natural numbers*.

$Y \stackrel{d}{=} \{y_i : i\in\omega\}$ is called the set of *variable symbols* and is disjoint from everything we use. Logical symbols: $\{\wedge,\neg,\exists\}$. Other symbols: $\{\leftarrow$, IF, THEN, (,), :$\}$. The set of "label symbols" is ω itself.

L_t denotes the set of all *first order formulas* of type t possibly with free variables (elements of Y of course), see e.g. [10] p.22. We shall refer to "*terms* of type t" as defined in e.g. [10] p. 22.

Now we define the set P_t of *programs* of type t.

The set U_t of *commands* of type t is defined by:

$(j : y \leftarrow \tau) \in U_t$ if $j\in\omega$, $y\in Y$ and τ is a term of type t.

$(j :$ IF λ THEN $v) \in U_t$ if $j,v\in\omega$, $\lambda\in L_t$ is a formula without quantifiers.

These are the only elements of U_t.

If $(i:u)\in U_t$ then i is called the *label* of the command $(i:u)$.

By a *program* of type t we understand a finite sequence of commands (elements of U_t) in which no two members have the same label. Formally, the set of programs is:

$$P_t \stackrel{d}{=} \{\langle (i_0:u_0),\dots,(i_n:u_n)\rangle \;:\; n\in\omega,\quad (\forall e\le n)(i_e:u_e)\in U_t,\quad (\forall e<k\le n)\, i_k\ne i_e\}.$$

For every $p \stackrel{d}{=} \langle (i_0:u_0),\dots,(i_n:u_n)\rangle \in P_t$ we shall use the notation $i_{n+1} \stackrel{d}{=} \min(\omega\setminus\{i_m : m\le n\})$.

<u>EXAMPLE:</u> Let t contain the function symbols "+,·,0,1" with arities "2,2,0,0 " respectively. Now the sequence

$\langle (0\!: y_1 \leftarrow 0),(1\!:$ IF $y_1=y_2$ THEN $4),(2\!: y_1 \leftarrow y_1+1),(3\!:$ IF $y_2=y_2$ THEN $1)\rangle$

is a program of type t. See Figure 1.

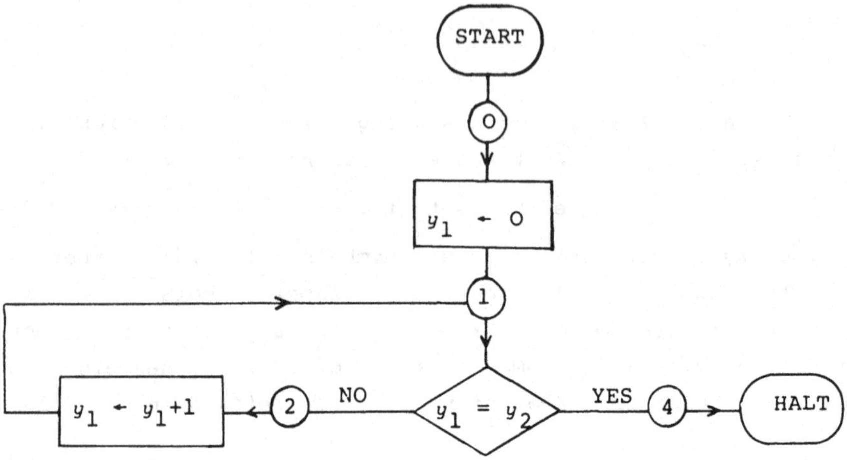

FIGURE 1

2. SEMANTICS

Let $p \in P_t$ be a program and $\mathfrak{A}$ be a structure or model of type t, see [10]p.20. The universe of a model denoted by $\mathfrak{A}$ will always be denoted by A.

V_p denotes the variable symbols occurring in p. Note that V_p is a finite subset of Y.

By a valuation (of the variables of p) in $\mathfrak{A}$ we understand a function $q : V_p \rightarrow A$ (cf. [8]p.55).

Let τ be a term occurring in p. Now $\tau[q]_{\mathfrak{A}}$ denotes the value of the term τ in the model $\mathfrak{A}$ at the valuation q of the variable symbols, cf. [10]p.27 Def.1.3.13. We shall often write $\tau[q]$ i.e. we shall omit the subscript $\mathfrak{A}$.

From now on we work with the *similarity type of arithmetic*. I.e. t is fixed to consist of "+,·,0,1" with arities "2,2,0,0". We shall omit the index t since it is fixed anyway.

$\mathfrak{N}$ denotes the standard model of arithmetic, that is $\mathfrak{N} \stackrel{d}{=} \langle \omega,+,\cdot,0,1 \rangle$ where +,·,0,1 are the usual.

EXAMPLE: Let $V_p=\{y_1,y_2\}$, $q(y_1)=2$, $q(y_2)=3$, $\tau=((y_1+y_2)+y_2)$. Then $\tau[q]_{\mathfrak{N}}=8$.

$PA \subseteq L$ denotes the (recursive) set of the *Peano-axioms* (together with the induction axioms), see [10]p.42 Ex.1.4.11 (axioms 1-7). We shall only be concerned with models of the Peano-axioms.

We are going to define the *continuous traces* of a program in a model of PA.

DEFINITION 1 Let $\mathfrak{A} \models PA$ be an arbitrary model (of Peano arithmetic). Let $p \in P$ be a program with set V_p of variables.

A *trace* of p in $\mathfrak{A}$ is a sequence $s \overset{d}{=} \langle s_a \rangle_{a\in A}$ indexed by the elements of A such that (i) and (ii) below are satisfied.

(i) $s_a : V_p \cup \{\lambda\} \to A$ is a valuation of the variables (of p) into $\mathfrak{A}$, where $\lambda \in Y \setminus V_p$ is a variable not occurring in p. λ can be conceived of as the "control variable of p". (We could call s_a a "*state*" of p in the model $\mathfrak{A}$.)

(ii) To formulate this condition, let $p = \langle (i_0:u_0),\dots,(i_n:u_n)\rangle$ and recall the notation $i_{n+1} \overset{d}{=} \min(\omega\setminus\{i_m : m\le n\})$. Now we demand

$s_0(\lambda) = i_0$ and for any $a\in A$,

if $s_a(\lambda) \notin \{i_m : m\le n\}$ then $s_{a+1} = s_a$ else

for all $m\le n$ such that $s_a(\lambda) = i_m$, conditions a) and b) below hold.

a) if $u_m =$ "$y_w \leftarrow \tau$" then

$s_{a+1}(\lambda) = i_{m+1}$ and for any $x\in V_p$,

$$s_{a+1}(x) = \begin{cases} \tau[s_a]_{\mathfrak{A}} & \text{if } x=y_w \\ s_a(x) & \text{otherwise.} \end{cases}$$

b) if $u_m =$ "IF χ THEN v" then

$$s_{a+1}(\lambda) = \begin{cases} v & \text{if } \mathfrak{A} \models \chi[s_a] \\ i_{m+1} & \text{otherwise, and} \end{cases}$$

$s_{a+1}(x) = s_a(x)$, for every $x\in V_p$.

By this we have defined traces of a program in $\mathfrak{A}$ as sequences

$\langle s_a \rangle_{a\in A}$ "respecting the structure" of the program. End of Def.1.

DEFINITION 2 The sequence $\langle s_a \rangle_{a\in A}$ is continuous in $\mathfrak{A}$ if $\langle s_a \rangle_{a\in A}$ satisfies the induction axioms, that is if for any $\varphi\in L$ with free variables in V_p we have

$$\mathfrak{A} \models ((\varphi[s_0] \wedge \bigwedge_{a\in A} (\varphi[s_a] \to \varphi[s_{a+1}])) \to \bigwedge_{a\in A} \varphi[s_a]).$$

By a *continuous trace* of p in $\mathfrak{A}$ we understand a trace $\langle s_a \rangle_{a\in A}$ of p which is continuous. End of Def.2.

Note that in the standard model $\mathfrak{N}$ every trace is continuous.

Intuitively, a trace $\langle s_a \rangle_{a\in A}$ is continuous if whenever a first order property $\varphi\in L$ changes during time (A), then there exists a *point of time* $(a\in A)$ when this change is just happening:

$\mathfrak{A} \models \varphi[s_0]$ and $(\exists a\in A)\ \mathfrak{A} \not\models \varphi[s_a]$ together imply that

$(\exists a\in A)(\mathfrak{A} \models \varphi[s_a]$ and $\mathfrak{A} \not\models \varphi[s_{a+1}])$.

DEFINITION 3 Let $p = \langle (i_0 : u_0), \ldots, (i_n : u_n) \rangle \in P$ and $\psi\in L$ be such that the free variables of ψ are in V_p. Let $\mathfrak{A} \models PA$.

The pair (p,ψ) is said to be *partially correct* in $\mathfrak{A}$ w.r.t. continuous traces if for any continuous trace $\langle s_a \rangle_{a\in A}$ of p in $\mathfrak{A}$ and for any $a\in A$ $s_a(\lambda) \notin \{i_m : m\leq n\}$ implies $\mathfrak{A} \models \psi[s_a]$.

$\mathfrak{A} \models^{pc} (p,\psi)$ denotes that the pair (p,ψ) is partially correct in $\mathfrak{A}$ w.r.t. continuous traces. End of Def.3.

3. DERIVATION SYSTEM (rules of inference)

In the following definition we recall the so called Floyd-Hoare derivation system. This system serves to derive pairs (p,ψ) (where $p\in P$ and $\psi\in L$) from theories $T\subseteq L$.

DEFINITION 4 Let $p = \langle (i_0, u_0), \ldots, (i_n : u_n) \rangle \in P$, let $\psi\in L$ and let $T\subseteq L$. The set of labels of p is defined as

$$\mathrm{lab}(p) \stackrel{d}{=} \{i_m : m\leq n+1\} \cup \{v : (\exists m\leq n) u_m = \text{"IF } \chi \text{ THEN } v\text{"}\}.$$

Note that lab(p) is finite.

A *Floyd-Hoare derivation* of (p,ψ) from T consists of a mapping Φ : lab(p) $\rightarrow L$ together with classical first-order derivations listed in (i)-(iv) below.

Notation: When $z \in$ lab(p) we write Φ_z instead of $\Phi(z)$.

(i) A derivation $T \vdash \Phi_{i_0}$.

(ii) To each command $(i_m : y_j \leftarrow \tau)$ occurring in p a derivation $T \vdash (\Phi_{i_m} \rightarrow \Phi_{i_{m+1}}(y_j/\tau))$, where $\varphi(y/\tau)$ denotes the formula obtained from φ by substituting τ in place of y in the usual way, cf. [8]p.61.

(iii) To each command $(i_m$: IF χ THEN $v)$ occurring in p derivations $T \vdash ((\chi \wedge \Phi_{i_m}) \rightarrow \Phi_v)$ and $T \vdash ((\neg\chi \wedge \Phi_{i_m}) \rightarrow \Phi_{i_{m+1}})$.

(iv) To each $z \in (\text{lab}(p) \setminus \{i_m : m \leq n\})$ a derivation $T \vdash (\Phi_z \rightarrow \psi)$.

The existence of a Floyd-Hoare derivation of (p,ψ) from T is denoted by $T \overset{FH}{\vdash} (p,\psi)$. <u>End of Def.4.</u>

<u>REMARKS:</u> If T is decidable then the set of Floyd-Hoare derivations (of pairs (p,ψ) where $p \in P$ and $\psi \in L$, from T) is also decidable. If T is recursively enumerable then the Floyd-Hoare derivable pairs are also recursively enumerable, i.e. $\{(p,\psi) : T \overset{FH}{\vdash} (p,\psi)\}$ is recursively enumerable.

<u>4. COMPLETENESS</u>

Notation: $\text{Mod}(T) \overset{d}{=} \{\mathfrak{A} : \mathfrak{A} \models T\}$ for any $T \subseteq L$.

<u>THEOREM 1</u> Let $T \supseteq PA$ be arbitrary. Let further $p \in P$ and $\psi \in L$ be also arbitrary. Then $T \overset{FH}{\vdash} (p,\psi)$ if and only if (p,ψ) is partially correct in every model of T w.r.t. continuous traces.

In concise form:

$$T \overset{FH}{\vdash} (p,\psi) \iff (\forall \mathfrak{A} \in \text{Mod}(T))\, \mathfrak{A} \overset{pc}{\models} (p,\psi).$$

<u>Proof.</u> The proof can be found in [3] which appeared in MFCS'81 pp. 162-171. <u>QED</u>

The condition $T \supseteq PA$ can be eliminated from the above theorem. Moreover, the restriction that t is the similarity type of PA can be eliminated, too. This generalization of Thm.1 above is Thm.9 of [4] on p.56 there (see also Prop.12 there), and it is also stated in Part II of [7] which is available in the literature. A somewhat modified version of this general theorem is Thm.3.3 of [13].

A drawback of our present approach is that the meanings of programs in $\mathfrak{A}$ are continuous traces and that these continuous traces are not elements of $\mathfrak{A}$, they are just functions $s : A \to A$ satisfying certain axioms formulated in the metalanguage (and not in L). This drawback is completely eliminated in the approach of [4], and of [7]. There the meanings of programs in a model $\mathfrak{M}$ are elements of $\mathfrak{M}$ and all requirements are formulated in the subject language L, e.g. continuity of traces is formulated by a set IA^q of formulas in L.

The present approach is also extended to treat total correctness in the quoted papers, see e.g. Thm.7 on p.51 of [4]. The generality of that approach enables one to investigate the lattice of logics of programs (or dynamic logics), see the figure on p.109 of [4], and for more results and detailed proofs in this direction see [19]. The proof methods in the quoted general works are similar to the model theoretic proofs in the book Henkin-Monk-Tarski-Andréka-Németi [18]. The algebraization of our general dynamic logic (of programs) yields Crs_α -s defined in the quoted book.

5. AN EXAMPLE FOR NONSTANDARD TRACES

So far we restricted ourselves to models of Peano's arithmetic PA. Specially, our similarity type t was required to contain the symbols $+, \cdot, 0, 1$ with arities $2,2,0,0$ respectively. However, all what we really used in our definitions, e.g. in the definition of continuous traces, was 0 and succ where succ is the successor function.

Let the similarity type d consist of the symbols 0, succ, pred of arities $0,1,1$ only. Here succ is the successor and pred is the predecessor, i.e. the standard model of type d is $\underset{\sim}{\omega} \overset{d}{=} \langle \omega, 0, \mathrm{succ}, \mathrm{pred} \rangle$ where $(\forall n \in \omega)[\mathrm{succ}(n) = n+1$ and $\mathrm{pred}(n+1) = n]$ and $\mathrm{pred}(0) = 0$. Let $Pa \overset{d}{=} \{\varphi \in L_d : \underset{\sim}{\omega} \models \varphi\}$. It is well known that Pa is decidable. Of course $PA \models Pa$.

In the present section we shall use Pa instead of PA and d

instead of t. Our aims with this change are simplicity and better understanding of the basic methods underlying the so called nonstandard time semantics approach.

DEFINITION 5 The definition of continuous traces of programs $p \in P_d$ in models of Pa should be clear, namely replace in Definitions 1,2 the statements "Let $\mathfrak{A} \models PA$" by "Let $\mathfrak{A} \models Pa$" and replace $a+1$ everywhere by succ(a). End of Def.5.

PROPOSITION 2 Let $T \subseteq L_d$ and assume $T \supseteq Pa$. Let $p \in P_d$ and $\psi \in L_d$ be arbitrary. Assume $T \stackrel{FH}{\vdash} (p,\psi)$. Then (p,ψ) is partially correct in every model of T w.r.t. continuous traces. In concise form:

$T \stackrel{FH}{\vdash} (p,\psi) \Rightarrow (\forall \mathfrak{A} \in \text{Mod}(T))\ \mathfrak{A} \stackrel{pc}{\models} (p,\psi)$.

Proof. Let $T \supseteq Pa$, $p = \langle (i_0 : u_0), \ldots, (i_n : u_n) \rangle \in P_d$ and $V_p = \{y_1, \ldots, y_k\}$. Assume $T \stackrel{FH}{\vdash} (p,\psi)$. We want to show partial correctness of (p,ψ) w.r.t. continuous traces in models of T.

Let $\mathfrak{A} \models T$ and let $\langle s_a \rangle_{a \in A}$ be a continuous trace of p in $\mathfrak{A}$. Let $\langle \Phi_z \rangle_{z \in \text{lab}(p)} = \Phi : \text{lab}(p) \to L$ belong to a Floyd-Hoare derivation of (p,ψ) from T. Recall that $y_1, \ldots, y_k$ are the variables occurring in p. Therefore we may use y_0 as "control variable" (i.e. for λ). Define

$$\Phi(y_0, y_1, \ldots, y_k) \stackrel{d}{=} \bigwedge_{m=1}^{n} (y_0 = i_m \to \Phi_{i_m}(y_1, \ldots, y_k)) \wedge$$

$$\wedge \left(\left(\bigwedge_{m=1}^{n} y_0 \neq i_m \right) \to \psi(y_1, \ldots, y_k) \right).$$

Now $\Phi \in L$ and $\mathfrak{A} \models \Phi[s_0] \wedge \bigwedge_{a \in A} (\Phi[s_a] \to \Phi[s_{\text{succ}(a)}])$. (This is true because $\Phi : \text{lab}(p) \to L$ belongs to a Floyd-Hoare derivation of (p,ψ) and $\langle s_a \rangle_{a \in A}$ is a trace of p in $\mathfrak{A}$.)

Since $\langle s_a \rangle_{a \in A}$ is, in addition, continuous, $\mathfrak{A} \models \bigwedge_{a \in A} \Phi[s_a]$. Let $a \in A$ be such that $s_a(\lambda) \notin \{i_m : m \leq n\}$. Then $\mathfrak{A} \models \Phi[s_a]$ implies $\mathfrak{A} \models \psi[s_a]$, by the definition of Φ. This means $\mathfrak{A} \stackrel{pc}{\models} (p,\psi)$ since $\langle s_a \rangle_{a \in A}$ was an arbitrary continuous trace of p in $\mathfrak{A}$.

We did this proof for programs p satisfying $V_p = \{y_1, \ldots, y_k\}$. Note that this does not restrict generality. QED

Proposition 2 above shows that it is useful to construct continuous traces of programs in models of Pa, too, since if the output of a continuous trace of the program $p \in P_d$ in a possibly nonstandard model

$\mathfrak{A} \models Pa$ does not satisfy the output condition ψ then $Pa \not\vdash^{FH} (p,\psi)$ i.e. then the partial correctness of (p,ψ) is not Floyd provable from Pa.

EXAMPLE

Let the similarity type d consist of the symbols 0,succ,pred of arities 0,1,1.

1.
We define the program $p \in P_d$ by the block-diagram on Figure 2.

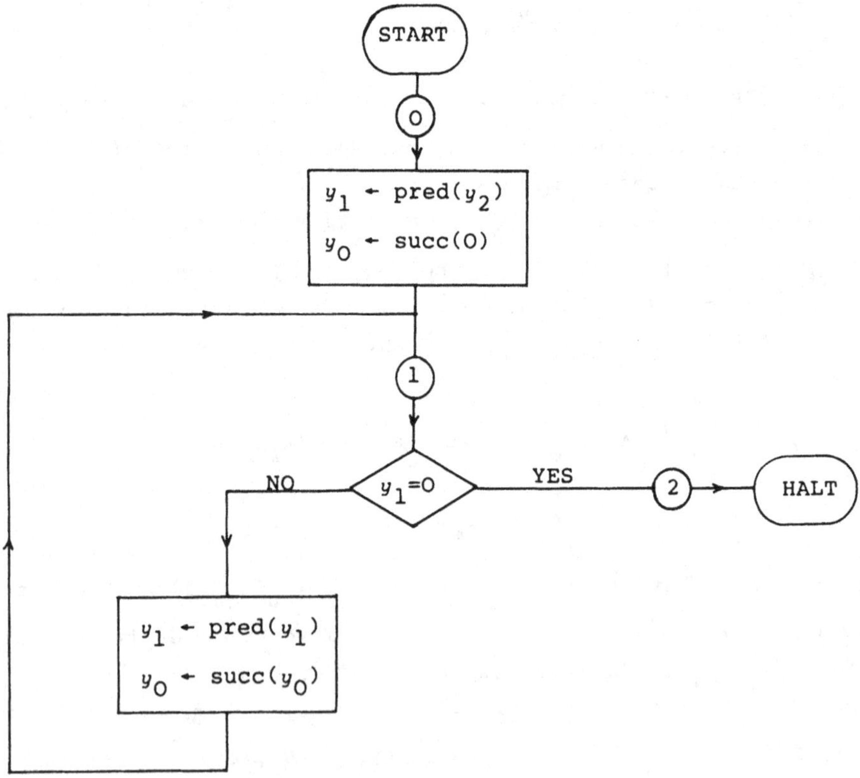

FIGURE 2

Clearly $p \in P_d$. Let ψ be $y_0 = y_2$. Then $\psi \in L_d$ and the free variables of ψ are in V_p. We shall call ψ the *output condition*, because we shall consider partial correctness of the statement (p,ψ).

2.

Next we construct a nonstandard model $\mathfrak{A}$ of our simplified number theory Pa.

Z denotes the set of integers, i.e. $Z \stackrel{d}{=} \omega \cup \{-n : 0<n\in\omega\}$. We define $A \stackrel{d}{=} (\{0\}\times\omega)\cup(\{1\}\times Z)$. See Figure 3.

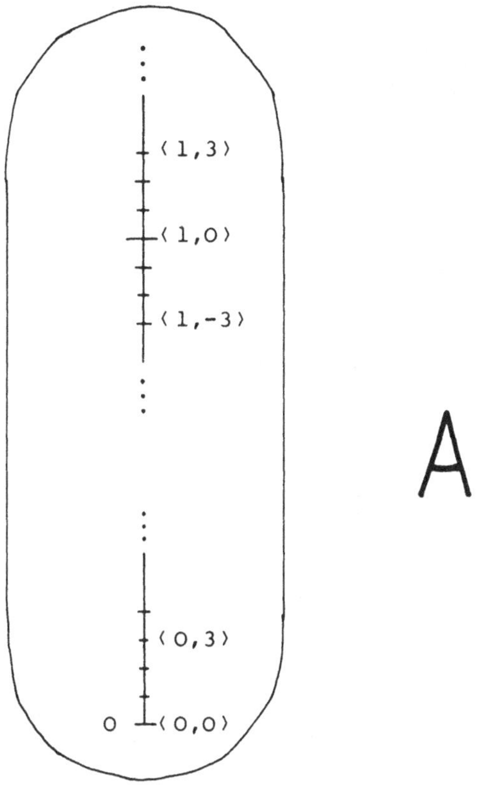

FIGURE 3

Now we define a model $\mathfrak{A}$ of similarity type d such that the universe of $\mathfrak{A}$ is A defined above, and the function symbols succ, pred,0 are defined on A as follows:

Let $\langle a,b\rangle\in A$. Then $\text{succ}(\langle a,b\rangle) \stackrel{d}{=} \langle a,b+1\rangle$, $\text{pred}(\langle a,b+1\rangle) \stackrel{d}{=} \langle a,b\rangle$, $\text{pred}(\langle 0,0\rangle) \stackrel{d}{=} \langle 0,0\rangle$. We define 0 of $\mathfrak{A}$ to be $\langle 0,0\rangle$.

We shall call $\langle 0,b\rangle\in A$ a standard number and $\langle 1,b\rangle$ a *nonstandard* number.

3.

Next we construct a continuous trace f of p in $\mathfrak{A}$.

Recall from Definition 1 that a trace of p in $\mathfrak{A}$ is a sequence $s = \langle s_a \rangle_{a \in A}$ of valuations $s_a : \{y_0, y_1, y_2, \lambda\} \to A$ of the variables where λ is the control variable. We shall identify this sequence s with a 4-tuple $\langle f_0, f_1, f_2, f_\lambda \rangle$ of sequences $f_i : A \to A$ such that $f_0 \overset{d}{=} \langle s_a(y_0) : a \in A \rangle, \ldots, f_\lambda \overset{d}{=} \langle s_a(\lambda) : a \in A \rangle$. Clearly $f_i : A \to A$ for $i \in \{0,1,2,\lambda\}$.

Note that we can consider f_i to be the history of the content of the program variable y_i during execution of p i.e. during time. For $a \in A$ we can say that $f_i(a)$ is the content of the variable y_i at time point a.

Now let $f_0 : A \to A$ and $f_1 : A \to A$ be as indicated on Figure 4. See also Figure 5.

That is:

$$f_0(\langle a_0, a_1 \rangle) \overset{d}{=} \begin{cases} \langle a_0, a_1 \rangle & \text{if } a_0 = 0 \text{ or } a_1 < 0 \\ \langle 1, 0 \rangle & \text{otherwise,} \end{cases}$$

$$f_1(\langle a_0, a_1 \rangle) \overset{d}{=} \begin{cases} \langle 1, -a_1 \rangle & \text{if } a_0 = 0 \\ \langle 0, -a_1 \rangle & \text{if } a_0 = 1 \text{ and } a_1 < 0 \\ \langle 0, 0 \rangle & \text{if } a_0 = 1 \text{ and } a_1 \geq 0. \end{cases}$$

We define

$f_2(a) \overset{d}{=} \langle 1, 0 \rangle$ for every $a \in A$, and

$$f_\lambda(\langle a_0, a_1 \rangle) \overset{d}{=} \begin{cases} \langle 0, 0 \rangle & \text{if } a_0 = a_1 = 0 \\ \langle 0, 1 \rangle & \text{if } (a_0 = 0,\ a_1 > 0) \text{ or } (a_0 = 1,\ a_1 < 0) \\ \langle 0, 2 \rangle & \text{if } a_0 = 1 \text{ and } a_1 \geq 0. \end{cases}$$

Now it is easy to see that $f \overset{d}{=} \langle f_0, f_1, f_2, f_\lambda \rangle$ is a trace of p in $\mathfrak{A}$, continuity of which will be proved below.

4.

PROPOSITION 3 Let d, $p \in P_d$, $\mathfrak{A}$, f be as defined above. Then f is a continuous trace of p in $\mathfrak{A}$.

Proof. For every $a \in A$ let $s_a : V_p \cup \{\lambda\} \to A$ be the valuation of the variables of p into $\mathfrak{A}$ be defined by $s_a(y_i) \overset{d}{=} f_i(a)$ for $i \in \{0,1,2\}$ and $s_a(\lambda) \overset{d}{=} f_\lambda(a)$. According to our convention made earlier, we identify the sequence $\langle s_a \rangle_{a \in A}$ with f and therefore we shall say that we want to prove that f is a continuous trace of p in $\mathfrak{A}$.

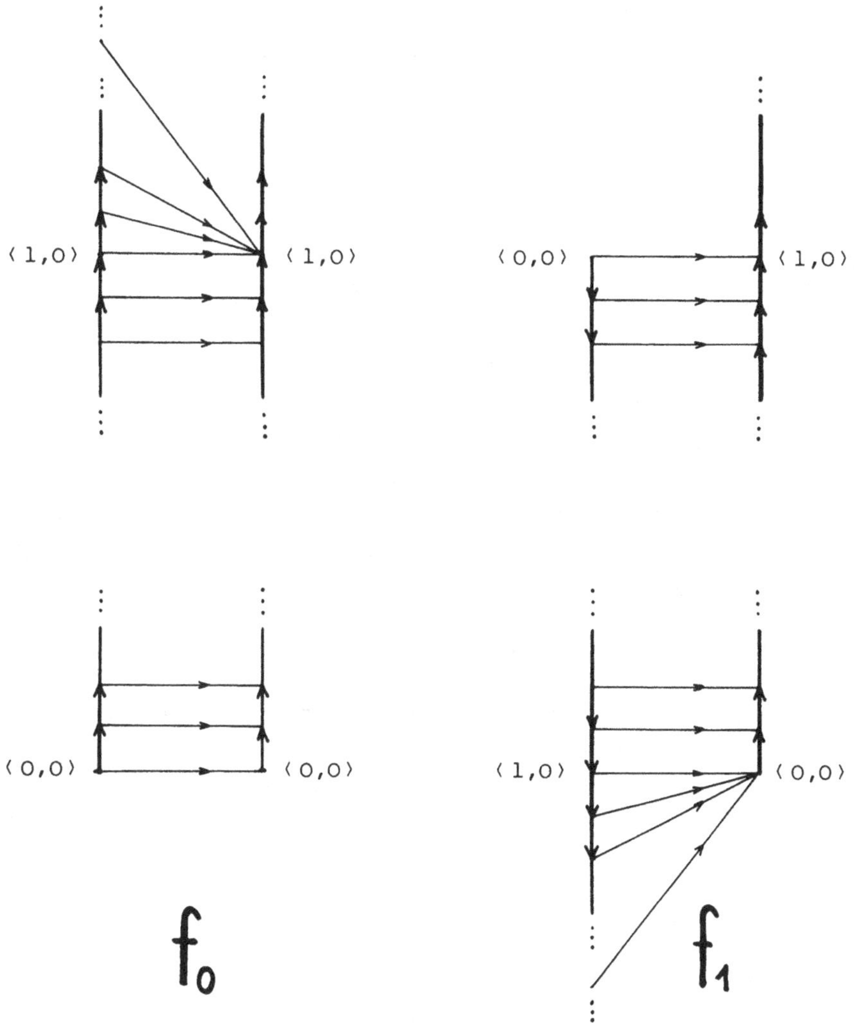

FIGURE 4

We shall use the following *notation*: Let $\varphi \in L_d$ with free variables in $V_p \cup \{\lambda\}$ and let $a \in A$. Therefore it is meaningful to write that $\mathfrak{A} \models \varphi[s_a]$ because $s_a : V_p \cup \{\lambda\} \to A$.

$\bar{f}(a)$ denotes the sequence $\langle f_0(a), f_1(a), f_2(a), f_\lambda(a)\rangle$. We define $\mathfrak{A} \models \varphi[\bar{f}(a)]$ to mean that $\mathfrak{A} \models \varphi[s_a]$.

In order to prove that f is a continuous trace of p in $\mathfrak{A}$, it is enough to prove for every $\varphi(y_0, y_1, y_2, \lambda) \in L_d$ that

$$\mathfrak{A} \models ((\varphi[\bar{f}(0)] \wedge \bigwedge_{a \in A} (\varphi[\bar{f}(a)] \to \varphi[\bar{f}(\mathrm{succ}(a))])) \to \bigwedge_{a \in A} \varphi[\bar{f}(a)]).$$

We shall prove this indirectly:

Assume that there is a $\varphi(y_0,y_1,y_2,\lambda)\in L_d$ such that

$$\mathfrak{A} \models (\varphi[\bar{f}(0)]\wedge \bigwedge_{a\in A} (\varphi[\bar{f}(a)] \to \varphi[\bar{f}(\mathrm{succ}(a))])) \tag{1}$$

but $\mathfrak{A} \not\models \bigwedge_{a\in A} \varphi[\bar{f}(a)]$ i.e. there is an $a\in A$ such that

$$\mathfrak{A} \models \neg\varphi[\bar{f}(a)]. \tag{2}$$

Recall that $\bar{f} : A \to {}^4A$ is as represented on Figure 5, i.e.: for every $0<n\in\omega$ we have

$\bar{f}(\langle 0,n\rangle) = \langle\langle 0,n\rangle,\langle 1,-n\rangle,\langle 1,0\rangle,\langle 0,1\rangle\rangle$,

$\bar{f}(\langle 1,-n\rangle) = \langle\langle 1,-n\rangle,\langle 0,n\rangle,\langle 1,0\rangle,\langle 0,1\rangle\rangle$,

$\bar{f}(\langle 0,0\rangle) = \langle\langle 0,0\rangle,\langle 1,0\rangle,\langle 1,0\rangle,\langle 0,0\rangle\rangle$,

$\bar{f}(\langle 1,0\rangle) = \langle\langle 1,0\rangle,\langle 0,0\rangle,\langle 1,0\rangle,\langle 0,2\rangle\rangle$.

Note that f_2 is a constant function and f_λ is almost constant.

By (1) we have $\mathfrak{A} \models \varphi[\bar{f}(a)]$ for every standard number $a\in A$, i.e. we have that $(\forall n\in\omega)\ \mathfrak{A} \models \varphi[\bar{f}(\langle 0,n\rangle)]$ i.e.

$$\mathfrak{A} \models \varphi[\langle 0,n\rangle,\langle 1,-n\rangle,\langle 1,0\rangle,\langle 0,1\rangle] \text{ for all } 0<n\in\omega. \tag{3}$$

(See Figure 5.) Then a is a nonstandard number in (2) i.e. there is a $z\in Z$ such that $\mathfrak{A} \models \neg\varphi[\bar{f}(\langle 1,z\rangle)]$. (See Figure 6.)

Then, by (1), we have that $(\forall w\leq z)\ \mathfrak{A} \models \neg\varphi[\bar{f}(\langle 1,w\rangle)]$. Then there is an $m\in\omega$ such that $(\forall n>m)\ \mathfrak{A} \models \neg\varphi[\bar{f}(\langle 1,-n\rangle)]$, i.e.

$$(\forall n>m)\ \mathfrak{A} \models \neg\varphi[\langle 1,-n\rangle,\langle 0,n\rangle,\langle 1,0\rangle,\langle 0,1\rangle]. \tag{4}$$

(See Figure 5.)

Let F be a nonprincipal ultrafilter over ω. $\mathfrak{B}$ denotes the ultrapower ${}^{\omega}\mathfrak{A}/_F$. For $\mathfrak{B}$ see Figure 9. We define

$b \stackrel{d}{=} \langle\langle 0,n\rangle : n\in\omega\rangle/_F$,

$c \stackrel{d}{=} \langle\langle 1,-n\rangle : n\in\omega\rangle/_F$,

$d \stackrel{d}{=} \langle\langle 1,0\rangle : n\in\omega\rangle/_F$,

$e \stackrel{d}{=} \langle\langle 0,1\rangle : n\in\omega\rangle/_F$.

Clearly $b,c,d,e\in B$. Then, by Łoś lemma and (3) we have

$$\mathfrak{B} \models \varphi[b,c,d,e]. \tag{5}$$

By Łoś lemma and (4) we have

$$\mathfrak{B} \models \neg\varphi[c,b,d,e]. \tag{6}$$

We define succ^n for $n\in\omega$ as: $\mathrm{succ}^0(g) \stackrel{d}{=} g$ and $\mathrm{succ}^{n+1}(g) \stackrel{d}{=} \mathrm{succ}(\mathrm{succ}^n(g))$ for every $g\in B$. pred^n is defined similarly to succ^n.

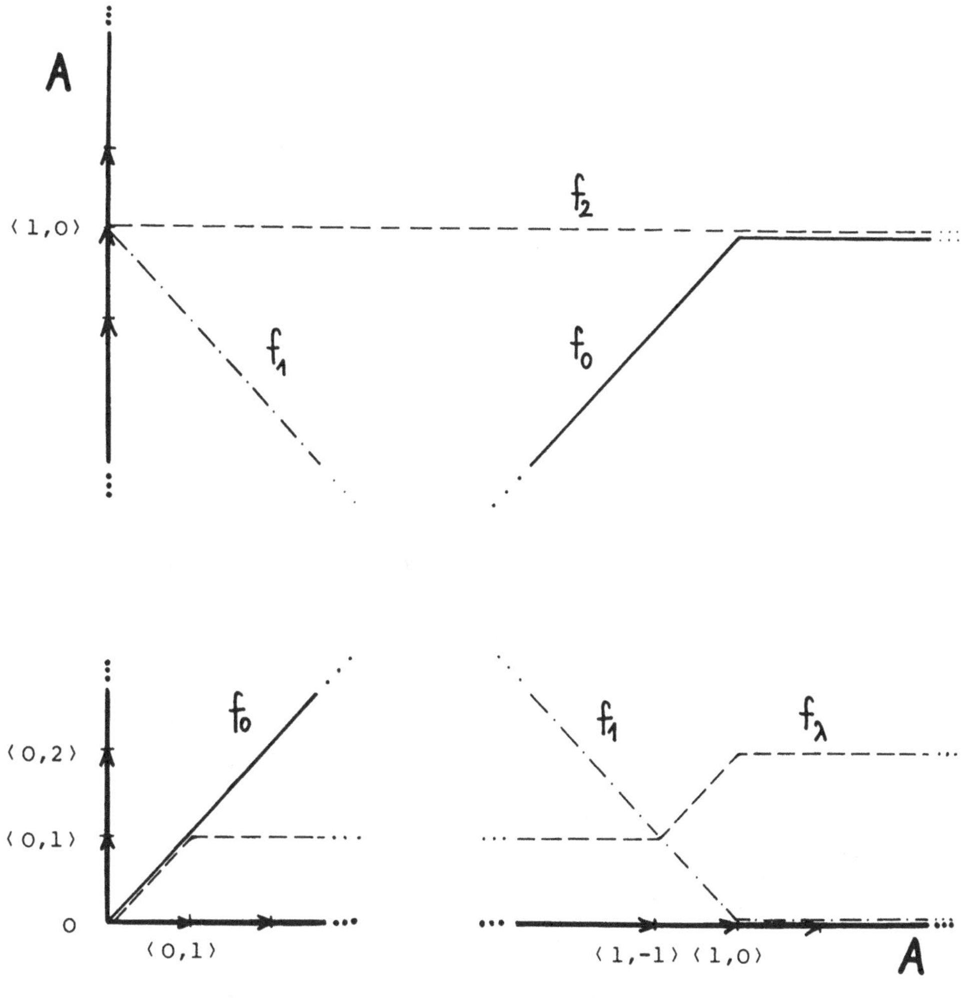

FIGURE 5

Clearly, $\mathcal{B}$ contains the following 2 "chains" Y,W illustrated on Figure 7. See also Figure 8.

More precisely, Y and W are the two subalgebras of $\langle B,\text{succ},\text{pred}\rangle$ generated by the elements b and c respectively. Then $b\in Y$ and $c\in W$ and Y is the smallest subset of B closed under succ and pred and containing b. Similarly for W and c. Then

$$\langle Y,\text{succ},\text{pred}\rangle \cong \langle W,\text{succ},\text{pred}\rangle.$$

Let $k : \langle Y,\text{succ},\text{pred}\rangle \to \langle W,\text{succ},\text{pred}\rangle$ be an isomorphism such that $k(b) = c$. For any $g\in B$ we define

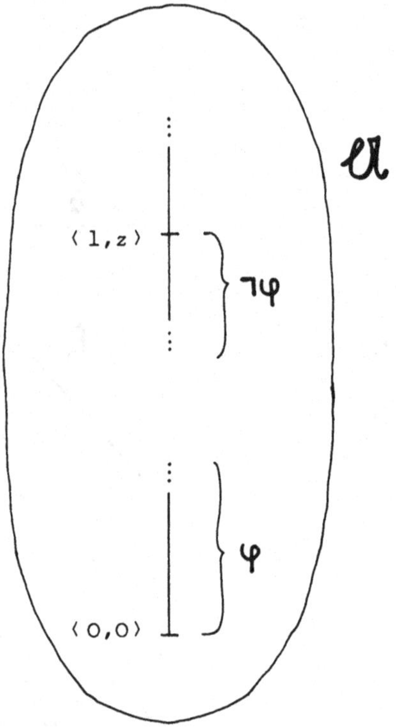

FIGURE 6

$$h(g) \overset{d}{=} \begin{cases} k(g) & \text{if } g \in Y \\ k^{-1}(g) & \text{if } g \in W \\ g & \text{otherwise.} \end{cases}$$

Then $h : B \to B$ is a function. Moreover, $h : \mathfrak{B} \to \mathfrak{B}$ is an automorphism of $\mathfrak{B}$. See Figure 9.
Therefore by (5) we have $\mathfrak{B} \models \varphi[h(b),h(c),h(d),h(e)]$, that is $\mathfrak{B} \models$ $\models \varphi[c,b,d,e]$. But this contradicts (6).

We derived a contradiction from the assumption (2). This proves $\mathfrak{A} \models \bigwedge_{a\in A} \varphi[\bar{f}(a)]$. This completes the proof. QED(Prop.3)

Clearly the "halting point" of the trace f of p in $\mathfrak{A}$ is the time point $\langle 1,0\rangle$. $f_0(\langle 1,0\rangle) = \langle 1,0\rangle$ and $f_2(\langle 1,0\rangle) = \langle 1,0\rangle$. Therefore the output condition $y_0=y_2$ of p is satisfied by trace f of p in $\mathfrak{A}$.

5.

Let $f_0' : A \to A$ differ from f_0 only on the nonstandard numbers and such that if $a\in A$ is nonstandard then $f_0'(a) = \mathrm{succ}(f_0(a))$. In more

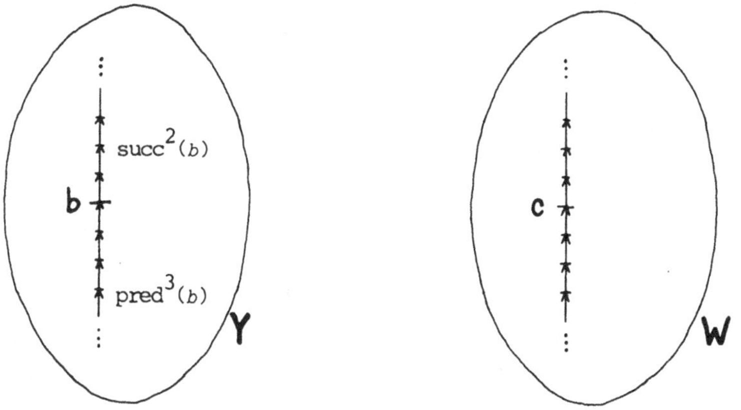

FIGURE 7

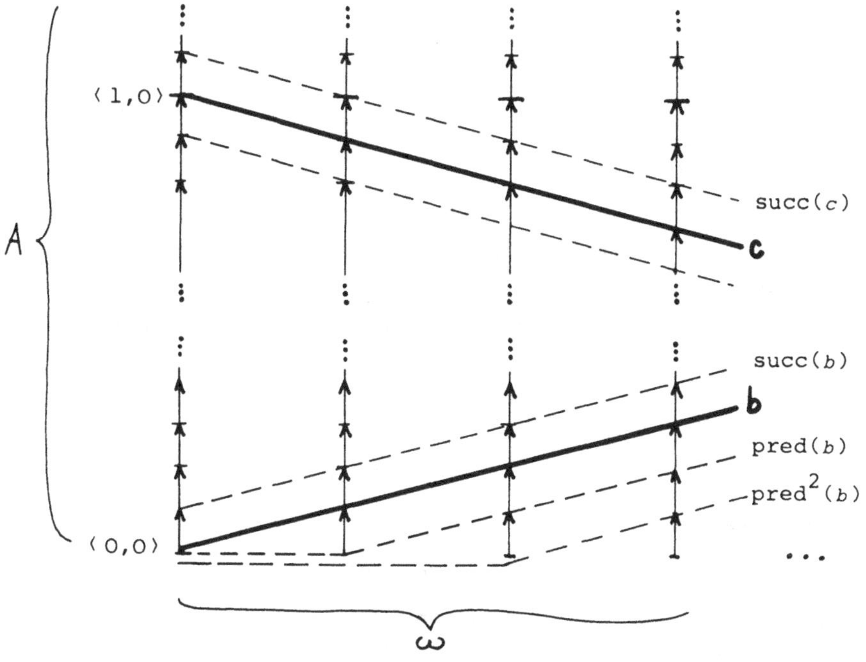

FIGURE 8

detail:

$(\forall n\in\omega)[f_0'(\langle 0,n\rangle) = \langle 0,n\rangle,\ f_0'(\langle 1,-n\rangle) = \langle 1,(-n)+1\rangle,\ f_0'(\langle 1,n\rangle) = \langle 1,n+1\rangle]$.

Let $f' \stackrel{d}{=} \langle f_0', f_1, f_2, f_\lambda\rangle$. By the constructions in the proof of Proposition 3 it is very easy to see that f' is continuous e.g. by using

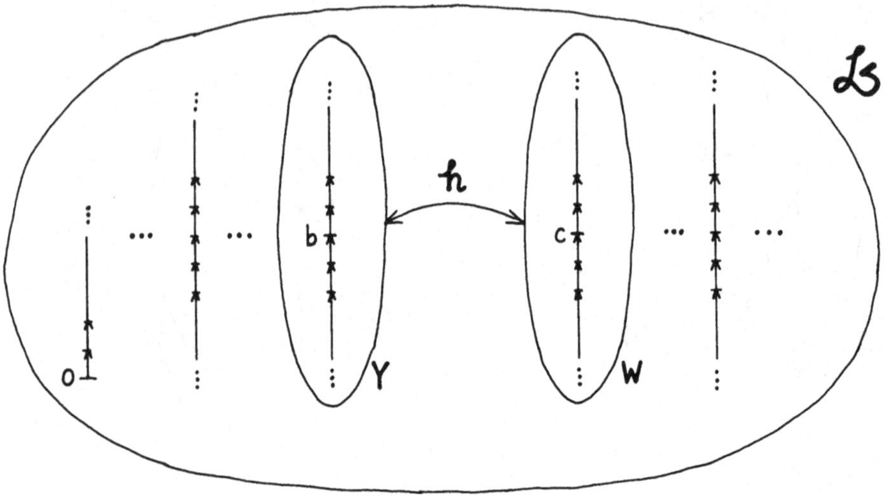

FIGURE 9

the fact that if we define

$$k(g) \overset{d}{=} \begin{cases} \text{succ}(g) & \text{if} \quad g \in W \\ g & \text{otherwise} \end{cases}$$

for all $g \in B$ then k is an automorphism of $\mathcal{L}$.

The trace f' of p terminates (at time point $\langle 1,1 \rangle$) with output $y_0 = \langle 1,1 \rangle$, $y_1 = \langle 0,0 \rangle$, $y_2 = \langle 1,0 \rangle$. Then for this output $y_0 \neq y_2$! Then in the sense of Definition 3 we have

$\mathfrak{A} \not\models^{pc} (p, y_0 = y_2)$.

6.

By Proposition 2 we have

$\{\varphi \in L_d : \mathfrak{A} \models \varphi\} \not\vdash^{FH} (p,\psi)$ and also $Pa \not\vdash^{FH} (p,\psi)$

since the continuous trace f' of p in $\mathfrak{A}$ terminates with an output not satisfying ψ.

7.

Let d' be the similarity type d expanded with the relation symbol $<$ with arity 2. We interpret $<$ in $\mathfrak{A}$ the lexicographical way i.e.: for every $\langle a_0, a_1 \rangle, \langle b_0, b_1 \rangle \in A$,

$\langle a_0, a_1 \rangle < \langle b_0, b_1 \rangle$ iff either $a_0 < b_0$ or $(a_0 = b_0$ and $a_1 < b_1)$.

Let $\mathfrak{A}'$ be the model $\mathfrak{A}$ expanded with the relation $<$ defined above. Then $\mathfrak{A}'$ is a model of similarity type d'. Let $f_i : A \to A$, $i \in \{0,1,2,\lambda\}$ be the functions defined in 3. above. Then $f = \langle f_0, f_1, f_2, f_\lambda \rangle$ is a trace of p in $\mathfrak{A}'$. But the trace f of p is not continuous in $\mathfrak{A}'$!

REFERENCES

[1] Andréka,H. Németi,I.: On the completeness problem of systems for program verification. (In Hungarian.) Math.Inst.Hung.Acad.Sci.--SZKI, 1977.

[2] Andréka,H. Németi I.: Completeness of Floyd Logic. Bull.Section of Logic (Wrowlaw), Vol 7, No 3, (1978), pp.115-120.

[3] Andréka,H. Németi,I.: A characterization of Floyd provable programs. Preprint, Math.Inst.Hung.Acad.Sci. No 8/1978. In: Mathematical Foundations of Computer Science'81 (Proc. Strbské Pleso Czechoslovakia) Ed.: J.Gruska, M.Chytil, Lecture Notes in Computer Science 118, Springer, Berlin, 1981. pp.162-171.

[4] Andréka,H. Németi I.: A complete first order dynamic logic. Preprint, Math.Inst.Hung.Acad.Sci., No 810930,1980. pp.1-120.

[5] Andréka,H. Németi,I. Sain,I.: Completeness problems in verification of programs and program schemes. Mathematical Foundations of Computer Science MFCS'79 (Proc. Olomouc, Czechoslovakia) Lecture Notes in Computer Science 74, Springer, Berlin, 1979. pp.208-218.

[6] Andréka,H. Németi,I. Sain,I.: Henkin-type semantics for program schemes to turn negative results to positive. In: Fundamentals of Computation Theory FCT'79 (Proc. Berlin) Ed.: L.Budach, Akademie, Berlin. 1979. pp.18-24.

[7] Andréka,H. Németi,I. Sain,I.: A complete logic for reasoning about programs via nonstandard model theory. Theoretical Computer Science Vol 17 (1982) Part I in No 2, Part II in No 3. To appear.

[8] Bell,J.L. Slomson,A.B.: Models and Ultraproducts. North-Holland, 1969.

[9] Biró,B.: On the completeness of program verification methods. Bull. Section of Logic, Wroclaw, Vol 10, No 2 (1981), pp.83-90.

[10] Chang,C.C. Keiser,H.J.: Model Theory. North-Holland, 1973.

[11] Cook,S.A.: Soundness and completeness of an axiom system for program verification. SIAM J. COMPUT. Vol 7, No 1, 1978, pp.70-90.

[12] Csirmaz,L.: On definability in Peano Arithmetic. Bull.Section of Logic (Wroclaw), Vol 8, No 3, 1979. pp.148-153.

[13] Csirmaz,L.: Programs and program verifications in a general setting. Theoretical Computer Science Vol 16 (1981), pp.199-211.

[14] Csirmaz,L.: On the completeness of proving partial correctness. Acta Cybernetica, Tom 5, Fasc 2, Szeged, 1981. pp.181-190.

[15] Csirmaz,L. Paris,J.: A property of 2-sorted Peano models and

program verification. Preprint, Math.Inst.Hung.Acad.Sci., 1981.

[16] Dahn,B.I.: First order predicate logics for Kripke-Models. Dissertation(B). Humboldt Univ., Berlin, 1979.

[17] Hájek,P.: Making dynamic logic first-order. In: Mathematical Foundations of Computer Science MFCS'81 (Proc.Strbské Pleso, Czechoslovakia) Ed.: J.Gruska, M.Chytil, Lecture Notes in Computer Science 118, Springer, Berlin, 1981. pp.287-295.

[18] Henkin,L. Monk,J.D. Tarski,A. Andréka,H. Németi,I.: Cylindric Set Algebras. Lecture Notes in Mathematics 883, Springer-Verlag, Berlin, 1981. v+323p.

[19] Németi,I.: Nonstandard dynamic logic. In: Proc. Workshop on Logics of Programs (May 1981, New York) Ed.: D.Kozen, Lecture Notes in Computer Science, To appear.

[20] Richter,M.M. Szabo,M.E.: Towards a nonstandard analysis of programs. In: Proc. 2nd Victoria Symp. on Nonstandard Analysis (Victoria, British Columbia, June 1980) Lecture Notes in Mathematics. Ed.: A.Hurd, Springer Verlag, 1981.

[21] Sain,I.: There are general rules for specifying semantics: Observations on abstract model theory. CL & CL Budapest, Vol 13, 1979. pp.251-282.

[22] Sain,L.: First order dynamic logic with decidable proofs and workable model theory. In: Fundamentals of Computation Theory FCT'81, (Proc.Szeged, 1981) Ed.: F.Gécseg, Lecture Notes in Computer Science 117, Springer, Berlin, 1981. pp.334-340.

[23] Salwicki,A.: Axioms of Algorithmic Logic univocally determine semantics of programs. In: Mathematical Foundations of Computer Science MFCS'80 (Proc. Rydzyna, Poland) Lecture Notes in Computer Science 88, Springer, Berlin, 1980. pp.552-561.

ON SOME EXTENSIONS OF DYNAMIC LOGIC

Ewa Orłowska
Institute of Computer Science
Polish Academy of Sciences
00-901 Warszawa, PKiN
Poland

1. Introduction

Program logics should provide tools to study algorithmic properties, namely:

- to express properties of programs in the formalized language of a program logic,
- to prove these properties using deductive system of the logic.

The question arises what are the properties of program logics which enable us to accomplish theses two tasks.

The problem of expressible algorithmic properties can be formulated in two ways. Usually, we formulate it from the point of view of a language, namely we try to define a powerful formalized language in which the complex program structures have their counterparts. From the semantical point of view formulas of a formalized language are considered as sets of states. Hence the problem of expressible algorithmic properties can be stated semantically as the problem of a characterization of sets of states which are definable by formulas of the language. Thus the definability of all subsets of the set of states is the desirable property of a program logic.

As far as the second task is concerned, it is not sufficient when the deductive system of a logic enables us only to recognize tautologies, i.e. algorithmic properties valid for all programs. It is more important to prove properties of special classes of programs. Hence holding of the strong completeness theorem for formalized theories and the compactness theorem are the desirable properties of a program logic.

In the paper we define the logic QPDL which is the extension of propostional dynamic logic PDL (Pratt[5], Fischer and Ladner [2]). QPDL is obtained from PDL by adding to the language of PDL quantifiers binding propositional variables and modal S5 operators. We give the finite axiomatization of QPDL and prove the completeness theorem for formalized theories based on QPDL and the compactness theorem.

We define the formalized theory based on QPDL such that in models of this theory all subsets of the set of states are definable by means of formulas. We also consider what is called normalized models. In such models any two distinct states can be distinguished by a formula. We present the formalized theory based on QPDL such that for any model of the theory there is an algorithmically equivalent normalized model

2. Formalized language of QPDL

Set of symbols of the language of QPDL is the union of the following disjoint sets:

infinite, denumerable set Var of propositional variables, denoted by $p, q, \dots$;

denumerable set Con of program constants, denoted by $R_0, R, R_1, R_2, \dots$

set $\{\neg, \rightarrow\}$ of sentential connectives ;

set $\{+, \cdot, *\}$ of program connectives ;

set $\{\forall\}$ consisting of the general quantifier ;

set $\{(\,,\,)\,,\,[\,,\,]\}$ of brackets .

Set Prog of program expressions is the least set satisfying the following conditions:

Con $\subseteq$ Prog ,

if $K, K_1, K_2 \in$ Prog then $K_1 + K_2$, $K_1 \cdot K_2$, $K^* \in$ Prog .

Set For of formulas is the least set satisfying the following conditions:

Var $\subseteq$ For ,

if $A, B \in$ For then $\neg A, A \rightarrow B \in$ For ,

if $A \in$ For and $K \in$ Prog, then $[K]A \in$ For ,

if $A \in$ For and $p \in$ Var then $\forall p A \in$ For .

We admit the usual definition of free and bound propositional variable. We will say that formula B is free for variable p in A(p) if no free occurrence of p in A(p) lies within the scope of a quantifier binding a variable which is free in B .

3. Semantics of QPDL

Semantics of QPDL is defined by means of the notion of a model and a satisfiability of formulas in a model.

By a model we mean system

$$M = (S\,,\,D\,,\,m)$$

where

S is a non-empty set, whose elements are called states,

D is a non-empty subset of set 2^S, called the domain of propositions,

m is mapping from set Prog into set $2^{S \times S}$, such that:

R_0 is an equivalence relation,

$m(K)$ is reflexive, for each $K \in$ Prog,

$m(K_1+K_2) = m(K_1) \cup m(K_2)$,

$m(K_1 \cdot K_2) = m(K_1) \circ m(K_2)$,

$m(K^*) \supseteq (m(K))^*$.

Given model M, by a valuation we mean any function v from set Var into set D. Let Val(M) be the set of all valuations which can be defined for model M.

We will say that formula A is satisfied in model M in state s by valuation v (M,s,v sat A) if the following conditions are satisfied:

M,s,v sat p iff $s \in v(p)$ for $p \in$ Var,

M,s,v sat $\neg$A iff non M,s,v sat A,

M,s,v sat $A \to B$ iff non M,s,v sat A or M,s,v sat B,

M,s,v sat [K]A iff for any state $s' \in S$ such that $(s,s') \in m(K)$ we have M,s',v sat A,

M,s,v sat $\forall pA$ iff for any set $P \subseteq D$ we have M,s,v(p/P) sat A, where v(p/P) denotes the valuation v' such that $v'(p) = P$ and $v'(q) = v(q)$ for any variable $q \neq p$.

We define sentential operations $\vee$, $\wedge$, $\leftrightarrow$, $\langle K \rangle$, $\exists$ as follows:

$A \vee B = \neg A \to B$,

$A \wedge B = \neg(A \to \neg B)$,

$A \leftrightarrow B = (A \to B) \wedge (B \to A)$,

$\langle K \rangle A = \neg [K] \neg A$,

$\exists pA = \neg \forall p \neg A$.

It is easily seen that according to the given semantics formulas $[R_0]A$ and $\langle R_0 \rangle A$ are interpreted in the same way as in modal logic S5, so in the following we will write $\Box A$ and $\Diamond A$ instead of $[R_0]A$ and $\langle R_0 \rangle A$, respectively.

A formula A is said to be valid in model $M = (S,D,m)$ if for each valuation $v \in$ Val(M) and each state $s \in S$ we have M,s,v sat A. A formula A is said to be a tautology of QPDL ($\vdash A$) if it is valid in any model for QPDL. A formula A is said to be a semantical consequence of set Γ of formulas ($\Gamma \models A$) if, for any model M for QPDL, A is valid in M whenever all formulas from Γ are valid in M. A set Γ of formulas is satisfied in model M by state s and valuation v (M,s,v sat Γ) if M,s,v sat A for every $A \in \Gamma$. Set Γ is satisfiable if M,s,v sat Γ for some model M, state s and valuation v.

The admitted notion of model is analogous to the notion of Henkin generalized model for higher order logic. For the semantics based on these models we obtained the strong completeness result and compactness.

4 . Deductive system of QPDL

For all $K \in$ Prog and $A,B \in$ For we admit the following axioms and inference rules.

A1. All formulas having the form of tautologies of classical propositional calculus,

A2. $[K](A \to B) \to ([K]A \to [K]B)$,

A3. $[K]A \to A$,

A4. $\Box A \to [K]A$,

A5. $\neg [K]A \to \Box \neg [K]A$,

A6. $\forall p(A \to B) \to (A \to \forall pB)$, where p is not free in A ,

A7. $\forall pA \to A(p/B)$ for any formula B which is free for p in A(p) ,

A8. $[K] \forall pA \leftrightarrow \forall p[K]A$,

A9. $[K_1 + K_2]A \leftrightarrow [K_1]A \wedge [K_2]A$,

A10. $[K_1 \cdot K_2]A \leftrightarrow [K_1][K_2]A$,

A11. $[K^*]A \to A \wedge [K][K^*]A$,

A12. $A \wedge [K^*](A \to [K]A) \to [K^*]A$.

R1 $\dfrac{A\ ,\ A \to B}{B}$

R2 $\dfrac{A}{[K]A}$

R3 $\dfrac{A}{\forall pA}$

For $K = R_0$ axioms A1,A2,A3,A5 are axioms of modal logic S5. Axiom A8 is the Barcan-type formula.

The notions of a proof and a theorem are defined as usual. We will write $\vdash A$ if A is a theorem of QPDL. A formula A is said to be derivable from a set Γ of formulas ($\Gamma \vdash A$) if there are formulas $A_1,\dots,A_n \in \Gamma$, $n \geqslant 1$, such that $\vdash (A_1 \to (A_2 \to \dots (A_n \to A)\dots))$.

Set Γ of formulas is said to be inconsistent if condition $\Gamma \vdash 0$ holds, where 0 denotes a formula of the form $A \wedge \neg A$. Set Γ is said to be consistent if it is not inconsistent.

For the given deductive system we have the following theorems.

(4.1) Soundness theorem

(a) $\vdash A$ implies $\models A$,

(b) $\Gamma \vdash A$ implies $\Gamma \models A$,

(c) Γ satisfiable implies Γ consistent.

(4.2) Completeness theorem

(a) $\models A$ implies $\vdash A$,

(b) $\Gamma \models A$ implies $\Gamma \vdash A$,

(c) Γ consistent implies Γ satisfiable.

The proof of completeness theorem is by the Henkin method extended to modal logics by Gallin [3] and Cresswell [1].

(4.3) Compactness theorem

Γ is satisfiable if and only if every finite subset of Γ is satisfiable.

5. Definability of sets of states

Given model $M = (S,D,m)$ of QPDL, we will say that set $X \subseteq S$ is definable in M if there is a formula A and a valuation $v \in Val(M)$ such that $X = \{ s \in S : M,s,v \text{ sat } A \}$.

Let Def(M) be the family of all sets definable in M. Observe that set Def(M) is non-empty, since set D is non-empty. Moreover, it is closed under set-theoretical operations of union, intersection and complement, and sets $\emptyset$ and S belong to Def(M). Hence the following fact is true.

(5.1) Set Def(M) is a Boolean algebra.

We define binary relation $\sim$ in set S of states in such a way, that two states are in relation $\sim$ iff they cannot be distinguished by means of formulas of QPDL:

$s \sim t$ iff for each formula A and each valuation v Val(M) we have M,s,v sat A iff M,t,v sat A.

The following facts follow immediately from the given definitions:

(5.2) Relation $\sim$ is an equivalence relation.

(5.3) For any model $M = (S,D,m)$ the following conditions are equivalent:

(a) $s \sim t$,
(b) for any set $X \in Def(M)$ we have $s \in X$ iff $t \in X$.

We will say that model M is normalized if for any states s,t we have $s \sim t$ iff $s = t$.

The question arises, whether given a model M, we can construct a normalized model M' such that sets of formulas valid in M and in M' are equal. In the next section we define the extension of QPDL, having this property.

6. Theories based on QPDL

Consider the scheme of formulas which is the propositional counterpart of the comprehension axiom:

C(A) $\exists p \Box (p \leftrightarrow A)$, where p does not occur in A.

Let QPDL+C denote the theory obtained from QPDL by adjoining formulas C(A) for all $A \in For$ to the axioms of QPDL. It is easy to see that the following facts are true.

(6.1) If M is a model of QPDL+C then $Def(M) = D$.

(6.2) For any model M of QPDL+C the following conditions are eqivalent:
(a) $s \sim t$,
(b) for any set $P \subseteq D$ we have $s \in P$ iff $t \in P$.

Consider the scheme of formulas

Ot(K) $\Box \exists p \forall q ([K] q \leftrightarrow \Box (p \to q))$

(6.3) For any model $M = (S,D,m)$ of QPDL if M,s,v sat Ot(K) then for any state $s \in S$ there is the least set $P_s \subseteq D$ containing all states $s' \in S$ such that $(s,s') \in m(K)$.

Hence formula Ot(K) defines sets of outputs of program K.

Consider theory QPDL+C+Ot obtained from QPDL+C by adding formulas Ot(K) for all $K \in Prog$ to the axioms of QPDL+C.

(6.4) If $M = (S,D,m)$ is a model of QPDL+C+Ot then for any $K \in Prog$ if $s \sim s'$, $t \sim t'$, and $(s,t) \in m(K)$ then $(s't') \in m(K)$.

Given model $M = (S,D,m)$ of QPDL+C+Ot, we define the quotient model $M/_\sim = (S/_\sim, D/_\sim, m/_\sim)$ as follows. $S/_\sim$ is the set of all equivalence classes of relation $\sim$. Let $\|s\|$ denote the equivalence class determined by a state s. Let h be the mapping such that $\|s\| \in h(P)$ iff $s \in P$ for any $P \subseteq D$. By (6.2) this definition is correct. Moreover, function h is one-to-one. We define set $D/_\sim$ as the range of h. Mapping $m/_\sim$ is defined as follows:

$$(\|s\|, \|t\|) \in m/_\sim(K) \text{ iff } (s,t) \in m(K).$$

By (6.4) this definition is correct.

(6.5) For any model M of QPDL+C+Ot, for any formula A, any state s and any valuation $v \in Val(M)$ we have

$$M,s,v \text{ sat } A \text{ iff } M/_\sim, \|s\|, v_h \text{ sat } A$$

where v_h is the valuation from set $Val(M/_\sim)$ such that $v_h(p) = h(v(p))$ for any $p \in Var$.

As a corollary we obtain

(6.6) For any model M of QPDL+C+Ot there is a normalized model M' such that sets of formulas valid in M and in M' are equal.

7. Algorithmic properties expressible in QPDL+C+Ot

Consider formula $\langle K \rangle 1$, where 1 denotes a formula of the form $A \vee \neg A$. This formula expresses the stop property of program K. But due to axiom C we have the following theorem.

(7.1) For any model $M = (S,D,m)$ of QPDL+C+Ot set $\{j : \exists i (i,j) \in m(K)\}$ is definable in M.

Formula $A \rightarrow [K]B$ can be interpreted as the partial correctness assertion for K with respect to precondition A and postcondition B. Given model M of QPDL and valuation $v \in Val(M)$, let us consider the following sets of states:

$$pre_{M,v}(K,A) = \{s \in S : \text{for any } t \in S \text{ if } (s,t) \in m(K) \text{ then } M,t,v \text{ sat } A\},$$

$$post_{M,v}(K,A) = \{t \in S : \text{there is a state } s \text{ such that } (s,t) \in m(K) \text{ and } M,s,v \text{ sat } A\}.$$

(7.2) For any model M of QPDL+C+Ot the following conditions are satisfied:

(a) $s \in pre_{M,v}(K,A)$ iff M,s,v sat $[K]A$,

(b) $t \in post_{M,v}(K,A)$ iff there exists a state s such that $t \in P_s$ and M,s,v sat A, where P_s is the set defined by formula $Ot(K)$.

Let us now define the following two families of formulas:

$\langle K \rangle^1 A = \langle K \rangle A$,

$\langle K\rangle^{n+1}A = \exists p(\langle K\rangle^{n}(A\wedge p) \wedge \langle K\rangle (A\wedge \neg p))$ for $n\geqslant 1$,

$(K)^{n}A = \langle K\rangle^{n}A \wedge \neg \langle K\rangle^{n+1}$ for $n\geqslant 1$.

(7.3) For any model $M = (S,D,m)$, any state $s\in S$ and any valuation $v\in Val(M)$ the following conditions are satisfied:

(a) M,s,v sat $\langle K\rangle^{n}A$ iff the set $Z=\{t\in S : (s,t)\in m(K)$ and M,t,v sat has at least n elements ,

(b) M,s,v sat $(K)^{n}A$ iff the set Z has exactely n elements.

In a similar way as in the logic PAL [4] we can define the finite degree of nondeterminism property of programs. Moreover, in the logic QPDL+C+Ot the sets of states determined by such formulas are quaranted to be contained in the domain of propositions of models.

References

1. Creswell M.J.: A Henkin completeness theorem for T . Notre Dame Journal of Formal Logic 8 (1967) 186-190.
2. Fischer M.J., Landner R.L.: Propositional modal logic of programs. Proc.9th ACM Symp.on Theory of Computing Boulder,Col.(1977) 286-294
3. Gallin D.: Intensional and higher order modal logic. North Holland Mathematics Studies 19 (1975).
4. Mirkowska G.: PAL - propositional algorithmic logic. Fundamenta Informaticae, to appear.
5. Pratt V.R.: Semantical considerations on Floyd-Hoare logic. Proc. 17th IEEE Symp.on Foundations of Computer Science (1976) 109-121.

ON ALGORITHMIC LOGIC WITH PARTIAL OPERATIONS

Uwe Petermann
Karl-Marx-Universität Leipzig, Sektion Mathematik
DDR 7010 Leipzig, Karl-Marx-Platz 1

ntroduction

n theoretical considerations on algorithmic logic there is assumed as sual, that models of algorithmic theories are realizations assigning full operation to every operator. In applications (for instance disribing data structures by algorithmic theories) it is usefull to allow ealizations with partial operations too.

n the present paper we prove, that the deductive system of algorithmic ogic (see /BCP/, /Mir/, /Ban/) with some slight modifications remains vailable in a larger class of realizations. There are considered many orted algorithmic languages with partial operations, where the domain f each operation has a certain syntactical charactarization. Namely o every operator φ corresponds a predicate with the same arity s φ. There are considered only such realizations, in which the realiation of the predicate φ^{*} corresponding to the operator φ coincides ith the characteristic function of the domain of the operation φ_R. his assumption enables us to prove a completeness theorem.

urthermore there is given a syntactical characterization of the proramme property "there will be no failure during the execution of the rogramme".

ecause of lack of space the results are given without proof.

he terminology corresponds to that used in /Ra-Si/ and /BCP/. The xamples are suggested by /Sal1/ .

. Many sorted algorithmic languages with partial operations

.1. Let Srt be an at most countable set (not empty), called in the ollowing the set of sorts. By Srt^{*} we shall denote the set of all ords over Srt, O the empty word and by Srt^{+} the set of all not mpty words.

s the alphabet of an Srt-sorted algorithmic language with partial perations (shortly: alphabet) we understand the ordered pair $A=(\Sigma,D)$ here Σ is the disjoint union of the following sets:

V_σ, for each sort σ, where card$(V_\sigma)=\aleph_0$;
the set of individual variables of the sort σ,
V_0, where card$(V_0)=\aleph_0$; the set of propositional variables,
$\Phi_{\underline{\sigma},\sigma}$ for each ordered pair $(\underline{\sigma},\sigma) \in Srt^* \times Srt$, where card$(\Phi_{\underline{\sigma},\sigma}) \leq \aleph_0$;
the set of operators of the sort σ with the arity $\underline{\sigma}$,
$P_{\underline{\sigma}}$ for every $\underline{\sigma} \in Srt^*$, where card$(P_{\underline{\sigma}}) \leq \aleph_0$;
the set of predicates of the arity $\underline{\sigma}$,
L_0, a two-element set containing propositional constants **0** and **1**,
L_1, a one-element set containing the unary logical connective $\neg$ (negation),
L_2, a three-element set containing the binary connectives $\wedge$ (conjunction), $\vee$ (disjunction), $\Rightarrow$ (implication),
Q, a four-element set containing the iterational quantifiers $\bigcap, \bigcup$ (general and existential) and the classical quantifiers $\forall$, $\exists$,
π, a three-element set containing the programme connectives sequential composition, if-then-else, while-do, denoted by $\circ, \veebar, *$ respectively,
U, a set of auxiliary signs [,], (,) , / and
D is a family of 1-1 mappings $D = \{D_{\underline{\sigma}} : \bigcup_{\sigma \in Srt} \Phi_{\underline{\sigma},\sigma} \dashrightarrow P_{\underline{\sigma}}\}_{\underline{\sigma} \in Srt^*}$.
If Srt is a one-element set, the first part of the definition above is equivalent to the definition of an alphabet of an algorithmic language given in /Ban/. The family of mappings D has been introduced in order to assign to each operator a predicate characterizing its domain.
To a given alphabet an Srt-sorted algorithmic language with partial operations will be constructed in a similar way as presented in /Mir/ or /Ban/ respecting the modifications caused by the occurrence of different sorts of individuals.

1.2. Let $A = (\Sigma, D)$ be an alphabet in the sense of 1.1. Then by the Srt-sorted algorithmic language with partial operations for A we understand the system of subsets of Σ^* (T, F, S, FS, FST, FSF) where:
The set of classical terms T is the disjoint union of the sets T_σ of terms of sort σ, the set F is the set of classical open formulas, both constructed as usual (see /Ass/, for the one-sorted case /Ra-Si/). The occurrence of terms of different sorts must be respected as follows: if $\varphi(t_1 \ldots t_n) \in T$ (resp. F), where for i=1,...,n $t_i \in T_{\sigma_i}$, then the operator φ (resp. predicate φ) has the arity $\sigma_1 \ldots \sigma_n$.
The set S of substitutions is the set of all words over Σ^* of the form $[x_1/t_1 \ldots x_n/t_n a_1/\alpha_1 \ldots a_m/\alpha_m]$, where $x_1,\ldots,x_n$ (resp. $a_1,\ldots,a_m$) denote pairwise different individual (resp. propositional) variables (n as well as m may be equal to zero), $\alpha_1,\ldots,\alpha_m$ are open formulas and for each i=1,...,n holds: if $x_i \in V_{\sigma_i}$, then $t_i \in T_{\sigma_i}$.

The set FS denotes the set of all structured programmes obtained starting from substitutions as primitive programmes and making use of the programme connectives from $\mathcal{T}$ and the open formulas as Boolean expressions.
The set FST denotes the set of all generalized terms. It is defined as the least set containing T, which is closed under the construction rules used constructing T and under the additional rule: if $K \in FS$ and $t \in FST$, then $Kt \in FST$. For each $\sigma \in Srt$ FST_σ denotes the set of all generalized terms of the sort σ.
The set FSF of generalized formulas is defined as the least set satisfiing the following conditions:

i) $F \subseteq FSF$,

ii) if $\varrho \in P_{\underline{\sigma}}$, $t_1 \in FST_{\sigma_1}, \ldots, t_n \in FST_{\sigma_n}$ and the word $\underline{\sigma}$ is equal to the word $\sigma_1 \ldots \sigma_n$, then $\varrho(t_1 \ldots t_n)$ belongs to FSF,

iii) if $K \in FS$ and $\alpha \in FSF$, then $K\alpha$, $\bigcap K\alpha$, $\bigcup K\alpha$ belong to FSF too,

iv) if $\alpha, \beta \in FSF$ and x is an individual variable of the sort σ, then the words $\forall x\alpha$, $\exists x\alpha$, $\alpha \wedge \beta$, $\alpha \vee \beta$, $\alpha \Rightarrow \beta$, $\neg\alpha$ belong to FSF too.

From now on every element of the set $FS \cup FST \cup FSF$ will be called an expression. As an abbreviation we introduce the following denotations: Φ for $\bigcup_{\underline{\sigma} \in Srt^*} \bigcup_{\sigma \in Srt} \Phi_{\underline{\sigma},\sigma}$, P for $\bigcup_{\underline{\sigma} \in Srt^*} P_{\underline{\sigma}}$, Φ_o for $\bigcup_{\sigma \in Srt} \Phi_{o,\sigma}$, P_{db} for $\bigcup_{\underline{\sigma} \in Srt^*} D_{\underline{\sigma}}(\bigcup_{\sigma \in Srt} \Phi_{\underline{\sigma},\sigma})$, V_i for $\bigcup_{\sigma \in Srt} V_\sigma$. The identity of two expressions ε_1 and ε_2 will be denoted by $\varepsilon_1 : \varepsilon_2$. For each $\varphi \in \bigcup_{\underline{\sigma} \in Srt^*} \Phi_{\underline{\sigma},\sigma}$ $D_{\underline{\sigma}}(\varphi)$ will be denoted by φ^*.

1.3. Example. Let us regard a $\{E,D\}$-sorted alphabet A. There are three operators: one of the sort E with arity D, two of the sort D with arity ED (denoted by amb, del, ins respectively) and exactly four predicates: one with arity D, three with arity ED (denoted by amb*, del*, ins*, mb respectively). The algorithmic language for this alphabet may be used to formulate an algorithmic theory of dictionaries (see /Sal1/).

1.4. Now we shall define a mapping, which assignes to every element ε of $T \cup F \cup FS$ a certain generalized formula $db(\varepsilon)$ expressing something like: "There will be no failure during the computation of ε" or in other words "During the computation of the value of ε all operators will be available if necessary". This mapping $db: F \cup FS \cup T \longrightarrow FSF$ will be defined by induction on the lenght of expressions. One can observe, that the predicates from P_{db} play an important role in the definition of the mapping db.

$$db(\varepsilon) = \begin{cases} 1 \ldots\ldots\ldots\ldots\ldots\ldots & \text{iff } \varepsilon \in L_o \cup V_o \cup V_i \cup \Phi_o \\ \varphi^*(t_1 \ldots t_n) \ldots\ldots\ldots & \text{iff } \varepsilon \in T \ \& \ \varepsilon: \varphi(t_1 \ldots t_n) \\ db(t_1) \wedge .. \wedge db(t_n) \ldots\ldots & \text{iff } \varepsilon \in F \ \& \ \varepsilon: \varrho(t_1 \ldots t_n) \\ db(\alpha_1) \wedge db(\alpha_2) \ldots\ldots & \text{iff } \varepsilon \in F \ \& \ \varepsilon: \alpha_1 \circ \alpha_2 \ \& \circ \in L_2 \\ db(\alpha) \ldots\ldots\ldots\ldots\ldots & \text{iff } \varepsilon \in F \ \& \ \varepsilon: \neg\alpha \\ db(\varepsilon_1) \wedge .. \wedge db(\varepsilon_n) \ldots\ldots & \text{iff } \varepsilon \in S \ \& \ \varepsilon: [z_1/\varepsilon_1 .. z_n/\varepsilon_n] \\ db(K) \wedge (\neg K 1 \vee K db(M)) \ldots\ldots & \text{iff } \varepsilon \in FS \ \& \ \varepsilon: \bullet[KM] \\ db(\delta) \wedge ((\delta \wedge db(K)) \vee (\neg\delta \wedge db(M))) \ldots & \text{iff } \varepsilon \in FS \ \& \ \varepsilon: \times[\delta KM] \\ \neg \bigcup \underline{\vee}[\delta K[\,]] (\neg db(\delta) \vee (\delta \wedge \neg db(K))) \ldots & \text{iff } \varepsilon \in FS \ \& \ \varepsilon: \bullet[\delta K] \end{cases}$$

2. Realizations of algorithmic languages with partial operations

2.1. Definition: Let A be an alphabet in the sense of 1.1. Further le $\mathcal{R}$ be an ordered pair (I,R), where $I = \{I_\sigma\}_{\sigma \in Srt}$ is a family of non-empty sets, R a mapping assigning to every operator $\varphi \in \Phi_{\underline{\sigma},\sigma}$ a partial operation $\varphi_R: I_{\sigma_1} \times .. \times I_{\sigma_n} \dashrightarrow I_\sigma$, if $\underline{\sigma} = \sigma_1 .. \sigma_n$, to every operator $\varphi \in \Phi_o$ a certain element of I_σ, if $\varphi \in \Phi_{o,\sigma}$, to every predicate $\varrho \in P_{\underline{\sigma}}$ a mapping $\varrho_R: I_{\sigma_1} \times \ldots \times I_{\sigma_n} \longrightarrow B_o$, if $\underline{\sigma} = \sigma_1 .. \sigma_n$, and B_o denotes a two-element Boolean algebra.

Then $\mathcal{R}$ will be called a realization of the alphabet A, if and only if for every operator φ the mapping φ^*_R coincides with the characterist function of the domain of the operation φ_R.

2.2. Example of a realization of the alphabet presented in 1.3. Rega the ordered pair $(\{I_E, I_D\}, R)$. I_E denotes the set of all natural numbers , I_D the power-set of I_E. The mapping R is defined as follows: for every $n \in I_E$, $X \in I_D$ hold

$$del_R(n,X) = X \setminus \{n\}, \quad ins_R(n,X) = X \cup \{n\}, \quad amb_R(X) = \begin{cases} \min X & \text{iff } X \neq \emptyset \\ \text{undef.} & \text{iff } X = \emptyset \end{cases}$$

$$del^*_R(n,X) = ins^*_R(n,X) = \checkmark,$$

$$amb^*_R(X) = \begin{cases} \checkmark & \text{iff } X \neq \emptyset \\ \bot & \text{iff } X = \emptyset \end{cases}, \qquad mb_R(n,X) = \begin{cases} \checkmark & \text{iff } n \in X \\ \bot & \text{iff } n \notin X \end{cases}.$$

(the symbols $\emptyset, \setminus, \cup, \in$ above have their usual set-theoretical meaning, by $\checkmark$ resp. $\bot$ will be denoted the truth-values true and false).

2.3. Now we shall define meanings to programmes and generalized terms and formulas. For a given realization $\mathcal{R} = (I,R)$ of the alphabet A every element of the set

$$Val_{\mathcal{R}} = \Big\{ v \in (B_o \cup \bigcup_{\sigma \in Srt} I_\sigma)^V : V = V_i \cup V_o \ \& \text{for all } \sigma \in Srt, \text{ all } x \in V: v(x) \in I_\sigma \ \& \text{ for all } a \in V_o: v(a) \in B_o \Big\}$$

will be called a valuation. The meaning of a generalized term $t \in FST$ will be a partial mapping $t_R: Val_{\mathcal{R}} \dashrightarrow I_\sigma$, the meaning of a generalized formula $\alpha \in FSF$ will be a mapping $\alpha_R: Val \longrightarrow B_o$. In the case $\varepsilon \in T \cup F$ ε_R is defined similar as in /Ass/. The occurrence of parti

operations and of different sorts of individuals causes, that the following definition must be respected:
if $\underline{\sigma}=\sigma_1..\sigma_n$, $\varphi\in\Phi_{\underline{\sigma},\sigma_0}\cup P_{\underline{\sigma}}$, $v\in Val_{\mathcal{R}}$ and for all $i=1,...,n$ helds $t_i\in T_{\sigma_i}$, then

$$\varphi(t_1..t_n)_R(v)=\begin{cases} w \text{ .... iff for every } i=1,..,n\ t_{iR} \text{ assigns to } v \\ \qquad\qquad\qquad \text{a value } w_i \text{ and } \varphi_R \text{ assigns the value} \\ \qquad\qquad\qquad w \text{ to } (w_1,...,w_n) \\ \wedge \text{ .... iff } t_{iR}(v) \text{ is not defined for some} \\ \qquad\qquad\qquad i=1,...,n \text{ and } \varphi\in P \\ \text{not defined .... otherwise} \end{cases}$$

In order to assign meanings to programmes we first introduce the notion of configuration and direct successor mapping. Every element of the set $Val_{\mathcal{R}}\times FS^{*}$ will be called a configuration. One can think about configurations as about snapshots, reflecting the moment in a computing history after the completion or failure of the current action. The first component of a configuration may be interpreted as the actual memory state of a computer, the second one as the sequence of programme steps, which actually remain to be executed. The partial mapping of direct successor reflects the rules of transition from one configuration to another during the programme execution.
Now the definition of the mapping succ:

i) for an arbitrary valuation v and a not empty sequence of programmes $K_0...K_n$ we define (if c equals $(v,K_0...K_n)$):

$$succ(c)=\left\{\begin{array}{l} (v',K_1..K_n) \text{ .... iff } K_0:[z_1/\varepsilon_1..z_m/\varepsilon_m] \\ \qquad\qquad \text{and for every term } t \text{ being a subexpression of } \varepsilon_i \text{ for some } i=1,..,m\ t_R(v) \text{ is} \\ \qquad\qquad \text{defined and for all } z\in V_i\cup V_0\text{: } v'(z)=v(z) \\ \qquad\qquad \text{if } z\notin\{z_1,..,z_n\},\ v'(z)=\varepsilon_{iR}(v) \text{ otherwise} \\ (v,K_0''K_0'K_1..K_n) \text{ ...... iff } K_0:\circ[K_0''K_0'] \\ \left.\begin{array}{l} (v,K_0'K_1...K_n) \text{ .. iff } K_0:\times[\delta K_0'K_0''] \;\&\; \delta_R(v)=\vee \\ (v,K_0''K_1..K_n) \text{ .. iff } K_0:\times[\delta K_0'K_0''] \;\&\; \delta_R(v)=\wedge \\ (v,K_0'K_0K_1..K_n) \text{ .. iff } K_0:*[\delta K_0'] \;\&\; \delta_R(v)=\vee \\ (v,K_1....K_n) \text{ ....iff } K_0:*[\delta K_0'] \;\&\; \delta_R(v)=\wedge \end{array}\right\} \begin{array}{l}\text{and for every } t\in T \\ \text{being a subexpression} \\ \text{of } \delta\ t_R(v) \\ \text{is defined}\end{array} \\ \text{not defined .... otherwise} \end{array}\right.$$

ii) succ is not defined for any configuration of the form
(v , empty sequence) .

To a given programme K and a given valuation v now can be assigned a sequence of configurations $\{c_i\}_{i<\lambda}$ called the computation of K at v, which fulfills the following conditions:

i) λ is a ordinal number not greater than ω ,

ii) $c_0 = (v , K)$

iii) for every $i<\lambda$: either holds $c_{i+1}=succ(c_i)$
or $i+1=\lambda$ and $succ(c_i)$ is not defined.

The computation of K at v will be denoted by c(K,v). It will be calle successful, iff it is of finite length and the sequence of programmes at its last configuration is the empty one. The valuation at the last configuration of a successful computation will be called its result. One can find a similar semantics in /Sal2/. There is only the differe arising from the occurrence of partial operations: the computation of a programme interrupts, whenever a certain operator is not available. So two kinds of unsuccessful computations may be distinguished. Infinite computations representing looping and finite computations wit a nonempty sequence of programmes at their last configuration represe ting failing.

Now let us define the meaning ε_R to an arbitrary expression $\varepsilon \in FST \cup FSF$.

i) $\varepsilon \in FST \cup FSF$ and there exist $t_i \in FST$ for every i=1,...,n, there exist $\sigma \in Srt$ and $\varphi \in \Phi_{\sigma_1 \ldots \sigma_n, \sigma}$ (resp. $\varrho \in P_{\sigma_1 \ldots \sigma_n}$) with $\varepsilon: \varphi(t_1 \ldots t_n)$ (resp. $\varepsilon: \varrho(t_1 \ldots t_n)$).

Then:

$$\varepsilon_R(v)= \begin{cases} \varphi_R(w_1,\ldots,w_n) \text{ .... iff for every } i=1,\ldots,n\ t_{iR} \text{ assigns to v a value } w_i,\ \varphi_R \text{ a value to } (w_1,\ldots,w_n) \\ \text{not defined .... otherwise} \end{cases}$$

(respectively

$$\varrho_R(v)= \begin{cases} \varrho_R(w_1,\ldots,w_n) \text{ .... iff for every } i=1,\ldots,n\ \ t_{iR} \text{ assigns to v a value } w_i \\ \Lambda \text{ .... otherwise} \end{cases}$$
)

ii) ε is an expression of the form $K\alpha$, where $K \in FS$ and $\alpha \in FST \cup FSF$.

Then for every $v \in Val_{\mathcal{R}}$:

$$\alpha_R(v)= \begin{cases} \alpha_R(v') \text{ .... c(K,v) is successful and has the result} \\ \Lambda \text{ .... c(K,v) is unsuccessful and } \alpha \in FSF \\ \text{not defined ..... otherwise} \end{cases}$$.

iii) ε is an expression of the form $\bigcup K\alpha$, $\bigcap K\alpha$, where $K \in FS$ and $\alpha \in FSF$.

Then for every $v \in Val_{\mathcal{R}}$ we define:

$\bigcup K\alpha_R(v) = \underset{i \in \mathcal{N}}{\text{l.u.b.}}\ K^i\alpha_R(v)$

$\bigcap K\alpha_R(v) = \underset{i \in \mathcal{N}}{\text{g.l.b.}}\ K^i\alpha_R(v)$

(where K^0: , K^1:K, K^{i+1}:$\circ[K^iK]$)

iv) ε is of the form $\alpha_1 \wedge \alpha_2$, $\alpha_1 \wedge \alpha_2$, $\alpha_1 \Rightarrow \alpha_2$, $\neg\alpha_1$, $\forall x\alpha_1$, $\exists x\alpha_1$. Then for every $v \in Val_{\mathcal{R}}$ $\varepsilon_R(v)$ will be obtained from the always defined $\alpha_{iR}(v)$ (for i=1,2) in the usual way (see /Ra-Si/, /Ass/).

2.5. Lemma

Let $\mathcal{R}$ be an arbitrary realization of a given alphabet. For every term $t \in T$, every formula $\alpha \in F$, every programme $K \in FS$ and for every valuation $v \in Val_{\mathcal{R}}$ the following statements are true:

2.5.1. $t_R(v)$ is defined iff $db(t)_R(v) = \checkmark$.

2.5.2. for every term $t' \in T$, which is a subexpression of t the value $t'_R(v)$ is defined iff $db(t)_R(v) = \checkmark$.

2.5.3. The computation of K at v is successful iff $K\mathbb{1}_R(v) = \checkmark$.

2.5.4. The computation of K at v is either successful or of infinite length iff $db(K)_R(v) = \checkmark$.

This lemma points out, that the mapping db has in fact the property demanded in section 1.

The following lemma (published in /Mir/) remains true in the larger class of realizations regarded here.

2.6. Lemma

Let $\mathcal{R}$ be an arbitrary realization of a given alphabet. Then for every term $t \in FST$ and for every formula $\alpha \in FSF$ of the form $\varrho(t_1 \ldots t_n)$ ($\varrho \in P$, $t_i \in FST$ for i=1,...,n) there exist programmes K_t, $K_\alpha \in FS$, a term $t' \in T$ and a formula $\alpha' \in F$, that for every valuation $v \in Val_{\mathcal{R}}$ hold:

i) $t_R(v)$ is defined iff $K_t t'_R(v)$ is defined and if these two values are defined, then they are equal.

ii) $\alpha_R(v) = K_\alpha \alpha'_R(v)$

A mapping assigning to every term and every elementary formula an expression of the form mentioned above may be defined in the same way as in /Mir/. It will be denoted by χ.

3. The semantical consequence operation

Let A be an alphabet in the sense of definition 1.1. and let $\mathcal{L}$ be the corresponding algorithmic language. We say, a formula $\alpha \in FSF$ is valid in a given realization $\mathcal{R}$ of A iff for every $v \in Val_{\mathcal{R}}$ the equation $\alpha_R(v) = \checkmark$ holds (α is fulfilled by v). A realization $\mathcal{R}$ is called a model of a set of formulas $Z \subseteq FSF$, iff every formula $\alpha \in Z$ is valid in $\mathcal{A}$. A formula $\alpha \in FSF$ is called a semantical consequence of a set of formulas $Z \subseteq FSF$, iff α is valid in every model of Z. The mapping Cn assigning to a given subset of FSF the set of its semantical consequences is called the semantical consequence operation. Every formula which is a semantical consequence of the empty set of formulas is cal[led] a tautology. The mapping Cn is a closure operation, which has not the compactness property. One can prove, that the rules of inference $r_1, \dots, r_6$ are sound with respect to Cn (i.e. for every set of formula[s] $Z \subseteq FSF$ holds: if the premises of one of the rules $r_1, \dots, r_6$ belong t[o] Z, then its conclusion belongs to Cn(Z).).

$$r_1)\ \frac{\alpha,\ \alpha \Rightarrow \beta}{\beta} \qquad r_3)\ \frac{\{MK^i\alpha \Rightarrow \beta\}_{i\in\omega}}{M\bigcup K\alpha \Rightarrow \beta} \qquad r_5)\ \frac{[x/y]\alpha \Rightarrow \beta}{\exists x\alpha \Rightarrow \beta}$$

$$r_2)\ \frac{\alpha \Rightarrow \beta}{K\alpha \Rightarrow K\beta} \qquad r_4)\ \frac{\{\alpha \Rightarrow MK^i\beta\}_{i\in\omega}}{\alpha \Rightarrow M\bigcap K\beta} \qquad r_6)\ \frac{\alpha \Rightarrow [x/y]\beta}{\alpha \Rightarrow \forall x\beta}$$

(In the rules $r_1, \dots, r_6$ K and M denote programmes, α and β formulas an[d] in r_5 and r_6 x and y denote variables of the same sort, furthermore y does not occur neither in α nor in β .)
This means, that the same rules of inference proposed in /Ban/ in ord[er] to construct a syntactical consequence operation for the algorithmic logic (with full operations only) may be used in the situation with partial operations too.

4. Algorithmic theories with partial operations

The main aim of the present section is to introduce a syntactical con[se]quence operation C: $2^{FSF} \longrightarrow 2^{FSF}$. First we introduce two auxilia[ry] denotations: by $\overline{s\delta}$ we denote the expression obtained from an expressi[on] $\delta \in T \cup F$ by the simultaneous replacement of every variable z occuring [in] δ by the expression δ' , whenever the sequence of symbols z/δ' is a sub sequence of s ($s \in S$). By $s_1 \circ s_2$ we denote the sustitution obtained fro[m] the substitution s_2 by the replacement of every expression ε occuring in s_2 by $\overline{s_1\varepsilon}$ and adjoining to the so obtained sequence all sequences $z^{(1)}/\varepsilon^{(1)}$ whenever $z^{(1)}/\varepsilon^{(1)}$ is a sub sequence of s_1 and there is n[o] expression ε', for which $z^{(1)}/\varepsilon'$ is a subsequence of s_2. (For details see /Ban/)

4.1. Lemma

Every formula of one of the following forms is a tautology:

i) axioms of the classical propositional calculus (see /Ra-Si/)

ii) A1) $\neg 0 \wedge 1$

A2) $s\delta \Leftrightarrow (db(s) \wedge \overline{s\delta})$ .. where $s \in S$, $\delta \in F$

A3) $K\varrho(t_1 \dots t_n) \Leftrightarrow \varrho(Kt_1 \dots Kt_n)$ .... where $K \in FS$, $\varrho(t_1 \dots t_n) \in F$[...]

A4) $\varrho(t_1 \dots t_n) \Leftrightarrow \tau(\varrho(t_1 \dots t_n))$ .... see 2.6.

A5) $K(\alpha \wedge \beta) \Leftrightarrow (K\alpha \wedge K\beta)$

A6) $K(\alpha \vee \beta) \Leftrightarrow (K\alpha \vee K\beta)$

A7) $K(\alpha \Rightarrow \beta) \Leftrightarrow (K\mathbb{1} \wedge (K\alpha \Rightarrow K\beta))$

A8) $K(\neg\alpha) \Leftrightarrow (K\mathbb{1} \wedge \neg K\alpha)$

A9) $\bigcup K\alpha \Leftrightarrow (\alpha \vee K \bigcup K\alpha)$

A10) $\bigcap K\alpha \Leftrightarrow (\alpha \wedge K \bigcap K\alpha)$

A11) $\circ[KM]\alpha \Leftrightarrow K(M\alpha)$

A12) $\veebar[\delta KM]\alpha \Leftrightarrow (db(\delta) \wedge ((\delta \wedge K\alpha) \vee (\neg\delta \wedge M\alpha)))$

A13) $*[\delta K]\alpha \Leftrightarrow \bigcup \veebar[\delta K[\,]]\,(db(\delta) \wedge \neg\delta \wedge \alpha)$

where $K, M \in FS$, $\alpha, \beta \in FSF$, $\delta \in F$ (for A5)–A13))

A14) $\varrho(t_1 \ldots t_n) \Rightarrow (db(t_1) \wedge \ldots \wedge db(t_n))$ .... where $t_1, \ldots, t_n \in T$

A15) $[x/t]\alpha \Rightarrow \exists x\alpha$ ....

A16) $db(t) \Rightarrow (\forall x\alpha \Rightarrow [x/t]\alpha)$ ....

where $\alpha \in FSF$ and the term t and variable x are of the same sort (for A15), A16))

A17) $s_1(s_2\alpha) \Leftrightarrow (db(s_1) \wedge s_1 \circ s_2\alpha)$ .... where $\alpha \in FSF$, $s_1, s_2 \in S$

A18) $s\exists x\alpha \Leftrightarrow \exists y(s([x/y]\alpha))$ .....

A19) $s\forall x\alpha \Leftrightarrow \forall y(s([x/y]\alpha))$ .....

where $\alpha \in FSF$, the variable y does not occur in $s\alpha$ and is of the same sort as x (for A18), A19))

All formulas mentioned above will be called axioms, the set consisting of all axioms will be denoted by Ax. One can observe, that there are some differences to the axiom system presented in /Mir/ or /Ban/. They are caused by the proposed semantics here. The axiom schemes A2), A16), A17) have been modified, because the termination of a substitution s depends on the fact wether all terms being a subexpression of s are defined. The axiom schemes A12), A13) have been modified, because the computation of a programme interrupts, whenever an operator occurring in a test is not available. There will be admitted the rules of inference pointed out in section 3. in the construction of the syntactical consequence operation. Namely to every subset Z of FSF will be assigned the least set containing $Ax \cup Z$, which is closed under the rules $r_1, \ldots, r_6$. The so defined syntactical consequence operation we denote by C. For every set $A \subseteq FSF$ the triplet $(\mathcal{L}, C, A)$ will be called an algorithmic theory. An algorithmic theory is called consistent iff $C(A) \neq FSF$. Now the main result:

4.2. Proposition (Completeness theorem)

For every algorithmic theory with partial operations $\mathcal{T} = (\mathcal{L}, C, A)$ holds $C(A) = Cn(A)$.

In order to prove proposition 4.2. we can modify the proof of the completeness theorem given in /Ban/. The crucial point is to define canonical models for a given algorithmic theory. In /Ban/ there are considered realizations with the set of all terms as the set of individuals. In our case we must find suitable subsets of the set of terms of one sort in order to get the set of individuals of this sort. This is possible, because we can characterize the domain of each term syntactically. To a given ultrafilter ∇ in the Lindenbaum algebra $\mathfrak{A}(\mathcal{T})$ of the algorithmic theory $\mathcal{T}$ we construct a canonical realization $\mathcal{K}_\nabla = (\{I_{\nabla,\sigma}\}_{\sigma\in Srt}, R_\nabla)$, where

$I_{\nabla,\sigma} = \{ t \in T : \| db(t) \| \in \nabla \}$ for every $\sigma \in Srt$,

for every $\varphi \in \Phi_{\underline{s},\sigma}$, all $t_1 \in I_{\nabla,\sigma_1}, \ldots, t_n \in I_{\nabla,\sigma_n}$:

$$\varphi_{R_\nabla}(t_1,\ldots,t_n) = \begin{cases} \varphi(t_1\ldots t_n) \;\ldots\; \text{iff } \| db(\varphi(t_1\ldots t_n)) \| \in \nabla \\ \text{not defined} \;\ldots\ldots\; \text{otherwise} \end{cases},$$

for every $\varrho \in P_{\underline{\sigma}}$, all $t_1 \in I_{\nabla,\sigma_1}, \ldots, t_n \in I_{\nabla,\sigma_n}$:

$$\varrho_{R_\nabla}(t_1,\ldots,t_n) = \begin{cases} \vee \ldots\ldots\ldots \text{iff } \| \varrho(t_1\ldots t_n) \| \in \nabla \\ \wedge \ldots\ldots\ldots \text{iff } \| \varrho(t_1\ldots t_n) \| \notin \nabla \end{cases}.$$

As corollaries from proposition 4.2. we obtain:

4.3. Proposition (Model existence theorem)

An algorithmic theory with partial operations is consistent iff there exists a model for it.

4.4. Proposition (Deduction theorem)

Let $\mathcal{T} = (\mathcal{L}, C, A)$ be a consistent algorithmic theory with partial operations. Then for every closed formula $\alpha \in FSF$ and for every formula $\beta \in FSF$: β belongs to $C(A \cup \{\alpha\})$, iff the formula $\alpha \Rightarrow \beta$ belongs to $C(A)$.

4.5. Example

Let us consider an algorithmic theory with partial operations. Let $\mathcal{L}$ be the language corresponding to the alphabet obtained from that given in 1.3. adjoining a predicate eq with the arity EE. We shall consider the algorithmic theory $\mathcal{T} = (\mathcal{L}, C, A)$, where A is the set of all formulas of one of the forms given below:

D1) $* [amb^*(d)\ [d/del(amb(d))]]\, 1$

D2) $mb(e,d) \Leftrightarrow \circ[K_1 K_2]\, b$ ...... where $K_1 : [d_1/d\ b/0]$ and $K_2 : *[amb^*(d_1) \wedge \neg b\ \circ[[b/eq(amb(d_1),e)][d_1/del(amb(d_1),\ldots$

D3) $[d/ins(e,d')]\,(mb(e,d) \wedge (eq(e',e) \Rightarrow (mb(e',d) \Leftrightarrow mb(e',d'))))$

D4) $[d/del(e,d')]\,(\neg mb(e,d) \wedge (eq(e',e) \Rightarrow (mb(e',d) \Leftrightarrow mb(e',d'))))$

D5) $amb^*(d) \Leftrightarrow \exists e\ mb(e,d)$

D6) $del^*(e,d) \wedge ins^*(e,d)$

D7) $eq(e,e) \wedge (eq(e_1,e_2) \Rightarrow eq(e_2,e_1))$

D8) $(eq(e_1,e_1') \wedge \ldots \wedge eq(e_1,e_1')) \Rightarrow ((\varphi^*(e_1\ldots e_n) \Rightarrow eq(\varphi(e_1\ldots e_n),\varphi(e_1'\ldots e_n'))) \wedge (\varrho(e_1\ldots e_n) \Leftrightarrow \varrho(e_1'\ldots e_n')))$

where $\varphi \in \{amb, ins, del\}$, $\varrho \in \{amb^*, ins^*, del^*, mb\}$.

The data structure of dictionaries may be discribed by this algorithmic theory (see /Sal1/). The realization given in 2.2. is not a model of this theory (formula D1!). Replacing the set I_D by the set of all finite subsets of I_E and assigning to the predicate eq the identity on I_E we obtain a model for $\mathcal{T}$. Therefore $\mathcal{T}$ is consistent.
Furthermore let us prove, that the computation of the programme $\circ[K_1K_2]$ at an arbitrary valuation in any model of $\mathcal{T}$ is successful. Taking in account the lemma 2.5. and the completeness theorem it is sufficient to prove, that the formula $\circ[K_1K_2]\mathbf{1}$ is a syntactical concequence of A. In order to prove this we use the following derived rules of inference:

$$r_7)\quad \frac{\alpha \Rightarrow \beta,\ db(\beta) \Rightarrow db(\alpha)}{*[\beta M]\mathbf{1} \Rightarrow *[\alpha M]\mathbf{1}} \qquad\qquad r_9)\quad \frac{M\mathbf{1},\ \alpha}{M\alpha}$$

$$r_8)\quad \frac{\{M_0{}^i\mathbf{1} \Leftrightarrow M_2{}^i\mathbf{1}\}_{i\in\omega},\ \{M_0{}^i\delta \Leftrightarrow M_2{}^i\delta\}_{i\in\omega},\ \{M_0{}^i db(\delta) \Leftrightarrow M_2{}^i db(\delta)\}_{i\in\omega}}{*[\delta M_0]\mathbf{1} \Leftrightarrow *[\delta M_2]\mathbf{1}}$$

where $M_0 : \circ[\circ[M_1M_2]M_3]$.

Let us observe, that for $M_1 : [d_1/del(amb(d_1),d_1)]$, $M_3 : [\ ]$, $\delta : amb^*(d_1)$, $M_2 : [b/eq(amb(d_1),e)]$ the premises of r_8) may be derived from A (by the help of A2), A14) , A15)). Hence from D1) by $r_1 : *[\delta M_0]\mathbf{1} \in C(A)$. For $M : K_2$, $\alpha : amb^*(d_1) \wedge \neg b$, β : $amb^*(d_1)$ the rule r_7) is available. By the help of this rule and modus ponens we deduce, that $K_2\mathbf{1}$ is a theorem of A. For $\alpha : K_2\mathbf{1}$ and $M : K_1$ the rule r_9) is available and we can deduce, that $K_1K_2\mathbf{1}$ is a theorem of A and therefore by A11) $\circ[K_1K_2]\mathbf{1}$ too.

References

/Ass/ ... Asser,G., Einführung in die mathematische Logik III, BSB B.G.Teubner Verlagsgesellschaft, Leipzig 1981.

/Ban/ ... Banachowski,L., Investigations on properties of programs by means of extended algorithmic logic I, Fundamenta Informaticae Vol.I (1977), 93-119.

/BCP/ ... Banachowski,L.,Kreczmar,A.,Mirkowska,G.,Rasiowa,H.,Salwicki, A., An Introduction to Algorithmic Logic in: Mazurkiewicz,A., Pawlak,Z., Theoretical Foundations of Computer Science, Banach Centre Publ. Vol.2, Polish Sc. Publ., Warsaw 1977, 7-99.

/Mir/ ... Mirkowska,G., Algorithmic Logic and its Applications in the Theory of Programs, Fundamenta Informaticae Vol.I (1977)1-17.

/Ra-Si/.. Rasiowa,H., Sikorski,R., Mathematics of metamathematics, PWN, Warszawa 1970.

/Sal1/... Salwicki,A., On Algorithmic Theory of Dictionaries,manuscript 1980.

/Sal2/... -, Axioms of Algorithmic Logic univocally determine Semantics of programs in Proc. MFCS`80, Lect. Notes Comp. Sc. Vol.88, Springer Vlg. Heidelberg-New York-Berlin 352-361.

TOWARDS A THEORY OF PARALLELISM AND COMMUNICATIONS FOR INCREASING EFFICIENCY IN APPLICATIVE LANGUAGES

Alberto Pettorossi

IASI - CNR and Dept. of Computer Science
Via Buonarroti, 12
Roma, Italy

University of Edinburgh
Edinburgh, Scotland

Abstract

A new methodology for writing efficient programs is proposed through various examples. The basic ideas are: i) the use of the applicative stile of programming, so that correctness of programs can easily be proved, and ii) the improvement of program efficiency by the evaluation of functions applications using concurrent computing agents.

For increasing efficiency, communications among those agents are necessary, so that redundant evaluations of common subexpressions can be avoided.

In this paper we also introduce some preliminary ideas for a theory of such communications. We call them "helpful communications". They include "compulsory" communications, which effect program correctness, and "optional" communications, which do not effect program correctness, but only program efficiency.

Summary

1. A motto and an introductory example.
2. Program Transformations for establishing Communications.
3. Program Annotations for establishing Communications.
4. Towards a theory of "helpful communications".
5. Conclusions and final remarks.
6. Acknowledgments.
7. References.

1. A motto and an introductory example

In order to obtain programs which realize efficient computations, we can apply the motto:

Efficiency = Parallelism + Communications

What we mean by this motto will be explained by a preliminary example in this section. Other examples will be given in the following sections, in which we will also illustrate the use of some techniques, as program annotation [12] and program transformation [1], for taking advantage of the improvements in program efficiency one can realize by applying that motto.

Algorithms with good time efficiency can be obtained (i) by splitting a given problem in many subproblems and (ii) by solving them separately, using various computing agents which operate in a concurrent way.

Therefore, parallelism is necessary for achieving high efficiency. However, it is not enough. In fact, parallelism may have its serious disadvantages, especially if an exponential number of resources is required for realizing it. In order to avoid those disadvantages we need a way of making computing agents, which operate in parallel, to know some "facts" about the computations performed by the other agents. This information will be made available through communications and it will allow a "good" cooperation among the agents. "Good" means that a desired performance can be achieved, as, for instance, the reduction of an exponential number of resources to a linear one, or other similar improvements of the computational properties.

We will show this fact through a familiar example, which has the advantage of allowing the reader to concentrate on the issues concerning computing agents and communications.

Let us consider the following program for computing the Fibonacci numbers.

Program 1.1

```
1. fib(0) = 1
2. fib(1) = 1
3. fib(n+2) = fib(n+1) + fib(n)    for n ≥ 0
```

In order to compute fib(n+2) in an efficient way, we could compute in parallel fib(n+1) and fib(n) and then the final answer can be obtained by adding these two values together. But parallelism alone does not offer an efficient solution. In fact when computing fib(n+1), which is equal to fib(n) + fib(n-1), we will compute again fib(n), and indeed this phenomenon of recomputing values is so bad that, in general, we need to compute an exponential number of Fibonacci values.

However, we can apply the second half of our motto, namely "communications". Indeed we can establish a communication going from the agent which has to compute fib(n), say A2, to the agent which has to compute fib(n+1), say A1. (See also fig. 1)

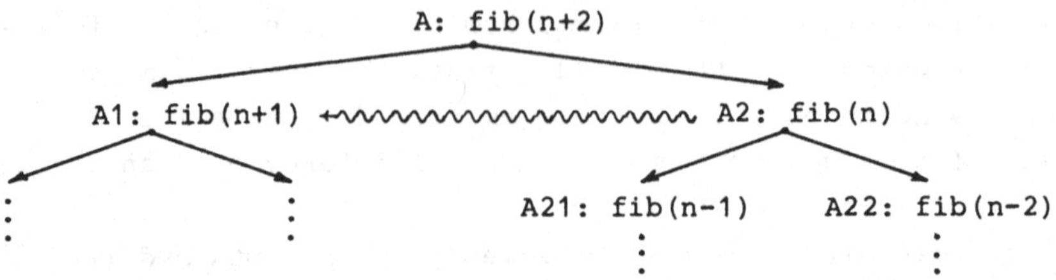

fig. 1 Establishing a communication for the evaluation of Fibonacci numbers.

This communication consists in the pair of values ⟨fib(n),fib(n-1)⟩ which A2 sends to A1. After receiving such a pair, A1 has only to add the arriving values together.

Therefore A1 is able to compute its result without duplicating the efforts of its "brother" A2. In this example, if we force an agent, to which the pair will be sent, to wait for it, the running time of the algorithm is linear. Also linear is the number of agents created during the computation.

Notice that a logarithmic running time for computing the Fibonacci numbers can be obtained using more sophisticated communications among agents [9].

In what follows we will be less informal about our notions of parallelism and communications and the examples we will give, will convey to the reader our intuitions. As a first approximation, we may consider that: (i) parallelism consists in concurrently computing distinct functions applications using distinct computing agents, and (ii) communications consist in properties, or relationships, of the results to be computed by those agents. For example, for the Fibonacci function, considering the computations of fib(n+1) and fib(n), the property representing the communication from agent A2 to agent A1 is the following property Prop. 1: "fib(n+1) = fib(n) + fib(n-1) for n > 0" (This property holds because it is equation 3 of Program 1.1).

How shall we express parallelism and communications in our programming language?

Parallelism needs not to be explicitely expressed, because we assume that the interpreter (or the compiler) determines a concurrent evaluation of distinct function applications by activating distinct computing agents.

Communications will be expressed in our programming languages by using two approaches: (i) the program transformation approach [1], and (ii) the program annotation approach [12]. We will discuss those approaches in some detail in the following sections.

Using the program transformation methodology we introduce new functions in the given program, so that the evoked computations simulate the occurrence of communications among computing agents, and therefore they achieve the desired efficiency.

A communication consists in a new function definition, and establishing a communication consists in transforming a given program, using such a new function. In the Fibonacci example, a communication instance is the pair of values ⟨fib(n),fib(n-1)⟩, which the agent computing fib(n) has to pass to the agent computing fib(n+1). So we can define the following "communication function":

R1. Rfib(n) = ⟨fib(n),fib(n-1)⟩, where we used the name Rfib for denoting that the "right" recursive call of the Fibonacci function in equation 3 will be transformed into another function returning two values, namely fib(n) and fib(n-1). Therefore we can establish such a communication by transforming Program 1.1 into the following:

```
                                                          Program 1.2
1. fib(0)     =1
2. fib(1)     =1
3'. fib(n+2)  =π1(Rfib(n+1)) + π2(Rfib(n+1))              by R1
              =u+v  where ⟨u,v⟩ = Rfib(n+1) for n≥0
4. Rfib(1)    =⟨1,1⟩                                      by 1. and 2.
5. Rfib(n+2)=⟨fib(n+2),fib(n+1)⟩                          by R1
              =⟨fib(n+1)+fib(n),fib(n+1)⟩                 by 3.
              =⟨π1(Rfib(n+1))+π2(Rfib(n+1)),π1(Rfib(n+1))⟩ by R1
              =⟨u+v,u⟩  where  ⟨u,v⟩=Rfib(n+1) for n≥0
```

where π1 and π2 denote the first and second projection function.

The Program 1.2 (which is essentially the same program derived in [1]) has linear running time: therefore establishing a communication improved time efficiency. It is interesting to see how for this program the "eureka step" introduced in [1], i.e. the pairing function definition, has been obtained as an instance of a communication between two recursive calls. Notice also that the established communication in this case completely destroys the possible concurrency among agents and the computation consists in a totally sequential evaluation of the following sequence of values: fib(0),fib(1),...,fib(n). In general, however, after establishing communications, some parallel evaluations are still possible as we will see later on.

The second method of implementing communications among concurrent computing agents, i.e. the program annotation method [12], will be introduced and discussed in sections 3. and 4.

2. Program Transformations for establishing Communications

In this section we will give some more examples of the application of the program transformation methodology for establishing communications among computing agents.

The programming language we will use for writing our programs is an applicative language very similar to HOPE [2]. It is a recursive equation language very well suited for program transformation. The reader is not expected to be familiar with it because we will use it in very simple and self-explanatory examples.

The examples we will give, show that, using suitable communications, one can obtain the same efficiency improvements which are associated with the introduction of an accumulator variable and the use of the lazy evaluation mechanism.

Let us first consider the well-known factorial function. Its definition can be written as follows:

Program 2.1

```
dec fact: num → num
fact(n) = 1              if n=0
      else n*fact(n-1)
```

In this program we can improve efficiency by avoiding explicit recursion and the management of the stack for implementing it. This effect can be achieved by establishing a communication between a call of the factorial function, to which we will refer as a "father-call", and its subsequent call, to which we will refer as the "son-call".

By establishing this communication, the father-call fact(n) (1) activates the son-call fact(n-1), telling it that it multiply its result by n and then (2) dies, whereby avoiding recursion.

Therefore fact(n) has to pass to fact(n-1), as an extra argument, the function λx. n*x, i.e. the multiplication by n, and fact(n-1) has to accept it.

The tentative functionality of the father-call is:

$$\text{num} \rightarrow \text{num} \times (\text{num} \rightarrow \text{num})$$

and the tentative functionality of the son-call is:

$$\text{num} \times (\text{num} \rightarrow \text{num}) \rightarrow \text{num}.$$

Starting from these functionalities, we can apply the minimal extension strategy for obtaining the functionality of the function fact, as it should be defined for allowing communications [11].

That strategy consists in:

1) making a diagram, called functionalities diagram, where nodes are <u>functions</u>, and arcs are <u>recursive calls</u> (denoted by ⟶) or <u>communications</u> (denoted by ⇝),
2) computing the minimal extension of the functionalities of the nodes related by ⟶, so that a unique functionality is derived for any recursively defined function.

In the case of the function factorial, the functionalities diagram is very simple and it looks like:

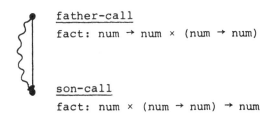

<u>father-call</u>
fact: num → num × (num → num)

<u>son-call</u>
fact: num × (num → num) → num

By applying the minimal extension strategy we must extend the functionalities num → num × (num → num) and num × (num → num) → num, so that a unique functionality is derived for the recursively defined function fact.

Thus we obtain the new function:

<u>dec</u> fact1: num × (num → num) → num × (num → num)

and the corrisponding program is the following:

<u>Program 2.2</u>

```
dec fact : num → num
dec fact1: num × (num → num) → num × (num → num)
fact(n)    =π1(fact1(n,λx.x))
fact1(n,f)=⟨ f(1),λx.x⟩           if n = 0
           else fact1(n-1,λx.(f(x)*n))
```

Notice that the function λx.x, in the definition of fact1, could be replaced by any other function, because the content of the communicated function does not matter if n = 0.

The reader may also notice that in Program 2.2 we rediscovered the "continuation" idea [13]: the function communicated from a father-call to its son-call is indeed a continuation.

Communications among computing agents can be very powerful and in the following example, as we anticipated, we will show how the <u>lazy evaluation</u> technique can be realized by suitable communications.

Let us consider a <u>leaf comparator</u> program, similar to the one given in [3]. It is a program for testing equality of the frontiers of two S-expressions, not taking into account atoms which are NIL.

Program 3.1

```
data Sexpr = atom ++ (Sexpr . Sexpr)
NIL is considered to be a particular atom and null(x) is true iff x = NIL.
data flatlist = [] ++ atom::flatlist
We will use the predicate empty(x) which is true iff x = [].
dec Eqleaves: Sexpr × Sexpr → bool
dec Eqflatlist: flatlist × flatlist → bool
dec Flatten: Sexpr → flatlist
Eqleaves (x,y) = Eqflatlist(Flatten(x),Flatten(y))
Flatten(x) = []                           if null(x)
           else [x]                       if atom(x)
           else Flatten(car(x)) ⟨⟩ Flatten(cdr(x))
Eqflatlist(x,y)= empty(y)                 if empty(x)
           else false                     if empty(y)
           else Eqflatlist(tl(x),tl(y)) if eq(hd(x),hd(y))
           else false
```

where ⟨⟩, hd and tl denote the append, head and tail functions on list. Suppose we want to compute Eqleaves((A.huge1), (B.huge2)) where huge1 and huge2 are two long S-expressions. In [3] a lazy evaluation technique has been used for computing the desired results in a fast way.

Here we will show that, through communications among computing agents, we can obtain the same efficient executions. Communications will be established using the program transformation methodology.

By definition we have:

```
Eqleaves((A.huge1),(B.huge2)) =
 empty(Flatten((B.huge2)))              if empty(Flatten((A.huge1)))
else false                              if empty(Flatten((B.huge2)))
else Eqflatlist(tl(Flatten((A.huge1)),
           tl(Flatten((B.huge2)))  if eq(hd(Flatten((A.huge1)),
                                         hd(Flatten((B.huge2)))
else false
```

The execution of Eqleaves can be speeded up if Flatten(x) communicates to the functions "empty" and "hd" the information they need for computing their results without waiting for Flatten to complete its work. This can be done by using null(x) instead of empty(Flatten(x)) and defining the function hdFlatten as follows:

dec hdFlatten: Sexpr → atom. It returns the leftmost atom different from NIL, occurring in a given S-expression. Otherwise it returns NIL.

```
hdFlatten(x) = x                          if atom(x)
           [else hdFlatten(cdr(x)) if null(a)
            else a
            where a =  hdFlatten(car(x))]
```

In order to make the efficiency improvement realized in the Eqleaves function by the use of the functions null(x) and hdFlatten(x) to work at any level of recursion, we need to transform the Eqflatlist call into a recursive call of Eqleaves.

This transformation can be done by defining the new function tlFlatten(x) which returns the S-expression x, after i) erasing its leftmost atom which is not NIL and ii) erasing all NIL's to the left of it. Otherwise it returns NIL.

For example: tlFlatten(((NIL.A).(NIL.B)))=(NIL.B). We also define tlFlatten s.t. tlFlatten(NIL) = NIL and tlFlatten(A) = NIL. Therefore we have:

```
dec tlFlatten: Sexpr → Sexpr
tlFlatten(x)=NIL                            if atom(x)
  else tlFlatten(cdr(x))                    if null(hdFlatten(car(x)))
  else cdr(x)                               if atom(car(x))
  else tlFlatten((cdr(car(x)).cdr(x)))      if null(hdFlatten(car(car(x))))
  else (tlFlatten(car(x)).cdr(x))
```

Now we can apply the "tupling strategy" [10] for defining a new function T and we obtain the following program:

```
dec Eqleaves: Sexpr × Sexpr → bool                              Program 3.2
dec T: Sexpr → ⟨bool,atom,Sexpr⟩
such that T(x)=⟨null(x),hdFlatten(x),tlFlatten(x)⟩
Eqleaves(x,y) =π1(b)                          if π1(a)
               else false                     if π1(b)
               else Eqleaves(π3(a),π3(b)) if eq(π2(a),π2(b))
               else false
where a,b = T(x), T(y)
T(x)=⟨true,NIL,NIL⟩                              if null(x)
   else ⟨false,x,NIL⟩                            if atom(x)
  [else ⟨false,π2(T(cdr(x))), π3(T(cdr(x)))⟩ if null(a)
   else ⟨false,a,cdr(x)⟩                         if atom(car(x))
   else ⟨false,a,π3(T((cdr(car(x)).cdr(x))))⟩if null(π2(T(car(car(x)))))
   else ⟨false,a,(π3(T(car(x))).cdr(x))⟩
   where a = π2(T(car(x)))]
```

By hand simulation, the reader may convince himself that Program 3.2 has the same efficient behaviour of the lazy evaluation mechanism.

3. Program Annotations for establishing Communications

In this section we will study another way of establishing communications among concurrent computing agents, namely the program annotation method [12]. This method consists essentially of extending the language in which we write our programs, for giving suitable suggestions to the interpreter (or compiler), so that the computations evoked by the programs might have the desired efficiency.

We will show this approach by examples. Let us consider the first one. Suppose we have binary trees, btrees for short, whose leaves are labelled by integer numbers, and we want to compute the set of all leaves of a given binary tree.

A first version of a program for accomplishing this task is the following:

```
                                                      Program 4.1
data btree(num) = niltree ++ tip(num) ++ btree(num) ∧ btree(num)
dec leaves: btree(num) → set(num)
leaves(nultree) = {}
leaves(tip(ℓ))  = {ℓ}
leaves(t1 ∧ t2) = leaves(t1) ∪ leaves(t2)
```

In order to compute the result, we need in any case to perform the complete visit of the given btree, but an increase of efficiency is possible if we speed up the set-union operation. No matter what algorithm we choose for implementing such an operation, it will require less time if we keep the sets involved as small as possible. This can be achieved by establishing some communications.

As soon as a computing agent has found a leaf value, say ℓ, it may communicate the number ℓ to all other agents. In this way, when another agent encounters the value ℓ, it may return {} instead of {ℓ}. Thus unioned sets may be smaller while program correctness is preserved. This argument will be made precise using the mathematical semantic definition of our applicative language with communications, which we will formally introduce in the following section.

We can annotate Program 4.1 for denoting the communications we mentioned, and we obtain Program 4.2.

```
                                                      Program 4.2
data btree(num) = niltree ++ tip(num) ++ btree(num) ∧ btree(num)
dec fastleaves: btree(num) → set(num)
fastleaves(niltree) = {}
fastleaves(tip(ℓ)) = {}                      if ℓ ∈ z /received(z)/
                    else {ℓ} /broadcast(ℓ)/
```

```
fastleaves(t1 ∧ t2) = fastleaves(t1) ∪ fastleaves(t2)
```

In this program we used broadcasting communications, i.e. communications which concern all computing agents. Their informal semantics can be explained as follows.

While the evaluation of fastleaves is performed, there exists a set of integer values, say s, which is accessible by all computing agents. The set s is initially empty and it is unioned with {ℓ}, when the communication /broadcast(ℓ)/ is realized. The meaning of the annotation /received(z)/ consists in binding the variaоle z to the value of the set s.

The annotations may denote optional or compulsory communications. If they denote optional communications, they are written between slashes (as in Program 4.2) and they do not affect program correctness. In that caөe a computing agent may refuse to send or receive information without affecting the result of the computation: it only does not take advantage of the work that other agents are doing or it does not help others in their work.

If the annotation /broadcast(ℓ)/ is not executed, then the value of the corresponding set of integers is left unchanged. If /received(z)/ is not executed, then the variable z is bound to the empty set.

Compulsory communications are denoted by annotations between exclamation marks. For a broadcasting communication no sequentiality is forced in sending or receiving operations and agents nead not to be synchronized with each other.

There exist also point-to-point and erasable communications and we will introduce them in the following example.

Suppose we would like to compute the value of an element of the Pascal triangle, i.e. a binomial coefficient, using the following recursive definition:

Program 5.1

```
B(n,m) = if m=0 or m=n then 1
      else B(n-1,m-1) + B(n-1,m)
```

Obviously if we compute B(n,m) by applying the definition in a straightforward way, we duplicate many computations and indeed in computing B(n,m) we will compute twice B(n-2,m-1), once in evaluating B(n-1,m-1) and once in evaluating B(n-1,m). This situation is somehow similar to the situation we discussed in section 1 concerning the Fibonacci function. But now, in order to avoid redundant computations, we need to organize the communicaitons in a more complex way. "Pairing" of values, as we did for the Fibonacci numbers, is no longer sufficient (it seems in fact necessary to have a potentially infinite tupling of values [10]) and the program transformation method seems not easily applicable for establishing the necessary communications. So we will present our solution to the problem using the program annotation method. We use point-to-point communications, whose primitives are:

i) send(v, line ℓ) for sending a value v to the line ℓ;

ii) receive(x, line ℓ) for giving to a variable x a value received via line ℓ.

Those primitives are elementary annotations.

The informal semantics of point-to-point communications can be explained as follows.

Each line is like a sequence of values initialized to an empty sequence. Sequentiality among agents is forced when they want to send values to the same line. Receiving values from the same line can be done in parallel by many agents. Thus, at any one time for the same line, either a sending operation or many receiving operations occur.

For each line, each agent is like a pointer to a value in the line, so that subsequent receiving operations performed by the same agent in the same line have access to the subsequent values stored in that line. If an optional sending operation is not performed, no value is appended to the specified line. If an optional receiving operation is not performed, or no values are available in the specified line for the given agent, then the variable occurring in the receiving operation is bound to the special value ␣, called "silence". The value ␣ is supposed to be different from any other user-defined value.

If an agent has to evaluate a compulsory annotation and the rules for accessing lines forbid that evaluation, the agent is blocked in case of a sending operation, or it binds the specified variable to ␣ in case of a receiving operation.

Using point-to-point communications, with line identifiers which are pairs of integers, we can write the following program for computing B(n,m):

```
                                                      Program 5.2
B(n,m)=if m=0 or m=n then 1
      else if x=PROMISE /receive(x,line⟨n,m⟩),receive(y,line⟨n,m⟩)/
           then y
           else b where b=B(n-1,m-1)+B(n-1,m)
                        /send(PROMISE,line⟨n,m⟩),send(b,line⟨n,m⟩)/
```

In Program 5.2 we used the convention that an optional annotation of the form /elem-annot1, elem-annot2, .../, if evaluated, it is sequentially evaluated from left to right, entirely. Thus never elem-annot2 can be evaluated before elem-annot1, and if elem-annot1 is evaluated also elem-annot2 will be evaluated by the same agent immediately afterwards.

When an agent is evaluating a non-elementary annotation, it uses all lines mentioned in the whole annotation (rule of global use of lines). For instance, if an agent is evaluating /send(v,line ℓ1), receive(x,line ℓ2)/, when it is receiving from line ℓ2 no other agent can send or receive from line ℓ1, because line ℓ1 is still considered in use for a sending operation.

Remembering that compulsory communications are between exclamation marks the following program is equivalent to Program 5.2:

Program 5.3

```
B(n,m)=if m=0 or m=n then 1
      else if x=PROMISE /receive(x,line⟨n,m⟩/
           then y !receive(y,line⟨n,m⟩)!
           else b where b=B(n-1,m-1)+B(n-1,m)
                     /send(PROMISE,line⟨n,m⟩),send(b,line⟨n,m⟩)/
```

Let us see how Program 5.2 or Program 5.3 works. If m=0 or m=n it is obvious. Otherwise the computing agent checks first whether or not the value in the line ⟨n,m⟩ is equal to PROMISE. If that value is equal to PROMISE, it means that another computing agent will compute the value of B(n,m): in fact after executing the annotation send(PROMISE, line⟨n,m⟩), the there will be the execution of send(b,line⟨n,m⟩) where b=B(n-1,m-1)+B(n-1,m)=B(n,m).

If the value in the line ⟨n,m⟩ is not equal to PROMISE, no other agent, for the time being, is computing B(n,m), therefore the computation proceeds by making the recursive call: B(n-1,m-1)+B(n-1,m) and, possibly, sending PROMISE and the value of B(n,m) to the line ⟨n,m⟩.

However Program 5.3 does not completely solve the problem of possible multiple evaluations of binomial coefficients.

Suppose that two agents almost at the same time are willing to compute B(n,m) for the first time with respect to any other agent. For both of them the test x=PROMISE fails, because they get ␣ in the line ⟨n,m⟩. So they both start computing B(n,m). In order to solve this problem we need a third kind of communications: the erasable communications.

The primitive operations available for erasable communications are:

i) send1 (v,line ℓ) for sending a value v to the line ℓ;

ii) receiveerase(x,line ℓ) for giving to a variable x a value received via line ℓ and erasing that value from the line.

The informal semantic of erasable communication is very similar to the one of point-to-point communications. However sequentiality among computing agents is also forced in receiving values from the lines. Moreover, when a value is received and erased from a line, it does not exist in that line for any subsequent access to that line by any agent.

If no values are available a receiveerase operation binds the specified variable to ⊔. Moreover it does not change the status of the line, which remains an empty sequence of values for the acting agent.

The following Program 5.4 makes use of erasable communications. and indeed avoids multiple execution of binomial coefficients.

Program 5.4

```
B(n,m)=Perm B(n,m)
      !∀i,j≥0 s.t. (i-j=n-m or (m≤i≤n and j=m))
      send 1 (GO,line Pij)!

Perm B(n,m)=if p=TAKEN   !receive(p,line T n m)!
            then res     !receive(res,line V n m)!
            else if p=GO !receiveerase  (p,line P n m)!
                 then res where res=B1(n,m) !send1(GO,line P n-2 m-1)!
                                            !send(TAKEN,line T n m),
                                             send(res,line V n m)!
            else Perm B(n,m)

B1(n,m)=if m=0 or m=n then 1
      else Perm B(n-1,m-1)+Perm B(n-1,m)
```

In this program we use 3 lines for each pair of values n and m. The line T n m is used for storing the value TAKEN denoting that the permission of computing B(n,m) has been taken by an agent.
The line V n m is used for storing the value of B(n,m), once it has been computed.
The line P n m is used for storing GO denoting that there is the permission of computing B(n,m).

Program 5.4 works as follows: permissions of computing the various values {B(i,j)} for any i and j such that i-j=m-n or (m≤i≤n and j=m) are sent to the lines Pij (see fig. 2).

In particular the permission of computing B(n,m) is given by sending GO to the line P n m, using the primitive send 1.

Permissions flow vertically (see fig. 2): in fact in computing B(n,m), a GO is sent to the line P n-2 m-1, which represents the line immediately "below" P n m. It is easy to show by induction that one and only one GO will be sent to any line Pij for i ≥ j ≥ 0, i ≤ n and j ≤ m.

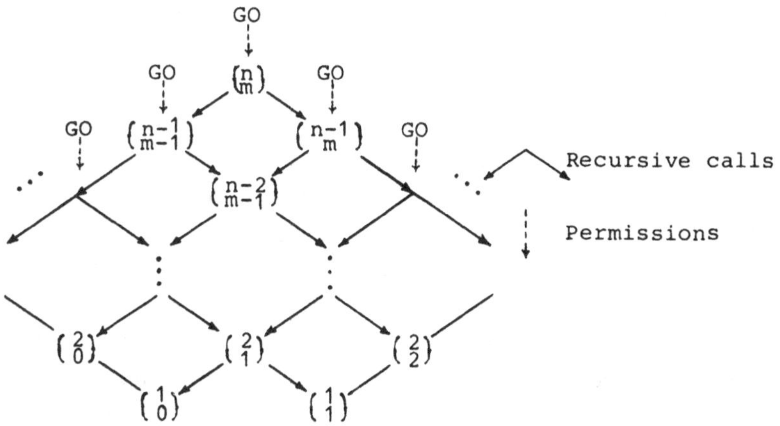

Fig. 2 The Pascal triangle with "permissions" and "recursive calls", when computing B(n,m).

The status of the lines for each pair i,j is changing from situation a to b, then c and finally d, as follows:

situation:	a	b	c	d
line Pij	⟨⟩	⟨GO⟩	⟨⟩	⟨⟩
line Tij	⟨⟩	⟨⟩	⟨TAKEN⟩	⟨TAKEN⟩
line Vij	⟨⟩	⟨⟩	⟨⟩	⟨B(i,j)⟩

where ⟨⟩ denotes an empty line, i.e. no values are stored in it. Again, one can prove this fact by induction on i,j. This fact also allows the proof of correctness of Program 5.4 by taking into account that in evaluating the annotation !send(TAKEN,line T n m),send(res, line V n m)! line T n m is not accessible, unless line V n m has already the value of B(n,m) (this is due to the rule of global use of lines).

In Program 5.4 we used a quantifier in annotating the expression defining B(n,m). One can consider that use as an abbreviation, because the same initialization can be achieved using the following recursive definitions:

```
B(n,m)=sendleft(n-1,m-1,n,m) !send1(GO,line P n m)!
sendleft(n,m,n0,m0)=sendleft(n-1,m-1,n0,m0) !send1(GO,line P n m)! if m>0
              else sendright(n0-1,m0,n0,m0) !send1(GO,line P n m)!
sendright(n,m,n0,m0)=sendright(n-1,m,n0,m0) !send1(GO,line P n m)! if n>m
              else PermB(n0,m0)              !send1(GO,line P n m)!
```

Program 5.4 avoids multiple evaluations of binomial coefficients, but it is not completely satisfactory, because of the following two problems:

i) busy waiting: since the line T n m is not accessible until the value of B(n,m) is computed, many computing agents may be forced to perform unuseful recursive calls to Perm B(n,m) while one of them is computing B(n,m).

ii) speed dependence: it is impossible to start the computation of a binomial coefficient for which the recursive function call could be activated, but there is no permission. On the contrary, for allowing any relative speed among the concurrently computing agents, we would like to be able to compute a value, even if the permission is not arrived yet (see fig. 3).

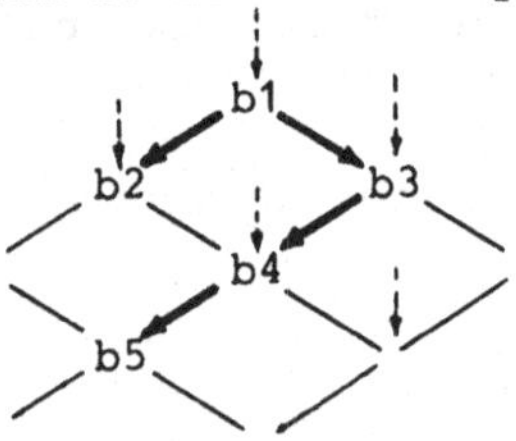

When computing b1, the computation of b3 and b4 may be much faster than that of b2. In that case we may want to compute b5, even if the permission to compute b5 is not arrived yet from b2.

Fig. 3 Allowing any relative speed among computing agents in the binomial coefficient computations.

In order to solve these problems, we need to introduce two extra primitive operations on lines:

i) receivetoken(x,line ℓ)

ii) receivetokenerase(x,line ℓ).

The infomal semantics of those annotations is the following:

- for the first one, the agent evaluating the annotation is blocked until a value different from ⊔ is available in line ℓ, then the variable x is bound to that value;
- for the second one: as for the first one, but the received value is also erased from the line ℓ.

Using these new primitives we can obtain the Program 5.5, which solves the above mentioned problems. In that program we use two lines:

i) V n m for storing the value of B(n,m), and

ii) S n m for storing the value PROMISE when a computing agent is computing B(n,m) or B(n,m) has been already computed.

Program 5.5

```
B(n,m)=if status=⊔/receiveerase(status,line S n m),send(PROMISE,
                            line S n m)/
        then res !send(res,line V n m)!   where res=B1(n,m)
```

```
        else res !receivetoken(res,line V n m)!
B1(n,m)=if m=0 or m=n then 1
        else B(n-1,m-1)+B(n-1,m)
```

4. Towards a theory of "helpful communications"

In this final section we will present some preliminary ideas for a theory of helpful communications, as introduced by examples in the previous sections.

We will give a formal definition of the syntax and the semantics of our programming language with annotations as follows.

A term t ∈ Terms is of the following form:

1.	g(t1,t2,...)	for any basic function $g \in G$
2.	f(t1,t2,...)	for any recursively defined function $f \in F$ $(F \cap G = \emptyset)$
3.	if t0 then t1 else t2	(conditional)
4.	t(z) where z = t1	(where clause; z is free in t)
5.	t annotation	(annotated term, where t is a term of the form 1 or 2 or 3 or 4)

An annotation is of the following form:

1. /elem-annot list/
2. !elem-annot list!

where elem-annot list is a list of elementary annotations of the form: elem-annot $\{,\text{elem-annot}\}_o^n$ or it is an empty list.

An elem-annot is of the following form:

1.1 broadcast(t)	1.2 received(x)
2.1 send(t,line ℓ)	2.2 receive(x,line ℓ)
	2.3 receivetoken(x,line ℓ)
3.1 send1 (t, line ℓ)	3.2 receiveerase(x,line ℓ)
	3.3 receivetokenerase(x,line ℓ)

A program is a function from F to Terms.

We will define the semantics of our language in an operational way, using a (nondeterministic) rewriting system, by which configurations are transformed into new configurations.

We assume that such transformations are performed by computing agents, which are associated to terms to be evaluated. Computing agents are elements of a domain, called Agents. The specific rule by which any term is associated to an agent will not be given here.

In a forthcoming paper we will address that issue, which is very important for allowing an high level of parallelism and efficiency of program executions. We will discuss that issue with respect to the architecture of the computer systems, the number of available processors and their allocation strategy.

A particular rule for associating agents to terms is to evaluate distinct recursive calls using distinct computing agents, possibly operating in parallel.

For instance, in Program 1.1 fib(n+2) may be evaluated by two distinct agents, one computing fib(n+1) and the other one computing fib(n)

The actual run-time association of agents to terms depends on the interpreter (or compiler) we use for implementing the rewriting system which defines the operational semantics.

A configuration is a pair of a process and a communication-environment (see fig. 4).

configuration:
- process: term or [agent;term;annotation] where term is not of the form 5.
- communication environment:
  - comm-structures: set of Values, line 1, line 2,...
  - comm-bindings: Var → Sets of Values ∪ Values

Fig. 4 A configuration and its components.

A process p is either a term t or a tuple [agent;term;annotation], where agent ∈ Agents.

The semantics of a blocked agent is expressed by the fact that the configuration, including the term to which that agent is associated, cannot be transformed into a new one.

A communication-environment CEnv is a pair [comm-structures, comm-bindings].

Comm-structures is the set {s,line 1,line 2,...} where s is a set of broadcast values, initialized to ∅, and line 1,line 2,... are lines mentioned in the given program initialized to ⟨⟩, i.e. empty lines.

Let Bool be the set {true,false} and V be the data domain used for expressing the input and output values of the user program.

Let Values be Bool ∪ V and Values' be Bool ∪ V ∪ {␣}.

For sets we have the following two primitive operations:

$\emptyset$: $\rightarrow$ sets of Values: $\emptyset$ is the empty set of Values

insert: Values $\times$ sets of Values $\rightarrow$ sets of Values: insert(v,s) = s $\cup$ {v}

In order to define lines let us give first some preliminary definitions.

A sequence σ of values is either an empty sequence denoted by ε, or it has an head (denoted by hd(σ)), which is a value, and a tail (denoted by tℓ(σ)) which is a sequence of values.

We will denote by "." the concatenation of values or sequences of values.

Given a sequence σ, the set of all the right subsequences of σ, denoted by Rsequences(σ), is defined as follows:

if $\sigma = \varepsilon$ then Rsequences(σ) = {ε}

if $\sigma = hd(\sigma)\cdot t\ell(\sigma)$ then Rsequences(σ) = {σ} $\cup$ Rsequences(tℓ(σ))

A line is a function from Agents to Rsequences(σ) for a particular sequence σ. Given a line ℓ: Agent $\rightarrow$ Rsequences(σ), if we assume that σ is the shortest possible sequence which satisfies the functionlity of ℓ, then σ is unique. This is why we will represent lines as sequences.

For clarity, we will also represent an empty line as $\langle\rangle$ and a line with one value v only, as $\langle v\rangle$. Lines is the set of all lines.

For instance, if Agents = {a1,a2}, Values = {true, false} $\cup$ $\mathbb{N}$ then the function {a1 $\mapsto$ 3.7.5, a2 $\mapsto$ 7.5} is a line. Notice that Rsequences(σ), i.e. the codomain of that line, is the set {ε,5,7.5,3.7.5}, which is indeed the set of all right subsequences of the sequence σ = 3.7.5.

That line can be pictorially represented as:

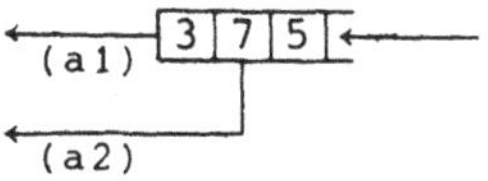

A line looks like a queue with one entry and many fronts one for each agent.

Now we give a formal definition of the lines as an abstract data type, by defining the following functions:

$\langle\rangle$: $\rightarrow$ Lines $\langle\rangle$ is the empty line.

$\forall$ a $\in$ Agents $\langle\rangle$(a) = ε

inline: Values $\times$ Lines $\rightarrow$ Lines

$\forall$ a inline(v,ℓ)(a) = ℓ(a).v

outline: Agents $\times$ Lines $\rightarrow$ Values' $\times$ Lines

outline(a,ℓ) = if ℓ(a) = ε then $\langle$ ␣, $\ell\rangle$ else $\langle$hd(ℓ(a)), $\ell'\rangle$

where $\ell' = \lambda$a1. if a1=a then tℓ(ℓ(a)) else ℓ(a1)

tokenoutline: Agents $\times$ Lines $\rightarrow$ Values $\times$ Lines

tokenoutline(a,ℓ)=if ℓ(a)$\neq\varepsilon$ then outline(a,ℓ)

else "agent a is blocked until ℓ(a)$\neq\varepsilon$, then outline(a,ℓ) is performed"

erase: Agents × Lines → Values' × Lines

erase(a,ℓ) = if ℓ(a)=ε then⟨ ␣, ℓ⟩ else ⟨hd(ℓ(a)), ℓ'⟩
where ℓ'=λa1. if ℓ(a1)=σ1.hd(a).tℓ(a) then σ1.tℓ(a
elseif a1=a then tℓ(a)
elseif ℓ(a1) ∈ Rsequences(tℓ(a)) then ℓ(a

tokenerase : Agents × Lines → Values × Lines

tokenerase(a,ℓ) = if ℓ(a)≠ε then erase(a,ℓ)
else "agent a is blocked until ℓ(a)≠ε, then erase(a,ℓ) is performed"

If we assume that the domain Agents is dynamically defined at each instant of the computation, then a newly created agent extends the domain of all existing lines. We assume that, given a line ℓ: Agents → Rsequences(σ), if a is a newly created agent then ℓ(a)=σ. In the case in which we consider the domain Agents statically defined, i.e. we assume that Agents is the domain of all agents, including those which will be generated during future steps of the computation, the conditions for newly created agents is implied by the initialization of any line as an empty line.

In order to clarify the given line definition, we give now an example of line transformation.

Let Agents be {a1,a2} and Values = {true,false} ∪ ℕ.

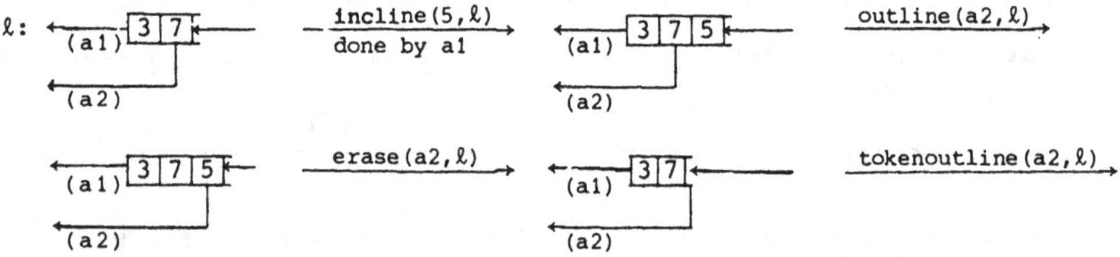

and the value 7 and the value 5

agent a2 is blocked until another agent performs an inline operation, say inline(9,ℓ), and we get:

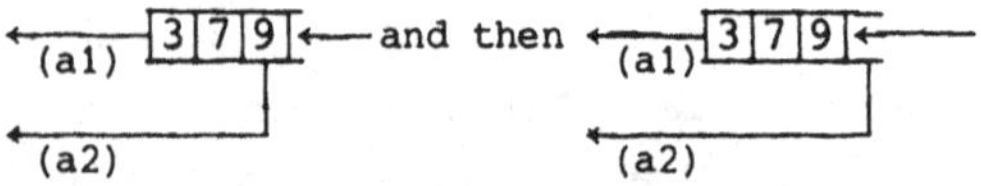

and the value 9

Starting from ℓ': 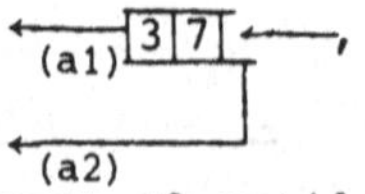 , takenerase(a2,ℓ') would have the effect of blocking the agent a2 until another agent does an inline operation, say inline(9,ℓ'). Afterwards we get: 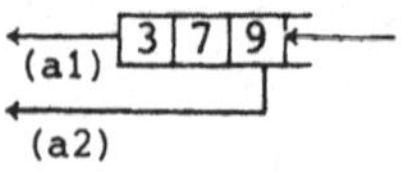 and then

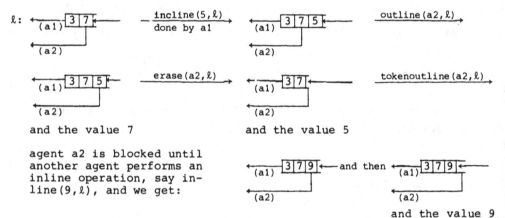

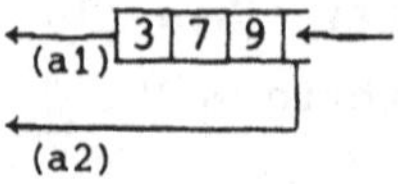

together with the value 9.

This ends the explanation of the comm-structures.

Comm-bindings is a function called Cbind, which associates a value with a variable occurring in point-to-point or erasable communications, and it associates a set of values with a variable occurring in broadcasting communications. It is initialized to the empty function. Now we can define the semantics of our programming language by specifying the transition function from configurations to configurations.

In writing such transition function we will write process1 → process2 meaning that the configuration changes only on its process component. Other changes of the configurations, when they occur, will be suitably specified in our rewriting rules.

We will write term 1 → term 2 meaning also that [ag;term 1;annotation] → [ag;term 2;annotation].

In particular this fact allows the concurrent evaluation of a term and its annotation.

In what follows v stands for an element of Values, and given a function f: A → B, we denote f|⟨a,b⟩ a function f', s.t. f'(x) = if x = a then b else f(x). By dom(f) we denote the domain of a function f. By t(x) we denote a term with 0 or 1 or more free occurences of x. The following rules specify the transition function from configurations to configurations. Let Prog be a given program.

1. g(t1,t2,...) $\xrightarrow{g(t1,t2,...)=v}$ v
2. f(t1,t2,...) ⟶ Prog(f)(t1,t2,...) and new agents are associated to subterms of Prog(f)(t1, t2,...)

Remark. In order to keep distinct the variables occurring in different recursive calls of f instead of Prog(f) we must use and α-conversion of it.

3.1 if t0 then t1 else t2 $\xrightarrow{t0=true}$ t1
3.2 if t0 then t1 else t2 $\xrightarrow{t0=false}$ t2

Remark. In a conditional, t0 and its annotation should be evaluated first.

4.1 e(z) where z=e1 $\xrightarrow{e1 \to e2}$ e(z) where z=e2
4.2 e(z) where z=v ⟶ e(z) and Cbind → Cbind|⟨z,v⟩

Remark. In a where clause e1 and its annotation should be evaluated first.

5. t !annotation! ⟶ [agi;t;annotation]
where agi is the agent name which has to evaluate t !annotation!

6.1 t /annotation/ ⟶ t

6.2 t /annotation/ ⟶ t !annotation!

Remark. By rules 6.1 and 6.2 we represent the fact that the evaluation of an annotation between slashes is optional.

7.1 [agi;t;elem-annot,elem-annot list] ⟶ [agi;t;elem-annot list]
and CEnv=[{s,line1,line2,...},
Cbind] changes of follows:

case elem-annot **of**

broadcast(v):	$s \rightarrow s \cup \{v\}$;
received(z):	Cbind →Cbind|⟨z,s⟩;
send(v,line ℓ):	ℓ → inline(v,ℓ);
receive(x,line ℓ):	ℓ → π2(outline(agi,ℓ)) **and** Cbind → Cbind|⟨x,π1(outline(agi,ℓ))⟩;
receivetoken(x,line ℓ):	ℓ → π2(tokenoutline(agi,ℓ)) **and** Cbind →Cbind|⟨x,π1(tokenoutline(agi,ℓ))⟩;
send1(v,line ℓ):	ℓ → inline(v,ℓ);
receiveerase(x,line ℓ):	ℓ → π2(erase(agi,ℓ)) **and** Cbind → Cbind|⟨x,π1(erase(agi,ℓ))⟩;
receivetokenerase(x,line ℓ):	ℓ → π2(tokenerase(agi,ℓ)) **and** Cbind → Cbind|⟨x,π1(tokenerase(agi,ℓ))⟩

end

7.2 [agi;t;empty list] ⟶ t

Remark. i) We can apply rule 7.1 only when the value v occurring in broadcast(v) or send(v,line ℓ) or send1(v,line ℓ) is an element of Values.

ii) When evaluating annotations according rule 7.1 we have to comply with the following metarules:

- broadcast(v) or received(z) may be done concurrently be any number of computing agents;
- for point-to-point communications, at any given moment, there could be only a send operation or many concurrent receive or receivetoken operations for any line;
- for erasable communications, at any given moment, there could be only a send or receiveerase or receivetokenerase operation for any line.

iii) After the use of rule 5 the agent agi which performs the rewriting of [agi;t;annotation] uses all lines mentioned in the whole annotation until it produces a process which is a term only. (Rule of global use of lines).

The metarules ii) and iii) are constraining the possible concurrent rewriting of configurations.

8.1 [agi;t(x);annot(x)] $\xrightarrow{\text{Cbind(x)=a}}$ [agi;t[a/x];annot[a/x]]

8.2.1 [agi;t(x);annot(x)] $\xrightarrow{x \notin \text{dom(Cbind)}}$ [agi;t[∅/x];annot[∅/x]] if received(x) occurs in annot(x).

8.2.2 [agi;t(x);annot(x)] $\xrightarrow{x \notin \text{dom(Cbind)}}$ [agi;t[⌴/x]; annot[⌴/x]] if receive(x,...) or receivetoken (x,...) or receiveerase(x,...) or receivetokenerase(x,...) occurs in annot(x).

9.1 t(x) $\xrightarrow{\text{Cbind(x)=a}}$ t[a/x]

9.2.1 t(x) $\xrightarrow{x \notin \text{dom(Cbind)}}$ t[∅/x] if the condition of 8.2.1 holds.

9.2.2 t(x) $\xrightarrow{x \notin \text{dom(Cbind)}}$ t[⌴/x] if the condition of 8.2.2 holds.

Remark. Rules 8.1, 8.2.1 and 8.2.2 are necessary for rewriting terms for which we want to evaluate the associated annotations. Rule 9.1, 9.2.1 and 9.2.2 are necessary when we do not want to evaluate their associated annotations.

As an example of application of the semantic rules we have given, let us see how the rewriting of B(n,m) is performed according to Program 5.5.

We start off with Cbind as an empty function and all lines as empty lines. The following is a possible sequence of rewriting of terms.

(A) if status=⌴ /...../ then ... $\xrightarrow{6.1}$ if status=⌴ then ... in case the annotation of the predicate of the conditional is not evaluated. Then we have rule 9.2.2: if ⌴=⌴ then ... $\xrightarrow{1.}$ if true then ... $\xrightarrow{3.}$ res !.....! where res=B1(n,m).

By recursion induction and rule 4.1 we finally get:

res !send(res,line V n m)! where res = $\binom{n}{m}$ $\xrightarrow{4.2}$

res !send(res,line V n m)! and Cbind(res) = $\binom{n}{n}$ $\xrightarrow{9.1}$

$\binom{n}{m}$!send($\binom{n}{m}$,line V n m)! $\xrightarrow{5.}$

[ag1;$\binom{n}{m}$;send($\binom{n}{m}$,line V n m)] $\xrightarrow{7.1}$ [ag1;$\binom{n}{m}$;empty list]

and V n m → inline($\binom{n}{m}$,V n m). Thus from now on in the line V n m we have the value $\binom{n}{m}$.

Eventually we get by rule 7.2 the result $\binom{n}{m}$.

(B) Starting from the term:

if status=⌴ /receiveerase(status,line S n m),send(PROMISE,line S n m)/ then ..., in case the annotation is evaluated, we get by rule 5:

[ag1; if status=⌴ then ...; receiveerase(status,line S n m), send(PROMISE,line S n m)].

Now there are two cases, as one can easily check by inspection:

i) line S n m is empty or ii) it has only the value PROMISE.

In case i), by rule 7.1, we get:
[ag1;if status=⊔ then ...; send(PROMISE,line S n m)] and S n m=⟨⟩ and Cbind(status)=⊔. Now the rewriting may nondeterministically proceeds according to case i.1 or i.2.

i.1: agent ag1 evaluates first the term: if status ⊔ then ...
In this case we get: if ⊔ = ⊔ then ... and then we get:
[ag1;if true then ...;send(PROMISE,line S n m)]. Now, before proceeding with the evaluation of the conditional, we should complete the evaluation of the annotation of the predicate of the conditional ifself, because of the remark for rule 3.
Eventually we get:
if true then ... and the line S n m will be equal to ⟨PROMISE⟩; i.e. a sequence with the value PROMISE only. From that time onwards the line S n m will be accessible by other agents, because the annotation has been completely evaluated and the rule of global use of line does not determine any constraint.

i.2: agent ag1 evaluates first the annotation send(PROMISE,line S n m). This leaves the line S n m as the sequence ⟨PROMISE⟩ and status $\notin$ dom(Cbind). The line S n m is then released, so that it can be accessed by other agents. Then we get if status=⊔ then ... which is rewritten by rule 9.2.2 into
if ⊔ = ⊔ then ... $\xrightarrow{1}$ if true then ...
In both cases we get the term:
res !send(res,line V n m)! where res=B1(n,m)
and the computation of B(n,m) is then achieved as in case (A), and the line V n m will be ⟨$\binom{n}{m}$⟩.

In case ii) in which S n m=⟨PROMISE⟩, since all lines are initialized to ⟨⟩, one can easily prove that the evaluation of B(n,m) is being performed by a computing agent which follows case (A) and leaves the line V n m equal to ⟨$\binom{n}{m}$⟩. Thus the computing agent which finds S n m=⟨PROMISE⟩ should wait for the value of B(n,m) from the line V n m. In fact we have:
[ag1;if status=⊔ then ...; send(PROMISE,line S n m)], S n m=⟨⟩ and Cbind(status)=PROMISE.
Now the computation nondeterministically proceeds by evaluating the condition status=⊔ (case ii.1) or the annotation send(...) (case ii.2).

ii.1: by rule 8.1 we get [ag1;if PROMISE=⊔ then ...;send(...)] $\xrightarrow{1.}$ [ag1;if false then ...;send(PROMISE,line S n m)]. By the remark for rule 3 we must evaluate the annotation send(...) first and we get:
[ag1;if false then ...;empty list] and S n m=⟨PROMISE⟩ $\xrightarrow{7.2}$ if false then ... $\xrightarrow{3.2}$ res !receivetoken(res,line V n m)!
Eventually by hypothesis, the line V n m will be ⟨$\binom{n}{m}$⟩ and the desired

result will be computed.

ii.2: by rule 7.1 we get: [ag1;if status=⊔ then ...;empty list] and S n m=⟨PROMISE⟩ $\xrightarrow{7.2}$ if status=⊔ then ... $\xrightarrow{9.1}$ if PROMISE=⊔ then ... $\xrightarrow{1}$ if false then ... $\xrightarrow{3.2}$ res !receivetoken(res,line V n m)!

And we get the desired result as in case ii.1.

This ends the example concerning Program 5.5.

Before closing this section, we would like to mention that we will develop a proof theory for the given rewriting system, so that semantic properties of programs written in our programming language can be easily proved. This will be the content of a forthcoming paper.

5. Conclusions and final remarks

We presented some examples for illustrating the motto: "efficiency = parallelism + communications". Efficiency in computations can be achieved by performing independent evaluations at the same time using various computing agents, which work in parallel. Sometimes, however, it could happen that more than one agent performs the same computation. In order to avoid such duplication of efforts we assumed that some communications are established among computing agents, so that an exchange of useful information may be realized and might produce an improvement of performances.

Communications, in our approach, need not to be the result of a computation, but they may as well be a property of such a result, which could be useful for increasing the efficiency of other computations. Another crucial property of such communications is that, in general, they need not to be performed and the correctness of the program is not effected by their presence. This fact indeed forced us to build a novel theory of communications, called "helpful communications", which is quite different from already known ones [4,5,6,7,8].

In particular if we compare our approach with the Kahn-McQueen's one, our lines are very similar to their queues, but ours are not "private" data structures. Any computing agent may access them, following a definite protocol, and they may get the information stored in them.

With respect to Milner's approach [8], the main difference consists in the fact that we can pass names of lines among computing agents, and this corresponds to an extension of the CCS language, where one assumes that names of ports can be passed.

A final important issue concerns the implementation of broadcast, point-to-point and erasable communications.

We will deal with that problem in a forthcoming paper, where we examine efficient implementations of our communication primitives using suitable VLSI design techniques and architectures. We think that the great development of the hardware technology during the last few year offers us interesting solutions for achieving high computational efficiency.

6. Acknowledgments

I would like to express my warm gratitude to Prof. R. Burstall, L. Cardelli, M. Gordon, G. Plotkin and R. Milner at Computer Science Department of Edinburgh University for many interesting conversations and providing the necessary stimulation.

Dr. A. Skowron at Mathematics Institute of Warsaw University gave me lots of ideas and great enthusiasm.

Many thanks to Roberta Venturini at KLIM for excellent typing.

7. References

[1] Burstall,R.M. and J. Darlington: *A Transformation System for Developing Recursive Programs*, J.A.C.M. Vol. 24, No. 1, Jan 77 pp. 44-67.

[2] Burstall,R.M., D.B. MacQueen and D.T. Sannella: *HOPE: An Experimental Applicative Language*, CSR-62-80 Computer Science Edinburgh University (1980).

[3] Henderson,P. and J.H. Morris, Jr.: *A Lazy Evaluator*, Proc. of POPL Conference Sigplan-Sigact Atlanta (1976) pp. 95-103.

[4] Hewitt,C. and H. Baker, Jr.: *Actors and Continuous Functionals*, Neuhold, E.J. (Ed.), Formal Descriptions of Programming Languages, Noth Holland, Amsterdam (1978).

[5] Hoare,C.A.R.: *Communicating Sequential Processes*, Comm. A.C.M. 21, 8 (Aug. 1978) pp. 666-677.

[6] Kahn,G. and D.B. MacQueen: *Coroutines and Networks of Parallel Processes*, in: Gilchrist, B. (Ed.), Information Processing 77, North Holland, Amsterdam (1977) pp. 993-998.

[7] Milne,G. and R. Milner: *Concurrent Processes and Their Syntax*, J.A.C.M. Vol. 26 pp. 302-321.

[8] Milner,R.: *A Calculus for Communicating Systems*, LNCS 92 Springer Verlag (1980).

[9] Pettorossi,A. and R. Burstall: *Deriving Very Efficient Algorithms For Evaluating Linear Recurrence Relations Using Program Transformation Technique*, (submitted for publication) (1980).

[10] Pettorossi,A.: *Transformation of Programs and Use of Tupling Strategy*, Informatica 77. Congress, Bled (Yugoslavia) (1977).

[11] Pettorossi,A.: *Organizing parallelism and communications for efficient distributed computations*, AICA Congress Bologna (1980).

[12] Schwarz,J.: *Using Annotations to Make Recursive Equations Behave*, D.A.I. Research Report No. 43, Edinburgh University (Sept. 1977).

[13] Strachey,C. and C.P. Wadsworth: *Continuations: A Mathematical Semantics for Handling Full Jumps*, Tech. Monograph PRG-11, Oxford University Computing Laboratory, Oxford (Jan 1974).

AN OPERATIONAL SEMANTICS FOR CSP

(Extended Abstract)

Gordon Plotkin

The present work is intended to illustrate a method of giving the operational semantics of programming languages. As an example a variant of Hoare's language, CSP, of communicating sequential processes is considered [Hoa]. At the same time some attempt is made to develop an approach to language analysis following a guiding principle of simplicity of the abstract syntax. This idea is independent of the semantic method used and can just as well be combined with other approaches, such as that of denotational semantics.

The operational semantics employs the well-known idea of transition systems, $\langle\Gamma, T, \rightarrow\rangle$, where Γ (ranged over by γ) is a set of configurations and $T \subseteq \Gamma$ is the set of final configurations and $\rightarrow\, \subseteq \Gamma \times \Gamma$ is the transition relation. A typical configuration could be $\langle c, \sigma\rangle$, where c is a command and σ is a store; further any store σ could be a final configuration (no command left to be executed). What is new is the specification of the transition relation. For this we follow the modern emphasis on structure and define the transition relation by structural induction on the abstract syntax by means of such rules as:

Sequence 1. $$\frac{\langle c_0, \sigma\rangle \rightarrow \langle c_0', \sigma'\rangle}{\langle c_0; c_1, \sigma\rangle \rightarrow \langle c_0'; c_1, \sigma'\rangle}$$

2. $$\frac{\langle c_0, \sigma\rangle \rightarrow \sigma'}{\langle c_0; c_1, \sigma\rangle \rightarrow \langle c_1, \sigma'\rangle}$$

Dijkstra's guarded command language underlies CSP [Dij]. Applying our principle of simplicity we try to minimise the number of syntactic categories in a non-artificial way and take guarded commands as being themselves commands so that for example if b is a Boolean expression and c is a command so is $b \rightarrow c$. As another application we do not wish to allow n-ary syntactic constructions (for every n) as implied by this syntax for conditions:

$$\underline{\text{if}}\ b_1 \rightarrow c_1 \,\square\, \cdots \,\square\, b_n \rightarrow c_n\ \underline{\text{fi}}$$

Rather we regard this, for each n, as a composite (= derived) construction from the above binary guarding construction, $b \rightarrow c$, a binary choice construction $c \,\square\, c$ and a unary conditional if c fi. The syntax for commands is then

$$c ::= a \mid \underline{\text{skip}} \mid c;c \mid b \Rightarrow c \mid \underline{\text{fail}} \mid c \,\square\, c \mid \underline{\text{abort}} \mid \underline{\text{if}}\ c\ \underline{\text{fi}} \mid \underline{\text{do}}\ c\ \underline{\text{od}}$$

where a ranges over primitive actions and b => c is a strong *guarding* construction, useful for concurrency, which does not allow any interruption by any process between the testing of b and the first action of c. The above *weak* guarding can be derived from the strong one by:

$$b \to c =_{\mathrm{def}} b \Rightarrow \mathrm{nil};\ c$$

This can be expressed by the rules:

Guarding 1. $\dfrac{\langle c, \sigma\rangle \to \gamma}{\langle b \Rightarrow c, \sigma\rangle \to \gamma}$ (if b is true in σ)

2. $\langle b \Rightarrow c, \sigma\rangle \to$ *failure* (if b is false in σ)

where *failure* is a new configuration standing for failure. The other constructs are specified along similar lines (and another new configuration, *abortion*, is needed).

The advantage of the strong guarding is that it allows the resolution of complex guarded commands in CSP containing input commands, such as b; A ? x → c, into b => (A ? x; c) and that in turn avoids the redundancy of input commands appearing in two places in the syntax.

The most complex construct in CSP is the parallel command

$$[P_1::c_1 || \ldots || P_n::c_n]$$

where, of course, the c_i can perfectly well contain further parallel commands. We view this as a *block* (with || replacing ;) and regard the process identifiers, P_i, as analogous to label identifiers; then the scope of the P_i can be taken, following the usual rules, as the whole of the block. With this idea we can analyse the parallel command into a binary *parallel* construction, c||c and a unary *labelling* construction P::c and a binary declaration construction *process* P;c as follows

process P_1;...; *process* P_n;
begin
$P_1::c_1 || \ldots || P_n::c_n$
end

(where *begin* ... *end* are just a pair of brackets). And we have a simple syntax for CSP

c::= (guarded command construction) | P?r | Q!w | c || c | P::c | *process* P; c

where r ranges over a set of input operations and w over a set of output operations and we have omitted certain details relating to non-interference between parallel processes. We have also omitted variable declarations, process arrays or guarded commands with ranges.

For the operational semantics we employ the well-known idea of labelled transition systems, $\langle\Gamma, T, M, \rightarrow\rangle$ where now M is a set of messages (= communications) and $\rightarrow \subseteq \Gamma \times M \times \Gamma$.. The rules for the guarded commands are the same as before, but with an m above the arrows for the messages. For CSP the appropriate messages with their intuitive meanings are:

ε - an internal action of a process

P ? v - P sends v to an unknown agent

Q ! v - an unknown agent sends a value v to Q

P,Q ? v - Q receives v from P

P,Q ! v - P sends v to Q.

Here are some typical rules

Output $\langle Q\,!\,w,\sigma\rangle \xrightarrow{Q!v} \sigma$ (where v is the value transmitted by w given store σ)

Labelling $$\frac{\langle c,\sigma\rangle \xrightarrow{P?v} \langle c',\sigma'\rangle}{\langle Q::c,\sigma\rangle \xrightarrow{P,Q?v} \langle Q::c',\sigma'\rangle}$$ (if $P \neq Q$)

Communication $$\frac{\langle c_0,\sigma\rangle \xrightarrow{P,Q?v} \langle c_0',\sigma'\rangle \langle c_1,\sigma\rangle \xrightarrow{P,Q!v} \langle c_1',\sigma\rangle}{\langle c_0 || c_1,\sigma\rangle \xrightarrow{\varepsilon} \langle c_0' || c_1',\sigma'\rangle}$$

This treatment omits consideration of Hoare's termination convention, which would require a little additional complication. (One adds a third component to the configurations, namely a set of process labels; these are intended to be the set of labels of all terminated processes.) Finally we note a great difference between this kind of operational semantics and the usual denotational semantics. We only specify one step of executions and do not say how to put these together to make up global behaviours or what it means for two such behaviours to be equal. There are many choices in general and we remain neutral between them. On the other hand any normal denotational semantics both automatically reflects such a choice and does not in general specify all the details of the execution sequences.

References

[Dij] Dijkstra, E.W. (1976) A Discipline of Programming. Prentice-Hall.

[Hoa] Hoare, C.A.R. (1978) Communicating Sequential Processes. CACM, Vol. 21, No. 8, 666-677.

PROGRAMMING LANGUAGES AND LOGICS OF PROGRAMS

S.R. Radev
Warsaw University, Warsaw, Poland

Abstract. We prove the completeness theorem for a class of logics of programs. As corollaries of our result, we obtain the completeness theorem for a large class of extensions of PDL.

Introduction. In recent years various authors have introduced modal logics to talk about computation processes. In general these logics cannot deal with the behaviour of the programs during the computation, or during some part of the computation. From the other side every extension of the program part of such a logic complicates the proof of the completeness theorem of the new logic. Meyer [2] shows that more of these logics differs only on the program part (the notion of what the program scheme is). That is why we divide the program part of the logics of programs from the logical part and the temporal semantics from the object semantics. The major points of our strategy are the following:

a. Considering every program as a language over a set of elementary actions;

b. Defining the semantics only on the elementary actions (object semantics);

c. Putting the logics of programs in standard form (standard syntax, semantics, axiomatics);

d. Considering the logics from that class as a fragments of any, large enough, logic.

In section 2 we define the notion of programming language (PL) together with the temporal semantics of the programs. That allows us to consider more than one semantics in a given formalization. In section 3 we give a standard axiomatization of the logics of programs, the completeness theorem for which is given in the section 4. Infinitary modal logic is large enough to treat these logics of programs as fragments of it.

2. Multi-Level Programming Languages.

2.1. Definition. A Multi-Level Programming Language (MLPL) is a triple $\mathcal{L} = (\mathbb{A}, \mathbb{P}, \mathbb{L})$ where:

i) $\mathbb{A} \neq \emptyset$ is at most countable set. The elements of $\mathbb{A}$ are called atomic programs;

ii) $\mathbb{P} \neq \emptyset$ is at most countable set. The elements of $\mathbb{P}$ are called programs;

iii) $\mathbb{L}: \mathbb{P} \longrightarrow (2^{\mathbb{A}^+} - \{\emptyset\})$ is a mapping such that for every $\alpha \in \mathbb{A} \cap \mathbb{P}$ $\mathbb{L}(\alpha) = \{\alpha\}$. For every $\alpha \in \mathbb{P}$ $\mathbb{L}(\alpha)$ is the set of the (partial computation) paths of the program α in the MLPL $\mathcal{L}$.

As usual the set of programs $\mathbb{P}$ in a logic of programs is defined inductively over the set of atomic programs $\mathbb{A}$. Respectively the meaning of every operator over programs is defined inductively. Hence the set of computation paths $\mathbb{L}(\alpha)$ of a given program α is definiable in a natural way. That is why we define the programming languages in such a way.

2.2. Definition. Let $\mathcal{L} = (\mathbb{A}, \mathbb{P}, \mathbb{L})$ be a MLPL. A model for $\mathcal{L}$ is any pair $\mathcal{F} = (U,R)$ where:

i) $U \neq \emptyset$ is a set;

ii) $R: \mathbb{A} \cup \mathbb{P} \longrightarrow 2^{U \times U}$ is a mapping such that for every $\alpha \in \mathbb{P}$

$$R(\alpha) = \bigcup_{w \in \mathbb{L}(\alpha)} R(w)$$

where $R(a_1 \ldots a_n) = R(a_1) \circ \ldots \circ R(a_n)$.

2.3. Definition. A MLPL $\mathcal{L} = (\mathbb{A}, \mathbb{P}, \mathbb{L})$ is standard if for every $a \in \mathbb{A}$ and every $\alpha \in \mathbb{P}$ there is a $\beta \in \mathbb{P}$ such that $\mathbb{L}(\beta) = \{a\} | \mathbb{L}(\alpha)$.

Roughly speaking the standard MLPL-s are these in which is definiable the concatenation operation.

3. Logics of standard MLPL-s.

Let $\mathcal{L} = (\mathbb{A}, \mathbb{P}, \mathbb{L})$ be a standard MLPL. We define the logic $L_{\mathcal{L}}$ which corresponds to the MLPL $\mathcal{L}$ as follows:

3.1. Definition. The set of all formulas of $L_{\mathcal{L}}$ is the least set such that:

i) $F \supset V_0$ where V_0 is a set of propositional variables;

ii) If $A, B \in F$, then $\neg A, A \wedge B \in F$;

iii) If $A \in F$ and $\alpha \in \mathbb{A} \cup \mathbb{P}$, then $\Box_\alpha A \in F$.

3.2. Definition. $\mathfrak{M} = (U,R,0,V)$ is a model for $L_{\mathcal{L}}$ if (U,R) is a model for $\mathcal{L}$, $0 \in U$ and V is a valuation $(V: V_0 \longrightarrow 2^U)$.

3.3. Definition. The validity of a formula A in the model $\mathfrak{M}$ at a point u (denote $\mathfrak{M},u \models A$) is defined inductively as follows:

i) For every propositional variable $A \in V_0$ $\mathfrak{M},u \models A$ iff $u \in V(A)$;

ii) $\mathfrak{M},u \models A \wedge B$ iff $\mathfrak{M},u \models A$ and $\mathfrak{M},u \models B$;

iii) $\mathfrak{M},u \models \neg A$ iff not $\mathfrak{M},u \models A$

iv) $\mathfrak{M},u \models \Box_\alpha A$ iff for every $v \in U$ $(u,v) \in R(\alpha)$ implies $\mathfrak{M},v \models A$.

A formula A is valid in the model $\mathfrak{M}$ if $\mathfrak{M},0 \models A$.

3.4. Axioms and rules of inference for $L_{\mathcal{L}}$.

A1) All instances of propositional tautologies.

A2) $\Box_\alpha A \Rightarrow \Box_w A$ for every $w \in \mathbf{L}(\alpha)$, every $\alpha \in \mathbf{P}$.

A3) $\Box_\alpha(A \Rightarrow B) \Rightarrow (\Box_\alpha A \Rightarrow \Box_\alpha B)$ for every $\alpha \in \mathbf{P} \cup \mathbf{A}$

R1) $\dfrac{A,\ A \Rightarrow B}{B}$ (modus ponens)

R2) $\dfrac{A}{\Box_\alpha A}$ for every $\alpha \in \mathbf{A} \cup \mathbf{P}$

R3) $\dfrac{A \Rightarrow \Box_w B \text{ for all } w \in \mathbf{L}(\alpha)}{A \Rightarrow \Box_\alpha B}$

A formula A is a theorem of $L_{\mathcal{L}}$ (denote $\vdash_{\mathcal{L}} A$) if there is a sequence $A_0,\dots,A_\mu,\dots,A_\nu = A$ $(\nu < \omega_1)$ such that for every $\rho \leq \mu \leq \nu$ A_μ is either axiom of $L_{\mathcal{L}}$ or is inferred by some rule from earlier formulas A_γ $(\gamma < \mu)$.

4. Completeness theorem for $L_{\mathcal{L}}$.

Let $\mathcal{A}_{\mathcal{L}}$ be the least fragment of $NM_T L_{\omega_1}$ where $T = \mathbf{A} \cup \mathbf{P}$ ($NM_T L_{\omega_1}$ is the infinitary propositional normal modal logic defined in [5]) such that for every $\alpha \in \mathbf{P}$ and every $A \in \mathcal{A}_{\mathcal{L}}$

$$\bigwedge \{ \Box_w A \mid w \in \mathbf{L}(\alpha)\} \in \mathcal{A}_{\mathcal{L}}$$

Let $\Gamma_{\mathcal{L}}$ be the set of all formulas from $\mathcal{A}_{\mathcal{L}}$ which are of the form $\Box_\alpha A \Leftrightarrow \bigwedge \{ \Box_w A \mid w \in \mathbf{L}(\alpha)\}$ for some $\alpha \in \mathbf{P}$ and some $A \in \mathcal{A}_{\mathcal{L}}$.

4.1. Lemma. For every formula A of $L_{\mathcal{L}}$ $\Gamma_{\mathcal{L}} \vdash_{\mathcal{A}_{\mathcal{L}}} A$ implies $\vdash_{\mathcal{L}} A$.

Proof: By simple verification that the following mapping T translates the proofs in the fragment $\mathcal{A}_{\mathcal{L}}$ from the theory $\Gamma_{\mathcal{L}}$ into proofs in the logic $L_{\mathcal{L}}$.

The mapping $T: \mathcal{A}_{\mathcal{L}} \longrightarrow F$ is defined inductively as follows:

$$T(A) =_{df} A \quad \text{when} \quad A \in V_0$$

$$T(\neg A) =_{df} \neg T(A)$$

$$T(A \wedge B) =_{df} T(A) \wedge T(B)$$

$$T(\Box_\alpha A) =_{df} \Box_\alpha T(A)$$

$$T(\bigwedge \Phi) =_{df} \Box_\alpha T(B) \quad \text{in the case when } \Phi = \{\Box_w B \mid w \in \mathbf{L}(\alpha)\}$$

4.2.<u>Theorem</u>.(Completeness theorem for $L_{\mathcal{L}}$) For every formula $A \in F$ A is a theorem of $L_{\mathcal{L}}$ if A is valid in every model for $L_{\mathcal{L}}$.

<u>Proof</u>: Follows immediately from the previous lemma and the completeness theorem for theories in countable fragments of $NM_T L_{\omega_1}$ [5] .

5. <u>$L_{\mathcal{L}}$ which corresponds to PDL</u>.

To obtain standard logic which corresponds to PDL is enough to define a standard MLPL which corresponds to the programming language used in PDL. The set of all programs in PDL is defined in [1] . We define the paths language for every program inductively as follows

$$\mathbf{L}(\alpha) = \{\alpha\} \quad \text{when } \alpha \in A$$

$$\mathbf{L}(\alpha \cup \beta) = \mathbf{L}(\alpha) \cup \mathbf{L}(\beta)$$

$$\mathbf{L}(\alpha \circ \beta) = \mathbf{L}(\alpha) \circ \mathbf{L}(\beta)$$

$$\mathbf{L}(\alpha^*) = (\mathbf{L}(\alpha))^*$$

It is clear that $\mathcal{L}_{PDL} = (\mathbf{A}, \mathbf{P}, \mathbf{L})$ is astandard MLPL. From the other side it is easy to see that in every model $\mathfrak{M}$ for $L\mathcal{L}_{PDL}$ the following equalities hold:

i) $R(\alpha \cup \beta) = R(\alpha) \cup R(\beta)$

ii) $R(\alpha \circ \beta) = R(\alpha) | R(\beta)$

iii) $R(\alpha^*) = (R(\alpha))^*$

Hence PDL has a completeness theorem ($L\mathcal{L}_{PDL}$ has a completeness theorem). In such a way one may obtain the completeness theorem for every extension of PDL for which there is a correspondence between path languages of programs and the relations in the models. For instance for the extension of PDL with "during" operation (see 8 , 9) one have to consider only one additional operation d such that for every program α $\mathbf{L}(d\alpha) = \{u \mid \text{there is } w \in \mathbf{L}(\alpha)$ such that u is initial subword of $w\}$

Another way of extension of a logic of programs is to extend the expressive power of the logic $L_{\mathcal{L}}$. That is when we consider larger fragments of the infinitary modal logic $NM_T L_{\omega_1}$ in which some program properties are expressible. Also some modalities which are expressible in $NM_TL_{\omega_1}$ may be considered in fragments of $NM_TL_{\omega_1}$: $\boxtimes_\alpha = \bigwedge_{w \in \mathbf{L}(\alpha)} \Diamond_w$ is one of these modalities. $\boxtimes_\alpha A$ says: "for every computation path w of α there is a computation of α over that path , such that A holds after that computation"

References.

[1] Harel, D. First-Order Dynamic Logic, Lecture Notes in Computer Science, Springer-Verlag, New York, 1979

[2] Meyer, A. Ten Thousand and One Logics of Programming, Bull. of EATCS, N 10,january, 1980

[3] Mirkowska, G. PAL- Propositional Algorithmic Logic, Fundamenta Informaticae, to appear.

[4] Pratt, V. Application of modal logic to programming, Studia Logica, vol. XXXIX 2/3, pp 257-274

[5] Radev, S. Infinitary Propositional Modal Logic and Programming Languages, PhD Thesis, Warsaw University, Institute of Mathematics,november 1981

[6] Rasiowa, H. Algorithmic Logic, IPI PAN Report N° 281, Warsaw, Poland, 1977

[7] Salwicki, A. Formalized algorithmic languages, Bull. de l'Acad. Pol. Sci.- vol. XVIII, 5, 1970, pp 227-232

[8] Segerberg K. Applying modal logic, Studia Logica, vol. XXXIX N° 2/3, pp 275-295

[9] Vakarelov, D. Expressibility of some "during" operations in PDL, unpublished manuscript, 1980

CONCURRENT PROGRAMS

Andrzej Skowron
Institute of Mathematics
Warsaw University
00-901 Warsaw, PKiN IX p/907

1.Introduction

One of the main research topics in computer science is concerned with parallel processing and related questions. Many models of parallel processes have been suggested by several authors, e.g. [BED 77], [DIJ 75], [KAR 69], [KEL 72], [KOT 79], [MAZ 77], [MIL 78], [PET 76,79], [WIN 80]. These models represent different approaches to investigation of concurrency.

In this paper we present a basis for a unified approach to problems related to concurrent programs. A basic concept which plays a crucial role in the paper is that of global instruction. The global instructions are obtained as a result of applying the mixing operation to elementary conditions and instructions operating on control variables and elementary conditions and instructions operating on program variables. We shall then construct a skeleton of a program which is built from a finite set of global instructions and two functions called strategy and collision. The strategy determines in the present memory state the family of subsets of the set of all active instructions in that state. Every element of that family can lead to the next state of computation. The collision function determines which instructions can be performed concurrently without leading to collision. By assigning a meaning to the control parts of global instructions occuring in a skeleton we obtain a schema of program. At the end by giving the meaning to those elementary instructions and conditions of schema, which operate on program variables we determine a concurrent program and its semantics. In Fig.1 the stages of program construction are presented.

Many models of concurrency which have been already developed and investigated can be considered as a particular cases of program considered in the paper. We will restrict our considerations to the finite programs (e.g. [KEL 72][DIJ 75]). The infinite programs (i.e. programs whose sets of global instructions are infinite or potentially infinite) can be introduced and considered using a slight modification of our investigations [SKO 80]. It allows us to investigate also such concurrent models as cellular structures or recursive concurrent programs.

The formalism presented here is supposed to be a foundation of concurrent programs theory. The author expects that the introduced formalism will play an important role in the creation of metatheory of concurrent programs, and will allow to investigate new classes of concurrent programs as well as existing ones, and can be a proper tool to compare different models of concurrency.

Here, we only mention this possibility by giving the example of how one can to apply the formalism to the optimal deadlock avoidance problem [SKO 80] [SUR 80]. We point out also the importance of program extension operation.

2. Basic notation

For any set X let P(X) be the family of all subsets of X, FIN(X) the family of all finite subsets of X and |X| the cardinality of X.

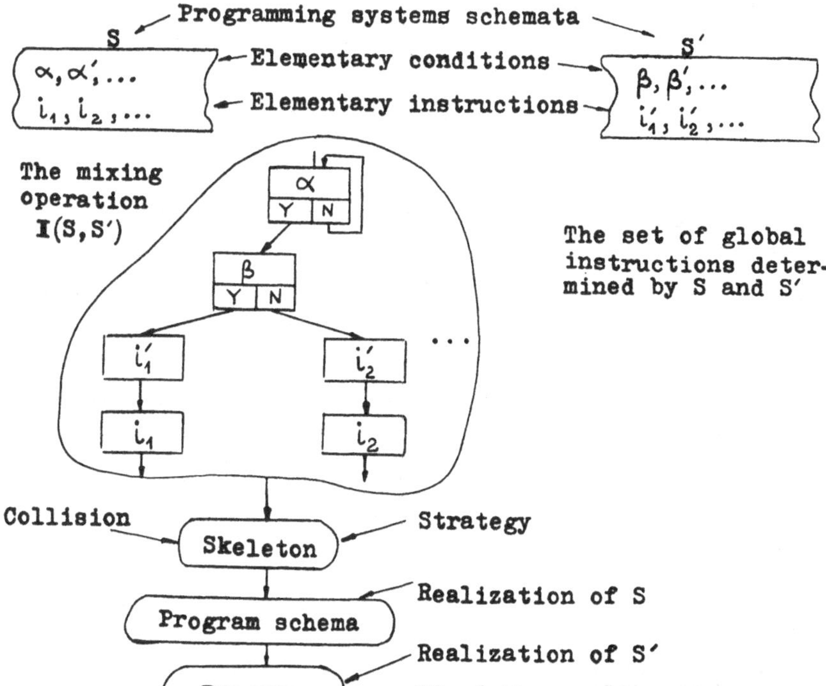

Fig.1 The construction stages of a program

If $f : X \longrightarrow Y$ then by Rgf we denote the counter-domain of f. If $A \subset X$, we shall denote by $f|A$ the restriction of f to the set A . The image of $A \subset X$ under f is denoted by $f(A)$ and the inverse image of $B \subset Y$ by $f^{-1}(B)$ for any function $f : X \longrightarrow Y$

By $\circ$ we denote the composition of relations.

If V is any set of variables and $U \neq \emptyset$, we shall denote by $Val(V,U)$ the set of all valuations of V in U, i.e. the set of all functions from V into U .

If $f : Val(X,U) \longrightarrow Val(X,U)$, $\alpha \subset Val(X,U)$ and Y is a set of variables, we shall denote by $[f]_Y$ the function from $Val(X \cup Y,U)$ into $Val(X \cup Y,U)$ such that $f_Y(v)(x) = v(x)$ if $x \in Y - X$ and $f(v)(x)$ if $x \in X$ and by $[\alpha]_Y$ the set $\{v \in Val(X \cup Y,U) : v|X \in \alpha\}$.

3. <u>Programming systems schemata</u>

Programming systems schemata consist of the elementary instructions and conditions. These instructions and conditions are used to compose the global instructions.

<u>A programming system schema</u> is an ordered system

$$(\Sigma , V , I , C , s)$$

where Σ is a finite alphabet , $|\Sigma| \geqslant 2$,

- V is a set of variables,
- I is a language over Σ , called the set of elementary instructions,
- C is a language over Σ , called the set of elementary conditions,
- $I \cap C = \emptyset$,
- s is a function from $I \cup C$ into $P(V)$, called the scope function.

The programming systems schemata are denoted by S, S', S ,.... .
If $x \in I \cup C$, then $s(x)$ is the set of variables on which x depends.

Example 1. Let T be a nonempty countable set, Σ a finite alphabet, V a set of variables (places) and let

$$[. , .] : FIN(V) \times FIN(V) \xrightarrow{1-1} \Sigma^*$$

$$[.] : FIN(V) \xrightarrow{1-1} \Sigma^* .$$

We define the programming system schema

$$S = (\Sigma , V, Rg[. , .] , Rg[.] , s)$$

where $s([A,B]) = A \cup B$, $s([A]) = A$ for $A,B \in FIN(V)$.

4. <u>Programming systems</u>

By attaching to the programming system schema the realization function which determine the meaning of each elementary instruction and condition we obtain the programming system. Formally :

<u>A programming system</u> is an ordered pair (S,R) , where S is a programming system schema and R is a function defined on $I \cup C$ such that for some nonempty set U :

1. for $i \in I$ $\quad i_R : Val(s(i),U) \longrightarrow Val(s(i),U)$,
2. for $\alpha \in C$ $\quad \alpha_R \subset Val(s(\alpha),U)$.

R is called the realization of S (in the domain U). By $\mathbf{S}$, $\mathbf{S}'$, $\mathbf{S}''$, ... we shall denote the programming systems.

Example 2. Let $\mathbf{S} = (S,R)$, where S is the programming system schema given in Example 1 and R is the realization of S in the set of natural numbers N defined as follows

$$[A,B]_R(v) = v' \overset{df}{\Longleftrightarrow} v'(p) = \begin{cases} v(p) & \text{if } p \in A \cap B \\ v(p)+1 & \text{if } p \in B - A \\ v(p)-1 & \text{if } p \in A - B \end{cases}$$

$$v \in [A]_R \overset{df}{\Longleftrightarrow} v(p) > 0 \quad \text{for } p \in A \ .$$

A programming system $\mathbf{S}$ is called recursive iff the following conditions hold:

1. the sets I,C are recursive,
2. the scope function s is recursive,
3. the domain of the realization of S is the set of natural numbers,
4. for any $i \in I$ i_R is a recursive function and for any $\alpha \in C$ α_R is a recursive set.

We shall consider only programming systems $\mathbf{S} = (S,R)$ with the following property: if <u>true</u> $\in C$ then $s(\underline{true}) \neq \emptyset$ and $R(\underline{true}) = Val(s(true),U)$, where U is the domain of R .

5. <u>Extensions of programming systems</u>

The extension of programs is the fundamental construction one can meet in the problem solving area. In this section we define the concept of programming system extension which will be used to define the program extension.

Two schemata of programming systems S and S' are called independent iff $\Sigma \cap \Sigma' = \emptyset$.

Let $\mathbf{S}$ and $\mathbf{S}'$ be programming systems whose schemata are independent and the domains of realization of $\mathbf{S}$ and $\mathbf{S}'$ are both equal to a nonempty set U . The programming system $\mathbf{S}'' = (S\ ,R\ )$ defined as follows

1. $S'' = (\Sigma \cup \Sigma' \cup \{\circ, \wedge\} , V \cup V', I'', C'', s'')$

   where $I'' = \{ i \circ i' : i \in I \,\&\, i' \in I' \}$

   $C'' = \{ \alpha \wedge \alpha' : \alpha \in C \,\&\, \alpha' \in C' \}$

   $s''(\alpha \wedge \alpha') = s(\alpha) \cup s'(\alpha')$

   $s''(i \circ i') = s(i) \cup s'(i')$

and

2. R'' is the realization of S'' in U such that

$$(i \circ i')_{R''} = [i_{R'}]_Y \circ [i_R]_X$$
$$(\alpha \wedge \alpha')_{R''} = [\alpha_R]_{Y'} \cap [\alpha_{R'}]_{X'}$$
where $X = s'(i')$, $Y = s(i)$, $X' = s(\alpha)$, $Y' = s'(\alpha')$,

is called the $\mathbf{S}'$-extension of $\mathbf{S}$ and is denoted by $Ext(\mathbf{S},\mathbf{S}')$. The schema of $Ext(\mathbf{S},\mathbf{S}')$ is denoted by $Ext(S,S')$ and its realization by $Ext(R,R')$.

6. <u>The mixing operation and global instructions</u>

The global instructions are kind of atoms which are used to form programs. These instructions are constructed by using the mixing operation $\mathbb{I}$.

Two independent schemata of programming systems S,S' are called disjoint iff $V \cap V' = \emptyset$.

The mixing operation $\mathbb{I}$ is defined on the set of pairs (S,S'), where S,S' are disjoint schemata of programming systems. The result $\mathbf{I}(S,S')$, called the set of global instructions (determined by S and S'), **consists of "drawings" (formally they are assumed to be the elements of $(\Sigma \cup \Sigma')^*$) of the following form :**

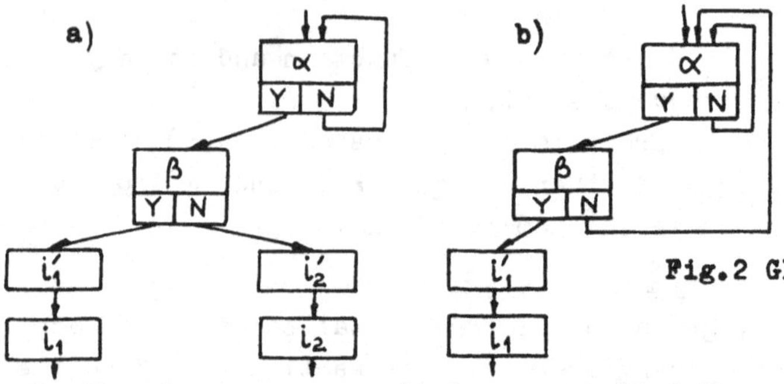

where $\alpha \in C$, $i_1, i_2 \in I$
$\beta \in C'$, $i'_1, i'_2 \in I'$

Fig.2 Global instructions

In the above case α, i_1, i_2 are called the control condition and instructions respectively and β, i'_1, i'_2 the working conditions and instructions respectively. By an input condition for a global instruction we understand a condition α (case a)) and a condition $\alpha \wedge \beta$ (case b)) (see Fig.1). The union of scopes of all elementary instructions and conditions which occur in a global instruction i we denote by $\hat{s}(i)$. If $\beta =$ <u>true</u> then we present the global instructions of Fig.2 in the simpler form (without β) :

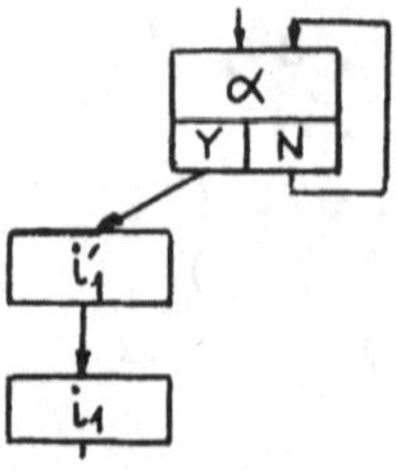

7. The realization of global instructions

Let $\mathbf{S}$, $\mathbf{S}'$ be two programming systems (with disjoint schemata) fixed for our considerations in this section. The set

$$\{v \in Val(V \cup V', U \cup U') : v|V \in Val(V,U),\ v|V' \in Val(V',U')\}$$

is called the set of global states and is denoted by $M_{\mathbf{S},\mathbf{S}'}$. If $v \in M_{\mathbf{S},\mathbf{S}'}$ then $v|V$ is the control part of v and $v|V'$ is the working part of v.

To every global instruction $i \in \mathbb{I}(S,S')$ corresponds the relation

$$\varrho \subset M_{\mathbf{S},\mathbf{S}'} \times M_{\mathbf{S},\mathbf{S}'}$$

such that

$$v \varrho v' \overset{df}{\Longleftrightarrow} \begin{cases} A_1 \vee A_2 & [\text{in the case a) of Fig.2}] \\ A_1 & [\text{in the case b) of Fig.2}] \end{cases}$$

where A_1 denotes the condition $v|s(\alpha) \in \alpha_R$ & $v|s'(\beta) \in \beta_R$ · & $v'|s'(i_1') = i_{1R}'(v|s'(i_1'))$ & $v'|s(i_1) = i_{1R}(v|s(i_1))$ & $v(x) = v'(x)$ for $x \notin s(i_1) \cup s'(i_1')$,

and A_2 denotes the condition $v|s(\alpha) \in \alpha_R$ & $v|s'(\beta) \notin \beta_R$ · & $v'|s'(i_2') = i_{2R}'(v|s'(i_2'))$ & $v'|s(i_2) = i_{2R}(v|s(i_2))$ & $v(x) = v'(x)$ for $x \notin s(i_2) \cup s'(i_2')$.

The relation ϱ is called <u>the realization of i</u> (determined by $\mathbf{S}$ and $\mathbf{S}'$) and is denoted by $\xrightarrow[\mathbf{S},\mathbf{S}']{i}$ (or $\xrightarrow{i}$).

According to the above definition the performance of the global instruction i in the state v is possible only if the input condition for i is satisfied in v. After performing i (if possible) in the state v the new state v' is determined by the appropriate elementary instructions.

If $i_1,\dots,i_n$ are global instructions from $\mathbb{I}(S,S')$ then by $\xrightarrow{i_1 \dots i_n}$ we denote the relation $\xrightarrow{i_n} \circ \xrightarrow{i_{n-1}} \circ \dots \circ \xrightarrow{i_1}$, where $\circ$ denotes the composition operation on relations. If $Y \neq \emptyset$ is a finite subset of $\mathbb{I}(S,S')$ then by $\xrightarrow{Y}$ we denote the relation

$$\bigcup_{\vec{Y} \in A} \xrightarrow{\vec{Y}}$$

where A is the set of all finite sequences $\vec{Y}$ of global instructions which are bijections from $|Y|$ onto Y.

8. The skeletons of programs

By a skeleton of program (over S and S') we shall understand **any triple** $\Phi = (Z, Str, Col)$

where $Z \in FIN(\mathbb{I}(S,S'))$,

Str is a function from $P(Z)$ into $P(P(Z))$, called the strategy of Φ, such that if $X \in P(Z)$ then $Str(X) \subset P(X)$,

Col is a function from $P(Z)$ into $\{0,1\}$ called the collision of Φ, with the following properties:

a) if $Y \in P(Z)$ and $Col(Y) = 1$ then for $i, i' \in Y$ **with** $i \neq i'$ $\hat{s}(i) \cap \hat{s}(i') = \emptyset$,

b) if $Y' \subset Y \subset P(Z)$ then $Col(Y) = 1$ implies $Col(Y') = 1$,

c) $Col(\{i\}) = 1$ for $i \in Z$.

S is called the control schema of Φ and S′ the working schema of Φ.

Examples of strategies.

1. Minimal strategy [HAC 76]

For every set of global instructions $\{i_1, \ldots, i_n\} \subset Z$

$$Str(\{i_1, \ldots, i_n\}) = \{\{i_1\}, \ldots, \{i_n\}\}.$$

2. Maximal strategy [BUR 80] [MÜL 79]

For every set of global instructions $\{i_1, \ldots, i_n\} \subset Z$

$$Str(\{i_1, \ldots, i_n\}) = \{Y \subset \{i_1, \ldots, i_n\} : Col(Y) = 1 \;\&\; \forall Y' \subset Z\, (Y' \supset Y \;\&\; Col(Y') = 1 \Rightarrow Y = Y')\}$$

3. Full strategy

For every set of global instructions $Y \subset Z$ $Str(Y) = P(Y)$.

4. i - forced strategy

For every set of global instructions $Y \subset Z$ $Str(Y) = \{X \in P(Y) : i \in X\}$.

9. Program schemata and programs

Let $\mathbf{S} = (S, R)$ be a programming system and S' a schema of programming system disjoint with S.

By <u>a program schema</u> (over $\mathbf{S}$ and S') we shall understand any triple

$$\mathcal{S} = (\Phi, R_{\mathcal{S}}, v_0)$$

where Φ is a skeleton over S and S'.

$R_{\mathcal{S}}$ is the restriction of the realization R (of S) to the elementary instructions and conditions which occur in the global instructions of Φ,

$v_0 \in Val(V, U)$, v_0 is called the initial control state of $\mathcal{S}$.

<u>A program</u> (over S and S') is any ordered system

$$P = (\mathcal{S}, R_P)$$

where $\mathcal{S}$ is a program schema over $\mathbf{S}$ and S'.

R_P is the restriction of the realization R' to the elementary instructions and conditions from S which occur in the global instructions of $\mathcal{S}$.

By M_P we denote the set $\{v \in M_{\mathbf{S}, S'} : v|V = v_0\}$. M_P is called the set of initial states of P.

Example 3. Petri Nets [HAC 76]

Let $\mathbf{S} = (S, R)$ be the programming system given in Example 2. A Petri net (over S and S'), where S' is disjoint with S, is any program schema $\mathcal{S}$ (over S and S') such that :

1. the global instructions of $\mathcal{S}$ are of the form

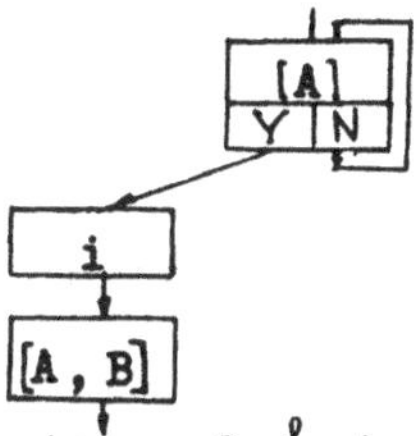

where $A, B \in FIN(V)$ **and** $i \in I'$,

2. the strategy of $\mathcal{S}$ is minimal.

10. The extensions of programs

In this section we assume that P is a program over **S** and **S**$'$. Let **S**$'$ be a programming system and f a one-to-one function from Z into $\Pi(Ext(S,S''),S')$ such that if $i \in Z$ and the instruction i is of the form presented in Fig.2a then f(i) is of the form presented in Fig.3a and if i is of the form presented in Fig.2b then f(i) is of the form presented in Fig.3b :

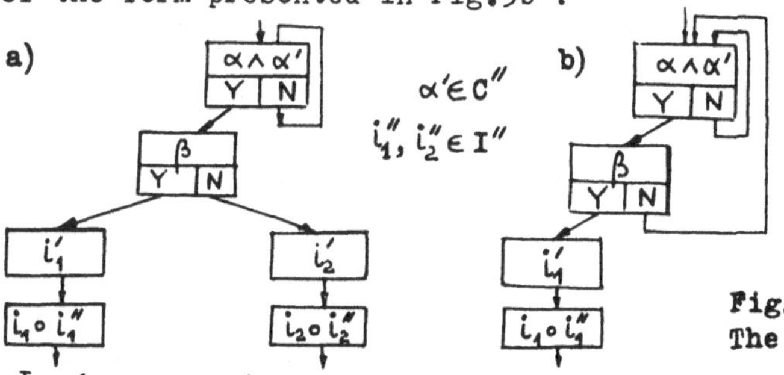

Fig.3
The definition of f(i)

Let $\Phi = (Z, Str, Col)$ be a skeleton of P and let **S**$''$ be a programming system. We assume that S$'$ and S$''$ are disjoint. By $f(\Phi)$ we shall understand the program skeleton over $Ext(S,S'')$ and S$'$ defined as follows: $f(\Phi) = (f(Z), Str', Col')$, where $Str'(Y) = \{f(\sigma) : \sigma \in Str(f^{-1}(Y))\}$, $Col'(Y) = Col(f^{-1}(Y))$ for $Y \subset f(Z)$.

S$''$ - extension of a program P (over **S** and **S**$'$) is any program P$'$ over $Ext(S',S'')$ and **S**$'$, whose skeleton has a form $f(\Phi)$ described above and an initial state $v_{P'}$ of P$'$ has the following property : $v_{P'}|V \cup V' \in M_P$. Thus, any **S**$''$ - extension of P (over **S** and **S**$'$) is a program over $Ext(S,S'')$ and **S**$'$.

11. The transition relation

Let P be a program over **S** and **S**$'$ and let $\perp \notin M_{S,S'}$.
If $v \in M_{S,S'}$, then by $Act_P(v)$ we denote the set of all these global instructions of P , for which the input conditions are satisfied in the state v . If $\sigma \in P(Z)$, then by $\overset{\sigma}{\underset{P}{\Longrightarrow}}$ we shall denote the relation in $M_{S,S'} \times (M_{S,S'} \cup \{\perp\})$ defined as follows :

$$v \overset{\sigma}{\underset{P}{\Longrightarrow}} v' \overset{df}{\Longleftrightarrow} \sigma \in Str(Act_P(v)) \;\&\; [(Col(\sigma) = 1 \;\&\; v \overset{\sigma}{\underset{S,S'}{\Longrightarrow}} v') \vee (Col(\sigma) = 0 \;\&\; v' = \perp)] .$$

The relation $\bigcup_{\sigma \subset Z} \overset{\sigma}{\underset{P}{\Longrightarrow}}$ is called the transition relation of P and is denoted by $\overset{\cdot}{\underset{P}{\Longrightarrow}}$.

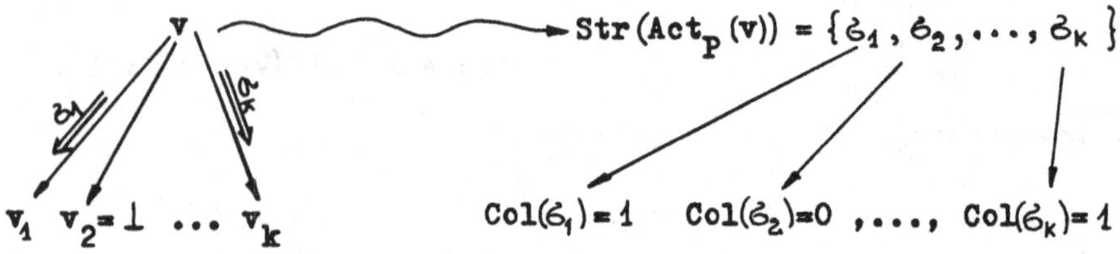

12. <u>Trace languages of programs</u>

Every program P (over S and S′) determine a language over $\Gamma = P(Z)$, where Z is the set of global instructions of P . If $v \in M_{S,S'}$ then by $L(P,v)$ we denote the language over Γ defined as follows :

$$\sigma_1 \ldots \sigma_n \in L(P,v) \overset{df}{\Longleftrightarrow} \exists v_1, \ldots, v_n \in M_{S,S'} \cup \{\bot\} \ (v \overset{\sigma_1}{\underset{P}{\Longrightarrow}} v_1 \overset{\sigma_2}{\underset{P}{\Longrightarrow}} \ldots \ldots \overset{\sigma_n}{\underset{P}{\Longrightarrow}} v_n) .$$

<u>The trace language of P</u> , denoted by $L(P)$, is the language $\bigcup_{v \in M_P} L(P,v)$. The set of all maximal chains in $(L(P), \sqsubseteq)$ where $\sqsubseteq$ is the relation "to be a prefix" is denoted by $L_m(P)$. $L_m(P)$ is the union of two disjoint sets: $L_F(P)$ and $L_\infty(P)$, where $L_F(P)$ is the set of all finite maximal chains and $L_\infty(P)$ is the set of all infinite chains in $(L(P), \sqsubseteq)$. We shall later on consider a chain from $L_m(P)$ as a sequence over Γ such that all prefixes of the sequence compose this chain.

13. <u>Computations</u>

Let P be a program over S and S′. <u>The set of finite computations of P</u> , denoted by $C_F(P)$, is defined in the following way :

$$(v_0, \ldots, v_n) \in C_F(P) \overset{df}{\Longleftrightarrow} (v_0 \in M_P) \& \quad \exists \sigma_1 \ldots \sigma_n \in L_F(P) \left[v_0 \overset{\sigma_1}{\underset{P}{\Longrightarrow}} v_1 \overset{\sigma_2}{\underset{P}{\Longrightarrow}} \ldots \quad \overset{\sigma_n}{\underset{P}{\Longrightarrow}} v_n \right].$$

It follows from the definition of $C_F(P)$ that if $(v_0, \ldots, v_n) \in C_F(P)$ then $v_n = \bot$ or $v_n \in \alpha_R$ for any input condition α of P .

<u>The set of infinite computations of P</u> , denoted by $C_\infty(P)$, is defined in the following way :

$$(v_0, \ldots, v_i, \ldots) \in C_\infty(P) \overset{df}{\Longleftrightarrow} \exists \sigma_1 \ldots \sigma_i \ldots \in L_\infty(P) \ \forall i \geq 1 [(v_{i-1} \overset{\sigma_i}{\underset{P}{\Longrightarrow}} v_i) \& (v_0 \in M_P)].$$

The union $C(P) = C_F(P) \cup C_\infty(P)$ is called the set of computations of P.

14. Problems of optimal deadlock avoidance

In this section we shall describe some results in the field of deadlock avoidance.

P1: Do exist for any program P over $\mathbf{S}$ and $\mathbf{S}'$ a programming system $\mathbf{S}''$ and a program P' over $Ext(\mathbf{S},\mathbf{S}'')$ and $\mathbf{S}'$ which is $\mathbf{S}''$-extension of P such that the following equalities hold:

$$(*) \qquad L_F(P') = \emptyset$$

$$h(L_\infty(P')) = L_\infty(P) \text{ }^{1)} \text{ ?}$$

The answer is YES [SUR 80]. Any program P with the properties (*) is called the solution of optimal deadlock avoidance problem.

P2: Do exist recursive programming systems $\mathbf{S},\mathbf{S}'$ and a program P over $\mathbf{S}$ and $\mathbf{S}'$ such that for every **recursive system $\mathbf{S}''$ and every $\mathbf{S}''$-extension of P the equalities (*) do not hold ?**

The answer is YES [SKO 80] .

P3: Does it exist an effective method which allows for arbitrary recursive programming systems $\mathbf{S},\mathbf{S}',\mathbf{S}''$ and a program P over $\mathbf{S}$ and $\mathbf{S}'$ to construct (**if there exists) $\mathbf{S}''$-extension of P which is the solution of the optimal deadlock avoidance problem?**

The answer is NO [SKO 80] .

Some interesting results for particular programming systems $\mathbf{S},\mathbf{S}',\mathbf{S}''$ and particular classes of programs over $\mathbf{S}$ and $\mathbf{S}'$ are given e.g. in [LAU 79] [ARN 80] [SUR 80] .

15. Cobegin...coend operation

We assume that $\mathbf{S} = (S,R)$ and $\mathbf{S}' = (S',R')$ are programming systems, R and R' are the realizations in a set $U \neq \emptyset$, and S,S' are disjoint.

Let $\varkappa : P(\mathbb{I}(S,S')) \longrightarrow \{0,1\}$. A program P over $\mathbf{S}$ and $\mathbf{S}'$ is called $\varkappa$-program if $Col = \varkappa | P(Z)$, where Col is the collision function of P and Z is the set of global instructions of P.

If P and P' [2] are $\varkappa$-programs over S and S' then cobegin $P \| P'$ coend is the program defined in the following way :

1. the set of global instructions of cobegin $P \| P'$ coend is the union of Z and Z',

1 **h erases the elementary conditions and instructions from S''**

2 **we assume $M_P = M_{P'}$, and $Z \cap Z' = \emptyset$**

2. the strategy Str'' of <u>cobegin</u> $P \| P'$ <u>coend</u> is defined as follows
$Str(X) = \{A \cup B : A \in Str(X \cap Z), B \in Str'(X \cap Z')\}$, where $X \in P(Z'')$,
3. the collision of <u>cobegin</u> $P \| P'$ <u>coend</u> is the restriction of $\varkappa$ to the family $P(Z'')$,

where Z, Z', Z'' are sets of global instructions of P, P' and <u>cobegin</u> $P \| P'$ <u>coend</u> respectively.

References

[ARN 80] Arnold A., Nivat M., Controlling behaviours of systems, some basic concepts and some applications, Lecture Notes in Comp. Sci.88, 1980, pp. 113-122

[BED 77] Bednarek A.R., Ulam S.M., Some remarks on relational composition in computational theory and practice, Lecture Notes in Comp.Sci.56, 1977, pp. 22-32

[BUR 80] Burkhard H.D., The maximum firing strategy in Petri nets gives more power, 3 th Conf.on Math.Problems of Comp.Sci., Zaborów, January 1980, ICS PAS **Reports No 411 ,1980**

[DIJ 75] Dijkstra E.W., Guarded commands, non determinancy and formal derivation of programs, Comm.ACM, vol. 18, No 8, August 1979, pp. 453-457

[HAC 76] Hack M., Decidability questions for Petri nets, Technical Report TR-161, Lab.for Comp.Sci. M.I.T., June 1976

[GEN 80] Genrich H.J., Lautenbach K., Thiagarajan P.S., Substitution systems: a family of system models based on concurrency, Lectures Notes in Comp.Sci.,vol.88, 1980, pp.698-723

[KAR 69] Karp R.M., Miller R.E., Parallel program schemata, J.Comp. Syst.Sci.vol.3, No2, 1969, pp, 147-195

[KEL 72] Keller R.M., Vector replacement system: a formalism modeling asynchronous systems, Princeton University, Technical Report No 117, 1972

[KOT 79] Kotov V.E., An integrated trigger function parallel system, Proc.of the 1st European Conf.on Parallel and Distributed Processing,Toulouse-France, February 14-16, 1979, pp. 191-197

[MAZ 77] Mazurkiewicz A., Concurrent program schemes and their interpretations,DAIMI PB-78,Aarhus Univ.Publ.July, 1977

[LAU 79] Lautenbach K., Thiagarajan P.S., Analysis of a resource allocation problem using Petri nets, Proc.of the 1st European Conf.on Parallel and Distributed Processing,Toulouse-France, February 14-16, 1979, pp. 260-266

[MIL 78] Milner R., Algebras for communicating systems,Internal Report CSR-25-78, University of Edinburgh, June 1978

[MÜL 79] Müldner T., On semantics of parallel programs, ICS PAS Reports No 348, 1979

[PET 76] Petri C.A., Non-sequential processes, ISF GMD, Bonn 1976

[PET 79] Petri C.A., Concurrency as basis of system thinking, Proc. 5th Scandinavian Logic Symposium, ed. Jensen, Mayoh and Møller, Aalborg Universitetsforlag 1979

[SKO 80] **Skowron A.,Concurrent programs /manuscript/**

[SUR 80] **Suraj Z.,Optimal deadlock avoidance /manuscript/**

[WIN 80] Winkowski J., Towards an algebraic description of discrete processes and systems, ICS PAS No 408, 1980.

AXIOMATIC APPROACH TO THE SYSTEM OF FILES

Lucjan Stapp

Institute of Mathematics

Warsaw Technical University

Abstract Two different points of view on sequential files are discussed: internal point of view representing the users and external one representing the system designers. The relational system of sequential file is presented, the axiomatization is done and there is proved that every model of the axiomatized theory is isomorphic with the standard model. An other axiomatized theory of file identificators is presented: consistency of the theory is proved. The "sum" of both theories gives an useful theory of sequential files with identificators.
At tthe end of the paper a class in the language LOGLAN 77 is presented. Every object of this class is a model of the last mentioned theory.

1. Introduction

There are two different points of view on files, one approach is represented by file users, the other by system designers. From the computer users point of view a file is a data set, with some operations, such as WRITE and READ in the case of direct access file or SKIP, REWIND, PUT and GET in the case of sequential file. It is well known that such data type can be considered as a relational system. The axiomatization of such system eases the goal of proving properties of programs operating in the system. But then the question arises: is every model of newly built theory "strongly connected" with our intuitions? And the first part of the paper is reserved to answer for the question.

All above problems are rather uninteresting for system designers. For them problems of access, allo cation in the memory and also problems of catalogues - inserting and deleting the unique information about file, are mostly interested. But both approaches are strongly connected, it is impossible to write on file or read from it, before finding in the catalogue all needed informations about the file under consideration. Hence before user starts to operate on file he has to"open" it. After finishing his actions on the file, he is obliged to "close" his file. Hence, there are two operations OPEN and CLOSE (we call them external following [10]), users and designers are interested in, and to have full representation of all file properties, one has to study both points of view.

The paper deals only with sequential files, since less degree of complication. Other kinds of files can be discussed analogously.

2. Internal properties of sequential file

This part of the paper deals with sequential file from the point of view of common user. For him the most interesting are the operations on the file and their properties.

There are usually 6 operation on sequential file: PUT, GET,SKIP, REWIND, OPEN and CLOSE, there is also one relation ENDofFILE. Their properties will be studed in the section.

It is assumed that records on files have standard form, we do not discuss their structure at all.

2.1 Sequential files as relational system

Let us consider a relational system called later a relational system of sequential files RSF. The universe of RSF consists of two disjoint nonempty sets R and SF. The elements of SF are called sequential files, shortly files, elements of R - records on files.

The following relations are primary in the RSF system

$\overline{\overline{R}}$ - identity in R,

OPF - nonempty subset of SF, when file f belongs to OPF, f is called an opened file,

EOF - nonempty subset of OPF, when file f belongs to EOF, f is in a state called "end of file" and reading from f is an unfeasible operation,

EF - a distinguished element of OPF, called an empty file, no record has been written on EF file

The following operations are in the RSF system

OPEN: $SF \longrightarrow OPF$

CLOSE: $SF \longrightarrow SF$

PUT : $R \times OPF \longrightarrow OPF$

GET : $OPF - EOF \longrightarrow R$

SKIP : $OPF \longrightarrow OPF$

REWIND: $OPF \longrightarrow OPF$

POS : $OPF \longrightarrow OPF$

The intuitions connected with OPEN, CLOSE, PUT, GET, SKIP and REWIND are obvious, the POS operation together with the EOF relation define an actual state of the file.

There are some assumptions (we call them suggestions) about relations and operations, and in this section we state them in a rather intuitive way. Let us consider the sequential file as a tape with cells filled from the left end, with the "head" pointing to one selected cell. Under such intuitive assumption our suggestions are as follows,

1. the result of OPEN operation is an opened file, with the "head" pointing to the first cell from the left,

2. the CLOSE operation is an opposite one to OPEN,
3. the other operations are defined only on opened files and the results are also opened files,
4. EOF(f) is true iff the pointed cell is the last filled one,
5. the result of the REWIND operation is afile with the "head" pointing before the first cell from the left, the operation does not change the content of cells,
6. the SKIP operation moves the "head" by one position to the right, if only it is not the last filled cell, the content of cells does not change,
7. every file has a finite number of filled cells,
8. there are no "holes" on the tape,
9. the result of the POS operation is the file obtained as a part of an argument, from the beginning of the tape to the cell pointed by the "head",
10. the PUT operation writes a record into the cell pointed by the "head" and makes this cell the last filled one,
11. the result of the GET operation is the record from the actually pointed cell.

Let us make two remarks

i). the first three suggestions define the external character of OPEN and CLOSE from the point of view of the other operations

ii). usually in practise the GET operation changes also the file by moving the "head" by one position to the right, in our model such operation may be obtained by superposition of GET and SKIP.

Our intuitions are rather inconvenient to prove formal properties of files, thus we propose the language of algorithmic logic to axiomatize all suggestions on sequential file.

2.2 Axioms and basic facts

To define the set of well formed expressions and formulas we shall follow the pattern of algorithmic logic [6] , [9] .

There are 3 disjoint sets of individual variables: V_0 – the set of propositional variables, V_R– the set of R variables and V_{SF}– the set of SF variables. We shall use the following notation: boo,bool,... $\in V_0$,r,r'... $\in$ f,f',... $\in V_{SF}$. For functors and predicates we shall use symbols of the previous section. We shall introduce a new identity predicate $\overline{\overline{SF}}$ to denote identity in the set SF.

The specific axioms are as follows

A1 OPF(OPEN(f))
the result of the OPEN operation is an opened file

A2 $\sim$OPF(CLOSE(f))
the result of the CLOSE operation is not an opened file

A3 OPEN(OPEN(f)) $\overline{\overline{SF}}$ OPEN(f)
the result of double superposition of OPEN is equal to the result of OPEN

A4 OPEN(CLOSE(f)) $\overline{\overline{SF}}$ REWIND(OPEN(f))
if file is opened than the superposition of CLOSE and OPEN is equal to the result of the REWIND operation

A5 OPF(f)$\Longrightarrow$[OPF(SKIP(f)) & OPF(REWIND(f)) & OPF(POS(f)) & OPF(PUT(r,f
the result of SKIP,REWIND,POS and PUT are opened files

A6 OPF(EF) & EOF(EF) & POS(EF) $\overline{\overline{SF}}$ EF
the properties of the distinguished element EF – the empty file

A7 OPF(f)$\Rightarrow$POS(REWIND(f)) $\overline{\overline{SF}}$ EF
the result of POS on rewinded file is the empty file

A8 OPF(f)$\Rightarrow$REWIND(REWIND(f)) $\overline{\overline{SF}}$ REWIND(f)
rewinding a rewinded file has no effect

A9 OPF(f)$\Rightarrow$REWIND(SKIP(f)) $\overline{\overline{SF}}$ REWIND(f)
rewinding after skipping is the same as rewinding only

A10 OPF(f)$\Rightarrow$[EOF(f)$\Rightarrow$SKIP(f) $\overline{\overline{SF}}$ f]
skipping has no effect, if the file is the state ENDofFILE

A11 OPF(f)$\Rightarrow$PUT(r,f) $\overline{\overline{SF}}$ POS(PUT(r,f))
the superposition of POS and PUT has the same effect as PUT

```
A12 OPF(f)⇒EOF(POS(f))
```
the result of POS is in the state ENDof FILE

```
A13 OPF(f)⇒begin
               while ~EOF(f) do f:=SKIP(f) od
            end true
```
every file has a finite number of elements

```
A14 OPF(f)⇒begin
               f':=REWIND(f);
               while ~(f =_SF f') do f':=SKIP(f') od
            end true
```
REWIND do not change the content of cells

```
A15 OPF(f)⇒begin
               f':=PUT(r,f);
               f1:=REWIND(f);
               f2:=REWIND(f');
               boo:=true;
               while boo &~EOF(f2) do
                 r1:=GET(f1);
                 if ~EOF(f1) then boo:=(GET(f1) =_R r1) else boo:=false fi;
                 f1:=SKIP(f1);
                 f2:=SKIP(f2);
               od
            end (boo & r =_R r1)
```
PUT does not change the beginning of the argument and puts the record at the end of the file

```
A16 f =_SF f1 ⟺ [OPF(f)⟺ OPF(f1)   &   begin
                                         f':=OPEN(f);
                                         f":=OPEN(f1);
                                       end (K boo  &  M boo)
```

where K is the following program

```
K:   begin
       boo:=true;
       f':=REWIND(f');
       f":=REWIND(f");
       while ~EOF(f') & ~EOF(f") & boo do
         boo:=(GET(f')  =_R GET(f"));
         f':=SKIP(f');
         f":=SKIP(f");
       od;
       boo:=boo & EOF(f') & EOF(f");
     end
```

and M is the following program

```
M:   begin
       f':=POS(f');
       f":=POS(f");
       K
     end
```

the above axiom defines the equality relation in SF, two files are equal when they have the same elements and their POS'es are also equal (i.e. "heads" are in the same position)

A17 - A21 axioms asserting that SKIP,POS,REWIND, PUT and GET are undetermined when $\sim$OPF(f), of the form
$\sim$ OPF(f)$\Rightarrow$SKIP(f)= <u>while</u> <u>true</u> <u>do</u> <u>od</u> f

A22 - A24 axioms of reflexibility, symmetry and transivity of $\overline{\overline{R}}$.

We admit logical axioms and rules of inference, as in[6] .

The system $\langle L,A,C\rangle$ where L is a language of algorithmic logic, A is the set of specific axioms defined above and C is the consequence operation defined by the logical axioms and the rules of inference will be called later the formal internal theory of sequential files (ITSF).

Before proving some facts about our theory let us remark that our axioms are strongly connected with the suggestions from the previous section.

Now let us formulate the following

<u>Proposition 1</u>

Let K be the program defined in the axiom A16. Then A12$\vdash$ K <u>true</u> ∎

Hence we have obtained that the equality in SF is strongly programmable in the other terms of the ITSF theory. Other properties of this relation are studied in the following

<u>Proposition 2</u>

For any f,f',f" $\in$ SF and any r $\in$ R the following are theorems in ITSF

(i) $f \overline{\overline{_{SF}}} f$ (in particular EF $\overline{\overline{_{SF}}}$ EF)

(ii) $f \overline{\overline{_{SF}}} f' \Rightarrow f' \overline{\overline{_{SF}}} f$

(iii) $[f \overline{\overline{_{SF}}} f'$ & $f' \overline{\overline{_{SF}}} f"] \Rightarrow f \overline{\overline{_{SF}}} f"$

(iv) $f \overline{\overline{_{SF}}} f' \Rightarrow [OPF(f) \Leftrightarrow OPF(f')]$

(v) $f \overline{\overline{_{SF}}} f' \Rightarrow OPEN(f) \overline{\overline{_{SF}}} OPEN(f')$

(vi) $f \overline{\overline{_{SF}}} f' \Rightarrow CLOSE(f) \overline{\overline{_{SF}}} CLOSE(f')$

(vii) $[f \overline{\overline{_{SF}}} f'$ & $OPF(f)] \Rightarrow [EOF(f) \Leftrightarrow EOF(f')]$

(viii) $[f \overline{\overline{_{SF}}} f'$ & $OPF(f)] \Rightarrow SKIP(f) \overline{\overline{_{SF}}} SKIP(f')$

ix) $[f \overline{\overline{\overline{SF}}}\ f' \ \&\ OPF(f)] \Rightarrow REWIND(f) \overline{\overline{\overline{SF}}}\ REWIND(f')$

x) $[f \overline{\overline{\overline{SF}}}\ f' \ \&\ OPF(f)] \Rightarrow POS(f) \overline{\overline{\overline{SF}}}\ POS(f')$

xi) $[f \overline{\overline{\overline{SF}}}\ f' \ \&\ OPF(f)\ \&\ \sim EOF(f)] \Rightarrow GET(f) \overline{\overline{R}}\ GET(f')$

xii) $[f \overline{\overline{\overline{SF}}}\ f' \ \&\ OPF(f)] \Rightarrow PUT(r,f) \overline{\overline{\overline{SF}}}\ PUT(r,f')$

Proof will be omitted here. ∎

2.3 Models

This section deals with the properties of models of the ITSF theory. We shall prove that a model exists (the theory is consistent) and that every model has a standard form. But before it, let us observe as a simple corrolary from Proposition 2, that in every model $\mathcal{M}$ of the ITSF theory the relation $\overline{\overline{\overline{SF}}}$ is a congruence. Hence we obtain

Proposition 3

If a relational system $\mathcal{M}$ is a model for the ITSF theory then the quotient model $\mathcal{M} / \overline{\overline{\overline{SF}}}, \overline{\overline{R}}$ is proper for identity. ∎

Now, let us assume that R is a fixed set, i.e. we know the form and length of records. Let $\overline{FSEQ(R)}$ be a set of all finite sequences over R of the form $r_1, r_2, \ldots, r_n$ and let FSEQ(R) be a subset of $\overline{FSEQ(R)} \times \omega$, such that

$f = ((r_1, r_2, \ldots, r_n), k) \in FSEQ(R) \Leftrightarrow 0 \le k \le n$

Let SF(R) be the following relational system

$\langle R \cup FSEQ(R) \times \{o,c\}\ ,\ \overline{\overline{R}}, ef, op, cl, eof, pu, ge, re, sk, po, eq, opd \rangle$

where relations and operations are defined as follows:

let $f \in FSEQ(R)$, $f = (r_1, r_2, \ldots, r_n), k)$ $0 \le k \le n$, then

1. $ef = ((\mathcal{E}, 0), o)$ where $\mathcal{E}$ is an empty sequence
2. opd $((f,w))$ is true iff $w = o$
3. $op((((r_1, \ldots, r_n), k), w)) = (((r_1, \ldots, r_n), 0), o)$
4. $cl((f,w)) = (f,c)$
5. $eof((f,w))$ is true iff $w = o$ and $n = k$
6. $re((f,o)) = (((r_1, \ldots, r_n), 0), o)$

7. $sk((f,o)) = \begin{cases} (f,o) & k=n \\ (((r_1,\dots,r_n),k+1),o) & k<n \end{cases}$

8. $po((f,o)) = \begin{cases} (((r_1,\dots,r_k),k),o) & k>0 \\ ef & k=0 \end{cases}$

9. $ge((f,o))$ is defined iff $\sim eof((f,o))$ and then

$ge((((r_1,\dots,r_k,r_{k+1},\dots,r_n),k),o)) = r_{k+1}$

10. $pu((((r_1,\dots,r_k,\dots,r_n),k),o),r) = (((r_1,\dots,r_k,r),k+1),o)$

11. $eq(f,f')$ is true iff $f=(((r_1,\dots,r_n),k),w)$ and

$f'=(((r_1',\dots,r_m'),k'),w')$ and $w=w'$ and $k=k'$ and $n=m$

and for any j, $1\leq j\leq n$, $r_j \overline{\overline{R}}\, r_j'$

12. re, sk, po, ge and pu are not defined for $w=c$.

It is easy to prove the following

<u>Theorem 1</u>

SF(R) is a model for the ITSF theory. ∎

<u>Corollary</u>

The ITSF theory is a consistent one. ∎

One can also prove the following

<u>Theorem 2</u>

If $\mathcal{M}$ is a model of the ITSF theory over the fixed set R of records, then the quotient model $\mathcal{M}/\overline{\overline{SF}}$ is isomorphic with the standard model SF(R). ∎

Proof of the theorem follows from the following

<u>Proposition 4</u>

Any element of SF is equal (in the terms of $\overline{\overline{SF}}$) with the file obtained from the empty file EF using certain finite iteration of the following operations: OPEN, CLOSE, PUT, REWIND, SKIP and POS. ∎

Thereby we have obtained that every model of the ITSF theory, proper for SF, is identical (with respect to isomorphism) with very simple relational system, strongly related to our intuitions.

To state that the ITSF theory is not a trivial one, let us formulte the following

Theorem 3

The internal theory of sequential files ITSF is an undecidable one.

Proof follows from the Dańko's undecidability criterion [3]. ∎

3. File descriptors and catalogues

This section of the paper deals with external problems of files, such as unique representation of file, catalogues, deleting and inserting the about a file in a catalogue. Also problems of allocation of a file to a process and hence problems of multiaccess and unique acess will be considered. As usuall in practice, a file is represented by its external name, but we do not consider problems connected with names such as safety or protection. When we shall speak "file" in this section, we will understand by it the unique file descriptor.

3.1 Relational system of file descriptors.

Let us consider a relational system called later a relational system of file descriprors RSD. The universe of the RSD system consists of 3 disjoint nonempty sets N, NF and K. The elements of N will be called external names of files, shortly names, the elements of NF - file descriptors and elements of K - catalogues of file descriptors or catalogues. The following relations are primary in the RSD system:

$=$ - identity in $N \times NF$

IDENT - nonempty subset of $N \times K$

MULTACC - nonempty subset of NF

FREE - nonempty subset of $N \times K$

NONE - a distinguished element of N

NEW - a distinguished element of NF

The following operations are in the RSD system:

NAME: $NF \longrightarrow N$

FIND: $N \times K \longrightarrow NF$

CATALOG: $N \times NF \times K \longrightarrow K$

PURGE: $N \times K \longrightarrow K$

REQUIRE: $NF \times K \longrightarrow K$

RELEASE: $NF \times K \longrightarrow K$

CHANGEACC: $NF \longrightarrow NF$

The intuitions connected with above relations and operations are as follows

1. NEW is the file descriptor, describing an oneaccessible reserved file which name is none,
2. NONE is not a name of any catalogued file,
3. NAME gives a name of file descriptor,
4. FIND finds a file descriptor of given name in given catalogue,
5. CATALOG puts a file descriptor with given name in given catalogue,
6. PURGE removes a file descriptor with given name from given catalogue,
7. in every catalogue is at most one file descriptor with given name,
8. CATALOG and FIND do not change properties of access and freeing,
9. IDENT(n,k) iff the file descriptor named n is an element of the catalogue k,
10. FREE(n,k) iff the file named n is free in the catalogue k, i.e. any demand of this file can be fullfilled,
11. REQUIRE is defined only on free files and is an operation of demandi file in the sence of file descriptor; after executing REQUIRE file i allocated to demanding job (process) and only to this job if the file is oneaccessible,
12. RELEASE is the opposite operation to REQUIRE ,
13. MULTACC(nf) iff nf is the file descriptor of multiaccessible file,

4. CHANGEACC is an operation which changes the kind of access of the file from oneaccessible to multiaccessible,

5. CHANGEACC does not change the kind of access for multiaccessible files,

6. every multiaccessible file is free in the catalogue the file under consideration is catalogued in.

3.2 The axioms

As in the part 2 of the paper, we shall use the language of algorithmic logic to formalize above intuitions.
There are 3 disjoint sets of individual variables V_N, V_{NF} and V_K of N, NF and K variables respectively. The elements of V_N will be denoted by n,n',... elements of V_{NF} by nf,nf',... and elements of V_K by k,k',... For functors and predicates we shall use the symbols of previous section.
We shall introduce a new predicate ONEACC to denote oneaccessible files.
The specific axioms are as follows

ax1. $ONEACC(nf) \Leftrightarrow \sim MULTACC(nf)$
the definition of the new predicate

ax2. $NAME(NEW) = NONE \ \& \ ONEACC(NEW)$
properties of NEW

ax3. $\sim IDENT(NONE,k)$
file without name is not in any catalogue

ax4. $\sim IDENT(n,PURGE(n,k))$
after deleting there is no file identificator with given name in the catalogue

ax5. $[\sim (NAME(nf) = n) \ \& \sim (n = NONE)] \Rightarrow [IDENT(NAME(nf),k) \Leftrightarrow IDENT(NAME(nf),PURGE(n,k))]$
PURGE removes at most one file descriptor

ax6. $\sim (n = NONE) \Rightarrow IDENT(n,CATALOG(n,nf,k))$
after inserting there is file descriptor with given name in given catalogue

ax7. $[\sim (NAME(nf) = n) \ \& \ \sim (n = NONE)] \Rightarrow [IDENT(NAME(nf),k) \Leftrightarrow IDENT(NAME(nf),CATALOG(n,nf',k))]$
CATALOG inserts at most one file descriptor

ax8. $[NAME(nf) = n \ \& \ \sim (n = NONE)] \Rightarrow FIND(n,CATALOG(n,nf,k)) = nf$

ax9. IDENT(n,k) ⟹ NAME(FIND(n,k)) = n

ax10. MULTACC(nf) ⟺ MULTACC(FIND(n,CATALOG(n,nf,k)))

ax11. FREE(n,k) ⟺ FREE(NAME(FIND(n,k)),k)
the above four axioms describe properties of FIND

ax12. FREE(n,k) ⟹ IDENT(n,k)
free file is in the catalogue

ax13. [ONEACC(nf) & FREE(NAME(nf),k)] ⟹ FREE(NAME(nf),REQUIRE(nf,k))

ax14. IDENT(NAME(nf),k) ⟹ FREE(NAME(nf),RELEASE(nf,k))
properties of REQUIRE and RELEASE

ax15. [IDENT(NAME(nf),k) & MULTACC(nf)] ⟹ FREE(NAME(nf),k)
multiaccessible file is free (if only catalogued)

ax16. MULTACC(CHANGEACC(nf))
the result of CHANGEACC is a multiaccessible file

ax17. NAME(nf) = NAME(CHANGEACC(nf))
CHANGEACC does not change names

ax18. ~IDENT(n,k) ⟹ FIND(n,k) = <u>while</u> <u>true</u> <u>do</u> <u>od</u>; nf

ax19. ~FREE(NAME(nf),k) ⟹ REQUIRE(nf,k) = <u>while</u> <u>true</u> <u>do</u> <u>od</u>; k

ax20. ~IDENT(NAME(nf),k) ⟹ RELEASE(nf,k) = <u>while</u> <u>true</u> <u>do</u> <u>od</u>;k

ax21. CATALOG(NONE,nf,k) = <u>while</u> <u>true</u> <u>do</u> <u>od</u>; k
axioms of undefining of FIND,REQUIRE,RELEASE and CATALOG in special cases.

ax22 - ax24 reflexibility, symmetry and transivity of = .

Now, the theory of file descriptors ATD is defined as formal system ⟨L,ax,C⟩, where L is a language of algorithmic logic, ax is the set of specific axioms defined above and C is the consequence operation defined by rules of inference (see [6]).

3.3 A model of ATD

Let us suppose that the universe of the relational system DM under consideration is as follows:
take the set ω of natural numbers as N, take $\omega\times\{0,1\}\times\{0,1\}$ as NF and take $\mathcal{K}$, a subset of the family of all finite subsets of NF,

$\{\subset 2^{FIN(NF)}$, such that if $a,b \in \{0,1\}$ then the following holds

$$k \in \mathcal{H} \Longleftrightarrow \{[(n,a,b) \in k \ \& \ (n',a',b') \in k \ \& \ n = n'] \Rightarrow [a \quad a' \ \& \ b \quad b']\}$$

There are following relations and operations in the DM system (names of appropriate operations and relations of RSD are in brackets): 0 (NONE), req(NEW), na(NAME), fi(FIND), cat(CATALOG), pur(PURGE), reqe(REQUIRE), rel(RELEASE), cha(CHANGEACC), mult(MULTACC), fr(FREE), id (IDENT) – defined as follows

1. $req = (0,0,1)$

2. $na(n,a,b) = n$

3. $$fi(n,k) = \begin{cases} (n,a,b) & \text{if there is } (n,a,b) \in k \\ \text{undef.} & \text{in opp. case} \end{cases}$$

4. $$cat(n,(n',a,b),k) = \begin{cases} k - \{nf \in k : na(nf) = n\} \cup (n,a,b) & \text{if } n > 0 \\ \text{undef.} & \text{if } n = 0 \end{cases}$$

5. $pur(n,k) = k - \{nf \in k:\ na(nf) = n\}$

6. $id(n,k) \Longleftrightarrow \exists nf \in k,\ na(nf) = n$

7. $$fr(n,k) = \begin{cases} \underline{\text{true}} & \exists\ nf = (n,a,b) \in k \ \ \& \ \ (a = 1 \vee b = 1) \\ \underline{\text{false}} & \text{in opp. case} \end{cases}$$

8. $mult(n,a,b) \Leftrightarrow b = 1$

9. $cha(n,a,b) = (n,a,1)$

10. $$reqe((n,a,b),k) = \begin{cases} k - \{nf \in k:\ na(nf) = n\} \cup \{(n,0,b)\} & \text{if } fr(n,k) \\ \text{undef.} & \text{in opp. case} \end{cases}$$

11. $$rel((n,a,b),k) = \begin{cases} k - \{nf \in k:\ na(nf) = n\} \cup \{(n,1,b)\} & \text{if } id(n,k) \\ \text{undef.} & \text{in opp. case} \end{cases}$$

There is easy to prove the following

<u>Theorem 4</u>

The DM system is a model of the ATD theory ∎

<u>Corollary</u>

The ATD theory is a consistent one.

∎

Contrary to the part 2 of the paper, in this instance there is no standard model. But the following theorem mirrors the very important role of the DM system

<u>Theorem 5</u>

Let M be a model of the ATD theory, such that the set of names is a denumerable one and every catalogue includes at most finite number of file descriptors. Then M is isomorphic with the DM system. ∎

<u>4. Catalogues and files</u>

In the section the system of files with descriptors will be described. All facts introduced before are helpful to build the new theory, which is an useful one.

4.1. Relational system of files with descriptors.

The relational system RSDF of files with descriptors is a "sum" of the system of sequential files RSF and the system of file descriptors RSD. In the RSDF system we introduce a new sort NSF SF NF, called the set of sequential files with descriptors or named sequential files. The following relations and operations are in the RSDF system

$\underset{D}{=}$ identity in NSF

new a distinguished element of NSF

eof nonempty subset of NSF

namefile: $NSF \longrightarrow NF$

confile: $NSF \longrightarrow SF$

open: $N \times K \longrightarrow NSF \times K$

op: $NSF \longrightarrow NSF$

close: $N \times K \longrightarrow NSF \times K$

cl: $NSF \longrightarrow NSF$

put: $NSF \times R \longrightarrow NSF$

get: NSF ⟶ R

skip: NSF ⟶ NSF

rewind: NSF ⟶ NSF

catalog: NSF × K ⟶ K

purge: NSF × K ⟶ K

changeacc: NSF ⟶ NSF

filename: NF × K ⟶ NSF

The operations namefile and confile are assumed to be protections, all the others exept filename can be defined using namefile and confile in terms of RSF and RSD. Filename is, roughly speaking, an opposite operation to namefile.

4.2 The axioms

The theory of named sequential files is obtained as a "sum" of ITSF and ADT. The set of variables is a sum of V_O, V_R and V_{SF} from ITSF, V_N V_{NF} and V_K from ADT. We also introduce a new sort of variables V_S to denote elements of NSF. The elements of V_s will be denoted by s,s',... All predicates and functors from ITSF and ADT are also functors and predicates in the theory under consideration. We also introduce new predicates and functors using symbols of the previous section. The set of specific axioms is also a sum of 3 sets: the set A of all specific axioms of ITSF, the set ax of all specific axioms of ADT and the set AX of axioms defined below

AX1. eof(s) = EOF(confile(s))

AX2. namefile(op(s)) = namefile(s)

confile(op(s)) = OPEN(confile(s))

AX3. namefile(cl(s)) = namefile(s)

confile(cl(s)) = CLOSE(confile(s))

AX4. get(s) = GET(confile(s))

AX5. namefile(put(r,s))= namefile(s)

confile(put(r,s))= PUT(r,confile(s))

AX6. namefile(skip(s))= namefile(s)

confile(skip(s))= SKIP(confile(s))

AX7. namefile(rewind(s))= namefile(s)

confile(rewind(s))= REWIND(confile(s))

AX8. catalog(s,k)= CATALOG(NAME(namefile(s)),namefile(s),k)

AX9. purge(s,k)= PURGE(NAME(namefile(s),k)

AX10. namefile(changeacc(s))= CHANGEACC(namefile(s))

confile(changeacc(s))= confile(s)

AX11. namefile(new)= NEW

confile(new)= EF

AX12. IDENT(NAME(nf),k) $\Rightarrow$ namefile(filename(nf,k)) $\equiv_{D}$ nf

AX13. $\sim$IDENT(NAME(nf),k) $\Rightarrow$ filename(nf,k)= <u>while</u> <u>true</u> <u>do</u> <u>od</u>; s

AX14. confile(filename(namefile(s),catalog(s,k)))) $\equiv_{SF}$ confile(s)

AX15. close(s,k)=
```
begin
  nf:=namefile(s);
  n:=NAME(nf );
  if IDENT(n,k) then k:=RELEASE(nf,k) fi;
  s:=cl(s);
end (s,k)
```

AX16. open(n,k) =
```
begin
  if IDENT(n,k) then
    nf:=FIND(n,k);
    if FREE(n,k) then
      k:=REQUIRE(nf,k);
      s:=filename(nf,k);
      s:=op(s);
    else while true do od;
    fi
  else s:=new;
  fi
end (s,k)
```

<u>Remark</u> in axioms AX2 – AX11 and AX13,AX15, AX16 "= " is understood as definition.

As in previous parts, we define the algorithmic theory of named sequential files NSFT.

Before stating some facts about models of NSFT, let us remark that the axioms AX13 and AX14 give us conditions about connections between elements of the set of catalogues K and files with descriptors,i.e. every catalogue includes at most one file descriptor connected (by namefile operation) with the given sequential file belonging to NSF. The above condition is rather natural from the intuitive point of view.
The model of the NSFT theory can be obtained as a "sum" of standard model for ITSF and the DM model for ATC, where S is a subset of a cartesian product (diagonal) of NF and SF, namefile and confile are projections and other operations are defined directly by axioms.
The model of the NSFT theoryare interesting mainly for system designers, because only models of NFST can be treated as proper file systems. The last two axioms (AX15 and AX16) can be treated as procedures defining open and close. The others are defined as in the"standard" model of NSFT, described above (as a corallary from theorems 2 and 5).
We shall try to describe how to program the whole file system in the section of the paper.

5. The type declaration

This section deals with the presentation of a type declaration in the language LOGLAN 77 [4] . First let us formulate some assumptions to simplify the discussion. All files will be input - output files, i.e. any process can write on its (allocated to this process) file and read from this file. Procedures to read, write , skip rewind etc. are programmed in differnt ways, depending on earlier defined kind of access To program the relational system of file descriptors, let us assume that there is a type describing dictionaries (for precisely definition see [9]), of the following form

```
type ARTofELEM: class; ..... fin;

type ELEMofDICT: class;
  var z: ARTofELEM;
  ...............
fin;

type DICTIONARY: class;
  type delete: procedure (x:ELEMofDICT);
    ..............
  fin;
  type insert: procedure (x:ELEMofDICT);
    ..............
  fin;
  type member: function (y:ARTofELEM):boolean;
    ..............
  fin;
  type amember:function (y:ARTofELEM):ELEMofDICT;
    ..............
  fin;
fin;
```

The intuitions connected with the above type declaration are as follows

(1) "delete" removes an element from the dictionary

(2) "insert" puts an element into dictionary

(3) "member" controls if there exists an element with the attribute y in the dictionary

(4) "amember" finds an element with given attribute y (if only is in the dictionary)

There are many different data structures to realize dictionaries such as hash lists, trees, 2-3 trees etc. (see [1]), but we do not interest to discuss the problem in the paper.

To simplify our declaration, let us also assume that there exists a type FILENAME, prefixed by ARTofELEM. Then the declaration of FILEIDENT is as follows

```
type FILEIDENT: ELEMofDICT class;
  var free,acc: boolean,
      name:FILENAME,
      SF:SEQFILE
fin;
```

The intuitions of free,acc and name result from section 3, SF is a pointer to "real" file.

Now let us present the declaration of the type CATALOG. Let us recall, that in LOGLAN 77 there is a system type "monitor". This type gives us a tool to synchronize parallel processes. The monitor is a data structure (for shared variables) and a set of procedures and functions operating on it (we call them "entry" ones). The shared variables are common for all processes, but an access to these data is possible only by use of entry procedures. It is proved (see [7]) that in every moment of parallel program computation at most one entry procedure of the monitor can be executed. The above gives us safety, when we operate on the catalogue, assure that in any moment at most one process changes a structure of the catalogue.

Let us also assume that there exists a procedure named ERROR, the result of this procedure is stopping the execution of program and signalizing an error. In axioms the suitable part is represented by "while true do od"

Under the above assumptions, the CATALOGUE type is as follows

```
type CATALOGUE: monitor class;
  var DICT:DICTIONARY;
  type CATALOG: entry procedure (x:FILEIDENT; n:FILENAME);
      var y:FILEIDENT;
      if DICT.member(n) then
        y:=DICT.amember(n);
        call DICT.delete(y);
      fi;
      x.name:= n;
      call DICT.insert(x);
  fin;
  type PURGE: entry procedure (n:FILENAME);
      var x:FILEIDENT;
      if DICT.member(n) then
        x:=DICT.amember(n);
        call DICT.delete(x);
      fi
  fin;
  type FIND: entry function (n:FILENAME):FILEIDENT;
      if DICT.member(n) then result(DICT.amember(n))
      else call ERROR fi;
  fin;
  type IDENT: entry function (n:FILENAME):boolean;
      result (DICT.member(n));
  fin;
  type REQUIRE:entry procedure (x:FILEIDENT);
      var n:FILENAME, y: FILEIDENT;
```

```
      n:= x.name;
      if DICT.member(n) then
        y:=DICT.amember(n);
        if y.free ∨ y.acc then
          call DICT.delete(y);
          x.free:=false;
          x.acc:=y.acc;
          call DICT.insert(x);
        else call ERROR fi
      else call ERROR fi
  fin;
  type RELEASE: entry procedure (x:FILEIDENT);
      var n:FILENAME;
      n:= x.name;
      if DICT.member(n) then
        call DICT.delete(amember(n));
        x.free:=true;
        call DICT.insert(x);
      else call ERROR fi;
  fin;
  DICT:=new DICTIONARY;
fin of CATALOGUE;
```

Now the question arises, where are our files stored? We assume that the files are stored on discs. Without loss of generality it is assumed, that records on the disc and records on the files have the same length. Let us also assume that the disc is represented by two types: DISCSTORMANAG and DISCFILESERVICE. First of them, DISCSTORMANAG, is a store manager analogous to that described in [8] . Under assumption, that the type REALADR describes a real adress on the disc, DISCSTORMANAG has the form as follows

```
type DISCSTORMANAG: monitor class;
  type occup: procedure (u.REALADR);
      ...............
  fin;
  type freeing: entry procedure (max:integer; w:REALADR);
      ...............
  fin;
  type firstfree:entry function (max:integer):REALADR;
      var u:REALADR; i:integer;
      ...............
      for i:= 1 step 1 to max do
        call occup (u+i);
      od;
      result (u);
  fin
fin;
```

he intuitions connected with the above procedures are as follows:

occup" occupies the disc records with given real adress,

firstfree" finds an adress of the first free of the sequence of "max"

ecords and occupies this sequence the result of the procedure is the

dress of the first free record,

freeing" is an opposite one to the above.

ISCFILESERVICE describes operations of real reading and writing on disc.

ence its declaration is as follows

```
ype DISCFILESERVICE:class;
 type READ: function (adr:REALADR):RECORD;
     ...............
 fin;
 type WRITE:procedure (adr:REALADR;r:RECORD);
     ...............
 fin
in;
```

ow,the DISC declaration is as follows

```
ype DISC:class;
 var DSM:DISCSTORMANAG, DFS:DISCFILESERVICE;
in;
```

inally we can declare the main type in the section - SEQFILE

```
ype SEQFILE:class (DISK:DISC; KAT:CATALOGUE; max:integer);
 var FI:FILEIDENT, CL:boolean, pos,length:integer,adroffirst:REALADR,
    BWM:BW;
 hidden protected pos,length,BWM,CL,adroffirst,BRACKET;
 type BW:monitor class;
     var BWbusy:boolean, BWq:head;
     type OCC: entry procedure;
         if BWbusy then call delay (BWq) fi;
         BWbusy:= true;
     fin;
     type FREE: entry procedure;
         BWbusy:= false;
         call continue (BWq);
     fin;
     BWq:= new head;
     BWbusy:= false;
 fin BW;
 type BRACKET: class;
     var rob:boolean;
     rob:= FI.acc;
     if rob then call BWM.OCC fi;
     inner;
```

```
        if rob then call BWM.FREE fi;
    fin;
    type put: BRACKET procedure (r:RECORD);
        var x:REALADR;
        x:=adroffirst+pos;
        call DISK.DFS.WRITE(x,r);
        pos:=pos+1;
        length:=pos;
    fin;
    type get: BRACKET function : RECORD;
        var x:REALADR;
        if (pos=length) then call ERROR fi;
        x:=adroffirst+pos;
        result (DISK.DFS.READ(x));
    fin;
    type skip: BRACKET procedure;
        if ~(length=pos) then pos:=pos+1 fi;
    fin;
    type rewind: BRACKET procedure;
        pos:=0;
    fin;
    type eof: BRACKET function:boolean;
        result (pos=length);
    fin;
    type op: procedure;
        CL:=false;
    fin;
    type close: BRACKET procedure;
        CL:=true;
        call KAT.RELEASE;
    fin;
    type catalog: BRACKET procedure (n:FILENAME);
        call KAT.CATALOG(FI,n);
    fin;
    type purge: BRACKET procedure;
        call KAT.PURGE(FI.name);
    fin;
    type changeacc: BRACKET procedure;
        FI.acc:=true;
    fin;
    pos:=0;
    length:=0;
    CL:=true;
    BWM:=new BW;
    FI:=new FILEIDENT;
    FI.name:=EMPTYNAME;
    FI.free:=false;
    FI.acc:=false;
    FI.SF:=this SEQFILE;
    adroffirst:=DISK.firstfree(max);
fin of SEQFILE;
```

To service defined above type of sequential file we need also extra procedure, with the following declaration

```
type open: function (n:NAMEFILE;KAT:CATALOGUE):SEQFILE;
  var NF:FILEIDENT, SF:SEQFILE, DISK:DISC,max:integer;
  if KAT.IDENT(n) then
     NF:=KAT.FIND(n);
     if NF.free ∨ NF.acc then
       call KAT.REQUIRE(NF);
       SF:=NF.SF;
       call SF.op;
       result (SF);
     else call ERROR fi;
  else
    DISK:= ...;
     max:= ...;
    comment fixing the disc, file will be stored on;
    SF:=new SEQFILE(DISK,KAT,max);
    call SF.op;
    result (SF);
  fi
fin;
```

The reader can verify that the relational system defined by the declaration of the type SEQFILE (i.e. every object of this type) is built in agreement with the model built in the end of section 4. Hence it is a model of the NSFT theory.

6. Final remarks

this paper aims to describe a method of building an important part of an operating system - the system of files. We have interested only in sequential files, but one can use the same method to describe direct files, sequential keyed files etc.

The most important is, in our opinion, the way to obtain the declaration of file system class in the high level language of programming. First the theory of files NSFT has been built as a sum of two simplier theories ITSF and ADT. A model of the NSFT theory gives us ideas for the declaration of the type SEQFILE. Some intuitions are obtained froma model of dictionaries ([9]) and a model of storage manager ([8]).

And we believe this is the way to program all components of the operating system.

Acknowledgment

The author is greatly indebted to prof. A. Salwicki for his help and useful remarks.

References

[1]. Aho,A.,Hopcroft,J.,Ullman,J., The Design and Analysis of Computer Algorithms, Addison-Wesley Publishing Co., Reading Ma., 1974

[2]. Brinch Hansen,P., The SOLO Operating System, Software - Practice & Experience 6,2,1976,141-205

[3]. Dańko,W.,A Criterion of Undecidability of Algorithmic Theories, to appear in Fundamenta Informaticae

[4]. LOGLAN 77 raport - internal raport of Institute of Computer Science, Warsaw University, December 1979

[5]. Mirkowska,G., Algorithmic Logic and Its Application in Program Theoty, Fundamenta Informaticae 1,1977,1-17,147-167

[6]. Mirkowska,G., On Formalized System of Algorithmic Logic, Bull. Acad.Pol.Sci,Ser math. astr. et phys.,19,1971,421-428

[7]. Muldner,T., Implementation and Properties of Certain Tools for Parallel Computation, to appear in Fundamenta Informaticae

[8]. Oktaba,H., On Algorithmic Theory of References, a manuscript

[9]. Salwicki,A., On Algorithmic Theory of Dictionaries,a manuscript

[10]. Sielberschatz,A., Kieburtz,R.B., The External Consistency of Abstract Data types, a manuscript.

A SEQUENT CALCULUS FOR KRÖGER LOGIC

M. E. Szabo *
Department of Mathematics
Concordia University, Montreal

0. INTRODUCTION. In [4,5], Kröger developed a variant of temporal logic as a basis for the analysis of computer programs. In this logic, the truth values of formulas vary along an ordinal time scale $[0,\omega^\omega)$, and the language involved is capable of expressing such ideas as "A and later B" and "If A then later B". Properties of programs are represented by formulas in the given language, and a program has a certain property if and only if the associated formula is provable in Kröger's logic. As a verification system, this logic is of course only as good as the ease with which formulas can be proved in the system. Since we are dealing with an infinitary extension of classical first order logic, there is no hope of making the discovery of proofs effective. What can be hoped for, however, is that the system enjoys a type of subformula property in the sense of Gentzen [7], and that the provable formulas can be characterized by a smooth cut-free sequent calculus in which the provability of a formula can be established in a direct way. It is the purpose of this paper to give such a characterization.

1. THE LANGUAGE L. The core language is a countable first order language with relation and function symbols, free and bound variables, based on the connectives $\neg$ and $\vee$ and the quantifier $\exists$, and the terms of L are defined as usual. The formulas, on the other hand, involve the additional propositional constants $I(\alpha)$, the temporal connectives (α), and the loop symbol @. Furthermore, each formula A has an associated time dependence $t(A)$ (Kröger calls it the thickness of A) influencing the validity of A at time α.

1.1. Definition. The formulas of L and their time dependences are defined as follows:

(1) For each $\alpha \in [1,\omega^\omega)$, $I(\alpha)$ is a formula and $t(I(\alpha)) = \alpha$.

(2) If R is an n-ary relation symbol and $t_1,\ldots,t_n$ are terms, then

* This research was supported in part by Grant No. A8224 of the National Sciences and Engineering Research Council of Canada. A preliminary version of this paper was first presented in December 1979 to a joint colloquium of the Mathematical Institute of the University of Warsaw and the Polish Academy of Science and the author wishes to extend to these institutions and to Professors Helena Rasiowa and Andrzej Salwicki his sincere thanks for their hospitality.

$R(t_1,\ldots,t_n)$ is a formula and $t(R(t_1,\ldots,t_n)) = 1$.

(3) If A is a formula, then $\neg A$ is a formula and $t(\neg A) = t(A)$.

(4) If A and B are formulas, then $(A \vee B)$ is a formula and $t(A \vee B) = \max(t(A),t(B))$.

(5) If A is a formula and $\beta \in [0,\omega^{\omega})$, then $(\beta)A$ is a formula and $t((\beta)A) = \beta + t(A)$.

(6) If A is a formula, then @A is a formula and $t(@A) = t(A) \times \omega$.

(7) If A(a) is a formula containing the free variable a and $t(A(a)) = 1$, and if the bound variable x and the constant I(1) do not occur in A(a), then $(\exists x)A(x/a)$ is a formula and $t((\exists x)A(x/a)) = 1$.

1.2. Notation. The following conventions simplify the description of our calculus:

(1) Capital Roman letters denote formulas.

(2) Capital Greek letters denote finite strings of formulas.

(3) Lower case Greek letters denote ordinals.

(4) The connectives $\wedge$, $\Rightarrow$, and $\Leftrightarrow$ and the quantifier $\forall$ are defined as usual.

(5) Outermost brackets are usually omitted. Thus αA denotes $(\alpha)A$.

(6) A^0 stands for I(1), and I(0) stands for the empty sequence.

(7) A^1 and $(-1)A$ stand for A.

(8) $A \Delta B$ abbreviates $A \wedge t(A)B$ and A^{n+1} abbreviates $A^n \Delta A$.

(9) $A \rightsquigarrow B$ abbreviates $A \Rightarrow t(A)B$.

(10) $\alpha(\alpha_1A_1,\ldots,\alpha_nA_n)$ stands for $(\alpha\alpha_1)A_1,\ldots,(\alpha\alpha_n)A_n$.

(11) Following Gentzen [7,8], pairs $\langle\Gamma,\Phi\rangle$ of strings of formulas (called sequents) are written as $\Gamma \rightarrow \Phi$.

2. THE KRÖGER LOGIC K AND THE ASSOCIATED SEQUENT CALCULUS S(K). We now describe the axioms and rules of the Kröger logic K [5] and present its sequential characterization S(K).

2.1. The logic K. The system K consists of the following axioms and rules of inference:

2.1.1. Axioms.

(1) All replacement instances of classical tautologies.

(2) All formulas of the form $A(a) \Rightarrow (\exists x)A(x/a)$.

(3) $(\alpha)\neg A \Leftrightarrow \neg(\alpha)A$.

(4) $(\alpha)(A \vee B) \Leftrightarrow (\alpha)A \vee (\alpha)B$.

(5) $(0)A \Leftrightarrow A$.

(6) $(\alpha)(\beta)A \Leftrightarrow (\alpha+\beta)A$.

(7) $A^n \Delta I(t(A) \times \omega) \Rightarrow @A$.

(8) $I(\alpha) \Rightarrow (\rho)I(\beta)$ for all $\rho + \beta \leqslant \alpha$.

(9) $I(\alpha) \Rightarrow (P \Leftrightarrow (\alpha)P)$ for all formulas obtainable by 1.1.2-4 and 1.1.7.

2.1.2. Rules of inference.

(1) If A and $A \Rightarrow B$ are provable, then B is provable.

(2) If $(\alpha)A(a) \Rightarrow B$ is provable and the free variable a does not occur in $(\alpha)(\exists x)A(x/a) \Rightarrow B$, then $(\alpha)(\exists x)A(x/a) \Rightarrow B$ is provable.

(3) If A is provable, then $(\alpha)A$ is provable.

(4) If $(\alpha)(A^n \Delta I(t(A) \times \omega)) \Rightarrow B$ is provable for all $n \in \omega$, then $(\alpha)@A \Rightarrow B$ is provable.

2.2. The calculus S(K). The system S(K) consists of the following axioms and rules of inference:

2.2.1. Axioms. All sequents of the form $A \rightarrow A$, with A obtainable by 1.1.1-2.

2.2.2. Rules of inference.

Classical rules

(C) All rules of Gentzen's calculus LK [7], with the exception of the cut.

Temporal rules

(T1) If $\Gamma \rightarrow \Phi$ is provable, then $\alpha\Gamma \rightarrow \alpha\Phi$ is provable.

(T2) If $\Gamma, A, \Delta \rightarrow \Phi$ is provable, then $\Gamma, (0)A, \Delta \rightarrow \Phi$ is provable and conversely.

(T3) If $\Gamma, \delta I(\gamma), \beta A, \Delta \rightarrow \Phi$ is provable and $-1 \leqslant \delta \leqslant \alpha < \beta \leqslant \delta + \gamma$, then $\Gamma, \delta I(\gamma), \alpha A, \Delta \rightarrow \Phi$ is provable.

(T4) If $\Gamma, \Delta \rightarrow \Phi, B, \Psi$ is provable and $\alpha = \rho + \beta$, then $\Gamma, \rho I(\beta), \Delta \rightarrow \Phi, \alpha B, \Psi$ is provable.

(T5) If $\Gamma, \alpha\beta A, \Delta \rightarrow \Phi$ is provable, then $\Gamma, (\alpha+\beta)A, \Delta \rightarrow \Phi$ is provable.

(T6) If $\Gamma \rightarrow \Phi, \alpha\beta B, \Psi$ is provable, then $\Gamma \rightarrow \Phi, (\alpha+\beta)B, \Psi$ is provable.

(T7) If $\Gamma, A, \Delta \rightarrow \Phi$ is provable, then $\Gamma, I(\alpha), \alpha A, \Delta \rightarrow \Phi$ is provable.

(T8) If $\Gamma, \rho I(\beta), \Delta \rightarrow \Phi$ is provable and $\gamma \leqslant \rho < \rho + \beta < \gamma + \alpha$, then $\Gamma, \gamma I(\alpha), \Delta \rightarrow \Phi$ is provable.

(T9) $\Gamma, \alpha I(\beta+\gamma), \Delta \rightarrow \Phi$ is provable iff $\Gamma, \alpha I(\beta), (\alpha+\beta)I(\gamma), \Delta \rightarrow \Phi$ is provable.

Mixed rules

(M1) If $\Gamma, \alpha A \vee \alpha B, \Delta \rightarrow \Phi$ is provable, then $\Gamma, \alpha(A \vee B), \Delta \rightarrow \Phi$ is provable.

(M2) If $\Gamma, \neg(\alpha A), \Delta \rightarrow \Phi$ is provable, then $\Gamma, \alpha(\neg A), \Delta \rightarrow \Phi$ is provable.

(M3) If $\Gamma, \alpha A(a), \Delta \rightarrow \Phi$ is provable and the free variable a does not occur in $\Gamma, \alpha(\exists x)A(x/a), \Delta \rightarrow \Phi$, then $\Gamma, \alpha(\exists x)A(x/a), \Delta \rightarrow \Phi$ is provable.

Loop rules

(L1) If $\Gamma, \alpha(A^n \Delta I(t(A) \times \omega)), \Delta \rightarrow \Phi$ is provable for all $n \in \omega$, then $\Gamma, \alpha @A, \Delta \rightarrow \Phi$ is provable.

(L2) If $\Gamma \rightarrow \Phi, A^n, \Psi$ is provable for some $n \in \omega$, then $\Gamma \rightarrow \Phi, @A, \Psi$ is provable.

This completes the description of the logic K and the sequential calculus S(K). Whereas the temporal rules of S(K) are specifically designed to yield a cut-free description of the Kröger logic, the mixed rules and the loop rules also make sense for other tense logics. Appropriate forms of these rules are in fact provable in Kawai's system for a logic of the traditional Prior type [3].

3. THE EQUIVALENCE OF THE SYSTEMS K AND S(K). In this section, we sketch a proof of the fact that K and S(K) determine the same set of provable formulas of L. In doing so, we shall make implicit use of standard definitions and results concerning Hilbert and Gentzen systems. For details, we refer to [7,8]. We note, in particular, that formulas A and $B \Rightarrow C$ are provable in K if and only if the sequents $\to A$ and $B \to C$ are provable in S(K), and that the formula $A \Leftrightarrow B$ is provable in K if and only if the formulas $A \Rightarrow B$ and $B \Rightarrow A$ are provable. We also recall that the sequential form of Kröger's rule (1) (modus ponens) is the following: If $\to A$ and $A \to B$ are provable, then $\to B$ is provable. This rule is a special case of Gentzen's cut: If $\Gamma \to \Phi, A, \Psi$ and $\Delta, A, \Lambda \to \Theta$ are provable, then $\Delta\Gamma\Lambda \to \Phi\Psi\Theta$ is provable.

In order to establish the adequacy of S(K) for K, we require the fact that the cut is an admissible rule of inference of S(K).

3.1. Theorem. If the sequent $\Gamma \to \Phi$ is provable in S(K), together with the cut, then $\Gamma \to \Phi$ is provable in S(K).

Proof. By double induction, exactly analogous to Gentzen's proof of the Hauptsatz for LK (cf. pp. 88-101 of [7]) and similar to cut elimination proofs in [8]. We omit the details since they are of no intrinsic interest in the present context. □

3.2. Corollary. A formula A is provable in K if and only if the sequent $\to A$ is provable in S(K).

Proof. In one direction, the corollary is clear from the standard interpretation of sequents of the form $A_1,\ldots,A_n \to B_1,\ldots B_m$ as formulas of the form $(A_1 \wedge \ldots \wedge A_n) \Rightarrow (B_1 \vee \ldots \vee B_m)$. In the other direction, we show that the axioms and rules of K are provable in S(K). For axioms of the form 2.2.1.1 and 2.2.1.2 in particular, the result is clear from [7]. The remaining axioms are proved as follows:

(3)

$$\dfrac{\dfrac{\dfrac{\dfrac{A \to A}{(\alpha)A \to (\alpha)A}\,(T1)}{(\alpha)A, \neg(\alpha)A \to}\,(M2)}{(\alpha)A, (\alpha)\neg A \to}}{(\alpha)\neg A \to \neg(\alpha)A} \qquad \dfrac{\dfrac{\dfrac{A \to A}{\to A, \neg A}\,(T1)}{\to (\alpha)A, (\alpha)\neg A}}{\neg(\alpha)A \to (\alpha)\neg A}$$

(4)
$$\dfrac{\dfrac{A \vee B \to A,B}{(\alpha)(A \vee B) \to \alpha A, \alpha B}\ (T1)}{(\alpha)(A \vee B) \to \alpha A \vee \alpha B} \qquad \dfrac{\dfrac{A \to A \vee B}{\alpha A \to \alpha(A \vee B)}\ (T1) \qquad \dfrac{B \to A \vee B}{\alpha B \to \alpha(A \vee B)}\ (T1)}{\alpha A \vee \alpha B \to \alpha(A \vee B)}$$

(5)
$$\dfrac{A \to A}{(0)A \to A}\ (T2) \qquad \dfrac{A \to A}{A \to (0)A}\ (T4)$$

(6)
$$\dfrac{\dfrac{\dfrac{A \to A}{\beta A \to \beta A}\ (T1)}{\alpha\beta A \to \alpha\beta A}\ (T1)}{\alpha\beta A \to (\alpha+\beta)A}\ (T6) \qquad \dfrac{\dfrac{\dfrac{A \to A}{\beta A \to \beta A}\ (T1)}{\alpha\beta A \to \alpha\beta A}\ (T1)}{(\alpha+\beta)A \to \alpha\beta A}\ (T5)$$

(7)
$$\dfrac{\dfrac{\dfrac{A^n \to A^n}{A^n, (t(A) \times n)I(t(A) \times \omega) \to A^n}}{A^n \wedge (t(A) \times n)I(t(A) \times \omega) \to A^n}}{A^n \wedge (t(A) \times n)I(t(A) \times \omega) \to @A}\ (L2)$$

(8)
$$\dfrac{\dfrac{I(\beta) \to I(\beta)}{\rho I(\beta) \to \rho I(\beta)}\ (T1)}{I(\alpha) \to \rho I(\beta)}\ (T8)$$

(9)
$$\dfrac{\dfrac{P \to P}{I(\alpha), \alpha P \to P}\ (T7)}{I(\alpha) \to \alpha P \Rightarrow P} \qquad \dfrac{\dfrac{P \to P}{I(\alpha), P \to \alpha P}\ (T4)}{I(\alpha) \to P \Rightarrow \alpha P}$$

The proofs of the premisses of (4) and (7) are along standard lines and so are the proofs of $A \to A$ and $P \to P$ for arbitrary formulas A and P.

The rules of inference of K are proved as follows:

(1) corresponds to the cut and is provable by Theorem 3.1.

(2) corresponds to (M3).

(3) corresponds to (T4).

(4) corresponds to (L1).

In view of the remarks made at the beginning of this section, the corollary therefore follows. □

Since the emphasis in this paper is on syntax, we omit the verification that the rules of S(K) are sound in the Kröger semantics. The details may be found in [6,9], where the system K is discussed in the context of nonstandard arithmetic.

It should be noted that Theorem 3.1 entails various conservative extension results: Classical logic with (α), I(α), and @ is conservative over classical logic with (α) and I(α), which is conservative over classical logic with (α) and it in turn is conservative over classical logic.

4. VERIFICATION OF A WHILE PROGRAM. We illustrate the utility of the subformula property of the provable formulas of K by comparing two proofs of a partial correctness formula for a while program. The formula and its K-proof are taken from [4].

We wish to prove the partial correctness of the following program:

$$(\pi) \qquad a:=1;\ b:=n;\ \underline{\text{while}}\ b > 0\ \underline{\text{do}}\ a:=2\times a;\ b:=b-1\ \underline{\text{od}}.$$

For this purpose we augment the language L of K by additional formulas of the form [a:=t], where a is a free variable and t is a term, and we take all formulas of the form

$$(*) \qquad [a:=t] \Rightarrow (A(t) \Leftrightarrow (1)A(a))$$

as additional axioms. In (*) it is assumed that A(t) is a formula by virtue of 1.1.2, 1.1.3, 1.1.4, and 1.1.7, and that A(a) results from A(t) by the replacement of all occurrences of t by a , and that the free variable a does not occur in A(t). The intended meaning of the formula [a:=t] is that "the variable a is currently being assigned the value t".

The statement of the corresponding extension of S(K) is simplified by the following notation:

$$\Delta(m\uparrow m+0) = [a(m):=t(m)]$$
$$\Delta(m\uparrow m+(n+1)) = \Delta(m\uparrow m+n)\ \Delta\ [a(m+n+1):=t(m+n+1)].$$

In the spirit of replacing axioms of K by rules of S(K), we augment the rules of S(K) as follows:

(*) If $\Gamma, (\alpha)[a:=t], (\alpha)I(1), \Delta \rightarrow \Phi$ is provable, then $\Gamma, (\alpha)[a:=t], \Delta \rightarrow \Phi$ is provable.

(**) If $\Gamma, (\alpha)A(t), \Delta \rightarrow \Phi$ is provable, then so is $\Gamma, (\alpha+1)A(a), (\alpha)[a:=t], \Delta \rightarrow \Phi$.

(***) If $\Gamma \rightarrow \Phi, (\alpha)(A(t) \wedge \Delta(1\uparrow n)), \Psi$ is provable, then $\Gamma \rightarrow \Phi, (\alpha+1)(A(a) \wedge \Delta(2\uparrow n)), \Psi$ is provable.

We remark that the semantics of assignment formulas of the form $(\alpha)[a:=t]$ is such that the deletion of formulas of the type $(\alpha)I(1)$ in (*) constitutes no loss of information.

In the representation of the program (π) and in its partial correctness statement, we use the following abbreviations:

$A \blacktriangle C \Delta @B \Delta (b \leqslant 0 \wedge I(1))$

$B \blacktriangle b > 0 \wedge [a:=2\times a] \Delta [b:=b-1]$

$C \blacktriangle [a:=1] \Delta [b:=n]$

$D \blacktriangle a = 2^{n-b} \wedge b \geqslant 0.$

In this notation, the program (π) is represented by the formula A and the partial correctness statement for (π) is represented by the formula $E \blacktriangle A \rightsquigarrow a = 2^n$.

In the system K, the proof of E given in [4] involves an induction on m in β^m and the following special axioms, provable formulas, and provable rules of inference:

(1) The axioms (*).

(2) The axioms $I(\alpha) \Rightarrow (P \Leftrightarrow (\alpha)P)$.

(3) The provable formulas $A \Delta B \Leftrightarrow A \wedge t(A)B$.

(4) The provable formulas $A \rightsquigarrow B \Leftrightarrow A \Rightarrow t(A)B$.

(5) The provable formulas $\alpha\beta A \Leftrightarrow (\alpha+\beta)A$.

(6) The provable rule: "If $A \wedge B \rightsquigarrow C$ and $C \wedge D \rightsquigarrow E$ are provable and $t(A) \leqslant t(B)$ and $t(C) \leqslant t(D)$, then $A \wedge (B \Delta D) \rightsquigarrow E$ is provable."

(7) The provable rule: "If $P \wedge A^n \rightsquigarrow Q$ is provable for all $n \in \omega$ and P and Q are formulas obtainable from 1.1.2, 1.1.3, 1.1.4, and 1.1.7, then $P \wedge @A \rightsquigarrow Q$ is provable."

The pattern of the proof of the formula E in [4] is the following:

$$\dfrac{C \overset{f}{\rightsquigarrow} D \qquad \dfrac{D \wedge I(1) \overset{g}{\rightsquigarrow} D \qquad \dfrac{D \wedge B^{m-1} \overset{h}{\rightsquigarrow} D \qquad D \wedge B \overset{i}{\rightsquigarrow} D}{D \wedge B^{m} \rightsquigarrow D}}{D \wedge @B \rightsquigarrow D}}{\dfrac{C \Delta @B \rightsquigarrow D \qquad D \wedge (b \leqslant 0 \wedge I(1)) \overset{j}{\rightsquigarrow} a = 2^{n}}{C \Delta @B \Delta (b \leqslant 0 \wedge I(1)) \rightsquigarrow a = 2^{n}}}\quad ,$$

where f uses (1) and (4); g uses (2); h is the induction hypothesis; i uses (1) and (3)-(6); and j uses (2) and (4). It should be noted, in particular, that the formula D, which plays a pivotal role in the proof, is not a subformula of E in any sense and must be divined in any attempt to prove E in the system K; so must the various axioms, provable formulas and provable rules which enter into the construction of the above proof.

This procedure is in sharp contrast with the following direct proof of E in S(K): Here too the proof involves an induction on m in B^{m}, and the induction basis and the induction steps are proved separately. In particular, we prove the formula

$$C \Delta I(1) \Delta I(\omega) \Delta (b \leqslant 0 \wedge I(1)) \Rightarrow (\omega+1)(a = 2^{n}),$$

and from the formula

$$C \Delta B^{m} \Delta I(\omega) \Delta (b \leqslant 0 \wedge I(1)) \Rightarrow (\omega+1)(a = 2^{n})$$

we derive the formula

$$C \Delta B^{m+1} \Delta I(\omega) \Delta (b \leqslant 0 \wedge I(1)) \Rightarrow (\omega+1)(a = 2^{n}).$$

The proofs go as follows:

(1)

$$\begin{array}{r}
[a:=1] \rightarrow [a:=1] \qquad n \leqslant 0 \rightarrow 1 = 2^{n} \\ \hline
[a:=1], n \leqslant 0 \wedge I(1) \rightarrow [a:=1] \wedge 1 = 2^{n} \\ \hline
[a:=1], [b:=n], (1)(b \leqslant 0 \wedge I(1)) \rightarrow (1)(a = 2^{n}) \\ \hline
[a:=1], [b:=n], I(1), (1)(b \leqslant 0 \wedge I(1)) \rightarrow (1)(a = 2^{n}) \\ \hline
[a:=1], [b:=n], I(1), (b \leqslant 0 \wedge I(1)) \rightarrow (1)(a = 2^{n}) \\ \hline
(\omega)[a:=1], (\omega)[b:=n], (\omega)I(1), (\omega)(b \leqslant 0 \wedge I(1)) \rightarrow (\omega+1)(a = 2^{n}) \\ \hline
(\omega)[a:=1], (\omega)[b:=n], (\omega)I(1), I(\omega), (\omega)(b \leqslant 0 \wedge I(1)) \rightarrow (\omega+1)(a = 2^{n}) \\ \hline
[a:=1], (1)[b:=n], (2)I(1), I(\omega), (\omega)(b \leqslant 0 \wedge I(1)) \rightarrow (\omega+1)(a = 2^{n}) \\ \hline
[a:=1], (1)[b:=n], (2)I(1), (3)I(\omega), (\omega)(b \leqslant 0 \wedge I(1)) \rightarrow (\omega+1)(a = 2^{n}) \\ \hline
[a:=1] \Delta [b:=n] \Delta I(1) \Delta I(\omega) \Delta (b \leqslant 0 \wedge I(1))) \rightarrow (\omega+1)(a = 2^{n})
\end{array}$$

and

$$
\begin{array}{rr}
 & \underline{[a:=1],(1)[b:=n],(2)B^{m},(2+2m)I(\omega),(\omega)(b \leqslant 0 \wedge I(1)) \rightarrow (\omega+1)(a = 2^{n})} \\
(2) & \underline{[a:=1],(1)[b:=n],(2)B^{m},I(\omega),(\omega)(b \leqslant 0 \wedge I(1)) \rightarrow (\omega+1)(a = 2^{n})} \\
 & \underline{[a:=1],(1)[b:=n],(2)B^{m},(2)(2m)B,I(\omega),(\omega)(b \leqslant 0 \wedge I(1)) \rightarrow (\omega+1)(a = 2^{n})} \\
 & \underline{[a:=1],(1)[b:=n],(2)B^{m},(2)(2m)B,(2+2(m+1))I(\omega),(\omega)(b \leqslant 0 \wedge I(1)) \rightarrow (\omega+1)(a = 2^{n})} \\
 & \underline{[a:=1],(1)[b:=n],(2)B^{m+1},(2+2(m+1))I(\omega),(\omega)(b \leqslant 0 \wedge I(1)) \rightarrow (\omega+1)(a = 2^{n})} \\
 & [a:=1]\ \Delta\ [b:=n]\ \Delta\ B^{m+1}\ \Delta\ I(\omega)\ \Delta\ (b \leqslant 0 \wedge I(1)) \rightarrow (\omega+1)(a = 2^{n}) \ .
\end{array}
$$

In [5], Kröger showed that the highly successful finitary Hoare verification system for computer programs [1,2] is faithfully embedded in the system K, augmented with assignment formulas. Our method therefore extends to the logic of Hoare and calculations similar to those above give an easy proof of the formula $A \sim B$, with

$$A \triangleq [r:=x]\ \Delta\ [q:=0]\ \Delta\ @(y \leqslant x \wedge [r:=r-y]\ \Delta\ [q:=1+q])\ \Delta\ (y > x \wedge I(1))$$

$$B \triangleq (\omega+1)(y > r \wedge x = r + y\times q),$$

which is the Kröger translation of Hoare's total correctness formula for the program

(ππ) r:=x; q:=0; <u>while</u> y ⩽ r <u>do</u> r:=r-y; q:=1+q <u>od</u>

discussed at length in [2].

REFERENCES

[1] K. R. APT, Ten years of Hoare's logic, to appear.

[2] C. A. R. HOARE, An axiomatic basis for computer programming, Communications of the Association for Computing Machinery 2 (1969), 576-583.

[3] H. KAWAI, Sequential calculus for a first order infinitary temporal logic, to appear.

[4] F. KRÖGER, Logical rules of natural reasoning about programs, in: Automata, languages, and programming (S. Michaelson and R. Milner, editors), Edinburgh University Press, Edinburgh 1976, pp. 87-98.

[5] F. KRÖGER, LAR: A logic for algorithmic reasoning, Acta Informatica 8 (1977), 242-266.

[6] M. M. RICHTER and M. E. SZABO, Towards a nonstandard analysis of programs, Proceedings of the Second Victoria Symposium on nonstandard analysis, Victoria, British Columbia, June 1980, to appear.

[7] M. E. SZABO (editor), The collected papers of Gerhard Gentzen, North-Holland Publishing Company, Amsterdam 1969.

[8] M. E. SZABO, Algebra of proofs, North-Holland Publishing Company, Amsterdam 1978.

[9] M. E. SZABO, Variable truth, to appear.

ON AXIOMATIZATION OF PROCESS LOGIC

M.K.Valiev
Institute of Mathematics,
Novosibirsk, 630090, USSR

Introduction

There is a number of generalizations [1,2,3,4,5] of propositional dynamic logic (PDL) of Fischer and Ladner [6] oriented to describe properties of execution sequences of programs (not only of input-output relations). Here we give decidability (with double-exponential time complexity) and Gentzen-type axiomatization results for some variants of Pratt's process logic (PL) [3] with formulas $a \sqcup p.q$ expressing "for any resulting execution sequence x of the program a either there exists a state s in x where p is true or q is true in the final state of x".

We consider in some details variant of PL where elementary programs are interpreted as sets of trajectories (with short notation TrPL) and give some comments on variant (FPL) with functional interpretations of elementary programs (note, however, that we do not include in FPL program inverse operator presented in TrPL). Cases when elementary programs are total functions, binary relations or total binary relations are similar. In all these cases formulas [a]p ("after a p is true" [6,1,2,3]) and $a \perp p$ (" p is true sometimes during any resulting computation of a" [3]) are expressed as $a \sqcup$false.p and $a \sqcup$p.false respectively. This unification of notions is the main reason for introducing $\sqcup$, jointly with the fact that there exists a nice axiomatization for $a;b \sqcup p.q$, contrary to $a;b \perp p$ see [2,3]. In FPL and other relational variants of PL two remaining operators from [1,2,3], $\sqcup\!\sqcup$ and $\int$, are also expressible: $a \sqcup\!\sqcup p$ is equivalent to p & $a\int p$, and for $a\int p$ there exists an inductive definition (in general case this inductive definition allows to eliminate formulas $a\int p$ with non-elementary a, and $A\int p$ is equivalent to $p \supset [A]p$, if A is a relation).

The abovesaid shows that operator $\sqcup$ allows to express in unified form a number of interesting program properties. There remain, however many program properties non-expressible in PL, too. In particular, there is no possibility in variants of PL discussed of taking into consideration properties of diverging computations. In this connection it may be useful to introduce a new operator $\sqcup\!\sqcup^{+}$, whose definition differs from the one of $\sqcup\!\sqcup$ by removing the word "resulting". Then a $\sqcup\!\sqcup^{+}$false.true and a $\sqcup\!\sqcup^{+}$p.false express $[a]^{+}$true ("all computations of a are resulting" [7]) and a $\perp$p with semantics defined as in [1,2] rather than in [3], respectively. It seems that our results can be extended to process logic PL^{+} with operators $\sqcup\!\sqcup$ and $\sqcup\!\sqcup^{+}$. However, we have so far such the results only for the important sublogic of PL^{+}, PDL^{+} (with operators [ ], $[\ ]^{+}$). We leave discussion of PDL^{+} and PL^{+} to another paper. Note that in [5] completeness and decidability results are given for a much more expressive variant of process logic, however, no elementary decision procedure is known for it.

It is not difficult to extend our results to TrPL augmented by $\sqcup\!\sqcup$, but adding $\int$ causes many difficulties. In [3] a Hilbert-type axiomatization is proposed for the latter case, claiming, however, that it is probably not complete (it should be noted that axiom $\neg$(a$\sqcup\!\sqcup\neg$p & & a$\perp$p) in [3] is not correct and should be removed, since a$\perp$p defined as in [3] is always true, when a has no resulting computations, but a$\sqcup\!\sqcup$p is not). Completeness of the part of this system dealing only with $\sqcup\!\sqcup$ and of (somewhat corrected version of) Gentzen-type system for $\sqcup\!\sqcup$ from [2] can be deduced from the completeness of our Gentzen-type system.

Although the usual programming constructs "if_then_else" and "while_do" can be expressed using tests, $\cup$ and $*$, it may be useful to have some explicit axiomatization for them. Such an axiomatization can be obtained using simple generalizations of Hoare's rules [8] for "if" and "while", and its completeness can be proved following lines below.

The proofs sketched below use idea of saturated sets due to [9] and generalized to PDL in [10]. Some improvements of the saturated sets approach allow to obtain complete Gentzen-type systems with a essentially restricted form of cut rule what makes them more suitable for formal proofs searching than Hilbert-type systems (e.g., see [11], [12]) and Gentzen-type system of [10] with unrestricted cut rule (note that Gentzen-type systems with induction rule [1,13,14] and the unusual formal system from [15] are still more suitable for proof searching, but completeness proofs for them are rather difficult).

The approach to completeness proofs outlined below gives two decision procedures at once: one based on proof searching, and second based on finite model property. However, both of these procedures have double-exponential time complexity vs. one-exponential procedure for PDL and DPDL obtained in [16,14,12]. The latter results are obtai ned under asumption of absence of program inverse operator $^-$ and can be generalized to FPL which also does not contain $^-$ as it is indicate above. No completeness and elementary decidability results are known for DPDL and FPL including $^-$, and it seems that existing proof method should be essentially improved to obtain results of this kind. We are to be successful [17] to use the saturated sets approach to obtain completeness and decidability results for logic of symmetric linear discrete time [18] corresponding to PDL restricted to programs A, A^-, A^*, A^{*-}, where A is total function. These results can be generalized to PDL with single total functional elementary program (no restrictio on program constructs) using simulation of equivalent transformations of regular expressions on cyclic groups by logical rules. It seems that this approach may be also useful in general case, but it needs more penetrating study of transformations of regular expressions on arbitrary free groups.

§1. TrPL: completeness and decidability.

1. Let us sketch briefly syntax of TrPL (syntax of FPL is obtain from the one of TrPL by removing operator $^-$).

There are two sorts of variables: propositional variables P,Q,.. and program variables A,B,... Notions of formula and program are defi in the following way:

1) propositional variables are (elementary) formulas, program variables are (elementary) programs;

2) if p and q are formulas, a and b are programs then $\neg p$, p & q $a \sqcup p.q$ are formulas, $a \cup b$, a;b, a^-, a^* and p? are programs.

2. We define now semantics of TrPL. A TrPL-model M = (S,T,V) is defined in the following way: S is a set (of states), T is a function binding to any elementary program A some set of finite sequences (trajectories) of states (note that there is no sense in introducing infinite trajectories because semantics of $\sqcup$ below uses only resulting trajectories), V is a function binding to any state s some set of elementary formulas (satisfiable in s).

T and V are extended to all the programs and formulas in such a way (using notation $s \models p$ instead $p \in V(s)$): 1) $T(a \cup b) = T(a) \cup T(b)$, 2) Let $t_1 \circ t_2$ denote the trajectory obtained by identifying the last state of t_1 with the first state of t_2 when they are the same. Then $T(a;b) = T(a) \circ T(b)$, where $T_1 \circ T_2$ denotes $\{t_1 \circ t_2 : t_1 \in T_1, t_2 \in T_2\}$, 3) $T(a^-) = \{t;$ inversion of t belongs to $T(a)\}$, 4) $T(a^*) = \{(s) : s \in S\} \cup$

$\cup T(a) \cup T(a;a) \cup \ldots$, 5) $T(p?) = \{(s) ; s \models p\}$, 6) $s \models \neg p$ iff non $s \models p$,) $s \models p \,\&\, q$ iff $s \models p$ and $s \models q$, 8) $s \models a \sqcup\!\sqcup p.q$ iff for any trajectory $s = s_0, s_1, \ldots, s_k)$ in $T(a)$ there exists j such that $s_j \models p$ or $s_k \models q$.

3. Let X and Y denote finite sets of formulas, and for any formula of the form $u \equiv v$ L_{uv} and R_{uv} denote Gentzen-type rules

$$\frac{X, v \to Y}{X, u \to Y} \qquad \frac{X \to v, Y}{X \to u, Y}$$

Then Gentzen-type deductive system AxTr for TrPL consists of the following rules:

I. Usual rules for propositional logic including cut rule (some restrictions on cut rule will be introduced below);

II. Rules L_{uv} and R_{uv} for the formulas $u \equiv v$ of the following forms:

$$(a \cup b) \sqcup\!\sqcup p.q \equiv a \sqcup\!\sqcup p.q \,\&\, b \sqcup\!\sqcup p.q$$
$$(a;b) \sqcup\!\sqcup p.q \equiv a \sqcup\!\sqcup p.(b \sqcup\!\sqcup p.q)$$
$$(a^*) \sqcup\!\sqcup p.q \equiv (p \vee q) \,\&\, a \sqcup\!\sqcup p.(a^* \sqcup\!\sqcup p.q)$$
$$(p?) \sqcup\!\sqcup q.r \equiv (p \supset q \vee r)$$
$$(a \cup b)^- \sqcup\!\sqcup p.q \equiv (a^- \cup b^-) \sqcup\!\sqcup p.q$$
$$(a;b)^- \sqcup\!\sqcup p.q \equiv (b^-;a^-) \sqcup\!\sqcup p.q$$
$$(a^*)^- \sqcup\!\sqcup p.q \equiv (a^-)^* \sqcup\!\sqcup p.q$$
$$(a^{--}) \sqcup\!\sqcup p.q \equiv a \sqcup\!\sqcup p.q$$
$$(p?)^- \sqcup\!\sqcup r.q \equiv (p?) \sqcup\!\sqcup r.q$$

III. Rules

$$\frac{X \to p}{X \to a \sqcup\!\sqcup p.q} \qquad \frac{p_1 \vee \ldots \vee p_k \vee w_1 \vee \ldots \vee w_m \to p \quad q_1, \ldots, q_k \to p, q, a^- \sqcup\!\sqcup W.Y}{a \quad p_1.q_1, \ldots, a \quad p_k.q_k \quad a \quad p.q,\ Y}$$

where $a \sqcup\!\sqcup W.Y$ denotes $\{a \sqcup\!\sqcup w.y :\ w \in W, y \in Y\}$, $W = \{w_1, \ldots, w_m\}$.

and rule

$$(\mathrm{Ind}) \ \frac{X \to r, Y \qquad r \to a \sqcup\!\sqcup p.r \qquad r \to p, q}{X \to a^* \sqcup\!\sqcup p.q,\ Y}$$

(more simple but less useful rule $\to p, q,\ a^- \sqcup\!\sqcup r.Y \quad r \to p \vdash a \sqcup\!\sqcup p.q, Y$ can be used instead of $\sqcup\!\sqcup 2$; in $\sqcup\!\sqcup 1$ and $\sqcup\!\sqcup 2$ a can be restricted to be A or A^-).

4. Soundness of AxTr is verified easily. It proves to be that AxTr is complete even for some notion of provability with strong restrictions on applications of cut rule and rules $\sqcup\!\sqcup 2$, (Ind) which is defined below (in fact, cut rule can be still more restricted).

Let $FL(p)$ denote closure of formula p defined similarly to that for PDL in [6], $\widetilde{FL}(p) = FL(p) \cup \{\neg q :\ q \in FL(p)\}$, and $FL'(p)$ be the set of disjunctions of conjunctions of formulas from $FL(p)$.

We say that a sequent $X \to Y$ is r-provable iff there exists an AxTr-proof for $X \to Y$ any formula in which has the form q or $a_1 \sqcup p.a_2 \sqcup p \ldots a_k \sqcup p.q$, where $p \in \widetilde{FL}(r)$, $q \in FL'(r)$, and a_i occur in formulas from FL(r) (note that if AxTr is augmented by some admissib rules (such as $X \to a \sqcup p.q \quad q \to s \vdash X \to a \sqcup p.s$) the notion of r-provability (in this extended system AxTr') can be still more restricted so that any sequent of any r-proof contains at most one formula differing from formulas in $\widetilde{FL}(r)$). A set X is r-consistent iff the sequent $X \to$ is not r-provable.

5. THEOREM. If $\neg r$ is r-consistent then $\neg r$ has a model of size $\exp(c|r|)$, where $|r|$ denotes the length of r.

This theorem shows completeness of AxTr and gives two decision procedures for TrPL. First procedure is based on searching of models of exponential size and has double-exponential time complexity. Secon procedure is based on proof searching: the set O(r) of sequents which can occur in r-proofs contains at most $\exp(\exp(\exp(c|r|)))$ elements (or $\exp(\exp(c|r|))$ elements, if proofs in AxTr' are considered), and r-provability of a sequent can be verified by usual Gentzen-type argument by successive searching of r-provable sequents from O(r) beginning from axioms (it also gives double-exponential time complexity for TrPL, if r-provability in AxTr' is considered).

6. We get now to the completeness proof for AxTr. It uses the notion of r-saturated sets similar to notions of complete pairs in [9] and saturated sequents in [10]. Namely, we say that a set $X \subseteq \widetilde{FL}(r)$ is r-saturated iff (1)X is r-consistent, and (2) for any p in FL(r) p belongs to X or $\neg p$ belongs to X.

The following simple lemma is true.

LEMMA 1. Any r-consistent subset of $\widetilde{FL}(r)$ can be extended to a r-saturated set.

7. We define now a finite model $M(r) = (S, T, \models)$ similar to model $S(\Omega)$ in [10](later it will be shown that M(r) is a model for $\neg r$):

(1) $S = \{X: X \text{ is r-saturated}\}$,

(2) $X \models P$ iff $P \in X$,

(3) Trajectory $(X_1, \ldots, X_k)$ belongs to T(A) iff

(i) if $A \sqcup p.q \in X_1$ then $p \in X_i$, for some i, or $q \in X_k$,

and (ii) if $A^- \sqcup p.q \in X_k$ then $p \in X_i$, for some i, or $q \in X_1$.

8. Let us introduce some notations. For any p in $\widetilde{FL}(r)$ p' denotes q, if p is of the form $\neg q$, and $p' = \neg p$, otherwise (p' has all needed properties of $\neg p$, and, moreover, p' is always in $\widetilde{FL}(r)$, contrary to $\neg p$). For any state X, program a and formula u in FL(r) let R(X,a,u)

denote the set $\{Y\colon$ there exists a trajectory $(X = X_0, X_1, \ldots, X_k = Y)$ in $T(a)$ such that $\neg u \in X_i$, for any $i\}$, and $X(a,u)$ be disjunction of all the formulas $\& Y_i$, where $Y_i \in R(X,a,u)$, $\&X$ denotes conjunction of formulas from X.

The following lemma is similar to lemma 4.6 in [10] and lemma 7 in [13].

LEMMA 2. The sequent $X \to a \sqcup u.X(a,u)$ is r-provable.

Proof (sketch). By induction on complexity of a.

Assume that $\neg u \in X$, otherwise rule $\sqcup 1$ can be applied.

Let $a = A$ (case $a = A^-$ is similar). Suppose that $\nvdash X \to A \sqcup u.X(A,u)$. Then $\nvdash X \to A \sqcup u.X(A,u), X'$, where $X' = \{q'\colon q \in X\}$.

Let $W = \{w\colon \vdash w \to u\}$. Then using rule $\sqcup 2$ and cuts to transfer some formulas right to left we obtain

$$\nvdash \{q\colon A \sqcup p.q \in X, \text{ and } p \in W\}, \neg u, \neg A^- \sqcup W.X' \cap \widetilde{FL}(r) \to X(A,u).$$

Let Y denote the antecedent of this sequent. $Y \subseteq \widetilde{FL}(r)$ and can be extended to a r-saturated set Z such that $\nvdash Z \to X(A,u)$. We now prove that it is impossible because $Z \in R(X,A,u)$.

To prove that $Z \in R(x,A,u)$ we have to show that there exists a trajectory $(X = X_0, X_1, \ldots, X_k = Z)$ such that

(1) $\neg u \in X_i$, for any i,

(2) if $A \sqcup p.q \in X$ then $p \in X_i$, for some i, or $q \in Z$,

(3) if $A^- \sqcup p.q \in Z$ then $p \in X_j$, for some j, or $q \in X$.

Choose as X_i the state containing $\{v_i, \neg u\}$, where $V = \{v_i\}$ is an enumeration of formulas v in $\widetilde{FL}(r)$ such that $\nvdash v \to u$. Then (1) is satisfied for chosen trajectory t, since $\neg u \in X$, by assumption at the beginning of the proof, and $\neg u \in Z$, by definition of Z. (2) is satisfied for t: if $p \notin X_i$, for any i, then $p \in W$, and $q \in Z$. If $p \notin V$ (i.e., $p \in W$) and $q \notin X$ (i.e. $q \in X'$) then $\neg A^- \sqcup p.q \in \neg A^- \sqcup W.X' \cap \widetilde{FL}(r)$, and $A^- \sqcup p.q \notin Z$. Hence (3) is also satisfied for t, and $Z \in R(X,A,u)$. This completes the proof of induction basis.

Induction step can be produced as in [10] using cut rule for $;$ or as in [13]. Sketch briefly the case $a = b^*;c$. Applying to the sequent $X \to b^* \sqcup u.c \sqcup X(b^*;c,u)$ rule (Ind) (with formula $X(b^*,u)$ as r) we reduce its provability to provability of sequents $X \to X(b^*,u)$, $X_i \to b \sqcup u.X(b^*,u)$ and $X_i \to u, c \sqcup u.X(b^*;c,u)$, where $X_1 \in R(X,b^*,u)$. First sequent is provable since, by assumption at the beginning of the proof, $\neg u \in X$, and $X \in R(X,b^*,u)$, consequently. Other premise sequents are provable using induction hypothesis and admissible rule $X \to a \sqcup p.q \vdash$ $\vdash X \to a \sqcup p.(q \vee r)$.

It is easy to verify that all the AxTr-proofs above are r-proofs.

REMARK. Possibility of proving lemma 2 (and lemma 7 in [13]) without using cut rule in fact is based on associativity of ; what could be reflected in syntax by giving hignest operator precedence to If we want to avoid such the syntactical convention we could explicit introduce in axiomatics rules for handling associativity of ; or use a slightly more difficult induction argument to prove a somewhat generalized form of lemma 2: $X \to a_1 \sqcup u.a_2 \sqcup u \ldots a_k \sqcup u.X(a,u)$ is r-provable, for any a equivalent to $a_1; a_2; \ldots; a_k$ up to associativity of ;.

9. LEMMA 3. If $\neg a \sqcup p.q \in X$ then there exists Y in $R(X,a,p)$ such that $\neg q \in Y$.

Proof. We have $\nvdash X \to a \sqcup p.q$, since $\neg a \sqcup p.q \in X$. Then $\nvdash a \sqcup p.X(a,$ $\to a \sqcup p.q$ (using cut on formula $a \sqcup p.X(a,p)$ and lemma 2). Then $\nvdash X(a,p) \to$ (using $\sqcup 2$), and $\nvdash X_i \to q$, for some i, where $X_i \in R(X,a,p)$. Hence, $\neg q \in$ since X_i is r-consistent.

REMARK. This proof coincides essentially with the proof of lemma 4.7 in [10]. Another proof using rule (Ind) but not using cut rul can be produced as in the proof of assertions (1)-(3) of lemma 8 in [1 (note that difficulties with assertion (4) of this lemma (see [14]) are automatically eliminated here by definition of M(r) thanks to using cut rule. Most of these difficulties can be also avoided by including in axiomatics reversions of some rules from [13] (see lemma 6 in [14]). In this way we obtain a more weak extension of axiomatics than by explicit introducing cut rule, but it has the same drawback to be less suitable for proof searching.

10. The following lemmas are proved by standard induction argumets on complexity of program a and formula p, respectively.

LEMMA 4. If $a \sqcup p.q \in X_0$ and $(X_0, X_1, \ldots, X_k) \in T(a)$ then $p \in X_i$, for some i, or $q \in X_k$.

LEMMA 5. For any p in FL(r) and state X of M(r)

$$X \models p \text{ iff } p \in X.$$

Since $\neg r$ is r-consistent there exists a state X such that $\neg r \in X$ Then application of lemma 5 concludes the completeness proof for TrPL

2. FPL: completeness and finite model property.

Here we give some comments on changes needed in the proofs above to obtain similar results for FPL.

1. As it is indicated above syntax and semantics of FPL are the same as that of TrPL except that operator $^-$ is removed, and elementary programs are interpreted as partial functions.

Gentzen-type system AxF for FPL is obtained from AxTr by removing all the rules including $^-$ and adding rules L_{pq} and R_{pq} for the axiom A⊔p.q ≡ p ∨ [A](p ∨ q) and rule

$$\text{(FM)} \qquad \frac{X \to Y}{[A]X \to [A]Y} \quad \text{(Y is non-empty)}$$

where [a]p is used as an abbreviation for a⊔false.p, and [a]X = {[a]p: p ∈ X}.

REMARK. If Y in (FM) is arbitrary (is singleton or has at most one element) we obtain axiomatizations for PL with interpretations of elementary programs as total functions, binary relations and total binary relations, respectively.

Notions of r-provable sequents and r-consistent sets for AxF are defined as that for AxTr.

THEOREM. If ¬r is r-consistent then ¬r has a (finite) FPL-model.

2. For the proof of the theorem we define first an infinite tree M(X) where X is a r-saturated set containing ¬r. Nodes of M(X) are labelled by r-saturated sets (label of a node z we denote by L(z)), and edges are labelled by elementary programs. M(X) is defined in the following way:

(1) The root of M(X) is labelled by X.
(2) Let L(y)=Y, and $\{Y^A_1,\dots,Y^A_m\}$ be the family of all the r-saturated sets containing {p: [A] p ∈ Y} ∪ {¬p: ¬[A] p ∈ Y}, then exactly m edges labelled by A go from y to nodes with labels $Y^A_1,\dots,Y^A_m$, respectively.

For any program a the set of a-trajectories in M(X) is defined in the obvious way. By T(a,p) we denote the set of a-trajectories such that labels of all states in them contain ¬p .

REMARK. Generally speaking M(X) can be partial (m can be = 0 above, if Y contains no formula of the form ¬[A]p). In the case of total elementary programs (i.e., when restriction that Y is non-empty is removed from (FM)) it is impossible, and M(X) will be total.

3. M(X) is non-deterministic (different edges with the same label can leave a fixed node), and any model defined on M(X) will be non-functional. To obtain a deterministic model D(X) for X we can apply to M(X) inductive process similar to that of Section 5 in [14]. This proves the completeness theorem for FPL, however, gives no finite model for X. To obtain a finite model we could attempt to factorize D(X) up to some finite equivalence relation on its nodes, but the factor model obtained can be non-functional, if D(X) contains sta-

tes x, y, u, v such that $y=A(x)$, $v=A(u)$, x and u are equivalent, y an v are not. In fact, the following is sufficient to obtain a finite model.

D(X) is constructed by a sequence of stages of constructing a sequence $\{F_i\}$ of finite subtrees of M(X) with properties: 1) $F_i \subseteq F_{i+1}$, 2) F_i is deterministic, for any i, 3) F_{i+1} is obtained from F_i in suc a way that a condition $\neg a_i \sqcup p_i . q_i \in L(s_i)$, $s_i \in F_i$, is fulfilled in F_{i+} (having in mind some process of enumeration of all conditions of thi form): (a) if F_i contains a node $t \in R(s_i, a_i, p_i)$ such that $\neg q_i \in L(t)$ then $F_{i+1} = F_i$, (b) otherwise, F_i contains a trajectory tr from s_i to a node t_i such that $\neg A_i;b_i \sqcup p_i . q_i \in L(t_i)$, for some A_i, b_i, all the nodes of tr contain $\neg p_i$, $tr \circ T(A_i;b_i) \subseteq T(a_i)$, and F_i contains no A_i-successor of t_i (existence of t_i can be deduced from the assertion (1) in lemma 6 below and from the fact (following from the definition of M(X)) that if $\neg A \sqcup p.q \in L(y)$ then $\{\neg p, \neg q\} \subseteq L(z)$, for any A-success z of y in M(X). Then F_{i+1} is obtained from F_i by adding a trajectory tr_i from t_i to a node $u_i \in R(t_i, A_i;b_i, p_i)$ such that $\neg q_i \in L(u_i)$.

Here we note that if $\neg A_i;b_i \sqcup p_i . q_i = \neg A_j;b_j \sqcup p_j . q_j$, and $L(t_i) = L(t_j)$, $i < j$, we can in fact merely identify A_i- (A_j-) successors of nodes t_i and t_j instead of adding tr_j to F_j. In this way after some finite number of stages we get a finite deterministic graph G(X) with $\leq 2^{|FL(r)|} \cdot |FL(r)| \cdot N$ nodes, where N denotes the maximal length of trajec tories tr_i used in the process of constructing G(X). Then a (finite) model for X is defined on G(X) as usual.

4. The following lemmas similar to lemmas 4.4 and 4.6 in [12] giv the possibility to obtain exponential upper bound for the size of G(X (for the simplicity we assume the following additional property of FL(r) which in fact already was used above in description of construc ting D(X): if $a \sqcup p.b \sqcup p.q \in FL(r)$ then $a;b \sqcup p.q \in FL(r)$).

LEMMA 6. Let $\neg a \sqcup p.q \in L(s)$, and $(s=s_0, s_1, \ldots, s_k) \in T(a,p)$, $k > 0$. Then for any $i < k$ there exists a formula $\neg A_i;b_i \sqcup p.q$ such that (1) $(s_0, \ldots, s_i) \circ T(A_i;b_i, p) \subseteq T(a,p)$, and (2) $(s_i, \ldots, s_k) \in T(A_i;b_i, p$.

LEMMA 7. If $\neg a \sqcup p.q \in L(s)$ then there exists an a-trajectory $(s=s_0, \ldots, s_k)$, $k \leq 2^{|FL(r)|} \cdot |FL(r)|$, such that $\neg p \in L(s_i)$, for any i, and $\neg q \in L(s_k)$.

REMARK. Similar lemmas can be also proved for the tree T(X) in [1 (moreover, the bound of lemma 7 can be replaced by $2^{|r|}$ in this case) however, analogue of lemma 6 in this case is more difficult to formu-late and to prove. In Section 5 of [14] analogue of lemma 6 without a sertion (2) is used which is sufficient to obtain finite model property for DPDL announced in [14]. Exponential upper bounds of model size for DPDL are implied by that for FPL and are also obtained in [12].

REFERENCES

1. Pratt V.R. A practical decision method for propositional dynamic logic. 10th Ann. ACM Symp. on Theory of Computing, 1978, 326-337.
2. Pratt V.R.Process logic:preliminary report. 6th Ann. ACM Symp. on Principles of Programming languages, 1979, 93-100.
3. Pratt V.R. Dynamic logic. Foundations of Computer Science, Mathematical Centre Tracts, 109, Amsterdam, 1979.
4. Nishimura H. Desoriptively complete process logic. Acta Informatica, 14 (1980), 359-369.
5. Harel D., Kozen D., Parikh R. Process logic: expressiveness, decidability, completeness. 21st IEEE Symp. on Foundations of Computer Science, 1980, 129-142.
6. Fischer M.J., Ladner R.E. Propositional dynamic logic of regular programs. J. of Comput. Syst. Sci., 18 (1979), 194-211.
7. Harel D., Pratt V.R. Nondeterminism in logics of programs. 5th ACM Symp. on Principles of Programming languages, 1978.
8. Hoare C.A.R. An axiomatic basis for computer programming. Comm. ACM, 12(1969), 575-580.
9. Schutte K. Vollstandige Systeme modaler und intuitionistischer Logik. Ergebnisse der Mathematik und ihrer Grenzgebiete, 1968, 42.
10. Nishimura H. Sequential method in propositional dynamic logic. Acta Informatica, 12 (1979), 377-400.
11. Kozen D., Parikh R. An elementary proof of the completeness of PDL. Theoretical Computer Science, 1981.
12. Ben-Ari M. Complexity of proofs and models in programming logics. Dissertation, Tel-Aviv Univ., 1981.
13. Valiev M.K. On axiomatization of deterministic propositional dynamic logic. Lect. Notes Comput. Sci., 74 (1979), 482-491.
14. Valiev M.K. Decision complexity of variants of propositional dynamio logic. Lect. Notes Comput. Sci., 88 (1980), 656-664.
15. Chlebus B. On the decidability of propositional algorithmic logic. Manuscript, 1980.
16. Pratt V.R. A near optimal method for reasoning about action. MIT/LCS Report TM-113, 1978.
17. Valiev M.K. Gentzen-style axiomatization of symmetric discrete linear time (to appear in the book of Russian authors on non-classical logics, Reidel Co.).
18. Prior A. Past, Present and Future. Clarendon Press, Oxford, 1967.

FILTRATION THEOREM FOR DYNAMIC ALGEBRAS WITH TESTS AND INVERSE OPERATOR

Dimiter Vakarelov
Bulgarian Academy of Sciences
Center of Mathematics and Mechanics
1090 Sofia, P.O.Box 373, Bulgaria

Key words: dynamic algebras, programming algebras, dynamic logic

1. Introduction. Dynamic algebras (DA) were introduced by Kozen [1,2,3] and Pratt [4,5] to provide algebraic semantics for propositional dynamic logic (PDL). Independently and for the same purpose such algebras, including tests and inverse operator, were introduced also by Longochev [6,7] under the name of programming algebras. For further information about dynamic algebras, their motivation and application in computer science the reader may consult the very suggestive paper [4] of Pratt. Recent results in that new area can be found in Reiterman and Trnkova [8].

In [4] Pratt proved the so-called filtration theorem for free separable DA-s and formulated as an open problem the extention of this result to DA-s with tests and inverse operator. He also characterized iteration in DA-s as a minimal solution of a special equation and asked whether an analogous result would hold for inverse operator. In the present paper we give a positive answer to the above two problems. Following Longochev [6,7] we reserve the term "programming algebra" for dynamic algebras with tests and inverse operator. The method which we use to prove the filtration theorem is an algebraic generalization of the Segerberg's [9] proof of the completeness theorem for PDL (without tests). As an application we obtain a Rasiowa-Sikorski style [10] completeness theorem for PDL with tests and inverse operator with respect to various algebraic semantics, including the standard Kripke semantics.

2. Programming algebras. Dynamic algebra is a two-sorted algebra $(B,P)=((B,0,1,\wedge,\vee,\Rightarrow,\neg),(P,\circ,\cup,*),[\,])$ where $(B,0,1,\wedge,\vee,\Rightarrow,\neg)$ is of the type (0,0,2,2,2,1), $(P,\circ,\cup,*)$ is of the type (2,2,1), $[\,]: P\times B\to B$ is an inter-sort operation and the following conditions are satisfied for any $a,b\in B$ and $\alpha,\beta\in P$:

1. $(B,0,1,\wedge,\vee,\Rightarrow,\neg)$ is a Boolean algebra

2a. $[\alpha](a\wedge b)=[\alpha]a\wedge[\alpha]b$, 2b. $[\alpha]1=1$

3. $[\alpha\circ\beta]a=[\alpha][\beta]a$

4. $[\alpha\cup\beta]a=[\alpha]a\wedge[\beta]a$

5a. $[\alpha*]a\leq a$, 5b. $[\alpha*]a\leq[\alpha][\alpha*]a$

5c. $a\wedge[\alpha*](a\Rightarrow[\alpha]a)\leq[\alpha*]a$

We abbreviate $\langle\alpha\rangle a=\neg[\alpha]\neg a$ for $a\in B$, $\alpha\in P$.

It is shown in [4] that 5abc are equivalent to

5' $\langle\alpha*\rangle a=\inf\{b\in B/a\vee\langle\alpha\rangle b\leq b\}$ or, dually, to

5'' $[\alpha*]a=\sup\{b\in B/b\leq a\wedge[\alpha]b\}$.

We say that (B,P) has an <u>inverse operator</u> if P has an one argument operator $^-:P\to P$ satisfying the following conditions for any $a\in B$ and $\alpha\in P$:

6a. $\langle\alpha\rangle[\alpha^-]a\leq a$, 6b. $a\leq[\alpha^-]\langle\alpha\rangle a$

<u>Lemma 1</u>. 6ab are equivalent to

6'. $[\alpha^-]a=\sup\{b\in B/\langle\alpha\rangle b\leq a\}$ or, dually, to

6''. $\langle\alpha^-\rangle a=\inf\{b\in B/a\leq[\alpha]b\}$.

<u>Proof.</u>($\longrightarrow$) Suppose 6a and 6b. Then by 6a $[\alpha^-]a\in\{b\in B/\langle\alpha\rangle b\leq a\}$. Suppose $\langle\alpha\rangle b\leq a$. Then by 2a we have $[\alpha^-]\langle\alpha\rangle b\leq[\alpha^-]a$ and by 6b $b\leq[\alpha^-]a$ which proves 6'.

($\longleftarrow$) Suppose 6'. Then $[\alpha^-]a\in\{b\in B/\langle\alpha\rangle b\leq a\}$ so we have 6a. From 6' we have also that for any $a,b\in B$ and $\alpha\in P$ $\langle\alpha\rangle b\leq a$ implies $b\leq[\alpha^-]a$. Putting here $a=\langle\alpha\rangle b$ we obtain $b\leq[\alpha^-]\langle\alpha\rangle b$ which is 6b.

We say that (B,P) has a <u>test operator</u> if (B,P) has an inter-sort operation $?:B\to P$ satisfying the following axiom for any $a,b\in B$:

7. $[a?]b=a\Rightarrow b$

Let us note that now all Boolean operations can be expressed by ?, [ ] and O.

We say that (B,P) is a <u>programming algebra</u> (PA) if it has an inverse operator and test operator.

Following Pratt [4] we define for $\alpha,\beta\in P$, $\alpha\approx\beta$ iff $(\forall a\in B)([\alpha]a=[\beta]a)$ and say that α and β are inseparable. A DA (B,P) is called <u>separable</u> if $\approx$ is the identity relation on P.

<u>Lemma 2.</u> In any PA (B,P) inseparability is a congruence relation.

<u>Proof.</u> For DA-s it is proved in [4] . To prove it for inverse operation suppose $\alpha\approx\beta$. Then $[\alpha^-]a=\sup\{b/\langle\alpha\rangle b\leq a\}=\sup\{b/\langle\beta\rangle b\leq a\}=[\beta^-]a$, that is $\alpha^-\approx\beta^-$.

Let (B,P) and (B',P') be PA-s. A pair (g,h) is called a homomorphism from (B,P) into (B',P') if g and h are homomorphisms from B into B' and from P into P' respectively and the inter-sort operations [ ] and ? satisfy the following conditions:

$g([\alpha]a)=[h(\alpha)]g(a)$, $h(a?)=g(a)?$.

Let $B_o \subseteq B$ and $P_o \subseteq P$ and define by simultaneous induction

$B_{n+1}=B_n \cup \{\neg a / a \in B_n\} \cup \{a \square b / a,b \in B_n,\ \square \in \{\wedge, \vee, \Rightarrow\}\} \cup \{[\alpha]a / \alpha \in P_n,\ a \in B_n\}$

$P_{n+1}=P_n \cup \{\alpha \circ \beta / \alpha, \beta \in P_n,\ \circ \in \{\cup, \circ\}\} \cup \{\alpha^{\circ} / \alpha \in P_n,\ \circ \in \{*,-\}\} \cup \{a? / a \in B_n\}$

If $B=\bigcup_{n=0}^{\infty} B_n$ and $P=\bigcup_{n=0}^{\infty} P_n$ we say that the pair (B_o, P_o) generates the algebra (B,P). Let (B,P) be PA and $\sum$ a set of PA-s. We say that (B,P) is a <u>free algebra</u> in $\sum$ if there exists a pair (B_o,P_o) which generates (B,P) and any pair (g_o,h_o) of functions $g_o: B_o \rightarrow B'$ and $h_o: P_o \rightarrow P'$ where $(B',P') \in \sum$ can be extendet to a homomorphism (g,h) from (B,P) into (B',P'). The elements of the sets B_o and P_o are called <u>free generators</u> of (B,P).

<u>3. Programming set-algebras.</u> Let U be a non-empty set. For $a \subseteq U$ and $\alpha, \beta \subseteq U \times U = U^2$ we define: $\alpha \circ \beta = \{(x,z) \in U^2 / \exists y \in U: (x,y) \in \alpha \text{ and } (y,z) \in \beta\}$, $\alpha^{\circ} = \{(x,x) / x \in U\}$, $\alpha^{i+1} = \alpha \circ \alpha^{i}$, $\alpha^{*} = \bigcup_{i=0}^{\infty} \alpha^{i}$, $\alpha \cup \beta = \{(x,y) / (x,y) \in \alpha \text{ or } (x,y) \in \beta\}$,

$\alpha^{-} = \{(x,y) / (y,x) \in \alpha\}$, $a? = \{(x,x) / x \in a\}$

$[\alpha]a = \{x \in U / (\forall y)((x,y) \in \alpha \rightarrow y \in a)\}$.

<u>Theorem 3.</u> The algebra $(2^U, 2^{U \times U}) = ((2^U, \emptyset, U, \cap, \cup, \Rightarrow, \neg), (2^{U \times U}, \circ, \cup, *, -), [\ ], ?)$ where $(2^U, \emptyset, U, \cap, \cup, \Rightarrow, \neg)$ is the Boolean algebra of subsets of U and the operations of $2^{U \times U}$ defined as above, is a separable algebra, called <u>programming set-algebra over U</u>.

The proof is by an easy verification.

<u>4. Filters in programming algebras.</u> Let (B,P) be a PA. A subset $x \in B$ is called a filter in (B,P) if it is a filter in the Boolean algebra B. By U we denote the set of all maximal filters in (B,P) (see [10] for the theory of filters in Boolean algebras). For any $\alpha \in P$ and $x \subseteq B$ define:

$$[\alpha]x = \{a \in B / [\alpha]a \in x\} \ ,\ R(\alpha) = \{(x,y) \in U^2 / [\alpha]x \subseteq y\}.$$

Then the following will hold:

<u>Lemma 4.</u> (i) If x is a filter in (B,P) then $[\alpha]x$ is a filter too.

(ii) For any $a \in B$, $\alpha \in P$ and $x \in U$:

$$[\alpha]a \in x \text{ iff } (\forall y \in U)(xR(\alpha)y \rightarrow a \in y)$$

For any $\alpha, \beta \in P$ and $a \in B$ we have:

(iii) $R(\alpha \cup \beta) = R(\alpha) \cup R(\beta)$, (iv) $R(\alpha^{-}) = R(\alpha)^{-}$

(v) $R(\alpha \circ \beta) = R(\alpha) \circ R(\beta)$, (vi) $R(a?) = \{(x,x) / x \in U,\ a \in x\}$.

<u>Proof.</u> (i) By a straightforward verification.

(ii) The "if" part is easy. For the "only if" part suppose $[\alpha]a \notin x$. Then $a \notin [\alpha]x$ and there exists a maximal filter y such that $a \notin y$ and $[\alpha]x \subseteq y$, that is $xR(\alpha)y$.

(iii) Suppose $R(\alpha \cup \beta) \nsubseteq R(\alpha) \cup R(\beta)$ for some $\alpha, \beta \in P$. Then for some $x,y \in U$ $[\alpha \cup \beta]x \subseteq y$, $[\alpha]x \not\subseteq y$, $[\beta]x \not\subseteq y$ and hence for some a, $b \in B$ $[\alpha]a \in x$, $a \notin y$, $[\beta]b \in x$, $b \notin y$. Let $c = a \vee b$. Then $c \notin y$, $[\alpha]a \leq [\alpha]c$, $[\beta]b \leq [\beta]c$ and hence $[\alpha]c \in x$, $[\beta]c \in x$, $[\alpha]c \wedge [\beta]c \in x$ and by axiom 4 $[\alpha \cup \beta]c \in x$, $c \in [\alpha \cup \beta]x$, $c \in y$ - a contradiction. Thus $R(\alpha \cup \beta) \subseteq R(\alpha) \cup R(\beta)$. The proof of the converse inclusion is easy.

(iv) Suppose $R(\alpha^-) \not\subseteq R(\alpha)^-$ for some $\alpha \in P$. Then for some $x,y \in U$ we have $[\alpha^-]x \subseteq y$, $[\alpha]y \not\subseteq x$ and hence for some $a \in B$ $[\alpha]a \in y$ and $a \notin x$. From axiom 6b we obtain $\neg[\alpha^-]\neg[\alpha]a \leq a$. This with $a \notin x$ imply $\neg[\alpha^-]\neg[\alpha]a \notin x$ and since x is a maximal filter - $[\alpha^-]\neg[\alpha]a \in x$ and $\neg[\alpha]a \in [\alpha^-]x \subseteq y$, so $\neg[\alpha]a \in y$ - a contradiction. This proves $R(\alpha^-) \subseteq R(\alpha)^-$. The proof of the converse inclusion is the same and makes use of the axiom 6a.

(v) Suppose $xR(\alpha \circ \beta)y$, i.e. $[\alpha \circ \beta]x \subseteq y$, $x,y \in U$. We shall construct $z \in U$ such that $xR(\alpha)z$ and $zR(\beta)y$. Let t be the smallest filter containing $[\alpha]x$ and $[\beta^-]y$. We shall show that t is a proper filter. Suppose the contrary. Then for some $a \in B$ $\neg a \in [\alpha]x$ and $a \in [\beta^-]y$. Then $[\beta^-]a \in y$, $\neg[\beta^-]a \notin y$ and since $[\alpha \circ \beta]x \subseteq y$ we obtain $\neg[\beta^-]a \notin [\alpha \circ \beta]x$ $[\alpha \circ \beta]\neg[\beta^-]a \notin x$. Applying axiom 3 we obtain $[\alpha][\beta]\neg[\beta^-]a \in x$ and $[\alpha]\neg[\beta]\neg[\beta^-]a \notin x$. By axiom 2a and 6a we have $\langle\alpha\rangle\langle\beta\rangle[\beta^-]a \leq \langle\alpha\rangle a$, so $\langle\alpha\rangle a \in x$, $\neg[\alpha]\neg a \in x$, $[\alpha]\neg a \notin x$, $\neg a \notin [\alpha]x$ - a contradiction. Thus t is a proper filter and hence is contained in a maximal filter z. From $[\alpha]x \subseteq t \subseteq z$ and $[\beta^-]y \subseteq t \subseteq z$ we obtain $xR(\alpha)z$, $yR(\beta^-)z$ and by (iv) $zR(\beta)y$. This proves $R(\alpha \circ \beta) \subseteq R(\alpha) \circ R(\beta)$. The proof of the converse inclusion presents no difficulies.

(vi) Suppose $xR(a?)y$, $x,y \in U$, $a \in B$. Then we have $[a?]x \subseteq y$. Suppose $b \in x$. Since $b \leq a \Rightarrow b$ we have $a \Rightarrow b = [a?]b \in x$, $b \in [a?]x \subseteq y$, $b \in y$, so $x \subseteq y$ and because x and y are maximal filters we have $x=y$. We have also $1 = a \Rightarrow a \in x$, hence $[a?]a \in x$, $a \in [a?]x \subseteq y$, $a \in y$, $a \in x$. This proves the inclusion $R(a?) \subseteq \{(x,x) / a \in x \in U\}$. For the converse inclusion suppose $a \in x \in U$ and $b \in [a?]x$. Then $a \Rightarrow b \in x$, $a \wedge (a \Rightarrow b) \in x$ and since $a \wedge (a \Rightarrow b) \leq b$ - $b \in x$, so $[a?]x \subseteq x$ and $xR(a?)x$.

<u>5. Sequential propositional dynamic logic (SPDL) and the existence of free separable programming algebras.</u> In this section we shall introduce a sequential formulation of PDL (including test and inverse operators) using only binary sequents.

<u>Language:</u> Φ_0 - an infinite set of Boolean (propositional) variables

Π_0 - a non-empty set of program variables

$\bot, \top, \wedge, \vee, \Rightarrow, \neg, [\,]$ - logical connectives

$\circ$, $\cup$, $-$, $*$, ? - program operators, ( ) - parentheses.

We define by simultaneous induction the following two sequences:

$\Phi_0, \Phi_1, \Phi_2, \ldots \quad , \Pi_0, \Pi_1, \Pi_2, \ldots$

$\Pi_{n+1} = \Pi_n \cup \{(\alpha \circ \beta)/\alpha,\beta \in \Pi_n,\ \circ \in \{\circ, \cup\}\} \cup \{\alpha^{\circ}/\alpha \in \Pi_n, \circ \in \{*, -\}\} \cup \{a?/a \in \Phi_n\}$

$\Phi_{n+1} = \Phi_n \cup \{\bot, \top\} \cup \{(a \Box b)/a,b \in \Phi_n,\ \Box \in \{\wedge, \vee, \Rightarrow\}\} \cup \{\neg a/a \in \Phi_n\} \cup$
$\quad \cup \{[\alpha]a/\alpha \in \Pi_n,\ a \in \Phi_n\}$

$\Pi = \bigcup_{n=0}^{\infty} \Pi_n$ - the set of <u>programs</u>; $\Phi = \bigcup_{n=0}^{\infty} \Phi_n$ - the set of <u>formulas</u>.

We abreviate $\langle\alpha\rangle a = \neg[\alpha]\neg a$. The expresions of the form $a \vdash b$ where a,b are formulas are called <u>sequents</u>.

<u>A xioms and rules:</u> $a \vdash a$, $\dfrac{a \vdash b,\ b \vdash c}{a \vdash c}$, $\bot \vdash a$, $a \vdash \top$

$(a \wedge b) \vdash a$, $(a \wedge b) \vdash b$, $\dfrac{c \vdash a,\ c \vdash b}{c \vdash (a \wedge b)}$, $a \vdash (a \vee b)$, $b \vdash (a \vee b)$

$\dfrac{a \vdash c,\ b \vdash c}{(a \vee b) \vdash c}$, $(a \Rightarrow b) \wedge a \vdash b$, $\dfrac{(c \wedge a) \vdash b}{c \vdash (a \Rightarrow b)}$, $(a \wedge \neg a) \vdash \bot$,

$\dfrac{(c \wedge a) \vdash \bot}{c \vdash \neg a}$, $\neg\neg a \vdash a$, $\dfrac{a \vdash b}{[\alpha]a \vdash [\alpha]b}$, $[\alpha]a \wedge [\alpha]b \vdash [\alpha](a \wedge b)$,

$\top \vdash [\alpha]\top$, $[\alpha \cup \beta]a \vdash [\alpha]a \wedge [\beta]a$, $[\alpha]a \wedge [\beta]a \vdash [\alpha \cup \beta]a$,

$[\alpha \circ \beta]a \vdash [\alpha][\beta]a$, $[\alpha][\beta]a \vdash [\alpha \circ \beta]a$, $[\alpha^*]a \vdash a$, $[\alpha^*]a \vdash [\alpha][\alpha^*]a$,

$\dfrac{a \vdash b,\ a \vdash [\alpha]a}{a \vdash [\alpha^*]b}$, $\langle\alpha\rangle[\alpha^-]a \vdash a$, $\dfrac{\langle\alpha\rangle b \vdash a}{b \vdash [\alpha^-]a}$, $[a?]b \vdash a \Rightarrow b$,

$a \Rightarrow b \vdash [a?]b$.

We say that a sequent $a \vdash b$ is provable if there exists a sequence $a_1 \vdash b_1, \ldots, a_n \vdash b_n$ with $a_n = a$, $b_n = b$ such that for all i $1 \le i \le n$, $a_i \vdash b_i$ is either an axiom or is obtained from some previous sequents by means of some of the rules. A formula a is provable if the sequent $\top \vdash a$ is provable.

For any $a,b \in \Phi$ and $\alpha,\beta \in \Pi$ define:

$a \dashv\vdash b$ iff $a \vdash b$ and $b \vdash a$ are provable sequents ,

$\alpha \sim \beta$ iff $[\alpha]p \dashv\vdash [\beta]p$ for some $p \in \Phi_0$ which does not appear in α,β

<u>Lemma 5.</u> (i) $\dashv\vdash$ is a congruence relation in Φ.

(ii) $\sim$ is a congruence relation in Π.

(iii) If $a \dashv\vdash b$ then $a? \sim b?$.

(iv) If $a \dashv\vdash b$ and $\alpha \sim \beta$ then $[\alpha]a \dashv\vdash [\beta]b$.

The proof of (i), (iii) and (iv) is not difficult. The proof of (ii) is analogous to that of lemma 2.

<u>Semantics.</u> Let (B,P) be a PA. Any pair (g_0, h_0) where $g_0 : \Phi_0 \to B$ and $h_0 : \Pi_0 \to P$ is called a valuation in (B,P). We extend g_0 and h_0 to $g : \Phi \to B$ and $h : \Pi \to P$ by induction as follows: 1. for $a \in \Phi_0$ and $\alpha \in \Pi_0$: $g(a) = g_0(a)$ and $h(\alpha) = h_0(\alpha)$; 2. for $a,b \in \Phi_n$ and $\alpha,\beta \in \Pi_n$: $g(a \Box b) = g(a) \Box g(b)$ $\Box \in \{\wedge, \vee, \Rightarrow\}$, $g(\neg a) = \neg g(a)$, $g([\alpha]a) = [h(\alpha)]g(a)$, $g(\bot) = 0$, $g(\top) = 1$, $h(\alpha \circ \beta) = h(\alpha) \circ h(\beta)$ $\circ \in \{\circ, \cup\}$, $h(\alpha^{\circ}) = h(\alpha)^{\circ}$ $\circ \in \{*, -\}$
$h(a?) = g(a)?$

We say that a sequent $a \vdash b$ is true in a PA (B,P) if for any valuation (g_o, h_o) in (B,P) we have $g(a) \leq g(b)$.

Lemma 6. Let (B,P) be a separable PA and (g_o, h_o) be a valuation from (Φ_0, Π_0) in (B,P). Then for any $a,b \in \Phi$ and $\alpha, \beta \in \Pi$ we have: (i) If $a \vdash\dashv b$ then $g(a)=g(b)$, (ii) if $\alpha \sim \beta$ then $h(\alpha)=h(\beta)$.

Proof. Condition (i) presents no difficulties. If g_o maps Φ_0 onto B then (ii) follows from separability of (B,P). If $g_o(\Phi_0)$ is a proper subset of B then by adding sufficient number of new variables to Φ_0 we can extend g_o to the new variables as to cover B and then to use separability again.

Lemma 5 enables us to form quotients $\Phi/\vdash\dashv$ and $\Pi/\sim$. We denote for any $a \in \Phi$ and $\alpha \in \Pi$ $|a| = \{b \in \Phi \,/\, a \vdash\dashv b\}$ and $\|\alpha\| = \{\beta \,/\, \alpha \sim \beta, \beta \in \Pi\}$. The new operations in $\Phi/\vdash\dashv$ and $\Pi/\sim$ are defined as follows:

$|a| \Box |b| = |a \Box b|$ $\Box \in \{\wedge, \vee, \Rightarrow\}$, $\neg|a| = |\neg a|$, $[\|\alpha\|]|a| = |[\alpha]a|$

$\|\alpha\| o \|\beta\| = \|\alpha o \beta\|$ $o \in \{\circ, \cup\}$, $\|\alpha\|^o = \|\alpha^o\|$ $o \in \{*, -\}$, $|a|? = \|a?\|$

Theorem 7. The algebra $\mathfrak{A} = (\Phi/\vdash\dashv, \Pi/\sim)$ with operations defined as above is a free separable PA in the class of all separable PA-s.

Proof. The proof that $\mathfrak{A}$ is a PA is long but easy. Let us show separability. $(\forall |a| \in \Phi/\vdash\dashv)([\|\alpha\|]|a| = [\|\beta\|]|a|)$ iff $(\forall a \in \Phi)([\alpha]a \vdash\dashv [\beta]a)$ iff $\alpha \sim \beta$ iff $\|\alpha\| = \|\beta\|$. The generators of $\mathfrak{A}$ are the sets $B_0 = \{|a| / a \in \Phi_0\}$ and $P_0 = \{\|\alpha\| \,/\, \alpha \in \Pi_0\}$. To prove that $\mathfrak{A}$ is a free algebra in the class of all separable PA-s let (B,P) be separable PA and $g_o : B_0 \longrightarrow B$, $h_o : P_0 \longrightarrow P$ be arbitrary functions. We define a valuation $(\tilde{g}_o, \tilde{h}_o)$ from (Φ_0, Π_0) into (B,P) as follows: for $a \in \Phi_0$ and $\alpha \in \Pi_0$ $\tilde{g}_o(a) = g_o(|a|)$ and $\tilde{h}_o(\alpha) = h_o(\|\alpha\|)$. Let $(\tilde{g}, \tilde{h})$ be the extention of $(\tilde{g}_o, \tilde{h}_o)$ to all formulas and programs. Then define $g(|a|) = \tilde{g}(a)$ and $h(\|\alpha\|) = \tilde{h}(\alpha)$. By lemma 6 this definition is correct. Now it is easy to see that (g,h) is a homomorphism from $\mathfrak{A}$ into (B,P) which extends (g_o, h_o). Thus $\mathfrak{A}$ is a free algebra in the class of all separable PA-s. The algebra $\mathfrak{A}$ is called the Lindenbaum algebra of the SPDL.

6. Filtration theorem for free separable PA-s. This is the name of the following theorem.

Theorem 8. Let (B,P) be a free separable PA and C be a finite subset of B. Then there exist a finite programming set-algebra (B',P') and a homomorphism (g,h) from (B,P) into (B',P') such that $g(a) \neq 1$ for any $a \in C$ and $a \neq 1$.

Proof. Let B_0 and P_0 be the sets of all free generators of (B,P). We consider B_0 and P_0 as sets of propositional and program variables respectively and build the sets $\tilde{B}$ and $\tilde{P}$ of all formulas and programs over B_0 and P_0. The elements of $\tilde{B}$ (of $\tilde{P}$) can be considered in two ways: as formulas (programs) and as elements of B (of P). When we want to say that two elements $a,b \in \widetilde{B} \cup \widetilde{P}$ are equal (different) as formulas or programs we will write $a \doteq b$ ($a \not\doteq b$). Obviously, it is possible for some $a,b \in \widetilde{B} \cup \widetilde{P}$ to have $a \not\doteq b$ and $a=b$. Since (B,P) is generated by (B_0,P_0) then for any $a \in B$ and $\alpha \in P$ there exist a formula $\widetilde{a} \in \widetilde{B}$ and a program $\widetilde{\alpha} \in \widetilde{P}$ such that $a=\widetilde{a}$ and $\alpha=\widetilde{\alpha}$. We denote by $\widetilde{C}$ a set of formulas such that for any $a \in C$ there exists only one formula $\widetilde{a} \in \widetilde{C}$ such that $a=\widetilde{a}$.

Let $M \subseteq \widetilde{B}$ and $N \subseteq \widetilde{P}$. We define the Fischer-Ladner closure of (M,N) - FL(M,N) to be the pair (Ψ, Θ) where Ψ and Θ are the smallest sets satisfying the following conditions:

FL1. $M \subseteq \Psi \subseteq \widetilde{B}$, $N \subseteq \Theta \subseteq P$.

FL2. Ψ is closed on subformulas and Θ is closed on subprograms.

FL3. If $[\alpha \cup \beta]a \in \Psi$ then $[\alpha]a \wedge [\beta]a \in \Psi$.

FL4. If $[\alpha \circ \beta]a \in \Psi$ then $[\alpha][\beta]a \in \Psi$.

FL5. If $[\alpha^*]a \in \Psi$ then $[\alpha][\alpha^*]a \in \Psi$.

FL6. If $[\alpha^-]a \in \Psi$ then $[\alpha]\neg[\alpha^-]a \in \Psi$

FL7. If $[b?]a \in \Psi$ then $b \Rightarrow a \in \Psi$.

FL8. If $[\alpha]a \in \Psi$ then $\alpha \in \Theta$.

FL9. If $a? \in \Theta$ then $a \in \Psi$.

As in [11] one can prove the following

Lemma 9. Let M and N be finite subsets of $\widetilde{B}$ and $\widetilde{P}$ respectively and $FL(M,N)=(\Psi,\Theta)$. Then Ψ and Θ are finite too.

Let $FL(C,\emptyset)=(\Sigma,\Omega)$ and U be the set of all maximal filters of (B,P). For $x,y \in U$ define the equivalence relation $x \sim y$ iff $x \cap \Sigma = y \cap \Sigma$ (in this context the elements of Σ are considered as elements of B). Denote $\widetilde{U}=U/\!\sim = \{|x| / x \in U\}$ where $|x| = \{y \in U / x \sim y\}$ and let (B',P') be the programming set-algebra over $\widetilde{U}$. It is easy to see that $\widetilde{U}$ is finite, so the same is (B',P'). For any $a \in B_0$ and $\alpha \in P_0$ define:

$g_0(a) = \{|x| \in \widetilde{U} / a \in x\}$.

$h_0(\alpha) = \{(|x|,|y|) \in \widetilde{U} \times \widetilde{U} / (\exists x',y' \in U)(x' \sim x \,\&\, y' \sim y \,\&\, x' R(\alpha) y')\}$.

where $R(\alpha)$ was defined in sec. 4. Since (B,P) is a free algebra in the class of all separable PA-s and (B',P') is a separable PA, then the pair (g_0,h_0) can be extended to a homomorphism (g,h) from (B,P) into (B',P'). It remains to prove that for any $a \in C$ and $a \neq 1$ we have $g(a) \neq 1$. We need the following two lemmas.

Lemma 10. For any $M \subseteq \widetilde{U}$ there exists $b \in B$ such that for any $x \in U$: $b \in x$ iff $|x| \in M$.

Proof. Since Σ is finite subset of $\widetilde{B}$ we have $\Sigma = \{b_1, b_2, \ldots, b_m\}$, since $\widetilde{U}$ is finite set we have $M = \{|x_1|, |x_2|, \ldots, |x_n|\}$. Define for any

$i=1,\dots,m \quad j=1,\dots,n \quad b_i^j=\begin{cases} b_i & \text{if } b_i \in x_j \\ \neg b_i & \text{if } b_i \notin x_j \end{cases}, \quad b^j=\bigwedge_{i=1}^{m} b_i^j, \quad b=\bigvee_{j=1}^{n} b^j$

Then for any $x \in U$ we have: $b^j \in x$ iff $x \sim x_j$ iff $|x|=|x_j|$; $b \in x$ iff $\exists j\ b^j \in x$ iff $\exists j\ |x|=|x_j|$ iff $|x| \in M$.

Lemma 11. For any $x,y \in U$, $\alpha \in \Omega$ and $a \in \Sigma$ the following holds:

(i) $xR(\alpha)y \longrightarrow |x|\,h(\alpha)\,|y|$

(ii) $|x|\,h(\alpha)\,|y| \longrightarrow (\forall a \in \tilde{B})(\ [\alpha]a \in x \cap \Sigma \longrightarrow a \in y)$

(iii) $g(a)=\{|x|\ /\ a \in x\}$.

First let us show how to end the proof of the theorem. Suppose $a \in C$ and $a \neq 1$. Then there exists a formula $\tilde{a} \in \tilde{C}$ such that $a=\tilde{a}$. Since $\tilde{C} \subseteq \Sigma$ we have that $\tilde{a} \in \Sigma$ and by lemma 11(iii) $g(\tilde{a})=\{|x|\ /\ \tilde{a} \in x\}$. Since $\tilde{a} \neq 1$ there exists a maximal filter x_0 such that $\tilde{a} \notin x_0$. So $|x_0| \notin g(\tilde{a})$ and $g(\tilde{a}) \neq U=1$.

Proof of lemma 11. We shall prove (i), (ii) and (iii) simultaneously by double inducion on the complexity of the construction of a and α.

1. Case $\alpha \in P_0 \cap \Omega$, $a \in B_0 \cap \Sigma$.

Claim (i). Suppose $xR(\alpha)y$. Since $x \sim x$ and $y \sim y$ we obtain $|x|\,h(\alpha)\,|y|$.

Claim (ii). Suppose $|x|\,h(\alpha)\,|y|$. Then for some $x',y' \in U$ we have $x \sim x'$, $y \sim y'$ and $x'R(\alpha)\,y'$, so $x \cap \Sigma = x' \cap \Sigma$, $y \cap \Sigma = y' \cap \Sigma$ and $[\alpha]x' \subseteq y'$. Suppose, by way of contradiction, that for some $a \in \tilde{B}$ $[\alpha]a \in x \cap \Sigma$ but $a \notin y$. Then by FL2 $a \in \Sigma$, so $a \notin y \cap \Sigma$, $a \notin y' \cap \Sigma$, $a \notin y'$, $a \notin [\alpha]x'$, $[\alpha]a \notin x'$, $[\alpha]a \notin x' \cap \Sigma$ and finaly $[\alpha]a \notin x \cap \Sigma$ - a contradiction.

Claim (iii). $g(a)=g_0(a)=\{|x|\ /\ a \in x\}$ - by the definition of g_0.

2. Case $\alpha \in \tilde{P}_{n+1} \cap \Omega$, $a \in \tilde{B}_{n+1} \cap \Sigma$. Induction hypothesis: for any $\alpha \in \tilde{P}_n \cap \Omega$ and $a \in \tilde{B}_n \cap \Sigma$ the assertion is true.

Claim (i). Suppose $xR(\alpha)y$ for some $x,y \in U$.

Subcase $\alpha \doteq \beta \cup \gamma$, $\beta,\gamma \in \tilde{P}_n$. Since $\beta \cup \gamma \in \Omega$ then by FL2 $\beta,\gamma \in \Omega$ so $\beta,\gamma \in \tilde{P}_n \cap \Omega$ and we can use the induction hypothesis. By lemma 4(iii) $xR(\beta \cup \gamma)y$ implies $xR(\beta)y$ or $xR(\gamma)y$ and by induction hypothesis $|x|\,h(\beta)\,|y|$ or $|x|\,h(\gamma)\,|y|$.

Subcase $\alpha \doteq \beta \circ \gamma$, $\beta,\gamma \in \tilde{P}_n$. Since $\beta \circ \gamma \in \Omega$ then by FL2 $\beta,\gamma \in \Omega$ so $\beta,\gamma \in \tilde{P}_n \cap \Omega$. By lemma 4(v) $xR(\beta \circ \gamma)y$ implies $xR(\beta)z$ and $zR(\gamma)y$ for some $z \in U$. By the induction hypothesis $|x|\,h(\beta)\,|z|$ and $|z|\,h(\gamma)\,|y|$, so $|x|\,h(\beta) \circ h(\gamma)\,|y|$ and hence $|x|\,h(\beta \circ \gamma)\,|y|$.

Subcase $\alpha \doteq \beta^*$, $\beta \in \tilde{P}_n$. By FL2 $\beta \in \tilde{P}_n \cap \Omega$. Suppose by way of contradiction that not $|x|\,h(\alpha^*)\,|y|$. Denote by $M=\{|z|\ /\ |x|\,h(\beta)^*\,|z|\}$. By lemma 10 there exists $b \in \tilde{B}$ such that for any $z \in U$ $b \in z$ iff $|z| \in M$. We have $|y| \notin M$, so $b \notin y$. Since $h(\beta)^*$ is a reflexive relation we have $|x|h(\beta)^*|x|$ so $|x|\in M$ and $b\in x$. From $xR(\beta^*)y$ and $b\notin y$ we obtain that $[\beta^*]b\notin x$. By axiom 5c $b\wedge[\beta^*](b\Rightarrow[\beta]b)\notin x$ and since $b\in x$ - $[\beta^*](b\Rightarrow[\beta]b)\notin x$. By lemma 4(ii) there exists $u\in U$ such that $xR(\beta^*)u$ and $b\Rightarrow[\beta]b\notin u$. So $b\in u$, $[\beta]b\notin u$ and again by lemma 4(ii) there exists $v\in U$ such that $uR(\beta)v$ and $b\notin v$. From $b\in u$ and $uR(\beta)v$ we obtain $|x|h(\beta)^*|u|$ and $|u|h(\beta)|v|$, so $|x|h(\beta)^*|v|$. This gives that $|v|\in M$ and that $b\in v$ - a contradiction. Hence $|x|h(\beta^*)|y|$.

<u>Subcase $\alpha\doteq\beta^-$.</u> $\beta\in\tilde{P}_n$. By lemma 4(iv) $xR(\beta^-)y$ implies $yR(\beta)x$, so by induction hypothesis $|y|h(\beta)|x|$, $|x|h(\beta)^-|y|$ and $|x|h(\beta^-)|y|$.

<u>Subcase $\alpha\doteq a?$</u>, $a\in\tilde{B}_n$. Since $a?\in\Omega$ then by FL9 $a\in\Sigma$, so $a\in\tilde{B}_n\cap\Sigma$ and we can apply the induction hypothesis. By lemma 4(vi) $xR(a?)y$ implies $x=y$ and $a\in x$. So $|x|=|y|$ and $|x|\in g(a)$. This implies $|x|g(a)?|y|$, so $|x|h(a?)|y|$.

<u>Claim (ii).</u> Suppose $|x|h(\alpha)|y|$.

<u>Subcase $\alpha\doteq\beta\cup\gamma$,</u> $\beta,\gamma\in\tilde{P}_n$. Suppose $[\beta\cup\gamma]a\in x\cap\Sigma$. By axiom 4 for PA-s we have that $[\beta]a\in x$ and $[\gamma]a\in x$. By FL3 and FL2 $[\beta]a$, $[\gamma]a\in x\cap\Sigma$. $|x|h(\beta\cup\gamma)|y|$ implies $|x|(h(\beta)\cup h(\gamma))|y|$ and $|x|h(\beta)|y|$ or $|x|h(\gamma)|y|$. Applying the induction hypothesis in both cases we obtain $a\in y$.

<u>Subcase $\alpha\doteq\beta\circ\gamma$,</u> $\beta,\gamma\in\tilde{P}_n$. Suppose $[\beta\circ\gamma]a\in x\cap\Sigma$. By axiom 3 for PA-s we have $[\beta][\gamma]a\in x$ and by FL4 that $[\beta][\gamma]a\in\Sigma$. $|x|h(\beta\circ\gamma)|y|$ implies $|x|h(\beta)\circ h(\gamma)|y|$ and $|x|h(\beta)|z|$ and $|z|h(\gamma)|y|$ for some $|z|\in\tilde{U}$. Applying the induction hypothesis we obtain $[\gamma]a\in z\cap\Sigma$ and $a\in y$.

<u>Subcase $\alpha\doteq\beta^*$,</u> $\beta\in\tilde{P}_n$. Suppose $[\beta^*]a\in x\cap\Sigma$. Then by FL5 and axiom 5b we have $[\beta][\beta^*]a\in x\cap\Sigma$. We shall show by induction that for any $i=0,1,\ldots$ if $|x|h^i(\beta)|z|$ then $[\beta^*]a\in z\cap\Sigma$.

<u>$i=0$.</u> Then $|x|=|z|$, $x\cap\Sigma=z\cap\Sigma$, so $[\beta^*]a\in z\cap\Sigma$.

<u>$i=k+1$.</u> Then $|x|h^{k+1}(\beta)|z|$ implies $|x|h(\beta)|u|$ and $|u|h^k(\beta)|z|$ for some $|u|\in\tilde{U}$. By induction hypothesis on β we have $[\beta^*]a\in u\cap\Sigma$ and by induction hypothesis on k we have $[\beta^*]a\in z$.

Suppose $|x|h(\beta^*)|y|$. Then $|x|h(\beta)^*|y|$ and since $h(\beta)^*$ is the reflexive and transitive closure of $h(\beta)$ we have $|x|h^i(\beta)|y|$ for some i. Then $[\beta^*]a\in y\cap\Sigma$ and by axiom 5a $a\in y$.

<u>Subcase $\alpha\doteq\beta^-$,</u> $\beta\in\tilde{P}_n$. Suppose $[\beta^-]a\in x\cap\Sigma$. Then by FL6 $[\beta]\neg[\beta^-]a\in\Sigma$. $|x|h(\beta^-)|y|$ implies $|x|h(\beta)^-|y|$, so $|y|h(\beta)|x|$. $[\beta^-]a\in x$ implies $\neg[\beta^-]a\notin x$. By the induction hypothesis $[\beta]\neg[\beta^-]a\notin y\cap\Sigma$ and since $[\beta]\neg[\beta^-]a\in\Sigma$ we have $[\beta]\neg[\beta^-]a\notin y$. From this we obtain: $\neg[\beta]\neg[\beta^-]a\in y$, $\langle\beta\rangle[\beta^-]a\in y$ and by axiom 6a for PA-s - $a\in y$.

<u>Subcase $\alpha\doteq b?$,</u> $b\in\tilde{B}_n$. Suppose $[b?]a\in x\cap\Sigma$. Then by axiom 7

and FL7 $b \Rightarrow a \in x \cap \Sigma$. From $|x|h(b?)|y|$ we obtain $|x|g(b)?|y|$, so $|x| = |y|$ and $|y| \in g(b)$. This by the induction hypothesis implies $b \in y$, which together with $b \Rightarrow a \in y$ give $a \in y$.

Claim (iii). We have to show that $g(a) = \{|x| \in \tilde{U} / a \in x\}$.

Subcase $a \doteq b \wedge c$, $b, c \in \tilde{B}_n$. By FL2 $b, c \in \tilde{B}_n \cap \Sigma$ and by the induction hypothesis $g(b) = \{|x| / b \in x\}$ and $g(c) = \{|x| / c \in x\}$. We have $g(b \wedge c) = g(b) \wedge g(c) = \{|x| / b \in x\} \cap \{|x| / c \in x\} = \{|x| / b \in x \text{ and } c \in x\} = \{|x| / b \wedge c \in x\}$.

Subcase $a \doteq \neg b$, $b \in \tilde{B}_n$. By FL2 $b \in \tilde{B}_n \cap \Sigma$ and by the induction hypothesis $g(b) = \{|x| / b \in x\}$. We have: $g(\neg b) = U \setminus g(b) = \{|x| / b \notin x\} = \{|x| / \neg b \in x\}$.

Subcase $a \doteq [\gamma]b$; $\gamma \in \tilde{P}_n$, $b \in \tilde{B}_n$. Since $[\gamma]b \in \Sigma$ by FL2 and FL8 $b \in \Sigma$ and $\gamma \in \Omega$, hence $b \in \tilde{B}_n \cap \Sigma$ and $\gamma \in \tilde{P}_n \cap \Omega$ and we can apply the induction hypothesis . We have $g([\gamma] b) = [h(\gamma)] g(b) = \{|x| / (\forall |y|)(|x| h(\gamma) |y| \rightarrow |y| \in g(b))\}$. We shall show first that $g([\gamma] b) \subseteq \{|x| / [\gamma]b \in x\}$. Suppose, by way of contradiction, that $|x| \in g([\gamma] b)$ but $[\gamma]b \notin x$. Then by lemma 4(ii) there exists $y \in U$ such that $xR(\gamma)y$ and $b \in y$. By the induction hypothesis, claim (i) and claim (iii) we have $|x| h(\gamma) |y|$ and $|y| \notin g(b)$. From $|x| \in g([\gamma] b)$ and $|x| h(\gamma) |y|$ we obtain $|y| \in g(b)$ - a contradiction. So $g([\gamma] b) \subseteq \{|x| / [\gamma]b \in x\}$. To prove the converse inclusion suppose, by way of contradiction, that $[\gamma]b \in x$ but $|x| \notin g([\gamma] b)$. Then there exists $|y|$ such that $|x| h(\gamma) |y|$ and $|y| \notin g(b)$. Since $[\gamma]b \in x$ and $[\gamma]b \in \Sigma$ then $[\gamma]b \in x \cap \Sigma$ and from inductive hypothesis, by claim (ii) we get $b \in y$, which by claim (iii) gives $|y| \in g(b)$ - a contradiction. So $\{|x| / [\gamma]b \in x\} \subseteq g([\gamma] b)$. Thus we have proved $g([\gamma] b) = \{|x| / [\gamma]b \in x\}$.

This ends the proof of lemma 11 and theorem 8.

The following theorem is an application of the filtration theorem.

Theorem 12. (Completeness theorem for SPDL). For any two formulas a and b the following conditions are equivalent:

(i) The sequent $a \vdash b$ is provable in SPDL.

(ii) $a \vdash b$ is true in any PA.

(iii) $a \vdash b$ is true in any separable PA.

(iv) $a \vdash b$ is true in any free separable PA.

(v) $a \vdash b$ is true in the Lindenbaum algebra of SPDL.

(vi) $a \vdash b$ is true in any programming set-algebra.

(vii) $a \vdash b$ is true in any finite programming set-algebra.

(viii) $a \vdash b$ is true in any finite PA.

Proof. (i)$\rightarrow$(ii) - by induction on the complexity of the proof of $a \vdash b$. (ii)$\rightarrow$(iii)$\rightarrow$(iv)$\rightarrow$(v) are obvious. (v)$\rightarrow$(i) - in a standard way showing that if $a \vdash b$ is not provable then $|a| \neq |b|$ in the

Lindenbaum algebra of SPDL. (iii)⟶(v)⟶(vi) - obvious. The implication (vii)⟶(vi) follows in a standard way from the Filtration theorem. (ii)⟶(viii)⟶(vii) are trivial. All this shows that the conditions (i)-(viii) are equivalent. Let us note that (i)⟷(vi) state the completeness of SPDL with respect to the standard Kripke semantics for SPDL.

Acknowledgements are due to S. Passy and G. Gargov for their helpful suggestions.

References

[1] Kozen, D. A representation theorem for models of *-free PDL, manuscript, July 1979.

[2] Kozen, D. On the duality of dynamic algebras and Kripke models, manuscript, may 1979.

[3] Kozen, D. On the representation of dynamic algebras, manuscript, October, 1979.

[4] Pratt, V. R. Dynamic algebras: examples, constructions, applications, manuscript, July, 1979.

[5] Pratt, V. R. Dynamic algebras and the nature of induction, manuscript, March, 1980.

[6] Longochev, I. A completeness theorem for PDL with test operator, master thesis, April 1980(Bulgarian, Math. Fac. Sofia univ.)

[7] Longochev, I. A completeness theorem for PDL with test operator, J. Theoretical and System Programming, Computing Centre SOAN SSSR 1981, Novosibirsk (in Russian)

[8] Reiterman, J. and Trnkovà, V. Dynamic algebras which are not Kripke structures, Lecture Notes in Computer Science 88, 1980, 528-538.

[9] Segerberg, K. A completeness theorem in the modal logics of programs, to appear in the Stefan Banach International Mathematical Centre, pubications series.

[10] Rasiowa, H. and Sikorski R. The Mathematics of Metamathematics, Warsaw, 3rd ed. 1970.

[11] Fischer, M. J. and Ladner, R. E. Propositional Modal Logic of Programs, Proc; 9th ACM Symp. on Theory of Comp. May 2-4,1977, pp 160-166.